SPQR in the USSR
Elena Shvarts's Classical Antiquity

LEGENDA

LEGENDA is the Modern Humanities Research Association's book imprint for new research in the Humanities. Founded in 1995 by Malcolm Bowie and others within the University of Oxford, Legenda has always been a collaborative publishing enterprise, directly governed by scholars. The Modern Humanities Research Association (MHRA) joined this collaboration in 1998, became half-owner in 2004, in partnership with Maney Publishing and then Routledge, and has since 2016 been sole owner. Titles range from medieval texts to contemporary cinema and form a widely comparative view of the modern humanities, including works on Arabic, Catalan, English, French, German, Greek, Italian, Portuguese, Russian, Spanish, and Yiddish literature. Editorial boards and committees of more than 60 leading academic specialists work in collaboration with bodies such as the Society for French Studies, the British Comparative Literature Association and the Association of Hispanists of Great Britain & Ireland.

The MHRA encourages and promotes advanced study and research in the field of the modern humanities, especially modern European languages and literature, including English, and also cinema. It aims to break down the barriers between scholars working in different disciplines and to maintain the unity of humanistic scholarship. The Association fulfils this purpose through the publication of journals, bibliographies, monographs, critical editions, and the MHRA Style Guide, and by making grants in support of research. Membership is open to all who work in the Humanities, whether independent or in a University post, and the participation of younger colleagues entering the field is especially welcomed.

ALSO PUBLISHED BY THE ASSOCIATION

Critical Texts
Tudor and Stuart Translations • *New Translations* • *European Translations*
MHRA Library of Medieval Welsh Literature

MHRA Bibliographies
Publications of the Modern Humanities Research Association

The Annual Bibliography of English Language & Literature
Austrian Studies
Modern Language Review
Portuguese Studies
The Slavonic and East European Review
Working Papers in the Humanities
The Yearbook of English Studies

www.mhra.org.uk
www.legendabooks.com

EDITORIAL BOARD

Chair: Professor Jonathan Long (University of Durham)
For *Germanic Literatures*: Ritchie Robertson (University of Oxford)
For *Italian Perspectives*: Simon Gilson (University of Warwick)
For *Moving Image*: Emma Wilson (University of Cambridge)
For *Research Monographs in French Studies*:
Diana Knight (University of Nottingham)
For *Selected Essays*: Susan Harrow (University of Bristol)
For *Studies in Comparative Literature*:
Dr Emily Finer, University of St Andrews, and
Professor Wen-chin Ouyang, SOAS, London
For *Studies in Hispanic and Lusophone Cultures*:
Catherine Davies (Institute of Modern Languages Research)
For *Studies in Yiddish*: Gennady Estraikh (New York University)
For *Transcript*: Matthew Reynolds (University of Oxford)
For *Visual Culture*: Carolin Duttlinger (University of Oxford)

Managing Editor
Dr Graham Nelson
41 Wellington Square, Oxford OX1 2JF, UK

www.legendabooks.com

SPQR in the USSR

Elena Shvarts's Classical Antiquity

Georgina Barker

LEGENDA
Modern Humanities Research Association
2022

Published by Legenda
an imprint of the Modern Humanities Research Association
Salisbury House, Station Road, Cambridge CB1 2LA

ISBN 978-1-83954-052-3 (HB)
ISBN 978-1-83954-053-0 (PB)

First published 2022

All rights reserved. No part of this publication may be reproduced or disseminated or transmitted in any form or by any means, electronic, mechanical, photocopying, recording or otherwise, or stored in any retrieval system, or otherwise used in any manner whatsoever without written permission of the copyright owner, except in accordance with the provisions of the Copyright, Designs and Patents Act 1988, or under the terms of a licence permitting restricted copying issued in the UK by the Copyright Licensing Agency Ltd, Saffron House, 6–10 Kirby Street, London EC1N 8TS, England, or in the USA by the Copyright Clearance Center, 222 Rosewood Drive, Danvers MA 01923. Application for the written permission of the copyright owner to reproduce any part of this publication must be made by email to legenda@mhra.org.uk.

Disclaimer: Statements of fact and opinion contained in this book are those of the author and not of the editors or the Modern Humanities Research Association. The publisher makes no representation, express or implied, in respect of the accuracy of the material in this book and cannot accept any legal responsibility or liability for any errors or omissions that may be made.

Trademark notice: Product or corporate names may be trademarks or registered trademarks, and are used only for identification and explanation without intent to infringe.

© Modern Humanities Research Association 2022

Copy-Editor: Dr Nigel Hope

CONTENTS

Acknowledgements		ix
Note on Conventions		x
Note on Abbreviations and Editions		xi
1	The Works and Days of Elena, a Poet from the Order of the Metamorphosis of the Self	1
	Shvarts's Biography	5
	Family history	5
	Childhood circles (1948–1966)	7
	Going underground (1967–1970s)	9
	Out in the open (1980s)	13
	Touring and mourning (1990s)	15
	Up in flames (2000s)	17
	Classical Reception	19
	Russia's classical tradition	21
	The Third Rome	21
	Romanticism and Modernism: Pushkin, Tsvetaeva, Mandel'shtam	23
	Stalinism and the Thaw: Brodskii and Kushner	25
	The Stagnation and post-Soviet era: Krivulin and Sedakova	27
	Conclusion	28
	Shvarts's Classical Reception	29
2	Classical Alter Egos	39
	The Alter Ego and Enstrangement	40
	The Celestial Bodies	45
	Narcissus	45
	Aphrodite/Venus	48
	Selene/Luna	57
	Odysseus	64
	The Katabasists	65
	Orpheus and Eurydice	68
	Inspired victims of Dionysus and Apollo	76
	Pythia	84
	Ariadne	88
	Conclusion	93
3	Kinfiia	95
	Lost and Translated	97
	Form	99
	Dialogue with Propertius	101
	Book I	102
	Book II	107
	Razroznennoe [*Oddments*]	109
	Conclusion	115

	Dialogue with Catullus and Other Classical Writers	116
	Book I	116
	Book II	124
	Razroznennoe [*Oddments*]	127
	Conclusion	130
	A Woman's Voice	131
	Just a *scripta puella*?	131
	The missing Sulpicia?	133
	Subverting elegy's gender subversion	133
	Textual bonding	135
	Conclusion	139
	Kinfiia's Rome or Shvarts's Russia?	139
	Anachronisms	139
	Anachorisms	141
	Biographical coincidences	144
	Poetic coincidences	148
	Conclusion	150
	The Apocrypha	150
	Dialogue with Propertius and other classical writers	152
	Shvarts's voice in the apocrypha	157
	Conclusion	159
	The End?	160
4	Rome	163
	1963–1996: The Russianness of Rome	163
	2001–2002: The Reality of Rome	175
	2006–2009: The Loss of Rome	182
	Conclusion	187
5	Homo Musagetes: Human, Leader of the Muses	189
	Horace in Russia	190
	Title	193
	Subtitle	194
	Epigraph	196
	Scythia vs Hyperborea	197
	Form	199
	I	200
	II	204
	III	206
	IV	209
	V	213
	VI	216
	VII	217
	VIII	220
	IX	224
	Conclusion	
6	Afterword	229
	Appendix	233
	Bibliography	335
	General Index	346
	Index of Elena Shvarts's Work	355

ACKNOWLEDGEMENTS

This book has been a decade (at least) in the making, so I have many people to acknowledge. My first thanks must go to Josie von Zitzewitz, who introduced me to the poetry of Elena Shvarts; and to Kirill Kozyrev, who opened up a wealth of Shvarts-related information — and his home — to me.

I am very grateful for the financial support I have received during the different phases of writing this book, from — in chronological order — the Wolfson Foundation, Russkiy Mir, the Institute for Advanced Studies in the Humanities at the University of Edinburgh, the Modern Humanities Research Association, the University of Exeter, and the Leverhulme Trust.

Several archives/libraries and their helpful, knowledgeable curators/librarians have been indispensable to my research: the Elena Shvarts Home Archive, and Kirill Kozyrev; Forschungsstelle Osteuropa (the Research Centre for East European Studies) at Bremen University, and Maria Klassen; Antichnyi Kabinet/Bibliotheca Classica Petropolitana, and Tat'iana Orlova; and Poriadok Slov bookshop.

Thank you to everyone who gave me interviews, information, and/or advice for this book: Boris Aksel'rod (a.k.a. Konstriktor, a.k.a. Vantalov), Boris Ostanin, Viacheslav Dolinin, Dmitrii Panchenko, Tat'iana Morozova, Pavel Uspenskii, Polina Barskova, Ilya Kutik, Iurii Orlitskii, Liudmila Zubova, Stephanie Sandler, Cathy Ciepiela, and Elena Cagnoli Fiecconi. Especial thanks go to my 'deciphering team', Kirill Kozyrev and Boris Ostanin, who helped me read Shvarts's handwriting.

Thank you to everyone who read drafts and gave me their insights: Katharine Hodgson, Pamela Davidson, Anna Vaninskaya, Calum Maciver, Donncha O'Rourke, Lisa Surridge, and Mary Elizabeth Leighton.

Thank you to the teachers who shaped my thinking about Russian and Latin: Sasha Smith, Philip Bullock, Peta Fowler, Elena Vladimirovna Eitingon, Marta Tomaszewski, and Jennifer Parsons.

Finally, I would like to thank all the people who supported me during the writing of this book by taking me away from it for a bit — my friends from Bristol, Oxford, Edinburgh, St Andrews, Exeter, and London (you know who you are). And, lastly and therefore most importantly, I thank my family — Catherine, Clive, Archie, Rosie, and Olivia — I could not have done this without you.

NOTE ON CONVENTIONS

* I use modified Library of Congress transliteration throughout. (Certain names appear in two forms, where convention/authorial preference conflict with this system.)
* All translations from Russian are mine unless otherwise noted.
* In most cases I only quote poetry in both Russian and English; I give non-poetic quotations in English only.
* Poem titles are translated at their first appearance in each chapter, and given solely in Russian for the rest of the chapter.
* I use italics to distinguish *poetic cycles* from 'standalone poems', contrary to the usual convention, since Shvarts primarily wrote poetry.
* St Petersburg is a city of many names. For simplicity, and because Shvarts's view of the city transcends its Soviet phase, I generally refer to the city as St Petersburg (or just Petersburg) unless I am specifically discussing the Soviet city of Leningrad.

NOTE ON ABBREVIATIONS AND EDITIONS

Elena Shvarts

* Writings cited solely by volume and page no. are from the five-volume collected works: *Sochineniia Eleny Shvarts*, 5 vols (St Petersburg: Pushkinskii fond, 2002–13)
* ZT: the 'Zelenaia tetrad'' [Green Notebook] of early poems, published posthumously: *Stikhi iz 'Zelenoi tetradi'. Stikhotvoreniia 1966–1974 godov*, ed. by Pavel Uspenskii and Artem Shelia (St Petersburg: Poriadok slov, 2018)
* BT: the 'Bremenskaia tetrad'' [Bremen Notebook] of drafts 1977–83: 'Tetrad'' so stikhami' (Bremen), Forschungsstelle Osteuropa, FSO 01–194 Švarc K3
* ESHA: Elena Shvarts Archive (St Petersburg) curated by Kirill Kozyrev. The six boxes in the archive are not catalogued or labelled, and contain loose papers, files with papers in, and notebooks. I have assigned the boxes letters based on the general category of their contents. I have assigned the files and notebooks abbreviations based on what is written on them, or their description.

    * D: *dokumenty* — official documents and prose
        D.prer: 'Preryvistaia povest'' [Discontinuous Story] file
        D.proza: 'Proza' [Prose] file
    * S: *stikhi* — poems
    * T: *tetradi* — notebooks
        T.A11: 'Al'bom 11' [Album 11] (1993)
    * P: *poemy, perevody* — long poems, poems in translation
    * M: mixed — documents, poems, long poems, childhood poems
        M.0, M.1, M.2: '0', '1', '2' files
        M.atom: atom-patterned file
    * J: juvenilia — childhood poems
        J.VT: 'Vtoraia' tetrad' [Second Notebook] (1962-63)
        J.ST: 'Stikhi' tetrad' [Poems Notebook] (blue, 1962?)

Roman Poets

* Cat.: Catullus, *The Poems of Catullus*, trans. by Guy Lee (Oxford: Oxford University Press, 1991)
* Odes/Epodes: Horace, *Odes and Epodes*, trans. by Niall Rudd (Cambridge, MA; London: Harvard University Press, 2004)
* Satires/Epistles: Horace, *Satires, Epistles and Ars Poetica*, trans. by H. Rushton Fairclough (London: Heinemann, 1926)
* Juv.: Juvenal, *Juvenal and Persius*, trans. by Susanna Morton Braund (Cambridge, MA: Harvard University Press, 2015)

* Prop.: Propertius, *Elegies*, trans. by G. P. Goold (Cambridge, MA; London: Harvard University Press, 2006)
* Mart.: Martial, *Epigrams*, trans. by D. R. Shackleton Bailey, 3 vols (Cambridge, MA; London: Harvard University Press, 1993)

CHAPTER 1

The Works and Days of Elena, a Poet from the Order of the Metamorphosis of the Self

> И каждый слог как мальчик наг
> Когда-то ночевал с Вергилием
> [And every syllable like a boy — naked —
> At one time spent the night with Virgil]
> E. A. Shvarts, 'Akh esli b vse zhili tak druzhno'
>   [Ah, if only everyone could live as harmoniously], 1974?

Elena Shvarts's greatest poems are works of genius. They transport the reader to see through the eyes and feel through the bodies of others — sometimes Shvarts's own, sometimes her alter egos'. They find beauty even in grime; no topic, exotic or mundane, is unworthy. They are profoundly bodily, both sensual and brutal, and often taboo-breaking. Female experience is central to them, but they are not feminist, or at least not politically feminist. They are apolitical, without ignoring contemporary reality or current events. They are religious, visionary, Dionysian; they strive constantly towards transcendence, even though transcendence always comes at the price of pain. They are theatrical, giving compelling glimpses of narrative, but without losing their lyric emotional focus. They are erudite, though never obviously so, and allusive, though never deferential; Shvarts's own voice always prevails. That voice is characterised most by its changeability, with metre and rhyme as wayward as the poems' contents, fitted to emotions and events, never allowed to confine expression.

Rhythm is the foundation of Shvarts's poetry: she writes that the jangling of keys first inspired words to their beat in her early teenagehood; this unforced, easy composing, she insists, produces her only true poetry (III.187, 230). In her poetic manifesto 'Poetika zhivogo' [Poetics of the Alive] (1996, IV.272–75) she describes her ideal rhythm:

> I by far prefer complex and broken, disjointed poetic music (similar to the music of the turn of the century, but not falling into the sonic collapse of contemporary music). [...] I have dreamed of finding a rhythm that would alter with every alteration in my flow of thought, with every new emotion or sensation.

Fig. 1.1. E.Sh. monogram. Photograph courtesy of Kirill Kozyrev.

As a result, Shvarts rarely keeps to one metre in a poem, saying: 'I can't ever bear to keep to one metre. I love to keep breaking step'. Her extremely unusual, and, in the Soviet period, subversive[1] approach to versification has been variously named 'polymetry',[2] 'heteromorphic verse',[3] 'polyrhythmy',[4] and 'verbal jazz'.[5] But Shvarts spoke out passionately against ignoring metre altogether, and descending to free verse, as Western poetry had done; in her eyes, by retaining rhythm Russian poetry was the only poetry that still had music and 'sacral meaning' (IV.180–81). For Shvarts saw the poet as a priest (III.194), in the Horatian and Pushkinian vatic mode.

Shvarts's writing process must have encouraged her belief in divine inspiration. It is clear from examining first drafts that Shvarts's poems generally came to her almost fully formed: there are usually only minor differences between draft and published

---

1   Emily Lygo, *Leningrad Poetry 1953–1975: The Thaw Generation* (Oxford, Bern, Berlin, New York: Peter Lang, 2010), p. 135.
2   Valerii Shubinskii, 'Elena Shvarts (Tezisy doklada)', in *Istoriia leningradskoi nepodtsenzurnoi literatury: 1950–1980-e gody: sbornik statei*, ed. by B. I. Ivanov and B. A. Roginskii (St Petersburg: Dean, 2000), pp. 110–15 (p. 114); Viacheslav Dolinin and others, *Samizdat Leningrada, 1950-e–1980-e: literaturnaia entsiklopediia*, ed. by Dmitrii Severiukhin (Moscow: Novoe literaturnoe obozrenie, 2003), p. 366.
3   Iurii Orlitskii, 'Geteromorfnyi (neuporiadochennyi) stikh v russkoi poezii', *NLO*, 73 (2005), <http://magazines.russ.ru/nlo/2005/73/or19.html> [accessed 3 June 2015].
4   Iuliia Ryzhenko, 'Chto takoe muzyka stikha? Ol'ga Sedakova o slovesnoi khoreografii — i o tom, zachem poetu nuzhno legkoe serdtse', *colta.ru* <http://www.colta.ru/articles/specials/1090?page=3> [accessed 3 June 2015].
5   Evgeniia Svitneva, 'Elena Shvarts. Dikopis' poslednego vremeni', *Novyi mir*, 9, 2001, 189–92 (p. 189).

versions, and I have found only one instance of her working out versification on paper (BT 134). The first thing that struck me when looking at Shvarts's papers is how awful her handwriting is, and how predominant are typewritten — and later, printed — pages. She began to use a typewriter aged fourteen (26/28 September 1962, v.299–300), and even enshrined her typewriter in the poem 'Moi mashinki' [My Typewriters] (1992, 1.282): 'На что мне радость и печаль, | Когда нет «Оптимы» со мной?' [What use to me is happiness or sadness | When my Optima isn't with me?]. The lasting impression I got from Shvarts's diaries and friends is that poetry was the central, all-consuming purpose of her life, and from childhood her entire self-worth was wrapped up in whether she was currently writing good poems.

Shvarts's poetics were unlike those of her contemporaries — especially metrically — and she did not belong or ascribe to any poetic school. Nevertheless, Shvarts and her group of poet friends have been called the 'Leningrad School' — which she repudiated as 'a fictive concept'.[6] Despite this, she clearly identified as a 'Petersburg poet': one in a long line of writers whose work was shaped by the classical façade and grimy underbelly of Peter the Great's improbable, northerly, force-fabricated, waterlogged city — and as such, transcending the political fluctuations that had turned the capital St Petersburg into the second city Leningrad. Much of her oeuvre could therefore be placed in the genre of the 'Petersburg Text'.[7] Various definitions have been posited for Shvarts's style. Many commentators take into account the highly allusive nature of her poetry: 'baroque',[8] 'neoclassicism',[9] 'neomodernism',[10] 'retromodernism'.[11] Others focus on her poetry's spiritual questing: 'rationalistic visionary',[12] 'Leningrad metaphysicism' (v.182).[13] Some combine the two features: 'metarealism',[14] 'metametaphorism'.[15] Another approach to defining her poetry has been via its influences. Shvarts has been compared to Silver Age poets of all stripes — Nikolai Zabolotskii, Marina Tsvetaeva, Vladimir Maiakovskii, Viacheslav Ivanov, Zinaida Gippius, Anna Akhmatova[16] — and Sedakova names Silver Age

---

6   Valentina Polukhina, *Brodsky through the Eyes of his Contemporaries* (Basingstoke: Macmillan, 1992), p. 218.
7   As exemplified by Aleksandr Pushkin, Nikolai Gogol', Fedor Dostoevskii, Aleksandr Blok, Andrei Belyi, Anna Akhmatova...
8   I. V. Ostapenko, 'Priroda v russkoi lirike 1960–1980-x godov: Ot peizazha k kartine mira' (PhD thesis, Kamenets-Podol'skii natsional'nyi universitet, 2012), pp. 32–33.
9   Ivan Zhdanov, 'Igra na ponizhenie', in 'Andegraund vchera i segodnia', ed. by Mikhail Aizenberg, *Znamia*, 6 (1998), 187–98 (p. 190).
10 A. A. Zhitenev, *Poeziia Neomodernizma* (St Petersburg: INAPRESS, 2012).
11 Sergei Zav'ialov, 'Retromodernizm v leningradskoi poezii 1970-x godov', in *'Vtoraia kul'tura': Neofitsial'naia poeziia Leningrada v 1970–1980-e gody*, ed. by Zhan-Filipp Zhakkar, Violen Fridli, and Iens Kherl't (St Petersburg: Rostok, 2013), pp. 30–52.
12 Shubinskii, 'Elena Shvarts', in Ivanov and Roginskii, p. 110.
13 Anton Nesterov, 'Germenevtika, metafizika i "drugaia kritika"', *NLO*, 61 (2003), 75–97.
14 Epstein, in Mikhail Epstein, Aleksandr Genis and Slobodanka Vladiv-Glover, *Russian Postmodernism: New Perspectives on Post-Soviet Culture* (New York; Oxford: Berghahn, 1999), p. 147.
15 Shubinskii, 'Elena Shvarts', in Ivanov and Roginskii, p. 113.
16 Olga Sedakova, 'L'Antica Fiamma Elena Shvarts', *Novoe Literaturnoe Obozrenie*, 3 (2010), https://magazines.gorky.media/nlo/2010/3/l-8217-antica-fiamma-elena-shvarcz.html [accessed 16

poets Velimir Khlebnikov and Mikhail Kuzmin as the poets closest to Shvarts in prosody.[17] Her forerunners have been traced further back, to Romanticism — Fedor Tiutchev.[18] They have been found in the Soviet era — Anna Barkova.[19] They have been found among her 'circle' of underground poets — Viktor Krivulin, Aleksandr Mironov, Oleg Okhapkin, Sergei Stratanovskii, and Vasilii Filippov.[20] Shvarts herself named Mironov as the closest to her of contemporary poets, and her 'antipode'.[21] And in her youth she idolised Tsvetaeva above all other Silver Age writers, which led to an unfortunate falling-out with the elderly Akhmatova (v.346, III.190–93). But ultimately, when asked who Shvarts learned her art from, her friend and fellow poet Ol'ga Sedakova replied 'all poetry at once', and, conversely, that 'Lena did not repeat anyone'.[22]

Elena Shvarts may not have repeated anyone, but she did rewrite a 'lost' Roman poet, as well as making many other poetic forays into classical antiquity. In this way, as my title puts it, Shvarts re-created Senatus Populusque Romanus in the Union of Soviet Socialist Republics. Shvarts's engagement with classical antiquity spans the entirety of her poetic oeuvre, with poems on classical themes as early as 1963 and as late as 2010. Classical antiquity is one of several major themes within her oeuvre; the others are religion and belief (of all kinds), the city (usually, but not always, St Petersburg), and poethood (Shvarts's theme of themes). Her classical poems intersect with all these other major themes. This is because classical antiquity is uniquely placed at the interstices of the drives and ideas motivating Shvarts's poetry, for a number of reasons. Ancient Greek and Roman culture is fundamental both to world culture and to pre-revolutionary Russian culture, with which Shvarts and her generation of poets strove to reconnect. Graeco-Roman mythology offers archetypal poets, gods, and believers. Ancient Rome is the archetypal city for Western cultures. Graeco-Roman literature is the basis of a huge range of modern poetic metres. Finally, the otherness of the ancient world provides an opportunity for escape and transcendence. And indeed, the ancient world inspired some of Shvarts's greatest poetry, and informed her commentary on the changing Russia

---

November 2013]; Shubinskii, 'Elena Shvarts', in Ivanov and Roginskii, p. 110; Aleksandr Ulanov, 'Postposlednii romantik?', *Znamia*, 9 (1999), 216–17; Stephanie Sandler, 'Thinking Self in the Poetry of Ol'ga Sedakova', in *Gender and Russian Literature: New Perspectives*, ed. by Rosalind J. Marsh (Cambridge: Cambridge University Press, 1996), pp. 302–25 (p. 313).

17   Nina-Inna Tkachenko, '"I ves' sostav moi budet napoen stradan'ia svetom..." Interv'iu s O. A. Sedakovoi v pamiat' poetessy Eleny Shvarts', *Gazeta KIFA* (2010), <http://gazetakifa.ru/content/view/3454/38/> [accessed 25 April 2019].

18   Ulanov; Iosif Nelin, '"i gornii angelov polet, i gad morskikh podvodnyi khod"', *Zvezda*, 10 (1997), 208–13 (p. 213).

19   Stephanie Sandler, 'Poetry after 1930', in *The Cambridge Companion to Twentieth-Century Russian Literature*, ed. by Evgeny Dobrenko and Marina Balina (Cambridge: Cambridge University Press, 2011), pp. 115–34 (p. 117).

20   Josephine von Zitzewitz, *Poetry and the Leningrad Religious-Philosophical Seminar 1974–1980: Music for a Deaf Age* (Oxford: Legenda, 2016), p. 226; Nikita Eliseev, '"Triumf" dlia Eleny', *Ekspert Severo-Zapad*, 5 (2004), <https://expert.ru/northwest/2004/05/05no-scult_50671/> [accessed 11 April 2019].

21   Eliseev.

22   Tkachenko; Sedakova.

in which she lived. So, in viewing Shvarts's oeuvre through the lens of classical reception, this book casts light on Shvarts's poetry as a whole and on her perceptions of contemporaneity.

This book follows Shvarts's transcendental and escapist encounters with classical antiquity from her wild youth to her defiant old age, from the oppressive Stagnation under Brezhnev, to the philistinic capitalism under Putin. Chapter 1 introduces Shvarts's life and times and the background to her classical reception. Chapter 2 addresses Shvarts's many classical alter egos — mythical characters whom Shvarts used to ventriloquise aspects of her self — from Narcissus to Ariadne. Chapter 3 explores her great classical cycle *Kinfiia* in depth, revealing its references within Latin literature and Russian culture. Chapter 4 turns to Shvarts's relationship with the city of Rome, in the abstract and the concrete. And chapter 5 analyses her lesser-known classical cycle *Homo Musagetes* in the light of its pervasive reception of Horace. The book will build a picture of a poet profoundly influenced by classical antiquity, and particularly by Ancient Rome.

This introductory chapter falls into two halves. The first half presents a biography of the poet. The second half gives the background to her poetry's use of Graeco-Roman antiquity: a summary of classical reception theory, a history of Russian classical reception, and details of Shvarts's personal acquaintance with Classics.

Shvarts's Biography

Elena Andreevna Shvarts was born in Leningrad on 17 May 1948.[23] She was self-willed, intellectual, beautiful, rowdy, theatrical, apolitical, religious, superstitious, animal-loving, chain-smoking, hard-drinking, nail-biting, a football fan, a technophile, a translator, a traveller, a Petersburger ... and, first and foremost, a poet. Shvarts felt that the contradictions within her character and poetry were perfectly encapsulated in her name, which contains oppositions within its meanings and provenances: 'Елена — светлая, Шварц — черная' [Elena is light, Shvarts is black];[24] *'Имя с окнами на запад и восток | Дал мне Бог'* [*A name with windows facing West and East | Was given me by God*].[25]

Family history

Shvarts's family history was important to her; she returns to the topic quite often in her diaries and memoirs.[26] Shvarts's parents were Dina Morisovna Shvarts

---

23 Sarah Clovis Bishop, 'In Memoriam: Elena Andreevna Shvarts (17 May 1948–11 March 2010)', *Slavonica*, 16.2 (2010), 112–30 (p. 113).
24 Eliseev.
25 'Dialog' [Dialogue], in *Nochnaia tolcheia* [*Night-Time Throng*] (1979, II.109–16).
26 While the diaries are reliable, a large part (mid-January 1964–early December 2003 (except November 2001)) is missing due to the flat fire; the memoirs sometimes need to be taken with a pinch of salt. See Josephine von Zitzewitz, 'From Underground to Mainstream: The Case of Elena Shvarts', in *Twentieth-Century Russian Poetry: Reinventing the Canon*, ed. by Katharine Hodgson, Joanne Shelton, and Alexandra Smith (Cambridge: Open Book Publishers, 2017), pp. 225–63 (pp. 250–51).

(1921–98), who was the literary manager of the BDT (Bol'shoi dramaticheskii teatr) [Bolshoi Drama Theatre], and Andrei Emel'ianovich (Andriy Omelianovych) Dzhedzhula (1915–71), who was a professor of history at the Taras Shevchenko National University of Kyiv.[27] Elena was their 'дитя любви' [love child] from a holiday romance at a southern coastal resort; Dzhedzhula asked Dina Shvarts to marry him — although he already had a wife in Kyiv. After the holiday the pair never met again, and Elena never met her father (III.204). Shvarts paints a lively picture of the possible intersection of her mother's Russian-Jewish ancestors and her father's Ukrainian-Ottoman Cossack ancestors in 'Predki' [Forebears] (III.205–07), with her Jewish forebears fleeing her Cossack forebears during the Khmelnytsky Uprising. Shvarts became interested in her absent father as a child (v.277, 281), but only briefly. It is her mother's recent family history that predominates in Shvarts's recollections. Shvarts's maternal grandfather Moris Abovich Shvarts was arrested on 30 December 1936 and shot in 1937, while her maternal grandmother Liubov' Izrailevna Rubina-Shvarts was arrested in 1937 and only returned from the GULag in 1947 (III.253–54, 206).[28] Her grandmother's sister, Berta Izrailevna Rubina, adopted Dina and her sisters Roza and Lilia after their parents were taken, which led to her expulsion from the Party and desertion by her fiancé (III.206–07). Berta managed to keep the girls alive through the Leningrad Blockade,[29] in part by boiling soup from leather from the factory where she worked, in part thanks to their evacuation from the city.[30] The middle sister Roza Shvarts (Panfilova) married and had children, and lived into her seventies;[31] however the youngest sister Lilia died after the war, aged sixteen, from falling off a tram (v.110, III.207). It was partly to compensate for this loss that Dina had Elena (III.207).

---

27 Aleksandr Petrushkin, 'Elena Andreevna Shvarts', *Megalit Evraziiskii Zhurnal'nyi Portal*, <http://www.promegalit.ru/personals/1917_shvarts_elena_andreevna.html> [accessed 17 April 2019]. While the index to Shvarts's diaries has Dzhedzhula's patronymic as 'Ivanovich' (v.398), Shvarts names her paternal grandfather as 'Emel'ian' (III.205), which is borne out by Dzhedzhula's entry on the Kyiv National University website: G. D. Kaz'myrchuk, 'Dzhedzhula Andriy Omelianovych', *Entsyklopediia Kyivs'kogo natsional'nogo universytetu imeni Tarasa Shevchenka* (2013), <http://eu.univ.kiev.ua/departments/istorychnyy-fakul%60tet/dzhedzhula-andriy-omelyanovych/> [accessed 17 April 2019].
28 'Spravka x2: Rehabilitation certificates for Moris Shvarts and Liubov' Rubina-Shvarts' (Bremen, 1956), Forschungsstelle Osteuropa, FSO 01–194 Švarc K2.
29 During which Dina's fiancé Sergei Antsiferov died (v.188).
30 Lilia in summer 1941 to Urzhum then Barnaul, Dina in February 1942 to Piatigorsk then Barnaul, Roza in April 1942 to Piatigorsk, Berta in summer 1942 to Orsk then Barnaul. Barnaul was where the sisters' mother, and Berta's sister, Liubov' Rubina-Shvarts was in exile, so Lilia, Dina, and Berta were reunited with her in evacuation. Roza Panfilova, 'Letter from Roza Panfilova July 2003', ESHA D.
31 Roza was born in 1924 (v.403) and still in correspondence with her niece in 2003, but very ill by then. Panfilova.

Childhood circles (1948–1966)

Shvarts's childhood was spent in the relatively liberal atmosphere — and ensuing artistic revival — of the Thaw, which began after the death of Stalin in 1953. She grew up with her mother and great-aunt Berta in the Egyptian Building on Kaliaev Street (now Zakhar'evskaia Street), and has attributed her early interest in writing to the presence of Thoth, the Egyptian god of writing, on the gates (III.233).[32]

FIG. 1.2. The Egyptian House, Zakhar'evskaia Ulitsa 23. My photograph, May 2019. I could not find the bird-headed god Thoth anywhere on the building's façade.

32 Barbara Heldt, 'The Poetry of Elena Shvarts', *World Literature Today*, 63.3 (1989), 381–83 (p. 381).

Fig. 1.3. Dina and Elena Shvarts on tour in Tbilisi, July 1959.
Photograph courtesy of Kirill Kozyrev.

Thanks to her mother, throughout her childhood Shvarts was immersed in the theatre, socialising and touring with the actors and directors, attending plays and even occasionally (reluctantly) performing in them; at the age of twelve she wrote that the theatre was 'the most sacred and vivid thing in my life' (v.286–87).

Many of her later habits are in evidence in her early diaries: the first entry describes her fighting at school, aged eight (v.257–58); by that time she is already writing poems (v.259); at ten she is a football fan (v.262); aged thirteen she has started smoking and drinking (v.294, 295, 3.182–83); at fifteen she decides that she believes in God (v.378). But the most important childhood experience for her career as a poet was her involvement in literary *kruzhki* [clubs; lit. little circles], which she began to attend aged eleven (v.273), and continued to attend throughout her adolescence.

The *kruzhok* was an integral part of the Soviet literary system, inherited from the pre-revolutionary intelligentsia, and used to channel young writers towards becoming fully fledged, ideologically sound members of the Union of Soviet Writers (of which the young Shvarts was aware: v.324, 337); *kruzhki* were extremely popular in the Thaw era.[33] As a child Elena Shvarts attended four *kruzhki*: the

---

33 Barbara Walker, 'Kruzhok Culture: The Meaning of Patronage in the Early Soviet Literary World', *Contemporary European History*, 11.1 (2002), 107–23 (p. 107); Lygo, p. 23; Josephine von Zitzewitz, 'From Underground to Mainstream', in *Twentieth-Century Russian Poetry*, ed. by Hodgson, Shelton, and Smith, p. 252.

schoolchildren's club 'Derzanie' [Daring] led by Aleksei Admiral'skii, Nina Kniazeva, Natal'ia Grudinina, and Irina Maliarova at the Palace of Pioneers (1959–?); a club for young prose-writers led by Iuliia Berezhnova at the Palace of Pioneers (1962);[34] a club led by Gleb Semenov at the House of Culture of the First Five-Year Plan (1963–?); and the Central LITO (literaturnoe ob"edinenie) [Literary Association] for poets led by Gleb Semenov at the House of Writers (1968–70).[35] Some of the leaders of these clubs became mentors to Shvarts: the teacher and philologist Iuliia Berezhnova, who heard Elena's first poetry reading, gave her books, introduced her to people, and always believed in her (III.187–88, v.317–18, 339–40); the poet and translator Natal'ia Grudinina, who took Elena on as an apprentice (v.314–15); and the poet Gleb Semenov, who taught Elena about poetic craft and saw her great talent, developing an inappropriately close relationship with her, until she outgrew him as a poet (v.331, 351, 366, and *passim*, 105). The *kruzhki* facilitated Shvarts's early entry onto the literary scene, and early acquaintance with fellow poets, some of whom (like Viktor Krivulin) would become her lifelong friends.[36]

Going underground (1967–1970s)

The freedoms of the late 1950s were gradually curtailed through the 1960s, especially with the accession of Brezhnev in 1964. The tightening of Party control was marked by conspicuous repressions of writers: Boris Pasternak in 1958, Iosif Brodskii in 1963–64, and Andrei Siniavskii and Iulii Daniel' in 1966.[37] The final nail in the coffin of the Thaw was the military suppression of the Prague Spring in 1968.[38] Most of Shvarts's poetic career, and the whole of her youth, would be spent in the Stagnation, without access to the usual prerequisites of a poetic career: opportunities to publish or give public readings — not to mention the dacha or car that members of the Writers' Union received. But Shvarts was in good company — the writers of her generation, 'eschewing any compromise with the censor',[39] formed independent literary groups where they gave private readings, and published their own work in *samizdat* [lit. self-publishing], handwritten or typed manuscripts

---

34 This may be the same as 'Derzanie': Bishop, p. 114.
35 Lygo, pp. 325–27; Kirill Kozyrev, 'Ot publikatora', *NLO*, 115 (2012), <http://magazines.russ.ru/nlo/2012/115/kk25.html> [accessed 3 March 2014]. For a description of the activities of the influential club 'Derzanie' (which included versification lessons, readings, and summer trips), see Lygo, pp. 49–50.
36 Writers who attended the same *kruzhki* as Shvarts (between 1953 and 1975) are, from Lygo's data: Mikhail Iasnov, Liudmila Zubova, Viktor Toporov, Evgenii Venzel', Sergei Stratanovskii, Viktor Krivulin, Elena Ignatova, Tat'iana Kurochkina, Tat'iana Tsar'kova, Mark Maz'ia, Nikolai Gol', Elena Pudovkina, Natal'ia Abel'skaia, Polina Bezprozvannaia, Elena Dunaevskaia, Petr Cheigin, Tamara Bukovskaia, Gleb Gorbovskii, Aleksandr Kushner, Aleksandr Mironov, Boris Kupriianov, Oleg Okhapkin. Lygo, pp. 325–27.
37 von Zitzewitz, *Poetry and the Leningrad Religious-Philosophical Seminar 1974–1980*, p. 4.
38 Jeremi Suri, 'The Promise and Failure of "Developed Socialism": The Soviet "Thaw" and the Crucible of the Prague Spring, 1964–1972', *Contemporary European History*, 15.2 (2006), 133–58 (pp. 157–58).
39 von Zitzewitz, *Poetry and the Leningrad Religious-Philosophical Seminar 1974–1980*, p. 4.

for circulation. This sub-culture of 'unofficial writers, artists, human rights activists, feminists, and Christian groups' became known as the underground.[40]

After leaving school, Shvarts entered the Philological Faculty of Leningrad State University, but found studying there 'boring and repugnant' (III.198). After half a year she lost her grant due to a (deliberate) bad mark and transferred to extramural study at the Theatrical Institute (III.198–99). She was nearly thrown out of the Theatrical Institute in 1969 for failing an exam on Party history (Shvarts criticised the invasion of Czechoslovakia and praised Pasternak), but was saved by the head of the Institute, who was a friend of her mother's (like nearly all the professors there), and she ultimately graduated with excellent marks (III.199–200).

At the age of 20 Shvarts married fellow poet Evgenii Venzel', 'for no discernible reason' (III.209). The couple continued to live apart after their marriage, and did not even tell their families it had taken place (III.210). The marriage was not a happy one: Venzel' was a heavy drinker, jealous, and violent, and on one occasion almost strangled Shvarts to death — afterwards he told her he stopped because 'I remembered what a good poet you are' (III.211). The domestic violence made its way into Shvarts's poetry (e.g. 'Gde my?' [Where Are We?] — see chapter 4). Having married in 1969, Shvarts and Venzel' divorced in 1974.[41]

When Shvarts left university the Stagnation was in full torpor — an era in which 'the phrase "unpublishable work" (*veshch' nepechatnaya*) began to be used to denote something of worth'.[42] In the early 1970s she succeeded in getting four poems published officially: two limerick translations in *Koster* [*Campfire*] (1970) and two poems in the Tartu University newspaper (1973) — her last official publications before *glasnost'*.[43] The 1973 publication followed a literary tour to Estonia, which Shvarts organised for herself and her fellow unofficial poets Oleg Okhapkin, Krivulin, Boris Kupriianov, Tamara Bukovskaia, and Venzel'. The tour — and the publication — took place because Estonia was far more liberal than Russia at that time, but the main reading was cancelled due to a request from Leningrad; this was Shvarts's last tour under the Soviet regime (IV.224–26). In 1974 Shvarts gave her only public reading of the 1970s at the House of Writers (III.195–96), arranged by Irina Maliarova — whose freedom to choose unofficial writers to read was subsequently curtailed.[44]

In stark contrast to this stunted official career, Shvarts's underground career was in full bloom by the mid-1970s, with her poetry appearing regularly in *samizdat* journals such as *37*, *Chasy* [*The Clock*], *Obvodnyi kanal* [*Bypass Canal*], and *Severnaia pochta* [*The Northern Post*].[45] Lack of an official career usually brought unofficial poets financial hardship, and necessitated taking menial jobs to avoid charges of *tuneiadstvo* [parasitism],[46] but Shvarts was supported by her mother: 'My mama,

---

40 Lygo, p. 115.
41 Elena Shvarts, 'Questionnaire for Article', ESHA D.
42 Lygo, p. 95.
43 Bishop, p. 115.
44 Lygo, p. 114.
45 Bishop, p. 115.
46 Lygo, p. 118.

Dina Shvarts, really didn't want me to do just anything. She would say: "I will keep you for as long as I live, and you mustn't do anything, only write poems".[47] Shvarts did do (poorly paid) translations of texts in English, German, and French,[48] work she got into with the help of El'ga Linetskaia (III.254), which she continued until late in life (v.110).

The underground was founded on private groups and readings, and Shvarts was no exception to this. Although she rarely read elsewhere, she gave poetry readings at home (III.196), and ran a private society called 'Obez'iana' [Simian] which held a 'Chimposium' at Shvarts's flat (8 Shkol'naia Street) on the 14th of each month from January 1975 until 1982. At each Chimposium the members drank invented cocktails and listened to two talks, one about poetry and one about a turning point in history. The talks were scored by a secret vote with coloured bootlaces — black = best, white = middling, red = worst — which the speaker then wore on their wrist or neck like a monkey's tail.[49] The leader of the Chimposium carried a large exotic bean-pod, which they used as a rattle to chair the meeting, and wore a metal bell attached to their tail.[50]

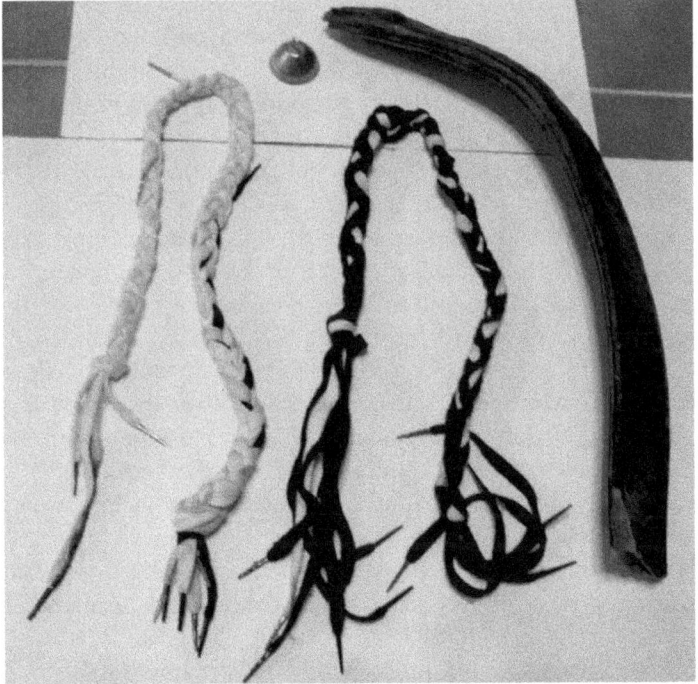

FIG. 1.4. Chimposium bootlace-tails, leader's bean-pod and tail-bell. Photograph by Viacheslav Dolinin, July 2020.

47 Eliseev.
48 Bishop, p. 115.
49 III.282–83; Dolinin and others, p. 465.
50 Viacheslav Dolinin, 'pro "obez'iannik"', 27 July 2020.

Every member of 'Obez'iana' had a simian nickname. Shvarts was called sister Chimp; other members included: Tat'iana Goricheva — sister Marikina, Boris Grois — brother Hanuman, Viacheslav Dolinin — brother Lemur, Natal'ia Kovaleva — sister Saimiri, Viktor Krivulin — brother Orang, Boris Ostanin — brother King Kong, Evgenii Pazukhin — brother Sloth (*Lenivets*), Arsenii Roginskii — brother Vega, Lev Rudkevich — brother Hamadryas Baboon (*Gamadril*), Sergei Stratanovskii — brother Jerboa (*Tushkanchik*),[51] Bella Ulanovskaia — sister Ouistiti, Mikhail Sheinker — brother Nila, and Vladimir Erl' — brother Tarsier (*Dolgopiat*).[52] On the grounds that every society in the USSR was infiltrated by the authorities, the group members lived in constant suspicion of an informer in their midst (III.285). The meetings of the Simian Society came to an end after a drunken Shvarts accidentally hit one of the other members (Ostanin) in the face with a bottle.[53] Shvarts was also connected with the 'Religiozno-filosofskii seminar' [Religious-Philosophical Seminar] (1974–80), founded by Stratanovskii, Goricheva, Krivulin, Pazukhin, and Dolinin: although she did not attend its meetings, she was friends with many of its members and published in its journal, *37*.[54] The group's mission was 'to enquire into the religious beginnings of European culture' out of a 'drive to find an antidote to the spiritual vacuum in late Soviet official culture'.[55] As a teenager Shvarts 'became fascinated by various religious and occult trends'; this was typical of her generation, who 'studied yoga, Buddhism and theosophy, later making a gradual move to Russian Orthodoxy', in what is known as the 1970s 'Religious Renaissance'.[56]

From 1978, Shvarts's poetry began to be published abroad, in *tamizdat* [lit. over-there publishing].[57] As a result, Shvarts was threatened with prison, and her mother was stopped from touring abroad with her theatre company; the director Georgii Tovstonogov was told this was because 'She is bringing her daughter up badly' (III.196). In 1979 Shvarts was awarded the Andrei Belyi Prize for unofficial literature, which in imitation (or mockery) of official culture bestowed on the recipient one ruble and 'a bottle of vodka, or '**бутылка белого**' (bottle of white), in honour of the prize's namesake'.[58] Although Shvarts was its second honouree, she was disappointed that it took 'quite a long time' for her to be awarded it, so Krivulin — the first honouree — invented and awarded her the Dante Prize, which took the form of an electric stainless-steel coffee percolator, to cheer her up (III.197).[59]

Shvarts's most constant companion through the 1970s and 1980s was her first dog, the poodle Iasha. Shvarts wrote about Iasha's human qualities — pride, shyness, grief, embarrassment, his smile — and said 'Although he was not a human, of

---

51   For some reason not simian. There may likewise have been a sister (?) Cheetah (III.282).
52   Dolinin and others, p. 465; Mikhail Berg, 'Momemury', <http://mberg.net/proza/momemuri/> [accessed 6 August 2020].
53   Boris Ostanin, Interview by Georgina Barker, St Petersburg, Russia, 2019. Shvarts also relates this incident, but misremembers Ostanin's nickname (III.286).
54   von Zitzewitz, *Poetry and the Leningrad Religious-Philosophical Seminar 1974–1980*, pp. 1, 21–22, 43.
55   Ibid., pp. 21, 1.
56   Bishop, p. 115; von Zitzewitz, *Poetry and the Leningrad Religious-Philosophical Seminar 1974–1980*, p. 4.
57   Bishop, p. 117.
58   Ibid., p. 116.
59   von Zitzewitz, *Poetry and the Leningrad Religious-Philosophical Seminar 1974–1980*, p. 12.

Fig. 1.5. 'Lena and Iasha'. Photograph courtesy of Kirill Kozyrev.

course, to me — he was more' (III.251). She dedicated *Letnee Morokko* [*Summer Moroque*] (1983, 1.164–76) to 'Достопочтенному другу [...] Яго Боевичу Неро — лучшему из пуделей [...] — с благодарностью за советы и критические замечания' [My venerable friend [...] Iago Boevich Nero — best of poodles [...] — with gratitude for advice and constructive criticism]. Iasha died in 1986.[60]

Out in the open (1980s)

The 1980s brought Shvarts a series of firsts and widening horizons due to liberalisations which snowballed through the 1980s Soviet Union, following the decline and death in 1982 of Brezhnev, and Gorbachev's policies of *perestroika* [restructuring] and *glasnost'* [openness] from 1985. In 1981 'Klub-81' [Club-81] became the USSR's first officially approved organisation for unofficial writers since 1932, with Shvarts as a member.[61] In 1983 in the House of Writers 'Klub-81' held its first public reading:

> Four hundred people crowded into a room built to seat two hundred fifty to hear Shvarts, Arkadii Dragomoshchenko, Viktor Krivulin, and Oleg Okhapkin, among others,[62] read from their work.[63]

In 1985 three poems by Shvarts were included in an anthology issued by 'Klub-

---

60 Vasilii Filippov, 'Pamiati Iashi' [In Memory of Iasha] (10 June 1986), *Vavilon*, <http://www.vavilon.ru/texts/filippov1-3.html> [accessed 27 April 2019].
61 Bishop, p. 116.
62 The other poets were Ol'ga Beshenkovskaia, Elena Ignatova, Boris Kupriianov, Vladimir Nesterovskii, Eduard Shneiderman. Boris Ivanov, *Istoriia Kluba-81* (St Petersburg: Izdatel'stvo Ivana Limbakha, 2015).
63 Bishop, pp. 116–17.

Fig. 1.6. Shvarts reads her poetry on stage at the House of Writers, 1983;
Sergei Korovin sits on the left and Viktor Krivulin sits on the right.
Photograph courtesy of Kirill Kozyrev.

81', her first official Soviet publication since 1973.[64] In 1988 she 'gave her first solo public reading in the packed main hall of the Leningrad Writers Union'.[65] In 1989 Shvarts had her first official book published in the USSR, *Storony sveta* [*Corners of the Earth*] — although three collections of her poetry had by then appeared in *tamizdat*.

That same year — the year the Berlin Wall fell, as Shvarts notes — she was allowed to travel abroad for the first time. This is how she describes the experience of leaving the Soviet Union:

> The first time I crossed the aerial border of my at that time large country was in the year of the fall of the Berlin Wall. Soviet power had been dragged irrevocably to its death bed, and one of the symptoms — a warning sign — of its incurability was that an unofficial poet was allowed to respond to an invitation and take part in a festival.[66] That first festival was called 'Child of Europe' — but on the contrary: when out of the clouds there appeared below

---

64 Ibid., p. 117.
65 Ibid., p. 123.
66 The festival was held in London in February 1989. Bishop, p. 124.

Fig. 1.7. Shvarts on tour in Germany, 1989. Left to right: Lev Rubinshtein, Shvarts, Dmitrii Prigov, Mikhail Sheinker. Photograph from Lev Rubinshtein's archive, published on OpenSpace.ru.

the even electric circles of German cities — then Europe was born for me. Later, when the golden thundering dish of night-time London lurched and stood vertical, something inside abruptly and irreparably changed. (IV.180)

Her own widened horizons combined with the USSR's and GDR's demise in Shvarts's mind and her poetry (see chapter 4). Among Shvarts's travelling companions on her 1989 Germany trip was her second husband, the literary critic Mikhail Sheinker.[67] Shvarts and Sheinker married in 1984 and divorced acrimoniously in 1995.[68]

Touring and mourning (1990s)

In her collection *Literaturnye gastroli* [*Literary Tours*] (IV.177–240) Shvarts describes her trips to an array of foreign locations:[69] Ohrid — Macedonia, Jerusalem — Israel, Paris — France, Helsinki — Finland, Peć — Serbia, Hoboken and New York —

---

67 Lev Rubinshtein, 'Lev Rubinshtein, Elena Shvarts, D. A. Prigov, Mikhail Sheinker. 1989 g. Germaniia. "Otpechatki": fotografii iz arkhiva L'va Rubinshteina', *OpenSpace.ru*, <http://os.colta.ru/photogallery/30314/281166/> [accessed 22 April 2019].
68 Shvarts, 'Questionnaire for Article'.
69 Some of her destinations are fantastical.

USA, Heidelberg — Germany, Kathmandu — Nepal, Copenhagen — Denmark, Belfast — Northern Ireland, Oslo — Norway, and Certaldo, Arezzo, Volterra, San Gimignano, and Rome — Italy. While her Italian visits took place in the 2000s (see chapter 4), the majority of the trips she describes will have taken place in the 1990s. This amount of travel represents a dramatic change in Shvarts's lifestyle.

Shvarts was also, finally, let in to the Writers' Union, which she joined in May 1990 — just at the point when the Union was becoming an irrelevance, and its standard perks no longer available. And in 1991 Shvarts joined the editorial board of an independent journal that had been allowed to start up — *Vestnik novoi literatury* [*Herald of New Literature*], which ran from 1990 to 1994.[70] Yet Russia's new freedom did not bring only benefits. Although the underground writers were now free to publish and travel and seek international fame, at home the public were losing interest in them and their work. Shvarts complained about the diminished respect poetry commanded in post-Soviet Russia:

> In those former times there was great interest in poetry. It wasn't published, it was banned, but if there was a reading somewhere, then people would gather there without any need for advertising. They would all but hang on the chandeliers to hear some poems. They would cry. Now hardly anyone cries when poems are read.[71]

Now it was no longer banned, unofficial poetry had lost its aura of sacred speech. It also had to compete with all the previously suppressed texts on taboo topics — such as Andrei Platonov's *Kotlovan* [*The Foundation Pit*], Vasilii Grossman's *Zhizn' i sud'ba* [*Life and Fate*], and Aleksandr Solzhenitsyn's *Arkhipelag GULAG* [*Gulag Archipelago*] — and it just could not keep the public's attention.

The other major events of Shvarts's 1990s were deaths. In 1992 Sheinker's and Shvarts's dog, the borzoi Dzhon, died. Shvarts dedicated a poem to Dzhon — and his soul to Morpheus.[72] In 1997 Shvarts was injured when she was run over by a car (v.63–64). But a far worse injury was to come the following year, when her mother died of cancer in April 1998.[73] Dina Shvarts was the person Elena loved most in the world, her most constant friend and support. Stephanie Sandler writes that 'for about four years, from 1998 to about 2002, her poems were nearly all shaped by her mother's death', and counts 69 poems of mourning in just two collections (of 1998 and 2001).[74] Shvarts's late diaries, too, are filled with grief; for example, on the eighth anniversary of her mother's death, Shvarts writes: 'Eight years already. For all these days I have been in an awful condition. As if grief has been physically killing me, suffocating me, and my heart has been hurting' (v.130). Shvarts felt that grieving for her mother became an intrinsic part of her — in 'Nesmyvaemoe

---

70 *Vestnik novoi literatury* 3 (Leningrad: Assotsiatsiia 'Novaia literatura', 1991), <https://imwerden.de/pdf/vestnik_novoj_literatury_3_1991__ocr.pdf> [accessed 6 August 2020].
71 Eliseev.
72 'Apologiia solntsevorotnogo sna' [Apology of Solstice Sleep] (1992, I.203–04).
73 *Solo na raskalennoi trube* [*Solo on a Red-Hot Trumpet*]; *Dikopis' poslednego vremeni* [*Maduscript of the Last Hour*]. Stephanie Sandler, 'On Grief and Reason, on Poetry and Film: Elena Shvarts, Joseph Brodsky, Andrei Tarkovsky', *Russian Review*, 66.4 (2007), 647–70 (p. 650).
74 Sandler, 'On Grief and Reason, on Poetry and Film', p. 650.

Fig. 1.8. 'cat and me', early 2000s. Shvarts's Optima typewriter is just visible in the background. Photograph courtesy of Kirill Kozyrev.

gore' [Indelible Grief] she says: 'My grief is so deep, it seems that if I died and met Mama there, it would still not go away but would remain like an indelible dark stain on the clothing of my soul' (III.269). Shvarts claims that it was only her sense of responsibility for her cat Murka that kept her alive after her mother died (v.130). Murka was with Shvarts until 2003, when she drowned in the Fontanka river.[75]

Up in flames (2000s)

In December 2003 Shvarts was awarded the Triumph Prize, worth 50,000 dollars, fulfilling Dina Shvarts's final prophetic dream, and changing Shvarts's life — or so she believed at the time (v.59). Shvarts joined an illustrious list of winners, including Thaw-era poets Bella Akhmadulina and Iunna Morits, as well as the singer-songwriter Boris Grebenshchikov.[76] In 2004 she was also the first winner of the Gogol' Prize for non-fiction.[77]

But her good fortune was not to last long: mere months after the Triumph award, on 30 March 2004, there was a fire in her flat (30 5-ia Krasnoarmeiskaia Street),

---

[75] Kirill Kozyrev, Interview by Georgina Barker, St Petersburg, Russia, 2019.
[76] Eliseev.
[77] 'Premii', *Soiuz pisatelei Sankt-Peterburga* (2019), <http://pisateli-spb.ru/award.html> [accessed 24 April 2019].

which was both psychologically and financially devastating. It was the night after Shvarts's return from America, she was taking a bath, and the first sign something was wrong was when the lights went off, around 5. a.m; when Shvarts got out to investigate, she found her bedroom ablaze (III.337–38). The possessions that were not burnt were either waterlogged when the firefighters put out the fire, or stolen in the aftermath (III.340). Most of her Triumph Prize money went on protracted renovations by cowboy builders and an even more protracted court case, as her downstairs neighbour sued her for damages (III.341, 346). In her second diary entry after her old diaries were lost in the fire, Shvarts writes: 'when everyone died, the flat became like a living entity for me. And now it's gone' (v.63).

The loss that Shvarts most laments from the fire is that of her old photographs, in which she was 'pretty and like a poet should be' (v.64).[78] A constant theme of her later diaries is ageing — in 2004 she was already imagining her death taking its place among the deaths of the great Russian poets:

> I suddenly worked out that I am already older than Brodskii; he did not quite live to 56. This is how it goes: first you outlive Lermontov, Esenin, then Maiakovskii, Blok, and then Tsvetaeva and Mandel'shtam, then Annenskii, and now Kuzmin lies ahead (with any luck). A ladder of sorts. My father and grandmother died at this age — 56. Perhaps I will, too ... (v.69)

And Shvarts did have ongoing health problems in her last years: in 2005 she was diagnosed with hepatitis, and admitted that 'the last eight years have been a delayed suicide [...] I have been drinking myself to death' (v.113). On top of this, she felt very alone — her close family was dead, she was on bad terms with both ex-husbands, many of her friends had died or emigrated, and few of those who remained had helped her after the fire (v.61, 66–68, 88, 169).

Shvarts continued to travel widely in her final decade. Her passport of 2004–09 contains visas for seven different countries: Germany (twice), Finland, Slovenia, USA, Italy (four times), Czechoslovakia, and the Netherlands (ESHA D). Her closest companion was her Japanese Chin dog, Khokku-Khoka, whom she bought as a puppy in 2006 (v.142). She trained him to do tricks, to the delight of neighbourhood children. When Khoka died in 2013, Shvarts's friend Kirill Kozyrev, who had looked after Shvarts in her last months and, afterwards, Khoka, had his ashes scattered on Shvarts's grave.[79] Shvarts's last great literary labour was her biography of the Italian poet Gabriele D'Annunzio (v.170, 206). In August 2009 Shvarts was diagnosed with cancer, which she called 'у рак ан' [hurricancer] (v.212–13, 217). Writing almost to the last, Elena Andreevna Shvarts died in St Petersburg on 11 March 2010, aged 61.[80]

---

78 Her diary entry of 23 April 2004 describes the burning of her early photographs as 'Будто самая главная часть тела сгорела' [As if the most important part of my body had burnt away] (v.61–62).
79 Kozyrev, 'Interview'.
80 Bishop, p. 112.

Fig. 1.9. Kirill Kozyrev and Boris Aksel'rod tending Dina and Elena Shvarts's grave in the Volkovo Cemetery.[81] My photograph, May 2019.

Classical Reception

The second half of this chapter deals with the underpinnings of Shvarts's interactions with classical antiquity. First it explains the theory behind classical reception, the lens through which this book examines Shvarts's poetry. There follows a concise history of classical reception in Russia, focusing on the parts of that history which have most influenced Shvarts's own classical reception. Finally, it addresses some of the mechanics behind Shvarts's use of classical antiquity.

In this book 'classical reception' embraces references to classical literature, myth, and history within Shvarts's work. 'Classical' refers here to Greek and Roman antiquity, from Greece's earliest extant literature (Homer: c. eighth century BC) to the end of the pagan period (c. AD 250).[82] 'Reception'[83] is the currently accepted term for later uses of Graeco-Roman antiquity, which aims to combine awareness of 'the historicity of texts' and 'the aesthetic response of readers'.[84] 'Reception'

---

81   Coincidentally, one of Shvarts's earliest poems, opening the 'неоконченный цикл' [unfinished cycle] *Smert'* [*Death*] (22 October 1964), begins: 'За Волковым кладбищем есть пустыри | Там души убитых зверей' [Beyond Volkovo Cemetery there are wastelands | There are souls of murdered beasts]. ESHA J.
82   Following the broader definition of Jan M. Ziolkowski, 'Middle Ages', in *A Companion to the Classical Tradition*, ed. by Craig Kallendorf (Malden, MA; Oxford: Blackwell, 2007), pp. 17–29 (p. 18); Christine Walde, in *Brill's New Pauly: The Reception of Classical Literature*, ed. by Christine Walde and others (Leiden; Boston: Brill, 2012), p. ix. For the history of the word 'classical', see *A Companion to Classical Receptions*, ed. by Lorna Hardwick and Christopher Stray, (Malden, MA; Oxford: Blackwell, 2008), pp. 76–81, 387.
83   Yielding 'receive', 'receptive', etc.; with antonym 'transmission', etc.
84   Charles Martindale, 'Introduction: Thinking through Reception', in *Classics and the Uses of Reception*, ed. by Charles Martindale and Richard F. Thomas (Malden, MA; Oxford: Blackwell, 2006), pp. 1–13 (p. 3).

understands that 'received' and 'receiving' texts alike are created by authors who are also readers, and who usually do not share the same frame of reference with each other, or indeed with their ensuing reader/receiver.

'Reception' is not a neutral term — there are no neutral terms for the act of making a classical reference: every term puts a different emphasis on the relative agency and priority of the 'received' and 'receiving' texts or authors.[85] I choose 'reception' above other terms partly for its 'dynamic and dialogic'[86] connotations, but mostly for its greater — but not exclusive — focus upon the receiving author as opposed to the ancient sources. This reflects the emphasis of this book, which takes the modern receiver (Shvarts) as its starting point, and her biographical and historical circumstances as the major prism through which her poetry is interpreted. For variety and nuance, I also use several other terms to express this overarching concept of reception. 'Intertextuality'[87] is a less author-centric word for the process, conveying both continuity and reciprocity. 'Intertextuality' generally refers to specifically textual references, so I use it more when Shvarts is clearly interacting with a concrete literary source — often from Russian poetry. 'Allusion' or 'allusivity' foregrounds authorial subjectivity more forcefully than 'reception'; my usage may have undertones of playfulness or greater implicitness,[88] requiring the reader's 'complicity'.[89] So I tend to use 'allusion' particularly when Shvarts is sharing (or not) an erudite reference with her reader. 'Influence' is used often, reflecting the importance to Shvarts of the predecessors whose words and topics she incorporates into her poetry. 'Reference' is used mostly interchangeably with 'reception', but sometimes connotes consultation with a specific source.[90] When wishing to signify a particularly characteristic or clichéd reference, I use 'motif' or 'topos'. Reception of classical antiquity via intermediary receivers — a common occurrence with Shvarts — is most often indicated by 'mediation'. Words I use more circumspectly are 'reworking' and 'imitation', because they suggest deviance/adherence from/to a specific 'model', implying value judgements.[91] 'Appropriation', which may imply lack of dialogue or resistance from the text being received, and 'tradition', which may imply the reverse, are also used circumspectly. I do not use 'rewriting' or 'emulation', since such modes of reception are not in keeping with Shvarts's personality. Nor do I use 'nachleben' or 'afterlife', as it implies that texts can die, which is certainly not the case as long as they continue to influence new readers/receivers like Shvarts.

---

85   Stephen Hinds, *Allusion and Intertext: Dynamics of Appropriation in Roman Poetry* (Cambridge: Cambridge University Press, 1998), p. xii.
86   Charles Martindale, 'Reception', in *A Companion to the Classical Tradition*, ed. by Kallendorf, pp. 297–311 (p. 300).
87   Julia Kristeva's term: Craig Kallendorf, 'Allusion as Reception: Virgil, Milton, and the Modern Reader', in *Classics and the Uses of Reception*, ed. by Martindale and Thomas, pp. 67–79 (p. 68).
88   Hinds, pp. 21–23.
89   Simon Goldhill, *Victorian Culture and Classical Antiquity: Art, Opera, Fiction, and the Proclamation of Modernity*, Martin Classical Lectures (Princeton, NJ: Princeton University Press, 2011), p. 244.
90   Hinds, p. 21.
91   See Alessandro Barchiesi, *Speaking Volumes: Narrative and Intertext in Ovid and Other Latin Poets* (London: Duckworth, 2001), p. 150.

As a practice and a field of study, classical reception dates back to classical antiquity itself.[92] Its long history, and especially its use to 'legitimate a social order and a set of institutions, beliefs, and values that are commonly associated with western civilization and "our" western cultural heritage',[93] makes classical reception a particularly revealing lens through which to examine European cultures. Russia is no exception, and, indeed, has a trajectory of classical reception that is unique in Europe.

Russia's classical tradition

Shvarts's engagement with classical antiquity — predominantly Roman — stems from a tradition of classical reception that is particular to Russia. Russia's initial access to the cultural legacy of the ancient world came via the Eastern Roman Empire — Byzantium — which outlived its Western counterpart by a millennium. Contact between early Russia and Byzantium was established when Prince Vladimir converted Kievan Rus' to Orthodoxy in 988,[94] but lost again after the Mongol invasion in the thirteenth century, until Russian states emerged from under the Tatar yoke in the fifteenth century. Crucially to Russia's later sense of belatedness in relation to the Classics, during this period the Russian states also missed the Renaissance, when Europeans reassessed their classical inheritance. In 1453, just decades before Muscovy regained its autonomy, Byzantium fell to the Ottoman Turks. It was out of these circumstances — Byzantium toppled and Russia established — that the idea emerged of Moscow (and by synecdoche, Russia) as the Third Rome.[95]

The Third Rome

Russia's positioning of itself as a legitimate heir to the Roman Empire began with Rus' acquiring Roman imperial trappings from the fallen Byzantium. In 1472 Ivan III married the niece of the last Byzantine emperor, and assumed the title 'Tsar' — derived from 'Caesar' — and the imperial symbol of the double-headed eagle.[96] But it was religion rather than imperial might that constituted the strongest link between Russia and Byzantium, and thence back to Rome. In the sixteenth century the Pskovian monk Filofei declared Muscovy to have succeeded the Second Rome, Byzantium, as the custodian of Orthodoxy. His messianic statement of Russia's capacity to preserve the legacy of a past in which it did not partake — 'Moscow is the Third Rome' — has endured within the Russian popular and literary con-

---

92 Walde and others, p. xiii.
93 Seth L. Schein, 'Our Debt to Greece and Rome: Canon, Class and Ideology', in *A Companion to Classical Receptions*, ed. by Hardwick and Stray, pp. 75–85 (p. 75).
94 John Fennell, *A History of the Russian Church to 1448* (London: Longman, 1995), p. 35.
95 Grigory Tulchinsky, 'Culture and Mythocracy', in *Re-entering the Sign: Articulating New Russian Culture*, ed. by Ellen E. Berry and Anesa Miller-Pogacar (Ann Arbor: University of Michigan Press, 1995), pp. 62–78 (pp. 65–66).
96 Judith E. Kalb, *Russia's Rome: Imperial Visions, Messianic Dreams, 1890–1940* (Madison: University of Wisconsin Press, 2008), p. 16.

sciousness, most notably in works by Nikolai Gogol', Osip Mandel'shtam, and Mikhail Bulgakov.[97] Shvarts's uses of the Third Rome myth are explored in chapter 4.

Despite Filofei's call to make Muscovy another Rome, in this period Ancient Rome was still alien to the Orthodox Russia. The seventeenth century saw a long conflict between Graecophiles and Latinists as Church and Tsars wrangled over which half of classical antiquity to adopt: Greek, seen as more 'Russian', aligned with Orthodoxy and the *narod* [common people]; or Roman, associated with Europe and modernisation. This early conflict is indicative both of how the two traditions would continue to be perceived, and of how classical antiquity was already bound up with Russia's self-identification.[98] But Rome had decisively won out over Greece by the time of Peter the Great's reforms.

In 1703 Peter the Great founded St Petersburg as part of his Westernisation of Russia, which came with many Roman trappings.[99] Peter's classicising reforms were taken up again by Catherine the Great, who presented herself as his natural successor.[100] During Catherine's reign it became 'a literary commonplace' for 'the glory-that-was-Rome' to signify 'the glory-that-was-to-be-Russia'[101] — and for the first time, under Catherine, Roman culture made more than just a symbolic impact on Russian culture. The Neoclassicists (primarily Antiokh Kantemir, Vasilii Trediakovskii, and Mikhailo Lomonosov) reformed the Russian language and metrics to conform more with Latin and Greek[102] and translated large quantities of classical literature.[103] It was Catherine who actually set in stone much of St Petersburg's Italianate, neoclassical look, which endures to this day;[104] Shvarts called Petersburg 'запад, вброшенный в восток' [west, flung into the east].[105] As the city that more than any other informs Shvarts's classical reception, and as the alternative capital of Russia, St Petersburg challenges Moscow's status as the Third Rome in Shvarts's poetry, in a very unusual take on the myth.

---

97 Nina Vasil'evna Sinitsyna, *Tretii Rim: Istoki i evoliutsiia russkoi srednevekovoi kontseptsii (XV–XVI vv.)* (Moscow: Indrik, 1998), pp. 7–9.
98 G. S. Knabe, *Russkaia antichnost': Soderzhanie, rol' i sud'ba antichnogo naslediia v kul'ture Rossii* (Moscow: Rossiiskii gosudarstvennyi gumanitarnyi universitet, 2000), p. 91.
99 Ibid., pp. 100–01; Kalb, p. 11.
100 For example, the Bronze Horseman, the statue of Peter which Catherine commissioned, is based upon a Roman statue of Marcus Aurelius and bears a Latin dedication. Kalb, p. 11.
101 Stephen L. Baehr, 'From History to National Myth: *Translatio Imperii* in Eighteenth-Century Russia', *Russian Review*, 37.1 (1978), 1–13 (p. 8). Lomonosov even attempted to demonstrate an 'equation' between Russian and Roman history in his 1766 *Drevniaia Rossiiskaia istoriia* [*Ancient Russian History*]. Baehr, p. 3. Catherine also encouraged allegories comparing her to Roman goddesses such as Minerva, and Roman rulers such as Augustus. Andrew Kahn, 'Readings of Imperial Rome from Lomonosov to Pushkin', *Slavic Review*, 52.4 (1993), 745–68 (p. 755).
102 Kahn, 'Readings of Imperial Rome from Lomonosov to Pushkin', pp. 747–48; Harold Segel, 'Classicism and Classical Antiquity in Eighteenth- and Early-Nineteenth-Century Russian Literature', in *The Eighteenth Century in Russia*, ed. by J. G. Garrard (Oxford: Clarendon Press, 1973), pp. 48–71 (pp. 50, 52, 55–56, 63–64); Knabe, *Russkaia antichnost'*, pp. 105, 113; Zara Martirosova Torlone, *Russia and the Classics: Poetry's Foreign Muse* (London: Duckworth, 2009), pp. 25–27.
103 Segel, p. 56.
104 See footnote above: Kalb, p. 11. [n. 101]
105 'Gde my?' [Where Are We?], *Chernaia paskha* [*Black Easter*] (1974, ll.77–83).

Romanticism and Modernism: Pushkin, Tsvetaeva, Mandel'shtam

Rome's supremacy as a cultural influence waned across the whole of Europe in the nineteenth century: Roman culture came to be seen as derivative of Ancient Greece, which was now in fashion. Themes from both sides of antiquity permeate the poetry of Russia's national poet Aleksandr Pushkin, who gained a thorough acquaintance with Classics as a teenager at his classical gymnasium.[106] In his most influential classical poems — 'K Ovidiiu' [To Ovid] (1821), 'Prorok' [Prophet] (1826),[107] 'Arion' (1827), 'Poet i tolpa' [The Poet and the Crowd] (1828), and 'Pamiatnik' [Monument] (1836) — Pushkin enters into communion with ancient poetic figures and refashions them in his own Romantic image.[108] Pushkin's fusion of classical and Romantic aesthetics to create an exotic yet home-grown view of the poet as a tormented, divinely inspired genius was hugely appealing to Shvarts, and Pushkinian echoes can be heard in many of her classical poems. Pushkin's formative influence specifically on Shvarts's classical reception is even evidenced in one of her childhood notebooks (see below).[109]

After the 'Golden Age' of Pushkinian Romanticism there came the 'Silver Age' of Russian modernism (1890s–1917) — a turn-of-the-century boom in Russian art of all kinds, so fervent and extensive that even at the time it was compared to the Italian Renaissance.[110] Silver Age artists and thinkers were fascinated with Graeco-Roman antiquity, partly because they saw the culture of their era as synthesising Russian and world culture.[111] Many believed it was the mission of Russia, as the Third Rome, to unite 'Eastern-based spirituality and Western secular imperialism', as embodied by Ancient Greece and Rome respectively.[112] And many embraced Friedrich Nietzsche's Apollo–Dionysus polarity[113] after the German philosopher

---

106 Andrew Kahn, *Pushkin's Lyric Intelligence* (Oxford; New York: Oxford University Press, 2008), p. 16.
107 While 'Prorok' has a primarily Christian context and lacks overt classical references, the Horatian vatic pose Pushkin strikes in the poem has led several later poets to echo 'Prorok' in classical contexts.
108 For Pushkin's classical reception, see Kahn, *Pushkin's Lyric Intelligence*; Kahn, 'Readings of Imperial Rome from Lomonosov to Pushkin'; Andrew Kahn, 'Ovid and Russia's Poets of Exile', in *A Handbook to the Reception of Ovid*, ed. by John F. Miller and Carole Elizabeth Newlands, Wiley Blackwell Handbooks to Classical Reception (Chichester: Wiley-Blackwell, 2014), pp. 401–15 (pp. 401–05).
109 ESHA J.VT, p. 94.
110 Pamela Davidson, *Cultural Memory and Survival: The Russian Renaissance of Classical Antiquity in the Twentieth Century*, Studies in Russia and Eastern Europe, 6 (London: UCL School of Slavonic and East European Studies, 2009), p. 2.
111 Knabe, 'Nekotorye teoreticheskie problemy kul'turnogo naslediia: vzaimodeistvie kul'tur i "russkaia antichnost'"', *Antichnoe nasledie v kul'ture Rossii*, ed. by G. S. Knabe (Moscow: Rossiiskii nauchno-issledovatel'skii institut kul'turnogo i prirodnogo naslediia, 1996), pp. 13–27 (p. 17); *Cultural Mythologies of Russian Modernism: From the Golden Age to the Silver Age*, ed. by Boris Gasparov, Robert P. Hughes, and Irina Paperno (Berkeley; Los Angeles; Oxford: University of California Press, 1992), p. 2.
112 Torlone, pp. 56–57; Philosopher-poet Vladimir Solov'ev was a particularly influential proponent of this idea: Kalb, pp. 17–18.
113 I.e. Nietzsche's transposition (in *The Birth of Tragedy*) of Apollo and Dionysus onto Schopenhauer's conception of humanity's 'fundamental drives', Representation and Will, which Nietzsche

was popularised by the Symbolists — foremost among them, Viacheslav Ivanov.[114] Shvarts has continued to depict Apollo and Dionysus together. But the area of Silver Age culture in which classical influence is most apparent is poetry, and the two most classically receptive Silver Age poets — Marina Tsvetaeva and Osip Mandel'shtam[115] — are also the two poets who have most influenced Shvarts. Shvarts even declared, aged fifteen, 'I will be like Tsvetaeva' (v.346).[116]

The Muscovite Tsvetaeva and Petersburger Mandel'shtam did not belong to the same poetic circles, but their love affair and ensuing friendship had a profound effect on both poets,[117] and the writing of both was shaped — and curtailed — by the brutalities of post-revolutionary and Stalinist Russia. Tsvetaeva was the daughter of the classically trained art historian Ivan Tsvetaev, but she attributed her interest in classical mythology to German sources: Romanticism and children's anthologies.[118] Tsvetaeva took a 'belligerently unscholarly approach' to classical reception,[119] and, like Pushkin before her and Shvarts after her, she used classical figures to express the pain of inspiration. The most prominent classical figures in Tsvetaeva's poetry are the Sibyl, Aphrodite, and Orpheus, all of whom Shvarts mobilises in her own poetry with reference to Tsvetaeva. Mandel'shtam coined the phrase 'тоска по мировой культуре' [yearning for world culture], which characterises his mixing of cultural references from all periods, with antiquity foremost among them.[120]

---

claimed must be combined for the creation of art. Martha C. Nussbaum, 'Nietzsche, Schopenhauer, and Dionysus', in *The Cambridge Companion to Schopenhauer*, ed. by Christopher Janaway (Cambridge: Cambridge University Press, 1999), pp. 344–74 (p. 358); James M. Curtis, 'Michael Bakhtin, Nietzsche, and Russian Pre-Revolutionary Thought', in *Nietzsche in Russia*, ed. by Bernice Glatzer Rosenthal (Princeton, NJ; Guildford: Princeton University Press, 1986), pp. 331–54 (p. 335).

114 Pamela Davidson, 'The Muse and the Demon in the Poetry of Pushkin, Lermontov, and Blok', in *Russian Literature and its Demons*, ed. by Pamela Davidson, Studies in Slavic Literature, Culture, and Society, 6 (New York; Oxford: Berghahn, 2000), pp. 167–213 (p. 188).

115 For Tsvetaeva's classical reception, see Torlone; Olga Peters Hasty, *Tsvetaeva's Orphic Journeys in the Worlds of the Word* (Evanston, IL: Northwestern University Press, 1996). For Mandel'shtam's classical reception, see Torlone; *Mandel'shtam i antichnost'*, ed. by Oleg Lekmanov (Moscow: Radiks, 1995); Victor Terras, 'Classical Motives in the Poetry of Osip Mandel'štam', *The Slavic and East European Journal*, 10.3 (1966), 251–67.

116 This declaration was occasioned by Shvarts's crushing meeting with Anna Akhmatova, so is partly a reaction against the other female poetic role model; however, Akhmatova's dislike of Shvarts may have been caused by Shvarts's impassioned panegyric of Tsvetaeva in her essay 'O Marine Tsvetaevoi' [About Marina Tsvetaeva] (1963, v.228–29).

117 Torlone, p. 132.

118 Hasty, p. 9; Torlone, pp. 94–95. She also attended various schools in Russia and abroad that taught Classics. Torlone, p. 92.

119 Maria Stadter Fox, cited in Torlone, p. 95.

120 Mandel'shtam spoke, rather than wrote, the phrase in the 1930s, as an answer to the question 'What is Acmeism?': M. Ia. Poliakov, in Osip Mandel'shtam, *Slovo i kul'tura*, ed. by Pavel Nerler (Moscow: Sovetskii pisatel', 1987), p. 9. The primacy of Classics in Mandel'shtam's 'world culture' is apparent from his clarification of what he yearns for: 'yesterday [...] has not yet really existed. I want Ovid, Pushkin, and Catullus to live once more, and I am not satisfied with the historical Ovid, Pushkin, and Catullus.' Osip Mandel'shtam, *Sochineniia v dvukh tomakh*, ed. by A. D. Mikhailov and P. M. Nerler (Moscow: Khudozhestvennaia literatura, 1990), II, p. 169. Classics was part of Mandel'shtam's studies at the progressive Tenishev School, the Philosophy Department of Heidelberg University, and the Philological Faculty of St Petersburg University. Torlone, p. 119.

He believed that 'Hellenism' — the riches of Ancient Greek culture — lived on in the Russian language, making every Russian word 'sounding and speaking flesh' and 'an acropolis kernel' — Russia's way of making its mark on world culture.[121] In Mandel'shtam's poetry idealised Hellenism gives way to a politicised antiquity, expressing his despair at the disappearance of the pre-revolutionary, cultured, European Russia. Shvarts takes up Mandel'shtam's Hellenism — not his poems about Homer and the Trojan cycle, but his poems about Aphrodite, Persephone, and the Muses. Shvarts frequently groups Tsvetaeva and Mandel'shtam together with Pushkin in her classical receptions (see chapters 2 and 5) — this poetic triad represents Shvarts's personal 'Russian classical antiquity'.

Stalinism and the Thaw: Brodskii and Kushner

The Stalinist era put the last nail in the coffin of Silver Age classicism. In 1932 all independent literary organisations were abolished, the Union of Soviet Writers was formed, and Socialist Realism was designated the only legitimate style of Soviet literature. Officially, Socialist Realism would remain in place right up to the fall of the USSR in 1991.[122] Socialist Realism stipulated for poetry 'Simplicity, normality, and freedom from complex historical-cultural associations'.[123] This greatly diminished both thematic and metrical variety within Soviet poetry, and made for a poor environment for classical reception. Still worse was Stalin's campaign against the intelligentsia — Russia's educated elite who were the bearers of its classical heritage. Perceived as class enemies by the Bol'sheviks, huge swathes of the intelligentsia were exiled, imprisoned, murdered, and, at the very least, deprived of a classical education and freedom of expression. But although Classics was banished from literature and suppressed in education, there was one area where classical influence remained prominent: high Stalinist architecture is markedly neoclassical.[124] The Stalinist regime, like the Tsarist regimes before it, still wanted to associate itself with Rome's imperial power.

After Stalin's death in 1953, and especially after Khrushchev's Secret Speech denouncing Stalin in 1956, there was a period of easing of repressions known as the Thaw, which lasted — with some fluctuations — into the mid-1960s.[125] The Thaw — in the view of Emily Lygo — started 'a flowering of poetry in Russia

---

121 'O prirode slova' [On the Nature of the Word] (1920–22), in Mandel'shtam, *Slovo i kul'tura*, pp. 58, 63. He relies implicitly on the Third Rome myth to establish Russia's inheritance of Greece.
122 Katerina Clark, 'Socialist Realism in Soviet Literature', in *The Routledge Companion to Russian Literature*, ed. by Neil Cornwell (London, New York: Routledge, 2001), pp. 174–83 (p. 174).
123 M. L. Gasparov, cited in Lygo, p. 135.
124 Davidson, *Cultural Memory and Survival*, p. 17.
125 The Thaw is associated with Khrushchev, who was removed in 1964. Some repressions continued under his rule (e.g. Pasternak's and Brodskii's repressions) and some aspects of Thaw freedoms continued for a few years after his replacement by Brezhnev (see, e.g., Evgenii Dobrenko and Ilya Kalinin, 'Literary Criticism during the Thaw', in *A History of Russian Literary Theory and Criticism: The Soviet Age and Beyond*, ed. by Evgeny Dobrenko and Galin Tihanov (Pittsburgh, PA: University of Pittsburgh Press, 2011), pp. 184–206). The year 1968 marks the definitive end of the Thaw (see above).

that can be compared in its scale and significance to the Silver Age'.[126] Classical reception was far from mainstream in this period — it is mostly absent from the works of the Thaw's civic 'stadium' poets — but it was important to two poets who began their careers in the Thaw, one in *samizdat*: Iosif Brodskii, and the other officially: Aleksandr Kushner.[127] Both Brodskii and Kushner were mentored by Akhmatova, and strove to reconnect with the Silver Age, bypassing the entire Socialist Realist period in an artistic act of rebellion. Brodskii saw his task as 'defending culture' against Soviet repression, and described himself as 'infected with normal classicism'.[128] Kushner explicitly associated Silver Age poets with Classics,[129] and consciously used classical references to talk about contemporary circumstances.[130] Both poets intensified and politicised their classical reception in the post-Thaw era.[131] After he was sentenced to hard labour in northern Russia for *tuneiadstvo*, Brodskii — following Mandel'shtam and Pushkin — wrote his exilic experience through Ovid, and in his subsequent poetry the Roman Empire would always stand for the Soviet Union.[132] Kushner likewise drew parallels — increasingly overtly after *glasnost'* — between the Roman Empire and the Soviet Union: their tyrants and their falls.[133] From her teenage participation in Leningrad's literary scene, Shvarts was acquainted with Brodskii and Kushner (v.335, 369); she was appalled, along with the rest of the Russian literary world, by Brodskii's arrest in 1963 (v.391–92). Both Brodskii and Kushner tried to promote Shvarts: Brodskii abroad and Kushner in the USSR.[134] But despite their shared classical reception and closeness in time, Shvarts vehemently denied any influence from her immediate predecessors, Brodskii in particular; she said that the 'coldness and rationality' of Brodskii's poetry was alien to her.[135] Sedakova confirms this, stating that Brodskii 'acts as a negative quantity' on Shvarts,[136] something that can be seen in *Kinfiia*.

126 Lygo, p. 1.
127 For Brodskii's classical reception, see Torlone; Dan Ungurianu, 'The Wandering Greek: Images of Antiquity in Joseph Brodsky', in *Russian Literature and the Classics*, ed. by Peter I. Barta, David H. J. Larmour, and Paul Allen Miller (Amsterdam: Harwood Academic, 1996), pp. 161–91; Andrew Kahn, 'Ovid and Russia's Poets of Exile', in *A Handbook to the Reception of Ovid*, ed. by Miller and Newlands, pp. 401–15 (pp. 410–14). For Kushner's classical reception, see David N. Wells, 'Classical Motifs in the Poetry of Aleksandr Kushner', in *Russian Literature and the Classics*, ed. by Barta, Larmour, and Miller, pp. 143–60.
128 Ungurianu, pp. 161–62.
129 Mandel'shtam learning Classics: 'Ne slishkom slozhen byl professorskii vopros' [The professor's question was not too difficult] (1988); Innokentii Annenskii and Apollo: 'Razmashistyi sovkhoz Temriukskogo raiona' [Sprawling state farm of the Temriukskii district] (1988); Tsvetaeva and Orpheus: 'O da, ona mogla b vnushit' Orfeiu' [Oh yes, she could have inspired Orpheus] (1990).
130 Wells, 'Classical Motifs in the Poetry of Aleksandr Kushner', p. 143.
131 Kushner's 1975 collection (unpublishable at the time) *Apollon v snegu* [*Apollo in the Snow*] refers in its title to the adverse conditions to writing classically inspired poetry in Russia. Wells, p. 146.
132 Kahn, 'Ovid and Russia's Poets of Exile', pp. 410–13; Torlone, pp. 175–78; Dan Ungurianu, in Barta, Larmour, and Miller, pp. 164–65.
133 Wells, 'Classical Motifs in the Poetry of Aleksandr Kushner', pp. 150–52.
134 Brodskii recited one of Shvarts's poems in Paris. Kushner recommended some of Shvarts's poems for publication in 1968. Eliseev; Lygo, p. 103.
135 Polukhina, p. 219.
136 Ibid., p. 250.

The Stagnation and post-Soviet era: Krivulin and Sedakova

The breath of fresh air that was the Thaw was all too brief. By the mid-1960s it was already giving way to the Stagnation, with renewed government repressions in all areas of Soviet life, including literature. But even in the inclement Stagnation era the Thaw's poetic flowering bore fruit: the unpublishable underground poets, Shvarts among them. They were inspired by a heady mix of previously unavailable literature, from all languages and periods, including antiquity, which was revealed to them — in Sedakova's words — 'like the latest news just in'.[137]

Of Shvarts's contemporaries, Krivulin and Sedakova are the poets whose work is most shaped by classical antiquity. Krivulin's classical reception was shaped by his religious belief and by his veneration of Silver Age poets, particularly Mandel'shtam. In his poetry Krivulin compared underground poets to early Christians persecuted by the Roman Empire, and used Mandel'shtamian classical images of death to signify the communist destruction of culture.[138] Krivulin's excessive admiration for European culture led him to be duped by Arno Tsart, Shvarts's Estonian alter ego; after hearing one of Shvarts's friends read the 'Estonian''s poems, Krivulin exclaimed (according to Shvarts): 'that's what Western culture means! Europe! You and I, Lena, we can't write like that' (III.326). Sedakova's classical reception is also shaped by religious belief, and by Western literary tradition. She is the most learned of her era of poets, speaking and translating extensively from several European languages, Old Church Slavonic, Latin, and Ancient Greek.[139] Her classical influences range from Virgil and Ovid to Anacreon to ancient gravestones.[140] Unsurprisingly, Sedakova is a very perceptive commentator on Shvarts's poetry. Both Krivulin and Sedakova were close friends of Shvarts's. Shvarts and fellow Petersburger Krivulin first met as teenagers at their *kruzhok* in 1963, and bonded over their mutual appreciation for each other's poetry (V.329, 334–35), remaining lifelong friends. Of Krivulin, Shvarts said 'he meant a lot to me, not even primarily as a poet, but more as an individual'.[141] Shvarts and the Muscovite Sedakova met aged 23 or 24,[142] had a shared interest in theology and translation, and corresponded all their lives.[143] Of Sedakova, Shvarts said 'her friendship and understanding have been a priceless gift of fate' (III.194).

---

137 Sedakova.
138 von Zitzewitz, *Poetry and the Leningrad Religious-Philosophical Seminar 1974–1980*, pp. 241, 69; Stephanie Sandler, 'A Poet Living in the Big City: Viktor Krivulin, among Others', in *Poetics, Self, Place: Essays to Honor Anna Lisa Crone*, ed. by Nicole Boudreau and Catherine O'Neil (Columbus, OH: Slavica, 2007), pp. 675–93 (pp. 685, 678).
139 Josephine von Zitzewitz, 'The "Religious Renaissance" of the 1970s and its Repercussions on the Soviet Literary Process' (DPhil thesis, University of Oxford, 2009), p. 122. Among the many writers Sedakova has translated is Horace. Polukhina, p. 237.
140 Olga Sedakova, Valentina Polukhina, and Robert Reid, 'Collective Analysis of Olga Sedakova's "The Wild Rose"', *Essays in Poetics*, 22 (1997), 237–57 (p. 246); Michael Wachtel, *The Development of Russian Verse: Meter and its Meanings* (Cambridge: Cambridge University Press, 1998), p. 294 n. 77.
141 Eliseev.
142 Tkachenko.
143 'Dorogaia Olia' (2001?), ESHA M.

Russian classical reception has, of course, continued among Shvarts's younger contemporaries and after her death.[144] Much of this has taken place on the internet and within the Russian diaspora. Two notable classically receptive poets are Il'ia Kutik and Polina Barskova,[145] who are, respectively, one and two generations younger than Shvarts. Kutik turns particularly to classical epic and history in his poetry; Barskova's imagination is sparked most by classical myth; like Shvarts, both make Classics convey their personal narratives, their attitudes towards Russian politics, and their own poethood. Both younger poets had fleeting contact with Shvarts: Kutik met her in 1985 at Klub-81 in Leningrad, where they were both giving a reading, and would encounter her again in 1995 in Hoboken, USA (IV.200–03);[146] the teenaged Barskova met her in 1996 in Elsinore, Denmark, where she went virtually unnoticed by the introspective Shvarts.[147] Barskova even wrote a poem about her impression of Shvarts, comparing her (explicitly) to Ophelia and (implicitly) to Helen of Troy.[148]

Conclusion

Classical antiquity has been used by Russia to define itself in relation to Europe since before it *was* Russia. Specifically *Roman* reception has tended to reflect on power, politics, empire. *Greek* reception is less easy to categorise, but has tended to reflect on spirituality, to be more aesthetic, and to be seen as more kindred. During the twentieth century much classical reception has stemmed from contemporary poets' desire to connect with classically influenced Russian literature suppressed in the Stalinist period, and with Europe, from which Russians were palpably divided for much of the twentieth century — the Mandel'shtamian 'yearning for world culture'. Shvarts was no exception to that yearning, and, as this chapter will argue, the yearning for world culture helped to shape Shvarts's recourses to antiquity.

---

144 For an indicative list, see Torlone, pp. 197–98.
145 For Kutik and Barskova's classical reception, see Georgina Barker, 'Russia's Classical Alter Ego, 1963–2016: Classical Reception in the Poetry of Elena Shvarts, Il'ia Kutik, and Polina Barskova' (PhD thesis, University of Edinburgh, 2017).
146 Ilya Kutik, 'A Small Question', 11 August 2020.
147 Polina Barskova, Interview by Georgina Barker, Amherst, Massachusetts, 2016.
148 'Elenograd' (1996/2010). Polina Barskova, 'pamiati vsiakikh besed i nabliudenii — davno', *pbarskova* (2010), <http://pbarskova.livejournal.com/20977.html> [accessed 13 November 2015].

Shvarts's Classical Reception

Shvarts made forays into classical studies in her early teens, which coincided with her first classically receptive poems. Aged fourteen she — a self-described autodidact — was studying Latin by herself (v.298–303) and even drew up a grammar study timetable.[149] Aged fourteen/fifteen she made a list of figures from Greek mythology:

> Greek gods mentioned by Pushkin: Apollo, Aphrodite, Zeus, Hermes, Eros, Proserpina, Morpheus, Bacchus, Satyr, Priapus, Mnemosyne, Nemesis, Parcae, Melpomene, Terpsichore, Pluto, Leda, Orpheus, Daphnis, Charon, Parnassus, Helicon, Hippocrene spring, Lethe and Styx.
>
> Muses: Terpsichore, Thalia, Calliope, ~~Eurydice~~ Euterpe, Melpomene, Clio, Urania, Erato, Polyhymnia.

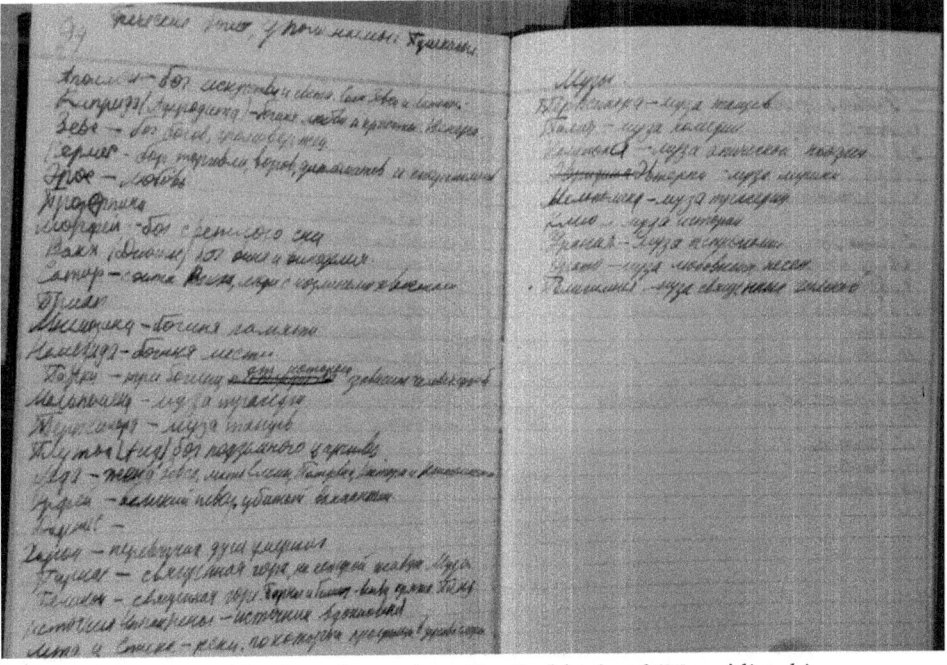

FIG. 1.10. 'Greek gods mentioned by Pushkin' and 'Muses' listed in Shvarts's childhood notebook. ESHA J.VT 94.

These two classical strands — Latin (encompassing Latin literature and Roman history) and Graeco-Roman myth — would come to define Shvarts's classical reception. This section first investigates Shvarts's interactions with Latin. It will demonstrate that, although she had no formal training in Latin, Shvarts read the Latin literature she receives in her poetry in the original.[150] It will then discuss how she gained access to classical texts in the USSR. Finally, it will hypothesise

---

149 From mid-September to late October 1962 Shvarts aimed to study for between one and five hours per day, except Sundays. ESHA J.ST.
150 Sedakova has also asserted that Shvarts could read Latin. Heldt, p. 381.

about the various personal and cultural factors that drew her more to Rome than to Greece.

Shvarts's familiarity with Latin is evidenced in the first instance by her habit of giving poems Latin titles or subtitles. Her first *samizdat* collection has its title and section titles all in Latin: *Exercitus exorcitans* [Army Exorcising] (1976), 'Praetoriani' [Praetorians], 'Equitatus' [Cavalry], 'Machinae obsidiales' [Siege Machines].[151] In the next twenty years she gives eight poems/cycles this Latin treatment: the subtitle 'Horror eroticus' for *Grubymi sredstvami ne dostich' blazhenstva* [Rough Methods Won't Get You Bliss] (1978, II.90–95); 'Laif-vita' [Life-vita] (1978);[152] 'Animus' (1982, 1.138); the subtitle 'natura culturata' for *Letnee Morokko* [Summer Moroque] (1983, 1.164–76); 'Cogito ergo non sum' (1988, 1.208–10); 'Genius loci' (1992, 1.307–08); 'Poetica — more geometrico' [Poetry — by Way of Geometry] (1994, 1.284); 'Arboreiskii sobor' [Arboreal Cathedral] (1996, 1.320). Further evidence for Shvarts's more than passing knowledge of Latin is her playful use of it. In one poem she puns on the similarity between the Latin word for 'bear' and the old name of Russia: 'Рус затравленный, урсус!' [Rus' baited, ursus!].[153] And Shvarts gives a Latin 'speaking name' to Kinfiia's aged slave — Priscus, which appropriately means 'former', 'ancient', 'old-fashioned'. In *Kinfiia* she uses Latin words wherever they are comprehensible in the Russian: 'муренам' [murenae/moray eels], 'таверне' [taberna/tavern], 'плебей' [plebeius/plebeian], 'тогу' [toga], 'мете' [meta/turning post], 'сенатор' [senator], 'цирковой' [circus], 'гетера' [hetaera], 'Лузитании' [Lusitania/Portugal]. Shvarts uses this technique again to add a Catholic feel to Lavinia's monastery in her great cycle *Trudy i dni Lavinii, monakhini iz ordena obrezaniia serdtsa* [The Works and Days of Lavinia, a Nun from the Order of the Circumcision of the Heart] (1984, II.164–221).[154] Lavinia herself has a Latin name: Lavinia was the daughter of Latinus King of Latium, the destined wife of Aeneas and mother of the Roman people, brought to literary prominence by her enigmatic blush in Virgil's *Aeneid* (XII.64–70).

Shvarts also wrote poems about Latin. Ancient languages are at the top of her list of the 'Filologicheskie razvlecheniia Demiurga' [Philological Amusements of the Demiurge] (1974, ZT 75):

> То клинописи нюхать порошок,
> То арамейским красить мамалыгу.
> Латынь он то в толстенной книге сушит,
> То дунет, и она — вертлявый мальчик милый,
> С которым спал разборчивый Вергилий...
> То в греческом он плещется китом
> И греется в его соленых брызгах

---

151 Elena Shvarts, *Voisko, Orkestr, Park, Korabl': chetyre mashinopisnykh sbornikov*, ed. by Artem Shelia and Pavel Uspenskii (Moscow: Common place, 2018).
152 From *Lestnitsa s dyriavymi ploshchadkami* [Staircase with Holey Landings] (1.69–94).
153 'Smutnye strofy' [Troubled Stanzas], in *Geopoliticheskii trilistnik* [Geopolitical Triptych] (1990), Elena Shvarts, 'Pesnia ptitsy na dne morskom', *Vavilon* (1995), <http://www.vavilon.ru/texts/shvarts3.html> [accessed 25 April 2019].
154 A. V. Markov, 'Latinizmy v poeticheskikh knigakh "Dikii shipovnik" Ol'gi Sedakovoi i "Trudy i dni monakhini Lavinii" Eleny Shvarts', *Vestnik Permskogo universiteta: rossiiskaia i zarubezhnaia filologiia*, 9.1 (2017), 122–29 (p. 126). *Laviniia*'s title also refers to Hesiod's *Works and Days*.

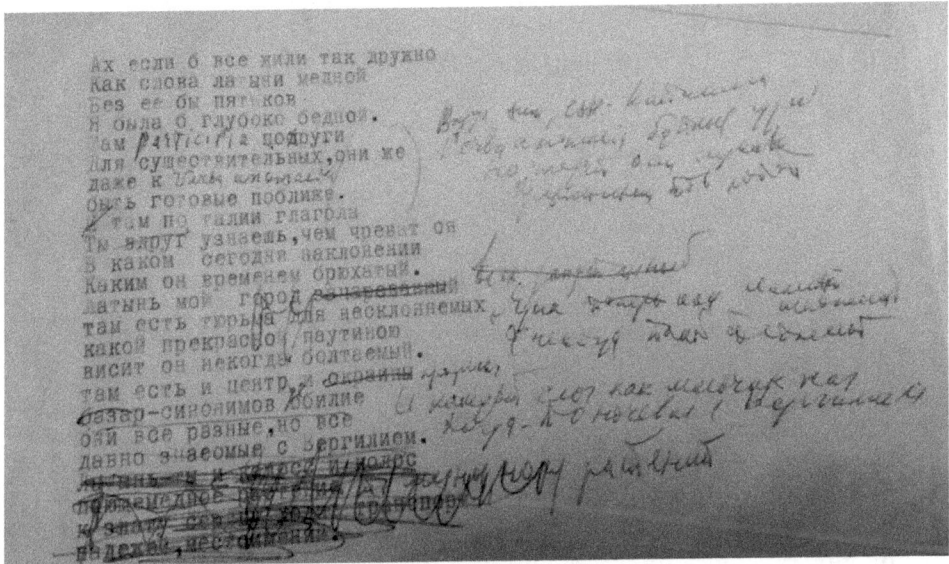

Fig. 1.11. 'Ah, if only everyone could live as harmoniously' (1974?), ESHA M.atom.

[Then sniffing cuneiform's powder,
Then dyeing polenta with Aramaic.
Then he presses Latin dry inside a big fat book,
Then blows on it, and it — is a sweet flighty boy,
Whom fussy Virgil has slept with...
Then he splashes about in Greek as a whale
And warms himself in its salty spray]

Shvarts's view of Latin is, at first, as a dead language found only in books, which God then breathes life into, life which she perceives through Virgil's adept use of the language. She sees Greek much less literally, connecting it with the sea, perhaps because of the Greek islands, or the seafaring in Homeric epic. The idea about Virgil having sex with Latin personified as a boy is shared with her unpublished poem 'Akh esli b vse zhili tak druzhno' [Ah, if only everyone could live as harmoniously] (also 1974?). (See the Appendix for a transcription and translation.)

In 'Akh esli b vse zhili tak druzhno' Shvarts imagines the grammatical parts of Latin as people in a city. She plays with the idea of grammar reflecting the internal state of a word-person:

там по талии глагола
Ты узнаешь, чем чреват он
В каком сегодня наклонении
Каким он времен[ем] брюхатый.

[there by a verb's waistline
You'll know what he's pregnant with
What mood he is in today
How tense the expectant father.[155]]

---

155 Literally: 'What tense he is pregnant with'.

Irregular verbs get a bad press, reflecting her difficulty in learning them:

> Вкруг sum, esse — Катилина
> Verba anomalia [братья ?] чудес!
> Но глядят они лукаво
> Правильными быть хотят
>
> [All around sum, esse — Catiline
> Verba anomalia [brothers ?] of marvels!
> But they look around slyly
> They want to be regular]

So do irregular nouns (in a line later redacted): 'там есть тюрьма для несклоняемых' [there are prisons for indeclinables]. And as well as the idea of Latin as a wanton boy in Virgil's bed, the poem also shares with 'Filologicheskie razvlecheniia Demiurga' the idea of Latin as a living language that has gone extinct (in two variants): 'какой прекрасной паутиною | висит он некогда болтаемый' [what a beautiful spider's web | left dangling, once chattered] (redacted); 'Язык как мамонт ископаемый | А некогда такой болтаемый' [Language like a fossilised mammoth | But once so chattered]. Finally (in redacted lines), punning on the similarity in Russian between 'koloss' [colossus] and 'kolos' [wheat ear], she turns Latin into a giant golden kernel, which its grammar travels up to like a convoy, or like prayers:

> Латынь — ты и колосс и колос
> поющемедное растение
> к злату сердцу ходит транспорт
> падежей, местоимений.
>
> [Latin — you are both helios and helianthus[156]
> a singing-copper plant
> towards the golden heart goes a transport
> of cases, of pronouns.]

This harmonises with Shvarts's personal note at the beginning of the poem: 'Без ее [латыни медной] бы пятаков | Я была б глубоко бедной' [Without its [copper Latin's] pennies | I would be profoundly poor]. Shvarts's thorough familiarity with and deep love of Latin is evident throughout 'Akh esli b vse zhili tak druzhno'.

Shvarts's short poem 'Nadgrobnaia nadpis'' imperatora Adriana' [Funerary Inscription of Emperor Hadrian] (n.d.)[157] adds to the long literary history of translations of Hadrian's last poem. Here is the original Latin version:

> Animula, vagula, blandula,
> hospes comesque corporis,
> quae nunc abibis in loca,

---

156 Literally: 'colossus and wheat ear'.
157 Elena Shvarts, 'Nadgrobnaia nadpis'' imperatora Adriana', *Novaia kamera khraneniia* <http://www.newkamera.de/shwarz/escwarz_12.html> [accessed 1 November 2014]. For the original, see *Minor Latin Poets, Volume II: Florus. Hadrian. Nemesianus. Reposianus. Tiberianus. Dicta Catonis. Phoenix. Avianus. Rutilius Namatianus. Others*, trans. by Arnold M. Duff and J. Wight Duff (Cambridge, MA: Harvard University Press, 1934), p. 444.

> pallidula, rigida, nudula,
> nec ut soles dabis iocos?
>
> [Soullet, wandererlet, charmerlet,
> body's guest and companion,
> what places now go you away into,
> pallidlet, rigidlet, nakedlet,
> nor, as you used, making jokes?]

And here is Shvarts's translation:

> Душенька странная бродяжка
> Гостья тела и собеседница
> Где ты теперь блуждаешь
> Смутным испуганным облачком,
> И уж шуткам своим не смеешься ты.
>
> [Lil' soul strange wanderer
> Guest of body and interlocutrix
> Where do you now meander
> Like a hazy frightened lil' cloud,
> And at your own jokes you no longer laugh.]

Analysis of Shvarts's translation suggests that she translated the poem from the original. The majority of the poem is faithful to the original: she chooses to retain Hadrian's diminutive in the first word; to address it in the second person; and to retain much of the original word order in the first four lines. But in other ways she departs from the original significantly. In the first line she changes 'blandula' [charming] to 'странная' [strange]. The fourth line is entirely different: 'Pallidula' [pale] becomes 'Смутным' [hazy], and 'rigida' [rigid] becomes 'испуганным' [frightened] — both reasonable substitutions; however, 'nudula' [naked] becomes 'облачком' [cloudlet], which is probably due not to poetic licence but to misunderstanding 'nudus' [naked] as 'nubes' [cloud]. The final line inexplicably changes 'dabis iocos' [make jokes] to 'шуткам своим [...] смеешься' [laugh at your own jokes]. The successes and mistakes in Shvarts's translation equally prove that she was working from a Latin text, without the aid of any crib.

In the Soviet Union, before freedom of information and the internet, it does not go without saying that Shvarts had access to the entirety of classical literature, in translation or otherwise. So I will demonstrate here that Shvarts could have got hold of classical works. Sadly, her library was devastated by the fire in her flat; scorched Russian editions of philosophers Sextus Empiricus, Aristotle, and Plato, and the comedies of Terence, are all that remain of her doubtless much larger personal Classics collection.

She is also attested as owning a Russian translation of the Roman poets Catullus, Tibullus, and Propertius, and a bilingual copy of the Roman poet Horace.[158] Besides her own books, Shvarts would have made extensive use of libraries: she signed up at the Leningrad Public Library — or 'Publichka' — aged eleven (v.273), and was

---

158 Dmitrii Panchenko, Interview by Georgina Barker, St Petersburg, Russia, 2019.

Fig. 1.12. Scorched classical books in Elena Shvarts's library. Photograph by Kirill Kozyrev.

able to use the Writers' Union library from childhood, thanks to her mother's membership (III.215–16). It was also common practice among the intellectuals of Shvarts's generation to make use of private collections for rare or pre-revolutionary books.[159]

These proofs of Shvarts's long-standing love and knowledge — albeit imperfect — of Latin, and of her access to classical literature in translation and in Latin, should be understood as background to my readings of Shvarts's classical reception over the course of this book.

While Shvarts was evidently well read in both Greek and Latin literature, her knowledge of Latin inclined her towards a greater interest in all things Roman. This is not to deny the great inspiration Shvarts evidently drew from classical myths, myths which mostly derive ultimately from Greece. But her sources for these myths tend to be either nebulous (i.e. from cultural knowledge rather than a particular text), or Russian poets' receptions, or Roman poets' versions. At a glance, her Romanophilia is perceptible in how many of her poems take Ancient Rome as their setting; none are set in Ancient Greece. But when you look deeper, her Romanophilia is most evident in the classical authors she chooses to strike up dialogue with: while the Greeks Sappho, Plato, and Homer occasionally get a look-in, she conducts extensive intertextual conversations with the Romans Propertius, Catullus, Ovid, Martial, Juvenal, and Horace in her classical cycles *Kinfiia* and *Homo*

---

159 von Zitzewitz, *Poetry and the Leningrad Religious-Philosophical Seminar 1974–1980*, p. 8.

Musagetes. But the Roman poets she returns to across her oeuvre and identifies with in particular are Catullus (Gaius Valerius Catullus, c. 84–54 BC[160]), Horace (Quintus Horatius Flaccus, 65–68 BC[161]), and Ovid (Publius Ovidius Naso, 43 BC–AD 18[162]). While the three poets lived through the same century, they inhabited vastly different Romes: Catullus — the late Republic, Horace — the Civil Wars then Augustus's Empire, and Ovid — Augustus's Empire then exile. But what all three have in common — and what distinguishes them from the other classical authors whom Shvarts received less frequently — is their changeability. Catullus wrote in a huge range of lyric metres, and spanned themes from love, through invective, to small-scale epic, from the personal to the mythical. Horace also wrote in a variety of lyric metres, spanning themes from love, through invective, to philosophy, from the personal to the national. Ovid was not metrically varied, but wrote changeability into his poetic persona, writing from various perspectives (including women) and even writing his national epic about changeability. I believe that it was their capacity to metamorphose themselves in their poetry that led Shvarts to return to Catullus, Horace, and Ovid. Catullus — besides his appearances in *Kinfiia* and *Homo Musagetes* — is Shvarts's source for her alter ego Ariadne. Shvarts even inhabits Catullus's clothing in her unpublished poem 'Kogda ia pod utro usnula' [When I fell asleep towards morning] (29 December 1983, ESHA M): she dreams she is looking out over Paris 'В дырявой рубахе Катулла' [In the holey shirt of Catullus] — perhaps motivated by poem XII where Catullus jokes about his poverty.[163] Horace — besides his appearances in *Homo Musagetes* and *Kinfiia* — features as a book being read by Shvarts in one poem, in another poem-pair Shvarts sets herself up as a Horatian satirist, and in one prose piece she aligns herself with Horace's biography (see chapter 5 for a detailed account of Shvarts's Horatian reception). Ovid — besides his appearances in *Kinfiia* — is Shvarts's source for her alter ego Narcissus. And it is in the case of Ovid that Shvarts makes her identification with the classical poet's changeability explicit. In 'Tri osobennosti moikh stikhov' [Three Characteristics of My Poems] (November 1996, IV.276–78) Shvarts pronounces that her poetry's third characteristic is 'An insurmountable attachment to metamorphoses. Like Ovid's.' She makes the same identification with Ovid more implicitly and emotionally in an unpublished prose piece about metamorphosis in Russian poetry:

> I think Ovid, like us nowadays, wasn't sure, when he was about to lift his eyes to himself in the mirror, whom he would see there, what he would see there — a tiger's muzzle, a bird's beak, or a Roman's face, puffy after yesterday's boozing.[164]

---

160 Catullus, *The Poems of Catullus*, trans. by Guy Lee (Oxford: Oxford University Press, 1991), p. xviii.
161 Horace, *Odes and Epodes*, trans. by Niall Rudd (Cambridge, MA; London: Harvard University Press, 2004), pp. 1–9.
162 Ovid, *Heroides; Amores*, ed. by G. P. Goold, trans. by Grant Showerman (Cambridge, MA; London: Harvard University Press, 1977), pp. 2–3.
163 Catullus also appears (crossed off) on her list of poetry to memorise. 'Lists: Vyuchit' liuboe iz sleduiushchikh stikhotvorenii. Rasskazat' o', ESHA D.
164 'Two prose pieces about metamorphosis: Russkaia poeziia nachalas' s ...; Apuleevskii osel

Shvarts's imagined step into Ovid's mind is palpable — especially when we remember that Shvarts was herself able to look into a mirror and see a Roman's face.

Another reason for Shvarts's Romanophilia can be found in the history of Russian classical reception and its fate in the twentieth century. Shvarts, along with her contemporaries in the Leningrad underground, felt cut off from the world outside the USSR: Europe and European culture, Classics and religion, and pre-revolutionary Russian culture, particularly the Silver Age. This severance from the non-Soviet world can be summed up with Mandel'shtam's phrase 'yearning for world culture'. The fact that so much of Shvarts's classical reception is mediated via Russian poets of the nineteenth century and the Silver Age especially shows that she was seeking connection not just with classical culture but with a Russia not alienated from global culture. In this context, it is enlightening to look at what Greece and Rome signified, taken separately. Historically, Russians felt that Ancient Greece was culturally kindred to them, due to the Greek origins of Russian Orthodoxy. Greece is therefore not as foreign or as global a cultural reference as Rome. And while Orthodoxy is one of the major themes of Shvarts's poetry — at least equal in scale and significance to her classical reception — she tends to see Christianity and pagan antiquity as antithetical, and certainly does not require classical Greek imagery to bolster her Russian Orthodox imagery. Historically Rome has also been seen as kindred to Russia when Russia is viewed as a political entity: a concept expressed in the 'Third Rome'. While Shvarts does not mind exploiting the Third Rome myth, Rome features far more often in her poetry as the quintessential representative of world culture: a concept expressed in the palindrome 'Рим и мир' [Rome and the Globe].[165] So when Shvarts was seeking escape from Soviet *byt* [humdrum everyday life] and cultural isolationism within a higher, globally connected cultural plane, shared with her poetic peers and predecessors alike, Ancient Rome — the global city — was an obvious destination.

This book will reveal the manifold ways in which Elena Shvarts re-created SPQR in the USSR and turned herself into a classical poet.

zabaven tem ...', ESHA D.prer.
165 The exact phrase 'Рим и мир' occurs four times in two poems (*Kinfiia* R.5 and 'Blagodarenie' [Thanksgiving]); the general idea is more widespread.

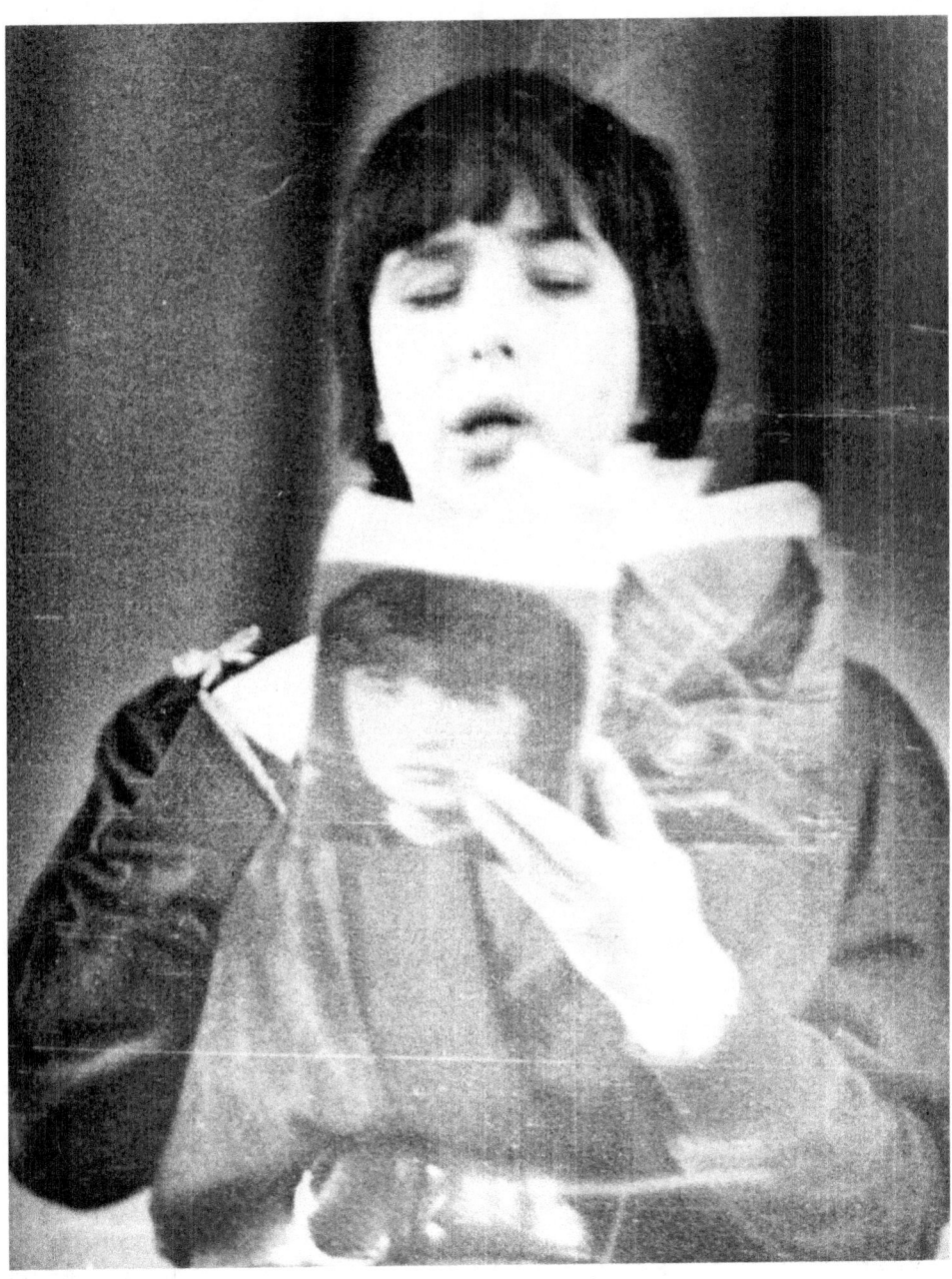

Fig. 1.13. Elena Shvarts reading her poetry.
Photograph courtesy of Kirill Kozyrev.

CHAPTER 2

❖

Classical Alter Egos

> Нарцисса я сужу за недостаток
> К себе любви
> [I find Narcissus guilty of an insufficiency
> Of self-love]
>
> — E. A. Shvarts, *Nochnaia tolcheia*
> [*Night-Time Throng*], 1979

A hallmark of Shvarts's classical reception is her appropriation of classical figures to represent facets of herself. Each classical figure reflects one or more aspect of her identity: as a woman, as a lover, as a drinker, as a mortal, and, most frequently, as a poet. I call these self-exploratory classical figures 'classical alter egos'.

FIG. 2.1. Doodled self-portrait. 'Perekhod cherez Neman i dal'she na Vitebsk' [Pificheskoe] (1976), ESHA M.2.

This chapter examines Shvarts's minor classical alter egos figure by figure to give a sense of the motivations and workings of Shvarts's identification with individuals from classical antiquity. With some of these figures Shvarts stages a very intense, one-off convergence between her self and theirs; with others, she returns to their character for self-expression in multiple poems: the alter egos in this chapter are 'minor' only as opposed to her major classical alter ego, Kinfiia, who is the subject of the next chapter. Shvarts's classical alter egos addressed in this chapter fall into two groups: the 'celestial bodies', who are mythical figures with special bodies, and the 'katabasists', who are descenders into the underworld. The celestial bodies are: the self-loving Narcissus, the goddess of love Aphrodite/Venus, the goddess of the moon Selene/Luna, and the Homeric hero Odysseus. The katabasists are: underworld gods Hades and Persephone, Odysseus again, the Dioscuri (twin brothers Castor and Pollux), the poet-musician Orpheus and his beloved Eurydice, various victims of the gods of poetic inspiration Dionysus and Apollo (including Marsyas and the rubbish dump Svalka), Pythia the Delphic oracle, and the deserted Ariadne.

The classical alter egos Shvarts chooses all stem from the mythical and literary side of classical antiquity, rather than the historical. (Shvarts's interest in history comes to the fore in association with Rome — see chapter 4.) Her preference for mythical/literary characters is because her alter egos are selective, and therefore intensified, versions of herself, and because Shvarts emphasises transcendental facets of her personality: mythical/literary characters are more suited to such hyper-real self-depictions. There is a remarkable gender balance among the minor classical alter egos: Shvarts turns equally to male and female characters for self-expression; however, Kinfiia tips the balance towards women. Most of her classical alter egos are tragic or suffering figures: Narcissus, Odysseus, Hades, Persephone, the Dioscuri, Orpheus, Eurydice, Dionysus, Marsyas, Pythia, Ariadne. Many are connected with forms of madness: Narcissus, Aphrodite/Venus, Selene/Luna, Orpheus, Dionysus, Pythia, Ariadne. And many represent poetry — whether as poets or inspirers or both: Orpheus, Eurydice, Dionysus, Apollo, Marsyas, Svalka, Pythia. These poetic classical alter egos all sacrifice either themselves or another person for the sake of poetic inspiration. Self-sacrifice is fundamental to Shvarts's self-image as a poet, and her use of classical guises to express this virtue is inherited from Russian poetic tradition. All the alter egos facilitate transcendence: the celestial bodies through bringing poet and heavens together; the katabasists through confronting mortality and returning to tell the tale. Before the chapter turns to look at Shvarts's classical alter egos in detail, it first addresses the concept of the alter ego and how it relates to Shvarts's poetic practice.

The Alter Ego and Enstrangement

The phrase 'alter ego' is manifoldly apt to describe Shvarts's poetic practice of setting up characters to mirror herself. As a Latin phrase, it suggests the classical source of many of Shvarts's alter egos. It is distinct from the pre-existing literary term 'persona', which implies the total or near-total assumption of a particular character by the author, something that could not even be consistently applied to Kinfiia, and certainly not to Shvarts's other classical alter egos. Yet by evoking the masked alter ego of a superhero, it retains some of the sense of 'persona': 'in Greek *prosopon* might be used for both face and mask, and [...] in Latin *persona* can mean mask, assumed character, or a "real" person'.[1] And finally, the term emphasises alterity, which is precisely where the utility of the alter ego lies: it can present a more extreme, fun, tragic, or ideal self.

A rare moment of literary self-criticism by Shvarts indicates the literary device behind her alter egos. In 'Neobiazatel'nye poiasneniia' [Optional Explanations], her introduction to *Mundus Imaginalis: Kniga otvetvlenii* [*Mundus Imaginalis: Book of Offshoots*] (1996), the book containing the *Kinfiia* cycle, Shvarts explains her motivation for writing from alter egos:

> This book consists of totally mismatched and unconnected parts — apart from one trait. That trait is being in stage make-up, speaking from under a mask, a reclothed (or reborn) author.
>
> Of course, composing such things carries a playful character and helps to take a new look at the familiar. The well-known principle of enstrangement. It's fun to transport your life from seventies Russia to, like, Ancient Rome — everything becomes funnier and prettier. I used Ancient Rome as something like maids' quarters or a kitchen — for gossip and settling scores; poems 'from yourself' don't give you that possibility.
>
> Besides — it is so good sometimes to run as far as possible away from yourself, in order to more surely return.[2]

Shvarts's alter egos are enacting *ostranenie* or 'enstrangement' (also known as 'estrangement' or 'defamiliarisation').[3] Enstrangement is not mentioned anywhere in the original draft of 'Neobiazatel'nye poiasneniia' (ESHA D); the term must have either occurred or been suggested to her at a later stage.

'Enstrangement' is the term coined by Russian Formalist Viktor Shklovskii in his 1917/19 essay 'Iskusstvo, kak priem' [Art as Device] for the artistic technique of making things strange, so as to deautomatise and thus prolong and heighten perception, in order 'to create the sensation of seeing, and not merely recognizing,

---

1   Shelley Hales, 'Aphrodite and Dionysus: Greek Role Models for Roman Homes?', in *Role Models in the Roman World: Identity and Assimilation*, ed. by Sinclair Bell and Inge Lyse Hansen (Ann Arbor: University of Michigan Press, 2008), p. 242.
2   Elena Shvarts, '"Mundus Imaginalis": Neobiazatel'nye poiasneniia', *Vavilon* (2001), <http://www.vavilon.ru/texts/shvarts1-6.html> [accessed 12 September 2016].
3   I follow Alexandra Berlina in following Benjamin Sher's translation of *ostranenie* as 'enstrangement': '*Ostranenie* is an unintentional neologism, an orthographic mistake on Shklovsky's part: derived from *strannyi* (strange), it should feature a double *n*. Sixty-seven years later Shklovsky (*O teorii prozy* (Moscow: Sovetskii pisatel', 1983), p. 73) commented: 'It went off with one "n", and is roaming the world like a dog with an ear cut off.' The missing ear draws attention: the word's incorrectness refreshes language and stimulates associations connected to strangeness. *Defamiliarization* and *estrangement* do not. [...] These two concepts suggest decreased emotional connection to people, fictional or real, which is the opposite of the intended effect of *ostranenie*. [...] in terms of effect *enstrangement* is close to Shklovsky's neologism, which is itself enstranging' (Berlina, in Viktor Shklovsky, 'Art, as Device', trans. by Alexandra Berlina, *Poetics Today*, 36.3 (2015), 151–74 (pp. 152–53).

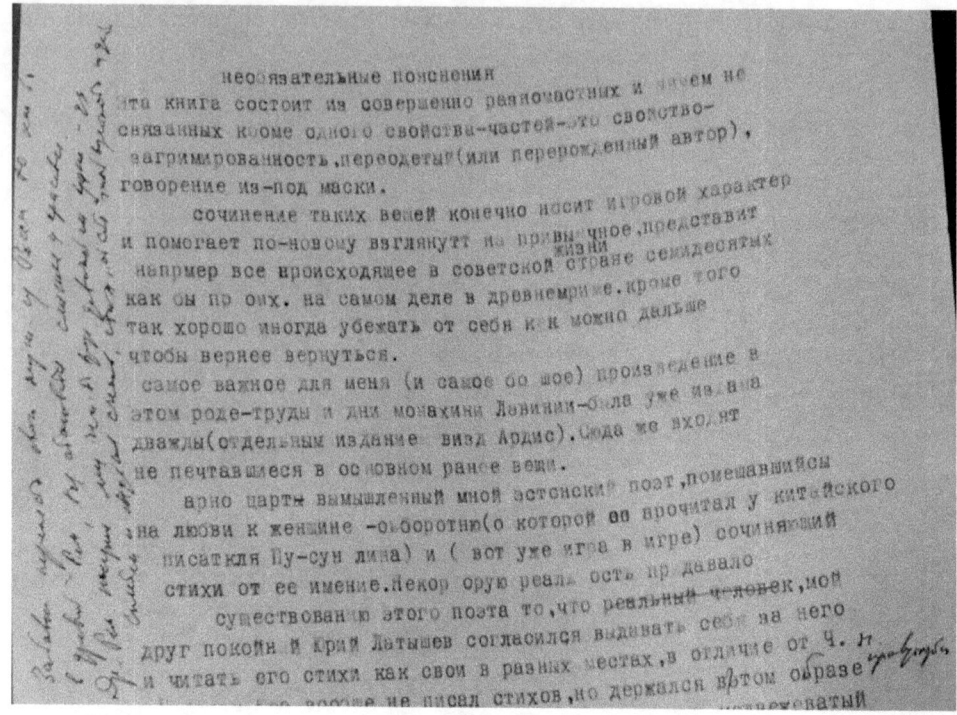

Fig. 2.2. 'Optional Explanations', ESHA D.

things'.[4] The classical world offers settings and characters that are particularly suited to enstrangement. For one, ancient Rome and Greece are indubitably foreign, both in place and in time; Shklovskii himself suggested foreignness as an enstranging mode (employing a classical reference as he did so): 'According to Aristotle, "poetic language" must have the character of the foreign, the surprising. It often is quite literally a foreign language'.[5] And the mythical figures Shvarts selects are larger than life, not only able to express magnified and transcendental aspects of Shvarts's character (as discussed above), but also capable of extraordinary, superhuman acts that further enstrange their everyday setting or references.

In 'Neobiazatel'nye poiasneniia' Shvarts also connects enstrangement with theatricality, a connection present in Shklovskii's original theory,[6] through three theatrical analogies: 'being in stage make-up, speaking from under a mask, a reclothed [...] author'. Shvarts had a lifelong association with the theatre: she essentially grew up in it, as her mother worked in the theatre all her life.[7] Shvarts even compares herself to a theatre in 'Pokhorony rifmy' [Burial of Rhyme] (1

---

4 Ibid., p. 162.
5 Ibid., p. 171.
6 Svetlana Boym, 'Poetics and Politics of Estrangement: Victor Shklovsky and Hannah Arendt', *Poetics Today*, 26.4 (2005), 581–611 (p. 587).
7 Dina Shvarts, *Dnevniki i zametki* (St Petersburg: Inapress, 2001). Of Elena's early years Dina writes: 'I divided myself between her and the theatre. Perhaps the theatre was more, I gave it my all. Perhaps, to the detriment of the child' (ibid., p. 267).

October 2006, III.135–36):

> К стене приклеены две горбоносых маски
> [...]
> Он мой двойник, подобна я театру
> В котором призраки твердят все ту же мантру.

[Two hook-nosed masks are stuck to the wall
[...]
It is my double, I am like a theatre
In which phantoms repeat the same old mantra.]

Her use of masks to evoke the theatre in this poem and persona-creation in 'Neobiazatel'nye poiasneniia' underscores the deep association for Shvarts between theatre, alter egos, and masks. Her interest in masks goes back at least to her time at university, when she wrote a 65-page undergraduate dissertation on 'Maski komedii del' arte vo f'iabakh Karlo Gotstsi' [Masks of Commedia dell' Arte in the Fiabe of Carlo Gozzi] (1971). In the dissertation she defined masks thus:

> A mask is fundamentally different from an ordinary specific character. First of all, a mask is far more theatrical in nature. Between an actor with a mask on their face and an actor without a mask there is the same relation as between a *lazzo* and a normal gesture. A mask is a kind of mythical being, a part of folk mythology, a type that lives in the people's consciousness and therefore possesses certain constant traits that make the type, the particular mask, recognisable.[8]

This definition displays Shvarts's high estimation of the power of taking on a pre-existing persona — the greater effect their words and actions have due to their already accrued cultural weight. The dissertation as a whole focuses on the innovations Gozzi made to the characters represented by masks — something Shvarts herself was already doing with the classical figures which she adapted into alter egos.

For Russians in the Thaw and Stagnation, enstrangement became a means of overcoming *byt*, 'the monster of everyday routine, opposed to the poetic and spiritual *bytie*'.[9] Shvarts hints at the drag of *byt* with 'It's fun to transport your life from seventies Russia'; fellow Thaw poet and bard Andrei Anpilov spells out the grimness of Soviet *byt* and its effect on poetry:

> Illusory social existence, *samizdat*, the expectation of being either searched or arrested. [...] that could not but stamp its mark on the face of poetry. Each strove to find their own sky, unpolluted by fear and banality. [...] To the geographical 'horizontal' of Soviet poetry, Thaw poetry counterposed a historical and aesthetic 'vertical'. Elena Shvarts, burning herself on contemporaneity, on time and place [...] flies away: to biblical subjects, to medieval China, to antiquity, to the eighteenth, nineteenth century, to a gypsy camp, to a monastery — wherever.[10]

---

8   Elena Shvarts, 'Maski komedii del' arte vo f'iabakh Karlo Gotstsi' (Bremen), p. 12, Forschungsstelle Osteuropa, FSO 01–194 Švarc K2.
9   Boym, 'Poetics and Politics of Estrangement', p. 587 n. 8.
10 Andrei Anpilov, 'Svetlo-iarostnaia tochka', *Novoe Literaturnoe Obozrenie*, 35 (1999), 362–72 (p. 370).

While Shvarts presents her refuge in alter egos as innocent playfulness and Anpilov presents it as a historical necessity, in fact the very act of artistic escapism was political, a form of resistance to Soviet reality and Socialist Realism: '"Art of estrangement" became a dissident art; in the Soviet artistic context of the 1960s [and beyond], estrangement represented a resistance to sovietization'.[11] Another facet of Shvarts's positioning of classical antiquity as the antipode to Soviet *byt* is her insistent connecting of her classical alter egos with pre-Soviet Russian literature.

Shvarts's alter egos tend to be highly intertextual — not only with classical texts, but also with Russian poetry from the pre-Soviet era. The Russian intertexts have the effect of Russifying Shvarts's classical alter egos, bringing her enstranged self-presentations back into the realm of the familiar for her reader. Josephine von Zitzewitz notes that Shvarts inherits some of her alter egos — especially the female ones — from her famous female poetic predecessors:

> The use of named mythical figures as a mouthpiece is yet another trait Shvarts inherited, consciously or not, from Akhmatova and Tsvetaeva. All three poets lent their voice to mythical female heroines whom the usual sources describe as passive and silent.[12]

Marina Tsvetaeva is indeed the foremost of the intermediaries through whom Shvarts receives her classical alter egos — more so than Akhmatova, whom Shvarts disliked — but almost as prominent as intermediaries are Osip Mandel'shtam and Aleksandr Pushkin. Her references to these great Russian poets align her classical alter egos — and, by extension, herself — with the figure of archetypal Poet. And it is not only the intertexts with specific Russian poems that make the classical alter egos familiar for a Russian readership. The figure of the alter ego itself is a reworking of a staple theme of Russian literature: the Double. The Double has been in circulation as a foundational Russian literary figure ever since Nikolai Gogol' and Fedor Dostoevskii imported it to Russia from British and German Romanticism.[13] Aware that her alter egos are doubles of the author, Shvarts frequently plays upon ideas of doubling in these poems to highlight her estrangement tactic.

Is Shvarts consciously engaging in enstrangement with her classical alter egos, as her quotation of the term would suggest? There is a certain knowingness, a certain outside view of the alter ego, which Shvarts writes into the poems explored below. In many of her classical alter ego poems, Shvarts's identification with the classical figure is not direct: she uses the classical character as a mirror, to see herself in. The alter ego poems often feature Shvarts herself as an observer, or they replace her with a representative, often an archetypal Poet figure. Most tellingly, they constantly use words and/or structures evoking mirroring — such as 'mirror', 'double', 'sister', 'daughter', 'masks' (in *Kinfiia*), reflections, pictures — or X-rays!, body-swaps,

---

11   Svetlana Boym, 'Estrangement as a Lifestyle: Shklovsky and Brodsky', *Poetics Today*, 17.4 (1996), 511–30 (p. 523).
12   Josephine von Zitzewitz, 'From Underground to Mainstream: The Case of Elena Shvarts', in *Twentieth-Century Russian Poetry: Reinventing the Canon*, ed. by Katharine Hodgson, Joanne Shelton, and Alexandra Smith (Cambridge: Open Book Publishers, 2017), pp. 225–63 (p. 247).
13   See John Herdman, *The Double in Nineteenth-Century Fiction* (Basingstoke: Macmillan, 1990), pp. 99–126.

orbiting, verbal consonances, spatial oppositions... The proliferation of such words and scenarios shows that Shvarts consciously wrote her alter egos to be enstranging.

The Celestial Bodies

The first half of this chapter explores a group of classical alter egos whom I call the 'celestial bodies': mythical figures who either have perfect bodies or are astronomical bodies, and whose bodies somehow merge with Shvarts's body.

Narcissus

The alter ego with whom this chapter starts its analysis — Narcissus, a classical figure who was famously reflected and unable at first to perceive his reflection as himself — is ripe with potential for reflections on alterity and similarity, doubling, and where the self begins and ends. Shvarts clearly saw this potential. When she compares herself to Narcissus, her extremely self-reflexive poem performs narcissism, playfully drawing attention to her use of an alter ego. Her hyperbolic opening statement that Narcissus, the original narcissist, did not, in her opinion, love himself enough, moves to the observation that the self is to be found and loved not externally, in one's reflection, but internally, inside oneself; and thence to a closing declaration of her deep-seated Russianness. Shvarts's criticism of Narcissus is supported by extensive reference to the Narcissus story from Ovid's *Metamorphoses* 3.

Here is 'Nartsissa ia suzhu za nedostatok' [I find Narcissus guilty of an insufficiency] from *Nochnaia tolcheia* [*Night-Time Throng*] (1979, II.III) in full:

> Нарцисса я сужу за недостаток
> К себе любви.
> Уж я-то не поверю отраженьям –
> В воде ль, в крови.
> Ах, angels, духи, когда бы вы могли
> Хоть на мгновенье
> Глухонемого 'я' извлечь коренья
> И стебли бледные из бешеной земли.
> Когда б устроили одно
> Мне с ним короткое свиданье,
> Чтоб прошептало мне оно
> Свои желанья.
> Его слегка поцеловав,
> Я буду знать, что я жива,
> Я буду знать, что 'я' во мне
> Спит в черноземной глубине.

> [I find Narcissus guilty of an insufficiency
> Of self-love.
> Me, now, I wouldn't trust reflections —
> In water, or in blood.
> Ah, *dukhi*, angels — when could you,
> For just a moment,
> Extract the roots and the pale stalks

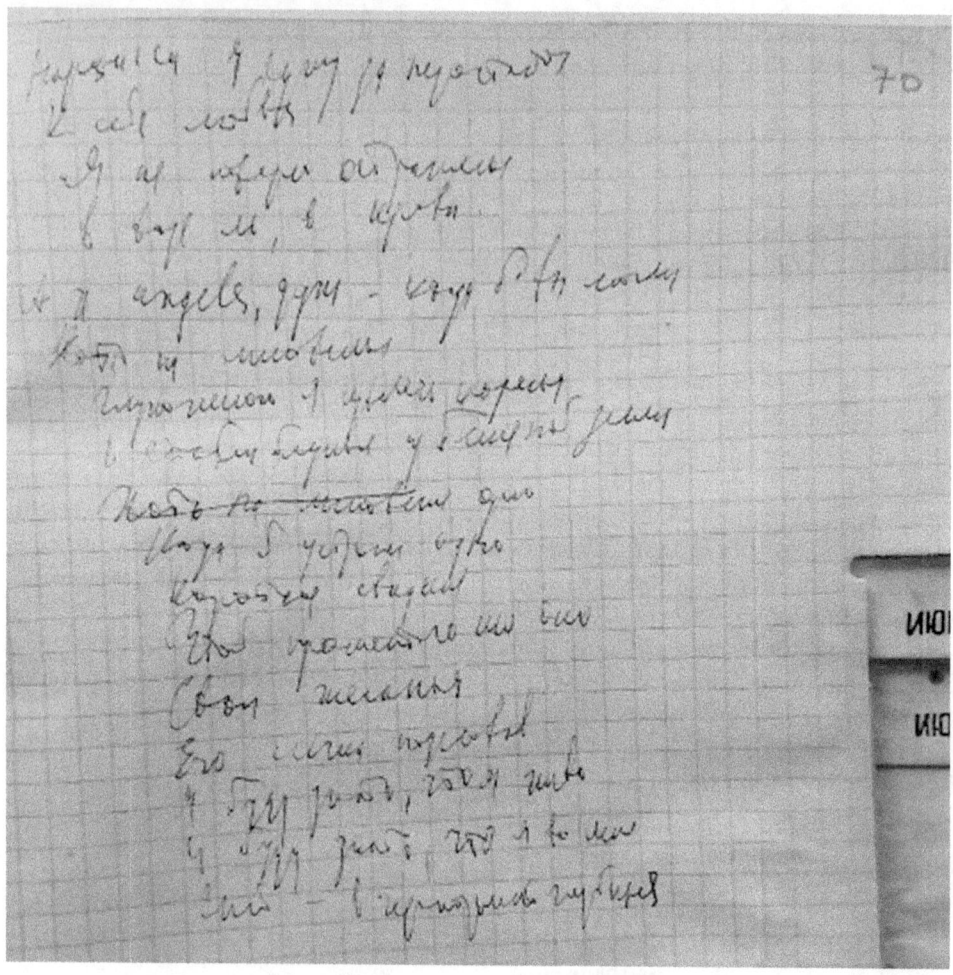

Fig. 2.3. 'I find Narcissus guilty of an insufficiency', BT 70 (between 27 and 31 December 1979). The draft of 'Nartsissa ia suzhu za nedostatok' was written almost exactly as published.

Of my deaf and dumb 'I' from mad soil.
When could you arrange one
Short date for me with it,
So it might whisper to me
Its desires.
Once I have lightly kissed it,
I will know that I am alive,
I will know that the 'I' inside me
Is asleep in black-earth depths.]

Throughout the poem Shvarts fits the Narcissus myth to herself, contrasting Narcissus's actions with hers. Whereas Ovid's Narcissus initially believes his reflection is another beautiful youth — 'while he drinks he is smitten by the sight of the beautiful form her sees. He loves an unsubstantial hope and thinks that substance which is only shadow' (*Met.* III.416–17)[14] — Shvarts claims not to be fooled by reflections, either in water, like Narcissus was, or in blood. This latter point is reinforced by the distinctly bloodless representation of her innards. Her depiction of her inner self as a speechless plant is reminiscent both of the crocus into which Narcissus metamorphoses, and of his silent reflection: 'as I suspect from the movement of your sweet lips, you answer my words as well, but words which do not reach my ears' (Ovid, *Met.* III.461–62, p. 157). The angels/spirits ('dukhi') whom she asks to uproot her self-plant tie the poem in with the angelic theme of *Nochnaia tolcheia*; they also serve as an addressee for Shvarts's echo of Narcissus's undirected wish, 'Oh, that I might be parted from my own body!' (*Met.* III.467, p. 157). Shvarts envisages a productive meeting/date with her self, culminating in a kiss. That Shvarts can successfully kiss her self fundamentally contradicts Ovid's scenario, in which Narcissus's kisses are thwarted by the water and the illusory nature of his reflection: 'often as I stretch my lips towards the lucent wave, so often with upturned face he strives to lift his lips to mine. You would think he could be touched — so small a thing it is that separates our loving hearts' (*Met.* III.451–53, p. 157). The kiss requites her self-love, leading to fertilisation; this again contradicts the *Metamorphoses* story, in which Narcissus wastes away and dies because his love is unrequited: 'so does he, wasted with love, pine away, and is slowly consumed by its hidden fire. [...] He drooped his weary head on the green grass and death sealed the eyes that marvelled at their master's beauty' (*Met.* III.489–503, p. 159). However, in another sense, the fertilisation that takes place also repeats the myth's conclusion, Narcissus's metamorphosis into a plant: 'In place of his body they find a flower, its yellow centre girt with white petals' (*Met.* III.509–10, p. 161). Shvarts achieves the multiple paradoxes of 'Nartsissa ia suzhu za nedostatok' by first condemning, then appropriating Ovid's pre- and post-metamorphosis Narcissus as her outer and inner self, and placing them in a sexualised union in imitation and defiance of the original story.

The Ovidian reception in 'Nartsissa ia suzhu za nedostatok' operates not only on a narrative level, but on a stylistic level as well: the verbal repetitiousness which abounds in this section of the *Metamorphoses* is also in evidence in Shvarts's poem, despite its short length. The words which she repeats most often are, fittingly, 'I' and its derivatives. Ovid's wordplay when Narcissus falls for his reflection has been seen as 'a reflexive parody' of his 'self-love of his own talent',[15] and since the eighteenth century Narcissus has been constantly adapted to symbolise the figure of the artist, or poet.[16] This subtext of the Ovidian Narcissus becomes the subtext of the Shvartsian Narcissus. When, in the final line, Shvarts predicts that kissing her self would result in a rooting of her self in earth, this earth is specifically Russian, from the (famously fertile) Black Earth region. So what Shvarts discovers

---

14   Ovid, *Metamorphoses*, trans. by Frank Justus Miller, 2 vols (Cambridge, MA: Harvard University Press, 1977), I, p. 153.
15   Philip R. Hardie, *The Cambridge Companion to Ovid*, Cambridge Companions to Literature (Cambridge: Cambridge University Press, 2002), p. 6.
16   Louise Vinge, *The Narcissus Theme in Western European Literature up to the Early 19th Century* (Lund: Gleerups, 1967), pp. 314, 329–30.

through her Narcissus-like encounter with herself is her poetry's fundamental Russianness — in spite of, or perhaps thanks to, its pervasive classical reception. This is supported by the poem's intertextual dialogue with Evgenii Baratynskii's anti-love poem 'Razuverenie' [Disillusion] (1821),[17] signalled by Shvarts in the third line, which echoes Baratynskii's 'Уж я не верю увереньям' [Now, I don't trust promises]. Whereas Baratynskii, wounded by his beloved, begs to be left to sleep undisturbed, Shvarts's beloved is neither another person nor a Narcissan reflection, but her self, which will sleep soundly even after Shvarts has dug up and kissed it.

Conspicuous by her absence from Shvarts's adaptation of Ovid's Narcissus story is the nymph Echo, who was among the many who fell in love with Narcissus, and who was introduced into the Narcissus myth by Ovid.[18] Shvarts's reasons for this omission are, of course, narcissistic: by cutting out extraneous figures she focuses the poem on her relationship with her self, thereby outdoing Ovid's Narcissus story for narcissism, as she promised at the start.

Aphrodite/Venus

Shvarts's classical alter egos tend to be unconventionally riotous. 'Afrodita uletaet v noch' na subbotu' [Aphrodite Flies off at the End of Friday Night] (15 June 1978, I.56) imagines the consequences of Aphrodite's Friday night on the town. (See the Appendix for the full poem.) The classical goddess visits contemporary Leningrad during the White Nights — 'В белой ночи по горло стояла столица' [The capital stood up to its neck in white night] — a time of year when the city is famously party-filled, and Aphrodite is imagined as not only an inspirer of debauchery, but debauched herself. 'Afrodita uletaet v noch' na subbotu' mingles the Aphrodites of Sappho, Tsvetaeva, and Mandel'shtam to create a very Shvartsian Aphrodite.

The goddess of love makes quite an entrance:

> Вдруг я услышала шелест и плеск,
> Запах розы и серы,
> Изнемогая, навзничь, сияя двойною луною зада
> В голубях и венках проплывала Венера.
>
> [All of a sudden I heard a rustle and a splash,
> I smelled rose and sulphur,
> Worn out, on her back, shining with the twin moon of her buttocks,
> Amidst pigeons and garlands Venus wafted past.]

Shvarts pairs conventional, romantic elements with irreverent and explicit elements to confound the reader's expectations: heavenly 'rose' with hellish 'sulphur', elevated 'shining' with crude 'buttocks'. While the raunchy depiction of Aphrodite is entirely Shvarts's, her entrance on a bird-drawn chariot is taken from Sappho's *Hymn to Aphrodite*: 'with chariot yoked: beautiful swift sparrows whirring fast-beating wings brought you above the dark earth down from heaven through the

---

17   Evgenii Baratynskii, 'Razuverenie', *Kul'tura.RF* <https://www.culture.ru/poems/25943/razuverenie> [accessed 8 February 2022].
18   Vinge, p. 40.

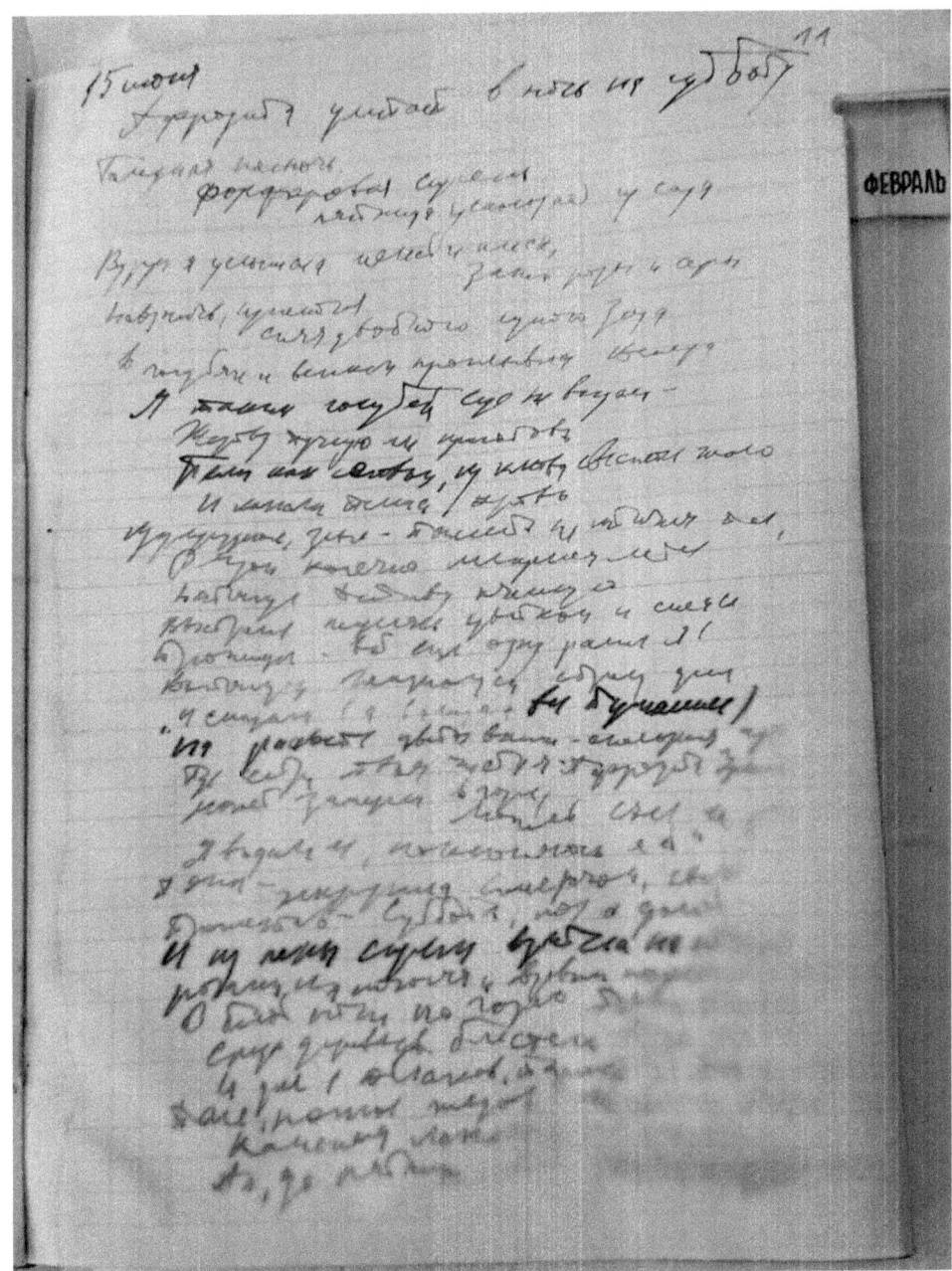

Fig. 2.4. 'Aphrodite Flies off at the End of Friday Night', BT 11 (15 June 1978). The draft version of 'Afrodita uletaet v noch'' na subbotu' shows only minor differences from the published version. Water damage sustained by the 'Bremen Tetrad'' during the fire in Shvarts's flat is particularly evident here.

mid-air' (LP 1.9–12).[19] In Shvarts's poem, Sappho's sparrows become doves or pigeons — although the Russian word 'голубь' means both, the modern urban setting means the birds are almost certainly not doves, but pigeons. The source of the change is Tsvetaeva's ironically titled 'Khvala Afrodite' [Praise to Aphrodite] (1921),[20] which is also based on Sappho's *Hymn to Aphrodite*. Tsvetaeva exclaims 'В широкие закатные ворота | Венерины, летите, голубки!' [Into the wide sunset gates | Of Venus, fly, doves!] Shvarts's 'голуби' have lost the diminutive 'к' of Tsvetaeva's 'голубки' (which can mean 'darlings' as well as 'doves'/'pigeons'). Although Shvarts's pigeons retain the beauty of Sappho's sparrows, they are also dangerous, sinister, vampiric, and unnatural:

> Я таких голубей еще не видала –
> Жертву тучную им приготовь.
> Пели, как соловьи, из клюва свесилось жало,
> Капала темная кровь.
> Изумрудные, алые — тяжесть не птичья тел.
>
> [I had never seen such pigeons —
> Prepare them a fatted victim.
> They sang, like nightingales, from their beaks dangled stings,
> Dark blood dripped.
> Emerald, scarlet bodies — of an unbirdly heaviness.]

Again, the difference from Sappho can be traced back to Tsvetaeva's 'Khvala Afrodite'. Tsvetaeva's doves are symbols of the dependence and depravity caused by love:

> Сколько их, сколько их ест из рук,
> Белых и сизых!
> Целые царства воркуют вкруг
> Уст твоих, Низость!
> [...]
> И полководец гривастый льнёт
> Белой голубкой.
>
> [How many of them eat out of your hands,
> How many, white and grey!
> Whole tsardoms coo around
> Your lips, o Baseness!
> [...]
> And a crested commander clings
> Like a white dove.]

By her alteration of Tsvetaeva's despicable doves into blood-sucking pigeons, Shvarts turns her concern about the potentially degrading nature of sexual desire into an image of physical pain. This emphasis on physical pain is very Shvartsian, and is typical of her self-image as a poet who must suffer for her inspiration; in this

---

19   *Greek Lyric*, I: *Sappho, Alcaeus*, ed. by David A. Campbell (Cambridge, MA; London: Harvard University Press, 1982), pp. 53–55.
20   Marina Tsvetaeva, *Stikhotvoreniia i poemy v piati tomakh* (New York: Russica publishers, 1980–90), II (1983), 133.

poem, love takes the place of poetic inspiration — but nevertheless provides the spur for producing a poem, and is therefore attended by similar imagery.

The same process — the addition of pain imagery indicative of an inspiration subtext — is evident in Shvarts's transformation of Cupid from Tsvetaeva's poem (Cupid is not present in Sappho's *Hymn to Aphrodite*). Tsvetaeva's Cupid shoots blunt arrows that free the poet from love, while Shvarts's Cupid shoots flower-arrows that are sharp like bee stings and that infect her with love.

Tsvetaeva:

> Тяжкоразящей стрелой тупою
> Освободил меня твой же сын.
>
> [With a heavy-smiting blunt arrow
> Your own son freed me.]

Shvarts:

> Натянул тетиву пчелиную,
> Выстрелил, не целясь, цветком и, смеясь,
> Пропищал — вот еще одну ранил я!
>
> [Bent his honeybee bow,
> Fired a flower without aiming, and, laughing,
> Squealed: 'That's another girl I've wounded!']

After Cupid shoots her, Shvarts is struck by love in a manner highly reminiscent of another poem by Sappho. Shvarts writes: 'в глазах все туманнее' [my sight was blurring]. In poem 31, one of Sappho's love symptoms is 'I see nothing with my eyes' (LP XXXI.11, p. 81). Once again, Shvarts privileges the pain of love, responding to the physicality and unromantic realism of Sappho's account of love.

Shvarts makes a contemptuously defiant address to Aphrodite and Cupid: '"На рассвете цветы ваши будут липкая грязь." ['By dawn your flowers will be slimy mud.']. (A similar interaction with Cupid, also influenced by Sappho, occurs in *Kinfiia* 1.4 'Kupidonu' [To Cupid], written four years earlier — see chapter 3.) This follows Tsvetaeva, who also defies Aphrodite: ' — Так о престол моего покоя, | Пеннорождённая, пеной сгинь!' ['So, o foam-born, perish in foam | Against the throne of my peace!']. By speaking to Aphrodite, Shvarts reverses the hierarchy of the Sappho poem, in which Aphrodite speaks to Sappho. Although Sappho's Aphrodite is benevolent and offering to do Sappho's bidding, whereas Shvarts's Aphrodite is hostile and attempting to overpower Shvarts's will, by the discrepancy in the amount of speech allotted to goddess and poet in the two poems Shvarts shifts the balance of power in her favour. In Sappho, Aphrodite speaks for ten out of 28 lines; in Shvarts, Aphrodite says only three words, and those in a whisper: 'суббота, пора домой' ['It's Saturday, time to go home'].

Instead of this Aphrodite, Shvarts requests Aphrodite Urania: 'Где сестра твоя чистая — Афродита Урания? | [...] | Я видала ее, поклоняюсь я ей".' ['Where is your pure sister — Aphrodite Urania? | [...] | I have seen her, I shall bow to her.']. Shvarts here employs the ancient tradition of two Aphrodites, Aphrodite Urania and Aphrodite Pandemos, schematised by Pausanias in Plato's *Symposium*:

> Does anyone doubt that she is double? Surely there is the elder, of no mother born, but daughter of Heaven [Uranus], whence we name her Heavenly [Οὐρανίαν]; while the younger was the child of Zeus and Dione, and her we call Popular [Πάνδημον].²¹

Plato's Pausanias assigns 'base' love (for women as well as boys, more physical than spiritual, and short-lived) to Aphrodite Pandemos and 'noble' love (for older boys, more spiritual yet also physical when there are good motives for reciprocal gratification, and eternal) to Aphrodite Urania.²² Since antiquity, perceptions of 'baseness' and 'nobility' have altered and the distinction simplified, so that Aphrodite Urania 'becomes, for philosophy and religion, the celestial goddess of pure and spiritual love and the antithesis of Aphrodite [Pandemos] [...], the goddess of physical attraction and procreation'.²³ Shvarts's suggestion of Aphrodite's sexual excess in her first description — 'Worn out, on her back' — confirms her identification as Aphrodite Pandemos. There is also the matter of Aphrodite's snatching of an 'old goat': 'взявши под мышку козла' [an old goat stashed under one arm]. The goat was associated with both Aphrodites in antiquity — they were frequently depicted riding goats and goats were sacrificed to them.²⁴ But this goat is clearly intended for a more Pandemos-type activity. Shvarts plays upon the Russian colloquial use of 'козёл' [goat] as an insult, usually for a man (e.g., 'arsehole'), making the 'goat' both an animal, with an appropriately lewd reputation, and a person, whom Aphrodite has presumably picked up to enjoy later.²⁵ Shvarts's opposition of Aphrodite Urania to Aphrodite Pandemos as 'archetypes' of the 'distinction between sacred and profane love'²⁶ expresses the dichotomy between her ideal and her actual approach to love and sex.

Aphrodite's departure is as a victorious general departing the battlefield, which figures sex as death: 'торжествуя, она оглядела | Поле, полное жертв' [triumphant, she surveyed | The field, full of victims]. This takes up Sappho's image of Aphrodite as her 'σύμμαχος' or 'fellow-fighter, ally' (LP 1.28, pp. 54–55)

---

21   Plato, *Lysis; Symposium; Gorgias*, trans. by W. R. M. Lamb (Cambridge, MA; London: Harvard University Press, 1925), pp. 108–09.
22   Ibid., pp. 108–21.
23   Mark P. O. Morford and Robert J. Lenardon, *Classical Mythology* (Oxford University Press, 1999), p. 116.
24   Rachel Rosenzweig, *Worshipping Aphrodite: Art and Cult in Classical Athens* (Ann Arbor: University of Michigan Press, 2004), pp. 70–75.
25   Aphrodite flying up with a personified goat is also reminiscent of the scene in Mikhail Bulgakov's *Master i Margarita* [*The Master and Margarita*] in which Margarita's maid and fellow witch Natasha flies naked on Margarita's next-door neighbour Nikolai Ivanovich, whom she has turned into a hog, and who, significantly, calls Natasha 'Venus': 'Она, совершенно нагая, с летящими по воздуху растрепанными волосами, летела верхом на толстом борове [...] — Венера! — плаксиво отвечал боров.' [Totally naked, with dishevelled hair flying in the wind, she flew mounted on a fat hog [...] 'Venus!', whined the hog in reply.] Mikhail Bulgakov, *Izbrannoe: roman 'Master i Margarita'; rasskazy* (Moscow: Khudozhestvennaia literatura, 1982), pp. 196–98. I am indebted to Ben Fletcher-Watson for this observation.
26   Morford and Lenardon, p. 116.

and turns it against the poet. The final line brings a surprising admission — Shvarts is addicted to Aphrodite's sex-bringing visits: 'Ах, до пятницы новой укола я в сердце не жду!' [Ah, I cannot wait till next Friday for a prick in the heart!]. This volte-face reflects a transition present in Sappho's poem, where at the beginning she pleads 'do not overpower my heart, mistress, with ache and anguish', yet at the end she asks 'Come to me now again and deliver me from oppressive anxieties; fulfil all that my heart longs to fulfil' (LP 1.3–4, 25–27, pp. 53–55).

Another reason for Shvarts's change of attitude may be found in Shvarts's other source for her Aphrodite. Shvarts discreetly acknowledges him in the very first lines, heralding Aphrodite's arrival: 'Бледная полночь, | Фарфоровая сирень' [Pale midnight, | Porcelain lilac]; and again as Aphrodite prepares to leave: 'из пены сирени' [from a foam of lilac blossom]. These lines echo the scene of Aphrodite's impending birth in Mandel'shtam's 'Silentium' (1910/1935): 'И пены бледная сирень | В черно-лазоревом сосуде' [And foam's pale lilac | In a black-azure bowl].[27] In 'Silentium' Mandel'shtam personifies his poetic ideal of *logos* (the word as flesh) as Aphrodite in her pre-corporeal, sea-foam state, and wishes his poetry to remain in the same pre-linguistic, musical state:

> Останься пеной, Афродита,
> И слово в музыку вернись,
> И сердце сердца устыдись
>
> [Remain foam, Aphrodite,
> And word, return to music,
> And heart, be shy of heart]

Mandel'shtam here connects the verbal with the sexual, and disavows them. Shvarts, in proclaiming her dependence on sex, also, via this Mandel'shtam reference, affirms her dependence on the word and poetry of a very earthly and corporeal nature.

In mingling Sappho, Tsvetaeva, and Mandel'shtam, and disagreeing with them all, Shvarts has moulded an Aphrodite in her own image, yet imbued with poetic tradition. She has both retained and reversed Sappho's alliance with Aphrodite, Tsvetaeva's criticism of Aphrodite, and Mandel'shtam's view of Aphrodite as an embodiment of poetic forces. An indication of Shvarts's mirroring of herself in an alter ego comes near the end of the poem, when mirrors make an appearance: 'Средь деревьев блестели везде зеркала' [Amidst the trees everywhere mirrors glinted]. But what makes this Aphrodite most recognisable as an alter ego of Shvarts is her crudity and violence and whimsy.

'Aphrodite' is specifically the Sapphic-Tsvetaevan-Mandel'shtamian love goddess for Shvarts: nowhere else does she appear as Aphrodite.[28] Elsewhere she is always Venus — in at least fourteen other poems.[29] The numbers suggest that Shvarts was

---

27   Osip Mandel'shtam, *Sochineniia v dvukh tomakh*, ed. by A. D. Mikhailov and P. M. Nerler (Moscow: Khudozhestvennaia literatura, 1990), I, pp. 70–71.
28   Except for one reference to an unpublished adolescent poem titled 'Afrodita' (which may be a very early version of 'Afrodita uletaet v noch' na subbotu') in a diary entry for 26 August 1963 (v.350).
29   Ten published poems: 'Rondo s primes'iu patriotizma' [Rondeau with a Dash of Patriotism]

more drawn to Venus than Aphrodite, but in those fourteen poems Venus is never so central nor so vivid as Aphrodite in her single poem. The imbalance probably stems from Shvarts's greater familiarity with the Latin name for the goddess, and from the fact that Venus can serve a dual function: due to the planet, Venus has celestial connotations which Aphrodite lacks; this makes her less human and, if anything, more dangerous. Danger — specifically, the threat that love/sex poses to the integrity of the poet and her body — is what Venus has in common with Aphrodite. Two distinct, yet overlapping, themes emerge in these Venus poems. The first is of very physical intrusion; the second is biblical.

Venus, willingly or unwillingly, invades Shvarts's body through her eye in three unpublished poems. In the second half of 'Razlilas' Venera v shest' luchei' [Venus spilled forth into six rays] (1980 and 1983),[30] 'Koren', koren' mandragory' [A root, a root of mandrake], Shvarts forces Venus to intrude her body: 'проглотил мой глаз Венеру | и она на сердце пала' [my eye gobbled up Venus | and she fell upon my heart]. In another poem composed the same day, 'Iz-za ugla Venera vyskochila' [Venus leapt out from behind the corner] (between 6 March and 16 April 1983, BT 159), Shvarts asks Venus to perform the same intrusion actively: 'Скользни в зрачок! Я буду вором | Найди во мне [другое] ты небо новое' [Slip through my pupil! I will be a thief | Find in me [another] a new sky]. And finally, in the aptly titled 'Opiat' Venera' [Venus Yet Again] (n/d, ESHA M.1), Venus forces the same intrusion on Shvarts:

> грудью прямо лезет в око.
> [...]
> Но легче когда ты на небе
> чем в теле заперта со мной.
>
> [via the chest she creeps straight into my eye.
> [...]
> But it's easier when you're in the sky
> than shut up in a body with me.]

These depictions of Venus connect with the ideas of bodily penetration and loss of sight in 'Afrodita uletaet v noch' na subbotu': when Cupid shoots Shvarts with an arrow and makes her sight blur. Love continues to be a thing half-wanted and half-unwanted, causing loss of control and judgement.

(1969, I.22–24), 'Moisei i kust, v kotorom iavilsia Bog' [Moses and the Bush God Appeared in] (early 1970s, I.38–39), 'Neugomonnyi istukan' [Indefatigable Idol] (1980, I.127–28), 'Gostinitsa Mondekhel'' [Hotel Mondehell] (1981, I.129–33), 'Ostrovok na Kamennom' [Islet on Kamennyi (Stony) Island] (1983, I.174–75), *Laviniia* II 'Temnaia Rozhdestvenskaia pesn'' [Dark Christmas Song] (1984, II.174–75), 'V monastyre bliz albanskoi granitsy' [In a Monastery near the Albanian Border] (1991, I.310–11), 'A v oknakh u tsygan' [But in gypsies' windows] (1996, I.348), 'Verchen'e' [Whirling] (1999, I.397), 'Malen'koe puteshestvie sredi ostrovov i zvezd' [A Little Journey among Islands and Stars] (1983). Four unpublished poems: 'Opiat' Venera' [Venus Yet Again] (n/d, ESHA M.1), 'Razlilas' Venera v shest' luchei' [Venus spilled forth into six rays] (1983, ESHA M.1), 'Pri lunnom zatmenii' [During a Lunar Eclipse] (1982, BT 131), 'Iz-za ugla Venera vyskochila' [Venus Leapt out from behind the Corner] (1983, BT 159).
30 ESHA M.1. The two parts of the poem also appear in BT 78 and 159, dating them between 5 and 17 March 1980, and between 6 March and 16 April 1983.

Shvarts's statement of unwilling dependence on Venus in 'A v oknakh u tsygan' [But in gypsies' windows] (1996, I.348) shows that her attitude to the love goddess remained the same over the nearly two decades since 'Afrodita uletaet v noch' na subbotu':

> Венера мне не сестр, а спицею холодной
> На древо знания пришпилена звезда
> Полярная —
>
> [Venus is not my sister, but, pinned with
> A cold needle to the tree of knowledge,
> My pole star —]

Shvarts describes Venus very differently from the customary depiction of the love goddess as hot and passionate; the 'cold needle' is reminiscent of the injection — 'prick' — at the end of 'Afrodita uletaet v noch' na subbotu'. The needle becomes a compass needle as the sentence resolves into the statement that Venus is Shvarts's guiding Pole Star. The star is conflated with Eve's apple, and Shvarts declares that she will eat this apple; her consumption of the Venus-apple repeats the bodily intrusions of Venus in the poems discussed above. This then brings about Venus's Satan-like fall from grace:

> как ягоду, как яблок,
> Я съем ее сегодня всю
> И демонов седых косматый облак
> Ее опустит вниз
>
> [Like a berry, like an apple,
> I will eat her all up today
> And the hirsute cloud of hoary demons
> Will cast her down]

This plays upon the planet Venus's — the morning star's — alternative name, Lucifer. Yet Shvarts's enthusiastic eating of the apple from the tree of knowledge returns Venus from a planet to the goddess of love, and the subtext from astronomy to sex, via the field in which both meanings are combined — the Bible.

Shvarts often sees Venus in apparently paradoxically Christian contexts. The poem 'V monastyre bliz albanskoi granitsy' [In a Monastery near the Albanian Border] (1991, I.310–11) presents a Venus described in some of the same voluptuous vocabulary — and the same position — as in 'Afrodita uletaet v noch' na subbotu': 'Я подняла глаза, увидела изнемогающую Венеру, | Сочащую любовь в пространство' [I raised my eyes, saw Venus growing worn out, | Exuding love into space]. The goddess is depicted hovering above the mountainous boundary between Orthodox North Macedonia and Muslim Albania. Throughout the poem Shvarts contrasts the known, beloved, and religiously correct environs of the Orthodox monastery with the unknown, alluring, yet religiously incorrect world across the border. Shvarts declares her love for both the Orthodox and the Muslim realms — a conclusion which has been foreshadowed by Venus oozing love over the border at the beginning.

Venus is a paradoxical — but strangely inevitable — presence at the Epiphany in *Laviniia* 11 'Temnaia Rozhdestvenskaia pesn'' [Dark Christmas Song] (1984, II.174–75). Unlike her lascivious depiction in 'Afrodita uletaet v noch' na subbotu', Venus is here called 'страшная Девица' [a fearsome Maiden], and she appears in the sky as both star and goddess, like in 'A v oknakh u tsygan'. In the sky she walks 'за Богом' [after God] — a synthesis of different religions that is typical of *Laviniia* — but which still reveals a definite hierarchy, with Christianity at the top. The same hierarchy is at work in the poem 'Moisei i kust, v kotorom iavilsia Bog' [Moses and the Bush God Appeared in] (early 1970s, I.38–39), where the Old Testament God is paradoxically called 'Творец и крови и Венеры' [Creator of both blood and Venus]. Here Venus may be a synonym for sex; it also suggests that the Roman goddess of love and the Abrahamic God both have passionate, carnal natures. In *Laviniia*, the birth which Venus oversees is not that of Christ, as would be expected, but of 'Другая Дева' [Another Virgin] — perhaps Mary, or even Lavinia herself. Venus objects:

> Венера в космосе кричала,
> Что Человек — он есть мужчина,
> Но ей блаженное мычанье отвечало,
> Что Дева, Дева — Микрокосм.
>
> [Venus shouted up in space
> That the Human — he is a man,
> But a blessed bleating answered her
> That the Virgin, the Virgin — is a Microcosm.]

A. V. Markov understands these lines as Venus objecting to the principle of a virgin birth, since she is Venus, the 'alchemical symbol for the union of contradictory elements', rather than Aphrodite, 'who gives her blessing to various kinds of love'.[31] Yet Shvarts's capitalisation of 'Human' suggests to me that Venus is not only objecting to the lack of sex in bringing about the birth, but to the fact that Jesus has not made his appearance in male form as expected. The response to Venus's complaint prioritises the inner world of a woman without a man: she is a microcosm. This response (from God?) is appropriate for the nun Lavinia, who is the 'creator' of an extensive fantastical poetic world. It also explains Shvarts's problem with Venus/Aphrodite, exhibited in their non-consensual interactions in poem after poem. Shvarts would prefer to be herself a 'microcosm', like her Narcissus alter ego; dependence on love and physical intimacy is unbefitting the poet, whose creative powers should be a whole unto themselves.

Shvarts's Aphrodite and Venus have much in common, especially the danger they represent. From the drug-like prick, to intrusion into Shvarts's body via her eye, to the forbidden apple, to the allure of other faiths, to the threat to the wholeness of virginity/creativity, the goddess of love always proffers a fatal temptation. However, Venus, due to her celestial side, is less human than her counterpart Aphrodite. The

---

31 A. V. Markov, 'Latinizmy v poeticheskikh knigakh "Dikii shipovnik" Ol'gi Sedakovoi i "Trudy i dni monakhini Lavinii" Eleny Shvarts', *Vestnik Permskogo universiteta: rossiiskaia i zarubezhnaia filologiia*, 9.1 (2017), 122–29 (p. 126).

following section will address an unambiguously celestial alter ego of Shvarts, who has starred alongside the planet Venus more than once.

Selene/Luna

Shvarts's close personal relationship with a deity personifying an astronomical body recurs with Selene/Luna, goddess of the moon. Venus and Luna are clearly linked in Shvarts's mind, as they appear together in two poems. In 'Gostinitsa Mondekhel'' [Hotel Mondehell] (1981, I.129–33) Shvarts claims identity and daughterhood with both Venus and Luna:

> И вернусь я Луной на Луну, и Венерой к Венере,
> Не узнают они, пусть разодранной, дщери?
> Семена мы и осыпи звезд.

> [And I shall return as Luna to Luna, and as Venus to Venus,
> Won't they recognise — even dismembered — their own daughter?
> We are the seeds and scree of stars.]

In 'Pri lunnom zatmenii' [During a Lunar Eclipse] (11 January 1982, BT 82) Luna's eclipse is construed as a deliberate attempt to scare Shvarts: 'Будто чулок бандитка на морду себе натянула' [As if the bandit pulled a stocking on over her own face]. Shvarts ends her draft of the poem with a face-to-face meeting with Venus, the morning star: 'Холодом счастья дохнула в лицо Венера' [Venus blew the cold of happiness in my face]. In the published version, 'Pri zatmenii Luny' [During an Eclipse of the Moon/Luna] (1982, I.136), Venus is absent, and her place in comforting Shvarts is taken by Shvarts's own poetry.

The moon was important to Shvarts from an early age, as her autobiographical writings show. She shared her generation's fascination with space exploration, on which topic she wrote several diary entries: on 11 November 1958 news of a scientist's discovery of a volcanic eruption on the moon's surface leads her to conclude joyfully that there is life on the moon; on 14 September 1959 she recounts in detail the landing of the second Soviet moon rocket; and on 28 October 1959 she excitedly reports the photographing earlier in the month of the dark side of the moon by another Soviet rocket (v.263, 271, 273).[32] Later diary entries show a more personal connection with the moon: on 1 November 1962 the nearly week-long absence of a moon disturbs Shvarts, who recalls reading that it is possible to drink the moon; on 14 December 1962 she reports doing just that — drinking moonlight in a glass of water — and claims she can still taste it (v.312, 315–16). Shvarts underscores her closeness with the moon in a prose account of her childhood, 'Komarovo', from the collection *Istinnye proisshestviia moei zhizni* [*True Events of My Life*]: she describes how, aged twelve, she was gazing at the full moon, feeling an intense excitement and connection with it, when the moon seemed to draw her blood towards it, starting her first period (III.330–31). The moon, then, is a prime candidate to be an alter ego in Shvarts's poetry.

---

32   The published diaries do not extend to 1969, so it is not possible to gauge her reaction to the American manned moon landings.

A difficulty arises, however, when trying to discern classical reception in Shvarts's depictions of the moon as an alter ego. The word most commonly used for the moon in Russian literary language is derived directly from Latin: 'luna'.[33] So this means that when writing 'luna' Shvarts may simply mean 'moon', or she may be referring to the Roman moon goddess; and as a poet she capitalises on the ambiguity. Therefore in this section I focus mainly on poems in which Shvarts names the moon by its Greek name, 'Selene' ('Selena' in Russian), except where it is clear (e.g. due to capitalisation and/or proximity to other classical references) that the personified Luna is intended as well as the moon. In these cases, I translate 'Luna' as 'Luna' rather than 'the moon', but ideally both should be understood simultaneously.

Selene, goddess and metonymy of the moon, is a frequent figure in Shvarts's poetry, appearing in three poems and one cycle: 'Nochnoe kupan'e' [Night Bathing] (1981 [1980], I.156), *Luna bez golovy* [*Luna Loses her Head*] (1987, II.147–52), 'Posledniaia noch'' [The Last Night] (1990, I.326–27), and 'Zabastovka elektrikov v Rime' [Electricians' Strike in Rome] (2002, III.48). In 'Zabastovka elektrikov v Rime' Selene is just an extension of the Roman setting (note that Shvarts chooses to underline the classical reference by using the Greek name for the moon). In 'Posledniaia noch'' Selene has some potential to be an alter ego: she is part of an anthropomorphised sky, in which a star is called 'brother' by Shvarts, and in the apocalyptic chaos not only is the cosmos humanised, but humans are mingling with nature. Selene comes closer to being an alter ego in 'Nochnoe kupan'e', a poem that expresses Shvarts's sense of oneness with the world, in a similar mode to 'Posledniaia noch''.

'Nochnoe kupan'e' begins with Shvarts as the sea: 'Была я морем и волной, | Кровинкою Господней' [I was the sea and a wave, | A blood drop of the Lord]. This launches a string of perspective-bending scenarios in which a big-small Shvarts encircles a big-small Earth. In the final lines Shvarts depicts herself orbiting Selene:

> Вокруг Селены быстро-мутной
> Ладьею утлой кружилась я
> На содрогающемся, смутном
> И темном сердце бытия.
>
> [Around Selene as a quick-dull
> Fragile boat I turned
> Upon the shuddering, troubled
> And dark heart of existence.]

The pull of the moon that Shvarts feels in this poem is similar to her description of its influence on her adolescent body in 'Komarovo'. Yet in 'Nochnoe kupan'e', as well as 'Posledniaia noch'', it is more the world that Shvarts identifies herself with; Selene is a personification of only one, distant aspect of this. In these poems Selene, unlike existence, is too serene to be Shvarts's alter ego.

---

33 There is also a folk word for the moon, 'mesiats' [month], but it is less common in literature.

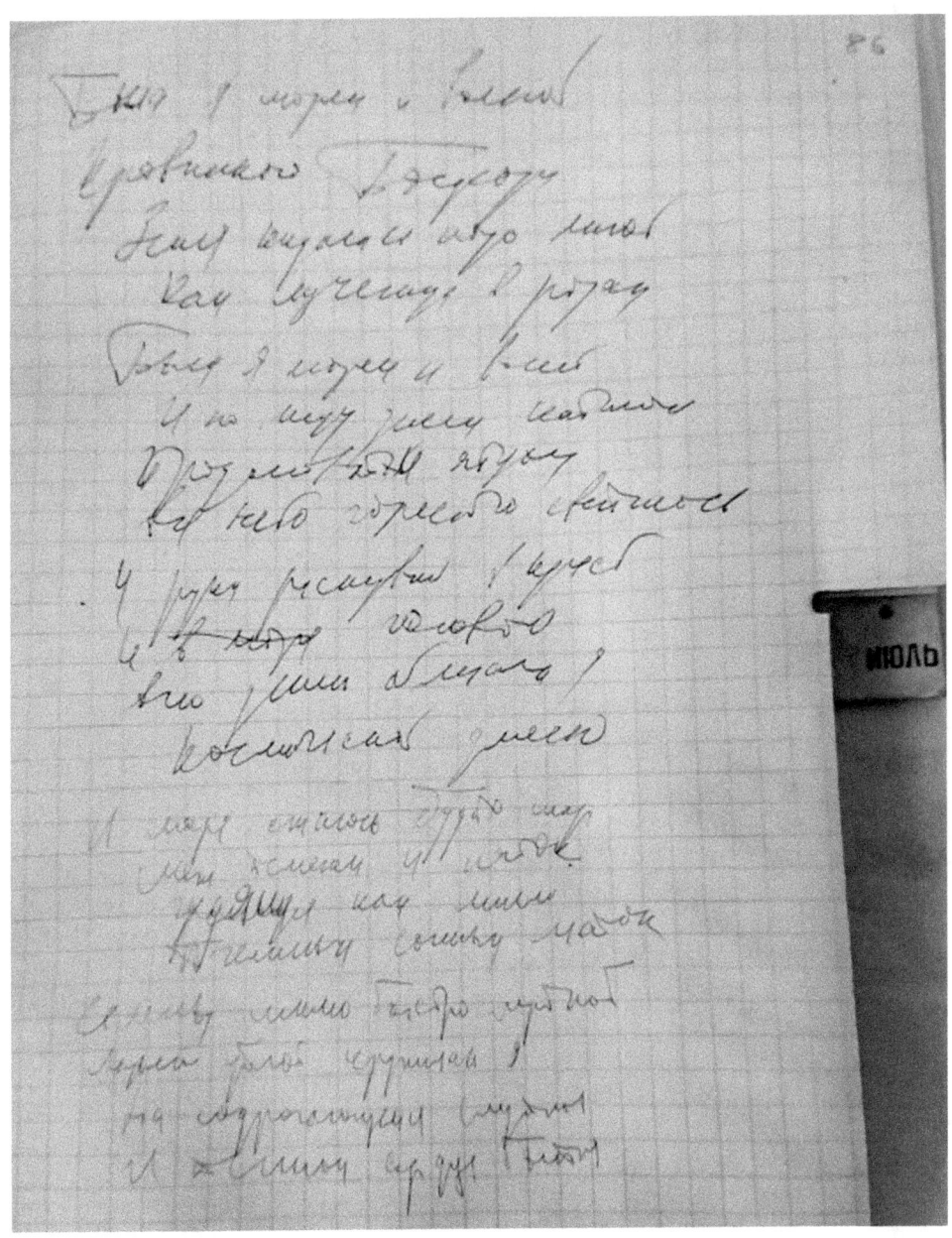

FIG. 2.5. 'Night Bathing', BT 86 (between 6 June and 7 August 1980). The draft version of 'Nochnoe kupan'e' (here untitled) shows only minor differences from the published version.

But Selene is troubled enough to be a true alter ego for Shvarts in the cycle *Luna bez golovy*. As the title says, the moon has lost her head, and the seven-poem cycle explores the ramifications of her loss upon Shvarts, who benefits from it in a way that binds them inextricably together. The moon is mostly called 'Luna' in the cycle, with 'Selene' used only in the first and third poems; throughout, Shvarts uses 'Luna' as a name — capitalised, personified, and with diminutives — in a way that she does not when talking about the moon elsewhere (e.g. in 'Afrodita uletaet v noch' na subbotu').

The opening couplet of the first poem encodes the name Selene in a way that closely ties Shvarts and Selene together, creating confusion over who is who, which continues into the third couplet:

> Се ли ты?
> Се ли она?
> В стакане темноты
> Горька Луна.
> И ты — моя сестра. И твой
> Я — сестр.
>
> [C'est toi là?
> C'est elle là?[34]
> In a glass of darkness
> Luna is bitter.
> And you are my sister. And your
> Sister am I.]

With the unusual wording of the first lines Shvarts suggests the closeness of the names 'Elena' and 'Selena', and through this her affinity with Selene. I. V. Ostapenko analyses the second line thus:

> a pun, emphasising the idea of the oneness of 'I' and the moon/Luna: the word 'selena' [...] is a homophone of the phrase 'se Lena' (in which 'se' is an obsolete form of the demonstrative pronoun 'this/that').[35]

The 'bitterness' of the moon in the glass is reminiscent of Shvarts's teenage tasting of the moon in a glass of water. The word 'bitter' also recalls the Russian tradition of shouting 'gor'ko' [bitter] at weddings to make the couple kiss, and so is suggestive of union and kissing. In the final couplet of poem 1, Saint Peter jingles the keys of heaven — complementing the celestial setting, but jarring with the classical references to Luna and Selene.

The one time Shvarts directly calls the moon 'Selene' in *Luna bez golovy* is in poem 3:

---

34   French gets closest to the sound of 'Se li ty? | Se li ona?' [Is this you? | Is this her?]. I have chosen it over English since the encoding of the syllables of 'Selena' is the crucial point of these lines.
35   I. V. Ostapenko, 'Priroda v russkoi lirike 1960–1980-x godov: Ot peizazha k kartine mira' (Kamenets-Podol'skii natsional'nyi universitet, 2012), p. 370.

> Я протяну к Селене,
> Такой же — и она мне.
> Мы с нею заговорщики,
> Мы шепчемся, шпионим.
>
> [I'll hold it out to Selene,
> So will she to me.
> We are conspirators,
> We whisper and spy.]

Tellingly, this is the point in the cycle when they are most equal and most friendly, so continuing Shvarts's identification of herself ('se Lena') with Selene from poem 1.

In poem 4, 'Telo Luny i golova ee zhe' [Luna's Body and her Head Too], Luna is personified, given bodily characteristics and affectionate diminutives of her name:

> Узкобедрая бежит Луна,
> Широких топот каблуков.
> Где же, Лунушка, твоя голова?
> На плечах одни полукружья рогов.
> Где же, Лунь, твоя голова?
> Высоко — во тьме облаков.
>
> [Narrow-hipped Luna runs,
> Clatter of wide heels.
> Where on earth, Lunushka, is your head?
> On your shoulders are only crescents of horns.
> Where on earth, Lun', is your head?
> It's high up — in the dark of clouds.]

Here Shvarts is playing the same game as in the first poem: making evident the similarity that also exists between 'Luna' and 'Lena' — the diminutive of 'Elena', the name she went by to her friends. There is only one letter's difference. At this point, Luna's body throws itself into Shvarts's body and gets tangled in her bones; crenellations rise around Shvarts's head, and a lake shines inside it; Luna's head (the moon) peers down, calling her lost body, and attacks Shvarts's head to try to find it, but cannot get to the lake; Shvarts tells Luna's head to return to the sky, since it is futile for Luna to attack Shvarts's head — it is like attacking herself. The shining lake inside Shvarts's head is a mirror of the moon — Shvarts is growing like her alter ego Luna.

Now that the reader knows where Luna's head is (it's the moon!), in poem 5 it is clarified exactly where — or who — her body is: 'Когда Луну вели на гильотину, | [...] | [...] тело спряталось в меня' [When Luna was led to the guillotine, | [...] | [...] her body hid itself inside me]. The confirmation that Luna's body *is* Shvarts affirms the punning upon Luna/Lena of the previous poem. As Shvarts is literally the embodiment of the moon, she is possessed of some of her powers, which leads to a confrontation between Shvarts and her larger alter ego:

> Я выхожу в полнолунье на крышу
> И ну — дразнить, сиять.
> Она ко мне летит, как ястреб,
> Я от нее — шустрее мыши

> [I go out at the full moon onto the roof
> And, well — to tease, to shine.
> She flies at me, like a hawk,
> I flee from her — nimbler than a mouse]

Yet despite Shvarts's evident joy in the possession of the moon's body, she claims that she and Luna both know that she will give it back: 'когда-нибудь — я тело верну и сращу | И забинтую шею своею кровью' [sometime — I will return the body and graft it back on | And I will bandage her neck with my own blood]. Even when envisaging her bodily separation from her alter ego, they are bonded by blood.

In poem 6 a lunatic is drawn to and contrasted with Luna. The lunatic is called Luna's 'double':

> Зима. Лунатик по карнизу
> Обломком Луны скользит
> [...]
> Ее двойник одет, она — нага
>
> [Winter. A lunatic on the cornice
> Slips on a fragment of Luna
> [...]
> Her double is clothed, she — is naked]

As in poem 5, the lunatic tries to climb as high as humanly possible, to be on a level with Luna. Luna is described not as a distant astronomical body, but as the most classically homely of homes, Ithaca:

> И тихо лунатик вплывает в Луну —
> Не как австронавт — от взгляда его плесневея,
> Скукожится вся, — а как в легкую дверь и родную страну,
> Где кинется сразу собака к нему,
> Как некогда было уже с Одиссеем.
>
> [And quietly the lunatic lands on Luna —
> Not like an astronaut — from his gaze she moulders,
> And quite shrivels up — but like at a light door and his native land,
> Where straight away his dog throws herself at him,
> Like already happened one time before, with Odysseus.]

At the end of the poem it is revealed that the lunatic is Shvarts herself:

> И вдруг я, жалкий лунатик, проснусь
> На брошенной в поле пустой колокольне.
> Как пуповина — откушенный луч,
> Мне больно, Луна, а тебе не больно?
>
> [And suddenly I, the pitiful lunatic, wake up
> In a field in an abandoned belltower.
> The bitten-off ray of light is like an umbilical,
> It hurts me, Luna, doesn't it hurt you too?]

Moonbeams are compared to an umbilical, connecting Luna and Shvarts as mother and daughter; Shvarts has been the moon's daughter once before, in 'Gostinitsa

Mondekhel'". Shvarts feels that the severing of this umbilical must hurt both her and her alter ego equally.

The increasingly violent and sacrificial imagery of the cycle comes to a head (!) in poem 7:

> Тело Луны
> [...]
> оно — Бог.
> И раз я его проглотила
> И оно во мне,
> Значит — мы с ним оба
> Суждены голове-Луне.
> Когда-нибудь я брошу свою головенку
> На футбольное поле — играй.
> А вместо нее — Луна,
> Сияющая, как рай.
> В пустые ее глазницы
> Поглядит человеческий род.

> [Luna's body
> [...]
> it is God.
> And since I swallowed it
> And it is inside me,
> That means me and it are both
> The destiny of the head-Luna.
> Some time I will throw my little head
> Onto the football field — play!
> But instead of it — Luna,
> Shining, like heaven.
> Through her empty eye sockets
> The human race will look.]

When Shvarts calls the body of Luna God, she ties the pagan Luna/Selene to Christian mythology. This explains some puzzling Christian images from earlier in the cycle: in particular, the cameo by Apostle Peter at the end of poem 1, and Shvarts's crenellated head in poem 4, which is reminiscent of Christ's crown of thorns. Moreover, Luna's beheading associates her with Christian martyrdom, while Luna's conflation with God reminds the reader of God's sacrifice of his son; all this allows Shvarts by the end of the cycle to represent her own severed head/Luna as Christlike in its/her suffering and compassion for humanity. The leap from moon to Christ is simultaneously achieved via the association of the moon with lunacy, and the special Russian category of lunatic, the *iurodivyi* [holy fool]. The holy fool, an outcast from society who can therefore speak truth to authority, and whose madness is a sign of divine inspiration, has featured in Russian literature since the medieval period; Shvarts often assumes a holy fool persona.[36]

---

[36] Josephine von Zitzewitz, *Poetry and the Leningrad Religious-Philosophical Seminar 1974–1980: Music for a Deaf Age* (Oxford: Legenda, 2016), pp. 122–24. Shvarts's most notable holy fool persona is the nun Lavinia, who, like Shvarts in 'Luna bez golovy', 'imitates and at times seems to exchange herself

Selene/Luna achieves a closer affinity with Shvarts as an alter ego than Venus/Aphrodite, and the poet chafes less at the merging of their bodies. The affinity arises partly due to the similarities Shvarts perceives between her name and Selene's and Luna's names, but mostly because — once she is no longer the serene celestial body — Selene/Luna represents lunacy, a state more conducive to Shvarts and her poetry than love.

In the first half of this chapter, we have seen three different 'celestial body' alter egos: Narcissus, Aphrodite/Venus, and Selene/Luna. The ideality of the celestial bodies allow them to represent states of mind for Shvarts — be it narcissism, love/sex, or madness/inspiration. This alignment of Shvarts's mental state with the celestial bodies' ideal form of that mental state is why their physicalities are so often mingled with the poet's.

Odysseus

A classical alter ego who bridges the two categories of alter ego in this chapter — celestial bodies and katabasists — is Odysseus. His descent into the underworld (discussed below) makes him a katabasist, but Shvarts also connects Odysseus with space travel and the stars, for example in poem 5 of *Luna bez golovy*. Odysseus is a relatively infrequent figure in Shvarts's poetry, but in the medium-length poem 'Malen'koe puteshestvie sredi ostrovov i zvezd' [A Little Journey among Islands and Stars] (March 1983)[37] Shvarts as the 'путник' [wanderer] makes Odysseus her classical alter ego, alongside Samuel Taylor Coleridge's Mariner.

'Malen'koe puteshestvie sredi ostrovov i zvezd' does what the title says: Shvarts/the wanderer sets sail among islands, which by the end of the poem have become stars. The poem is accompanied by prose comments in the margins, like stage directions. The characters and episodes Shvarts/the wanderer meets along the way are mostly fleeting, in a compression of the episodic layout of the *Odyssey*. The flow of events is highly associative, almost hallucinatory. This dreamlike quality, along with the sailor protagonist, explains the poem's subtitle, '*в манере Кольриджа*' [*in the style of Coleridge*], which refers to Coleridge's *The Rime of the Ancient Mariner*. However, there are no concrete references to the text of Coleridge's poem, while references to Homer's abound. Shvarts evidently discerned the parallels between the Mariner and Odysseus — both sailors lost at sea, both captains who lose their entire crews, and both returning safely home to tell their tales — and made a composite from Coleridge's style and Homer's plot.[38]

The Odyssean characters named in 'Malen'koe puteshestvie sredi ostrovov i

for Christ'. Sarah Clovis Bishop, 'Harmonious Disharmony: Elena Shvarts's *Trudy i dni Lavinii, monakhini iz Ordena Obrezaniia Serdtsa*', *The Slavic and East European Journal*, 56.2 (2012), 213–31 (p. 223).
37   Elena Shvarts, 'Non dolet', *Znamia*, 8 (2001), <http://znamlit.ru/publication.php?id=1502> [accessed 21 November 2019]; Elena Shvarts, 'Malen'koe puteshestvie sredi ostrovov i zvezd' (Bremen, 1983), Forschungsstelle Osteuropa, FSO 01–265 Pazuchin K35; Elena Shvarts, 'Malen'koe puteshestvie sredi ostrovov i zvezd' (St Petersburg, 1983), ESHA M.1.
38   Although in the opening section Shvarts copies Homeric diction, too: 'муж Одиссей богоравный' [godlike man Odysseus].

zvezd' are: Odysseus, Circe, Calypso, Boreas, a Siren, Polyphemus, and Lotus-eaters; several of these appear elsewhere in Shvarts's oeuvre.[39] There are almost as many references to aspects of Shvarts's self-mythology as a Petersburg poet, all of them somehow connected to water: a bath, St Petersburg, Peter I (founder of Petersburg as a naval power), Chernaia Rechka [Black River] — the site of Pushkin's fatal duel, the Neva, and Marina [Tsvetaeva]. There are also several non-Odyssean classical references, all but one of which connect with Shvarts's oft-inhabited classical alter egos: Venus, a 'mer-Amazon' (the odd one out), Apollo,[40] Delphi (Pythia), and vines (Dionysus).

The wanderer is unveiled unmistakeably as Shvarts at two points in 'Malen'koe puteshestvie sredi ostrovov i zvezd'. The first is the poem's first 'stage direction': *'Путник (или его душа) пускается в плаванье среди островов Греческого архипелага, но его мучает подозрение, что он плывёт не в лазурном море, а лежит дома в ванне и всё это ему только мерещится'* [*The wanderer (or his soul) sets off sailing among the islands of the Greek Archipelago, but he is plagued by the suspicion that he is not sailing on the azure sea but lying at home in the bath, and all this is just his imagination*]. Shvarts was known among her friends for composing poetry in the bath,[41] so this 'suspicion' is in all likelihood actually the case. The second is when Marina Tsvetaeva, Shvarts's favourite poet, appears. Tsvetaeva, called only 'Marina' in the poem, is admissible to this small odyssey due to her 'marine' name, but she is also incorporated into the Odyssean narrative, being introduced as a 'морская нимфа' [sea nymph].

Odysseus never reaches Ithaca in Shvarts's poem, only dreaming he is home (a dream induced by Calypso). Shvarts, on the other hand, reaches her destination, coming into communion with her frequent alter ego Venus, who is both the star and the personification of love, via the medium of another frequent alter ego, Dionysus, and his intoxicating, poetry-inspiring vines, which twine around Shvarts in her boat, as in the *Homeric Hymn to Dionysus* (VII). 'Malen'koe puteshestvie sredi ostrovov i zvezd' shows both what extensive familiarity Shvarts had with the *Odyssey*, and what personal resonance the *Odyssey* had for Shvarts. Odysseus's final outing in Shvarts's poetry is examined in the next section.

The Katabasists

The second half of this chapter explores a group of classical alter egos whom I call 'katabasists': mythical figures who made a *katabasis*, or a descent into the underworld, and lived to tell the tale. Shvarts's fascination with katabasists is motivated in part by the fact that Christ is also a katabasist (due to his death and resurrection), so, as in *Luna bez golovy*, many of Shvarts's classical alter egos explored below are shadowed by the figure of Christ.

---

39   Odysseus appears twice more: discussed above and below. Circe appears once more, in the unpublished poem 'Tsirtseia' [Circe] (1983) ESHA M.2. The image of the blinded cyclops Polyphemus is most compelling to Shvarts, appearing three more times: 'Burliuk' (1974, I.11), *Slepaia vesna* [*Blind Spring*] (1995, I.271–77), 'U Panteona' [*At the Pantheon*] (2002, III.49).
40   'A certain | Radiant god' who helps Shvarts against Boreas.
41   Kirill Kozyrev, Interview by Georgina Barker, St Petersburg, Russia, 2019.

One of Shvarts's earliest[42] adoptions of a katabasist alter ego is of Hades, the god of the underworld himself. In the poem 'Rasskaz Aida, proglochennogo Kronom' [The Tale of Hades, Swallowed by Kronos] (no later than February 1973, ZT 60) Shvarts vividly imagines Hades' experience of descending into his father's stomach, and subsequently growing up there. (See the Appendix for the full poem.) 'Rasskaz Aida, proglochennogo Kronom' can be seen as a metaphorical prefiguring of the real *katabasis* Hades will eventually undergo when he is made lord of the underworld.

Hades' wife Persephone makes two appearances in Shvarts's poetry as a miserable katabasist (rather than as queen of the underworld). Shvarts's long cycle *Lestnitsa s dyriavymi ploshchadkami* [*Staircase with Holey Landings*] (January–February 1978, I.69–94) is structured as a climb towards Heaven, with (katabastic) holes along the way. In one 'hole' poem, 'Ia opushchus' na dno morskoe' [I sink to the seabed], Shvarts hears 'визги пьяных Персефон, | И разъяренный бас Деметры' [shrieks of drunken Persephones, | And the enraged bass of Demeter].[43] At the end of *Elegii na storony sveta* [*Elegies on the Corners of the Earth*] (1978, I.100–04), the last lines of the 'Zapadnaia' [Western] elegy put Persephone in a contemporary setting, despondently looking at the phone — which holds the underworld of shades — and eating pomegranate seeds to quench her hunger and thirst. Her representation here as a modern woman and an alcoholic — as Shvarts often depicts herself — suggests Persephone as a minor katabasist alter ego.

Shvarts's most extensive treatment of the *katabasis* theme is in the cycle *Solntse spuskaetsia v ad* [*The Sun Descends into Hell*] (2002, III.6–11). It is subtitled 'Gimny k adventu' [Hymns for Advent], and the pagan image of the sun descending below the earth in the depths of winter is paralleled by the Christian image of Christ's birth (the annual celebration of which was set to coincide with the winter solstice). Each of the eight poems is based around something that matches the sun's descent underground: 1 — winter's warmth in hibernation under the snow; 3 and 6 — the sun, sinking into the underworld like a bucket down a well; 7 — Shvarts/Christ in the crib; and 8 — God's love in Shvarts's poetry, which will rise up above the universe if nurtured with a mustard seed (representing Heaven). In three of the cycle's eight poems, Shvarts draws matches for the underground sun — and alter egos for herself — from the katabasists of classical mythology: 2 — Orpheus; 4 — Odysseus; and 5 — the Dioscuri. Orpheus is an important figure within Shvarts's oeuvre more broadly, so will be discussed separately. I turn first to Odysseus and the Dioscuri.

Katabasist-Odysseus (as opposed to Wanderer-Odysseus of the previous section) is the match for the sun in poem 4 of *Solntse spuskaetsia v ad*, 'Zhazhda tenei' [The Shades' Thirst]:

> В безотрадной степи Персефоны
> У истоков Коцита
> Жертвенной кровью

---

42   I believe from the rather simplistic, childish style of the poem that it was written much earlier than its latest possible date of 1973, perhaps as early as 1966.
43   Orpheus has a brief cameo in another of the 'hole' poems, 'Laif-vita' [Life-vita].

> Поил
> Стадо теней Одиссей.
> [...]
> в декабре вкушают
> Немного падшего солнца.
>
> [In Persephone's desolate steppe
> By the springs of Cocytus
> Odysseus gave the flock of shades
> Sacrificial blood
> To drink.
> [...]
> in December they partake of
> A bit of fallen sun.]

This Odysseus comes from *Odyssey* Book 11, when he converses with the dead: 'I took the sheep and cut their throats over the pit, and the dark blood flowed. Then there gathered from out of Erebus the ghosts of those that are dead'.[44] Odysseus remains physically at the site of the sacrifice, but his conversation with the dead is figured by Homer as a *katabasis*; Shvarts, on the other hand, sets the scene firmly in the (curiously russified) underworld. She specifically calls the *blood* which Odysseus feeds to the shades 'A bit of fallen sun'. The key to why is found in the line 'Жаждут они вина нашей крови' [They thirst for the wine of our blood]: it is not the sheep's blood of Homer's story, but is instead human blood — presumably, of Odysseus himself, and therefore self-sacrificial blood. She calls the blood 'wine', a word redolent in this sacrificial context of the communion wine representing/embodying Christ's blood. This makes Odysseus the counterpart not only of the fallen sun but also of Christ.

At the beginning of poem 5 of *Solntse spuskaetsia v ad*, 'Kol'tso Dioskurov' [Ring of Dioscuri], Shvarts, watching the sun sinking, is reminded of a pair of sparrows joined in a ring that crashed to the ground in front of her and died. The sparrows are the first of Shvarts's alter egos in the poem; Shvarts felt a personal connection with sparrows, saying 'я ленинградский воробей' [I am a Leningrad sparrow] (29 April 2006, v.139). In turn, the 'Птичье кольцо живое' [Living bird ring] reminds her of the Dioscuri, the twins Castor and Pollux, one a mortal and one a demigod, who become her second alter egos in the poem.[45] Shvarts relates their tale — how Pollux was taken by his father Zeus to Olympus, while Castor languished in the underworld, but Pollux could not bear to be apart from his brother, and arranged for them both to spend half the year together in each place. Shvarts solidifies the

---

44 Homer, *The Odyssey*, trans. by A. T. Murray, 2 vols (Cambridge, MA; London: Harvard University Press, 1974), I, p. 403.

45 In her diary in April 2005 Shvarts notes with surprise the connection Oleg Dark had found between the Dioscuri and sparrows, which she had not known about when she linked them (v.88–89). Well may Shvarts have been surprised: the Dioscuri's connection with sparrows seems to date back to Robert Graves, who confuses '*xouthos*' [tawny] with '*strouthos*' [sparrow], and thus reads their 'tawny wings' in the *Homeric Hymn to the Dioscuri* (xxxiii) as 'sparrowy wings' and their ancestor Xuthus as 'Sparrow': Robert Graves, *The Greek Myths*, 2 vols (Harmondsworth: Penguin Books, 1962), I, p. 252.

comparison of the Dioscuri with the sparrow ring (and with the sun) by viewing their *katabases* and ascensions as a cycle:

> Так в колесо превратились —
> Вечно в прыжке под землю,
> Вечно в прыжке в небеса.
>
> [So they turned into a wheel —
> Eternally in a leap under the ground,
> Eternally in a leap into the heavens.]

Shvarts compares the unbreakable bond between the twins to that of her soul with an unnamed 'you', whom she calls her 'бессмертный, | Легкий и лучший двойник' [immortal, | Easy and better double]. The next line, in which he is 'Полный ко мне сострадания' [Full of compassion for me], all but announces that this third alter ego is Christ. The connection between the Dioscuri and Christ is their partial divinity, partial mortality. At the end of the poem she merges this Christ figure with herself, the sparrows, and the Dioscuri:

> Выведешь из Преисподней
> Ты самого себя
> Верю я — мы сольемся,
> Как два воробья на асфальте
> Как Диоскуры в полете.
>
> [You will lead yourself
> Out of the Underworld,
> I believe — we will coalesce,
> Like two sparrows on the asphalt,
> Like the Dioscuri in flight.]

The Dioscuri parallel the classical alter egos we have seen so far in one key aspect: duality.[46] Their duality allows Shvarts to exploit them as alter egos more multivalently than the other classical figures she uses in *Solntse spuskaetsia v ad*.

Orpheus and Eurydice

Orpheus first appears in Shvarts's poetry very early on — and in first-person direct speech — in '"Szhal'tes', milye teni' ['Sweet shades, take pity] (1967, ZT 21). (See Appendix for the full poem.) This Orpheus is approached primarily through the opera *Orfeo ed Euridice* by Christoph Willibald Gluck, who, Shvarts implies, is antiquated, just like the classical underworld which he depicted in his music. Opening the poem as Orpheus appealing to the dead to release Eurydice, the nineteen-year-old Shvarts briefly takes on his persona. But although Orpheus is at first able to move wild animals to tears with his song (as in his myth), by the end of the poem it is no longer Orpheus who is the musician, but Cerberus, who plays 'Chopsticks' (in Russian: 'The Dog Waltz') in a parody of Orpheus's and Gluck's

---

46 Narcissus's duality is self-evident; Aphrodite/Venus's duality is highlighted by Shvarts mentioning Aphrodite Urania; Selene/Luna's duality is introduced by Shvarts dividing the moon into body and head.

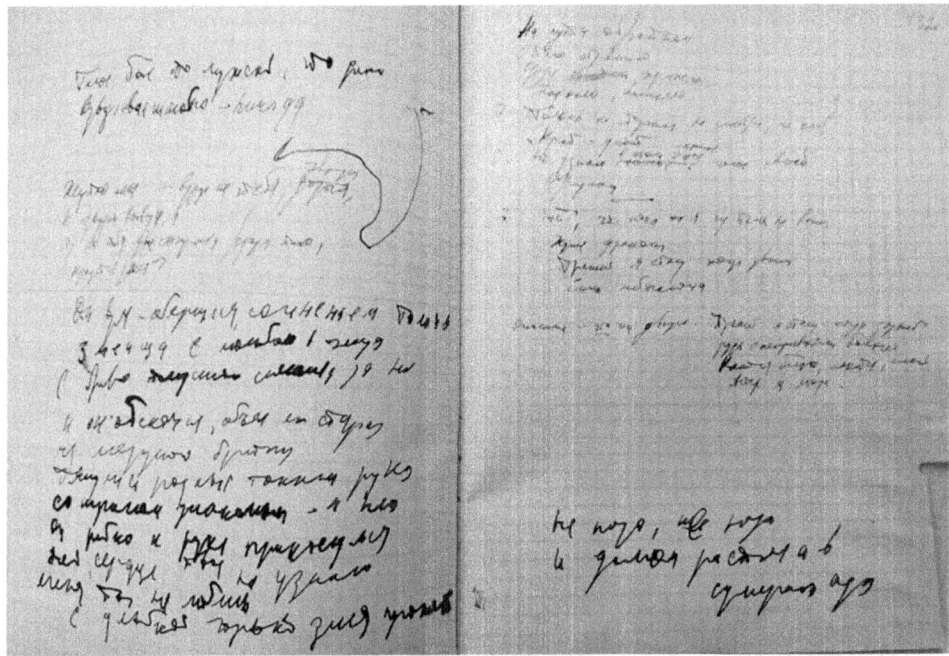

Fig. 2.6. 'Orpheus', BT 132 (between 11 and 24 January 1982). This draft varies considerably from the printed version. It was written in two (or maybe three) stints: recto, then verso continuing onto recto. In the first stint Shvarts wrote ll. 1–16, then a note to self: 'Описание — <u>что</u> он увидел' [Description — <u>what</u> he saw]. The differences from the print version (listed in the Appendix) create a Eurydice who is more masculine and less serpentine, and an Orpheus who is less loving, who fears the serpent even before he sees her.

lost musical prowess. Despite the tongue-in-cheek depiction of Orpheus here, he is still the katabasist-Orpheus (as opposed to the Argonaut-Orpheus) whom Shvarts would go on to depict throughout her life.[47]

Fifteen years later, it is both Orpheus and Eurydice whose voices Shvarts takes on. 'Orfei' [Orpheus] (1982, I.153–54) stages a dialogue between Orpheus and Eurydice as he is leading her out of the underworld. (See the Appendix for the full poem.) 'Orfei' hinges on the — literally — pivotal moment of the Orphic myth, the moment when on the path back to the living world Orpheus turns, despite having been forbidden to do so, sees Eurydice, and thus loses her for good. Feminists have come to see this moment as emblematic of the male gaze, by which artists — who are de facto male — define their female subjects for the enjoyment of their audience — who are also de facto male — thereby stripping those women of agency. Helen Sword sums up the effect of Orpheus's turn on the second most important figure in the Orphic myth: 'defined and manipulated by his powerful

---

47 There is evidence that Shvarts was planning something — perhaps a play — involving the Argonaut Orpheus alongside a host of other classical characters, but no published work seems to have come of her copious notes. ESHA T.A11 pp. 13–29.

gaze, Eurydice is, comparatively speaking, a mythological nobody. Her only obvious archetypal significance resides in a negative role: that of woman-as-Other, woman-as-death.'[48] Shvarts perceives the superficiality of Eurydice's depiction as defined by Orpheus's gaze. She presents a Eurydice who is literally Other when Orpheus looks at her — 'Змеища' [A huge serpent] — and an Orpheus whose love is not sufficient to see past Eurydice's exterior to the person within. Shvarts departs from the usual myth in that it is not the fact that Orpheus turns round that causes him to lose Eurydice, but that he does not recognise her when he does: ' — Нет, сердце твое не узнало, | Меня ты не любишь' ['No, your heart did not recognise me, | You do not love me']. Because of this, Shvarts's Eurydice makes the active choice not to follow Orpheus out of the underworld — unlike the powerlessness of the mythical Eurydice. Indeed, throughout 'Orfei', in Korneliia Ichin's analysis, Shvarts opposes an Orpheus who is perpetually fearful to a Eurydice who is 'the personification of faith, love, and sacred knowledge': it is Eurydice, in Shvarts's version, who guides Orpheus, who knows what exists in the underworld and what awaits in the world above.[49]

> *Эвридика*: По сторонам не смотри, не смей,
> Край — дикий.
> [...]
> Прежней я стану когда увижу
> Синь небосклона.
> Прежней я стану — когда задышит
> Грудь — с непривычки больно.
> Кажется, близко, кажется, слышно —
> Ветер и море.
>
> [*Eurydice*: Don't look about you, don't you dare, this —
> Is wild territory.
> [...]
> I will become my former self when I see the blue
> Of the horizon.
> I will become my former self when my chest begins
> To breathe — unaccustomedly, painfully.
> It seems like it's close, it seems like I can hear it —
> The wind and the sea.]

It must be this superior insight that allows Shvarts's Eurydice to break the mythical power of the male gaze, which she first endures and then judges flawed.

Eurydice's greater narrative control means that, although 'Orfei' is still titled for the poet-musician, it is Eurydice who is the real protagonist of the poem, as Aram Asoian concludes. But Asoian also claims that Shvarts makes a complete

---

48 Helen Sword, 'Orpheus and Eurydice in the Twentieth Century: Lawrence, H. D., and the Poetics of the Turn', *Twentieth Century Literature*, 35.4 (1989), 407–28 (p. 408).
49 Korneliia Ichin, '"Orfei" Eleny Shvarts v kontekste poeticheskoi traditsii', in *Poetika iskanii ili poisk poetiki: materialy mezhdunarodnoi nauchnoi konferentsii-festivalia 'Poeticheskii iazyk rubezha vekov i sovremennye literaturnye strategii' (16–19 maia 2003 goda)*, ed. by Natal'ia Fateeva (Moscow: Izdatel'stvo Instituta russkogo iazyka RAN, 2004), pp. 356–67 (p. 365).

break from the Orphic tradition, which is far from the case.⁵⁰ Firstly, Shvarts takes elements of her retelling from both the famous classical sources. Orpheus's fear derives from Ovid: he writes that Orpheus looks back 'afraid' (*Met.* x.56, p. 69). But the Ovidian influence on Shvarts's retelling of the Orpheus and Eurydice story is generally a negative one: by giving her Eurydice speech and letting *her* rather than the gods of the underworld judge the power of Orpheus's love, Shvarts counters Ovid's insistence that 'she made no complaint against her husband; for of what could she complain save that she was beloved?' (*Met.* x.60–61, p. 69). Instead, it is Virgil's retelling (which Ovid's version is here countering) that most resonated with Shvarts, and it is from Virgil that she derives Eurydice's reproach, the focus on her hands, and her melting away like smoke:

Shvarts:

> Тянулись родимые тонкие руки
> Со шрамом родимым — к нему.
> Он робко ногтей розоватых коснулся.
> [...]
> Не надо! не надо! —
> И дымом растаяла в сумерках ада.
>
> [Reached out familiar slender hands
> With their familiar scar — to him.
> Hesitantly he touched the pale pink fingernails.
> [...]
> 'Don't! Don't!'
> And she melted away like smoke in the twilight of hell.]

Virgil:

> She cried: 'What madness, Orpheus, what dreadful madness has brought disaster alike upon you and me, poor soul? [...] And now farewell! I am borne away, covered in night's vast pall, and stretching towards you strengthless hands, regained, alas! no more.' She spoke, and straightway from his sight, like smoke mingling with thin air, vanished afar. (*Georgics* IV.494–500)⁵¹

Equally important as Virgil as an influence on Shvarts's 'Orfei' is Tsvetaeva's 'Evridika — Orfeiu' [Eurydice to Orpheus] (1923).⁵² Tsvetaeva gives Eurydice similar capabilities of speech and choice over her fate. Indeed, Tsvetaeva's poem tips the balance further towards Eurydice than Shvarts's: it is a monologue, with Orpheus allotted no speech at all. Tsvetaeva's Eurydice is enjoying the peace, the passionlessness, the realness of death; she tells Orpheus (repeatedly) to leave her alone:

---

50 Aram Asoian, *Semiotika mifa ob Orfee i Evridike* (St Petersburg: Aleteiia, 2017), p. 72.
51 Virgil, *Eclogues. Georgics. Aeneid I–VI*, trans. by H. Rushton Fairclough, 2 vols (Cambridge, MA; London: Harvard University Press, 1999), I, p. 255.
52 Tsvetaeva, III (1983), 56. Tsvetaeva's 'Evridika — Orfeiu' is named on a typed list (date unknown) of poems Shvarts planned to memorise. 'Lists: Vyuchit' liuboe iz sleduiushchikh stikhotvorenii. Rasskazat' o', ESHA D.

> мне нужен покой
> Беспамятности... Ибо в призрачном доме
> Сем — призрак *ты*, сущий, а явь —
> Я, мёртвая... Что же скажу тебе, кроме:
> — 'Ты это забудь и оставь!'
>
> [I need the peace
> Of memorylessness... For in this phantom
> House — the phantom is *you*, the living man, and the reality —
> Me, the dead woman... What then shall I say to you, besides:
> 'You forget this and leave off!']

Ichin sees Shvarts's Eurydice's rather unspecific 'Не надо! не надо!' ['Don't! Don't!'] as a direct quotation of Tsvetaeva's penultimate line, 'Не надо Орфею сходить к Эвридике' [Don't come down to Eurydice, Orpheus], to the extent that without supplying the rest of Tsvetaeva's line, Shvarts's own line does not entirely make sense.[53] 'Orfei' is inextricably entwined with the poetic tradition behind the Orpheus myth.

Yet one element of 'Orfei' is completely without precedent: Eurydice's transformation into a serpent. Eurydice warns Orpheus: 'Знай, что пока я из тьмы не вышла, — | Хуже дракона' [Know that until I emerge from the dark, I am — | Worse than a dragon]; when he turns round he indeed sees 'Змеища' [A huge serpent]. Ichin argues that the serpent's bite (which kills Eurydice in the source myth) turns her into a 'тень-дракон' [shade-dragon].[54] The trodden snake is a potent association for Shvarts to draw on. She used it before in 'Zemlia, zemlia, ty esh' liudei' [Earth, earth, you eat people] (1981, I.155), calling the earth 'древняя змея' [ancient serpent] and saying 'тем, кто ходит по тебе, | Втираешь тлен в пяту' [you rub decay into the heels | Of those who walk on you]. The decaying — or snake-bitten — heel symbolises the mortality inherent in being human; mortality which, at the beginning of the poem, allows the generation of a string of natural phenomena symbolising poetry. Whose heel Shvarts has in mind in 'Zemlia, zemlia, ty esh' liudei' is not clear — the mortality of Achilles' heel is famous, but the snakebite and poetic associations point to Eurydice.[55] What Eurydice's transformation into a serpent does connect with, however, is Shvarts's own oeuvre, as will be explored below.

The year after 'Orfei', Shvarts returns to the couple in an unpublished fragment, 'Taiat' mozhet' [It could melt away] (after 22 July 1983, BT 184). Here is the fragment in full:

---

53 Ichin, p. 365.
54 Ibid.
55 The placing of 'Zemlia, zemlia, ty esh' liudei' after 'Orfei' in print editions — the *samizdat* collection *Korabl'* [Ship] and the initial two-volume collected works which Shvarts oversaw — also points to Eurydice being the primary classical reference here, before Achilles. Elena Shvarts, *Voisko, Orkestr, Park, Korabl': chetyre mashinopisnykh sbornikov*, ed. by Artem Shelia and Pavel Uspenskii (Moscow: Common place, 2018), pp. 264–65; Elena Shvarts, *Sochineniia Eleny Shvarts*, 5 vols (St Petersburg: Pushkinskii fond, 2002–13), I (2002), 153–55.

Таять может
остров тот весь
замшелая ступень
жирная
провал и свая ~~в лиры лесы~~
О, я — Орфей. Ты — робкая
~~И~~ робкая стень
О бородатая и в джинсах Эвридика
~~Тебе, наверное, в Аиде лучше жить~~
~~Хотя б меня из ада отпусти~~[56]

[It could melt away —
that whole island
the mossy step
greasy
the pit and stake ~~into lyre's scaffolds~~
O, I — am Orpheus. You — are timorous
~~And~~ a timorous wraith
O bearded and jeans-wearing Eurydice
~~You would, probably, have been better off living in Hades~~
~~At least let me go free from hell~~]

The Eurydice in this fragment is akin to the Eurydice of 'Orfei', who also has a beard. But here Shvarts puts her in jeans, making her a contemporary — and possibly masculine — figure. Unlike 'Orfei', Shvarts does not assume both voices; in 'Taiat' mozhet' she emphatically takes the part of Orpheus, which may be why this Eurydice takes on male characteristics.[57]

Shvarts mobilises Orpheus in her *Geopoliticheskii trilistnik* [*Geopolitical Triptych*] (May 1990)[58] lamenting the break-up of the Soviet Union. Poem 2 'Smutnye strofy' [Troubled Stanzas] has Shvarts wishing to become a modern-day Russian busker, whom she compares ironically to Orpheus:

О если я могла бы играть на флейте —
Кажется, лучшего и не надо!
Хорошо бы в метро за медяк случайный,
Как Орфей, выходящий один из ада.

[O if only I could play the flute —
Apparently, nothing better is needed!
It'd be good in the metro for the odd copper coin,
Like Orpheus, exiting hell alone.]

Shvarts's pessimism is expressed in the Orpheus she chooses: he is no longer with Eurydice, but has failed in his quest and lost her forever. The poem ends with a nod to an even more depressing Orpheus: the dismembered Orpheus — who appears more prominently in *Homo Musagetes* — when a 'каменная лира' [stone lyre] plays

---

56   The fragment is virtually illegible in places, so the transcription is not 100% reliable. The inserted word 'жирная' [greasy] could belong with either 'ступень' [step] or 'свая' [stake].
57   I am indebted to Boris Ostanin for this observation.
58   Elena Shvarts, 'Pesnia ptitsy na dne morskom', *Vavilon* (1995), <http://www.vavilon.ru/texts/shvarts3.html> [accessed 25 April 2019].

during the death of a bear (representing Russia) whose head is separate from its paws.

Coming full circle to Orpheus's appearance in *Solntse spuskaetsia v ad*, poem 2 'Orfei opiat' spuskaetsia v ad' [Orpheus Descends into Hell Yet Again] is like 'Orfei' in its representation of Eurydice, if not in its tone — and the poem's title wryly recognises Shvarts's repeated use of the Orphic theme. Once again, Eurydice herself thwarts Orpheus's attempt to return her to the world:

> Но она
> Простой саламандрой —
> Прозрачной, пустою летала,
> Сквозь пальцы текла...
> Отсветы влажные
> В ее сердцевине мерцали.
> Он быстро ее проглотил
> И хотел унести
> На горькую землю назад.
> Она же пламенным вихрем
> Опять изо лба унеслась
> И, танцуя, в огне растворилась...

> [But she
> A simple salamander —
> Transparent, empty flew,
> Flowed through his fingers...
> Moist gleams
> Glimmered in her core.
> He quickly swallowed her
> And wanted to carry her off
> Back to the bitter land.
> Yet she in a flaming whirlwind
> From his forehead sped away again
> And, dancing, dissolved in fire...]

Orpheus's swallowing of Eurydice is unsettling; it is an act apparently of violence and control, rather than love — paralleling his lack of love for her in 'Orfei'. Eurydice's representation as a salamander, which has long been connected with fire in folklore, underscores that she is in her natural element in Hell. Once Orpheus gets home, Eurydice burns inside him:

> Странный ожог терзал его сердце
> С тех пор —
> Там
> Прозрачною ящеркой
> Ты, Эвридика, плясала.

>   [A strange burn has torn at his heart
>   Since then —
>   There
>   A transparent lizard
>   You, Eurydice, have danced.]

Eurydice's fieriness — which makes her rather than Orpheus the match for the sun — and her representation as an amphibian/reptile connect her still further with the dragon-serpent Eurydice of 'Orfei'. Yet the Eurydice of 'Orfei opiat' spuskaetsia v ad' is not personified or humanised in the way that the Eurydice of 'Orfei' is. This is because she represents something — what, we will now discover.

The Eurydice of 'Orfei opiat' spuskaetsia v ad' corresponds with two of Shvarts's recurring self-representations. The first is as a fiery salamander (or serpent). Lavinia, Shvarts's most prolific alter ego, is told: 'Саламандрой | Была ты в прошлом' [You were | A salamander in the past].[59] In 'Salamandra' [Salamander] (2001)[60] Shvarts tells the salamander: 'Ты живешь и в сердце у меня' [You also live in my heart]. And in 'Chem byla i chem stala' [What I Was and What I Have Become][61] Shvarts turns into a dancing snake-like firebrand that is counterposed to a list of Shvarts's most important alter egos, and very reminiscent of the dancing lizard/serpent/salamander Eurydice:

>   А теперь я сделалась *головнёй*,
>   Говорящей
>   И танцующей на хвосте,
>   Как змея.
>
>   [But now I am become a *firebrand*,
>   Speaking
>   And dancing on my tail,
>   Like a serpent.]

The second is as a force penetrating the forehead. Eurydice's emergence from Orpheus's forehead connects with an incident in Shvarts's childhood that she relates in one of the mini-essays of *Opredelenie v durnuiu pogodu* [*Definition for a Rainy Day*]:

> **Ray**
> How I became a believer. I was about thirteen years old. I was sitting by the window, side-on, and I suddenly felt that the curtain was being sort of pierced by a ray, and that the ray entered my left temple. It wasn't a ray of sunlight, I don't think — this all happened in the late evening.
> Everything in my life changed immediately, I started seeing and understanding differently, it was like a thread into the unseen.
> Later (much) I saw a medieval miniature, where King David was shown in prayer, and on it was depicted just this — a ray came through a curtain and entered his temple. (III.229–30)

---

59   *Laviniia* 43 'Ognennyi urok' [Fiery Lesson] (1984, II.196).
60   Elena Shvarts, 'Dikopis' poslednego vremeni', *Vavilon* (2001), <http://www.vavilon.ru/texts/shvarts4.html> [accessed 13 September 2018].
61   Poem 3 of *Stikhi o Gore-Zloschast'e i beskonechnom schast'e byt' mechennoi Bozh'ei rukoi* [*Poems on Grief-Ill-Fortune and the Endless Joy of Being Marked by God's Hand*] (2004, III.81–85).

Imagery from this memory forms part of Shvarts's 'personal myth as a seer-poet', drawing on 'the Hindu concept of chakras (energy points on the body)', in which 'the "third eye" stands for the brow chakra, representing intuitive insight into things beyond ordinary sense perception'; and in one poem the 'ray of light is explicitly identified as poetic inspiration'.[62] When Eurydice becomes this ray of light in 'Orfei opiat' spuskaetsia v ad', she is not only the alter ego of the sun and Christ, but also the embodiment of poetry. This must be why Orpheus was able to internalise Eurydice by the end of 'Orfei opiat' spuskaetsia v ad': Shvarts cannot countenance the poet without inspiration.

Shvarts takes both Orpheus and Eurydice as alter egos — she does not prioritise Orpheus as 'the poet' or Eurydice as 'the woman', but sees them as a pairing where Eurydice embodies poetry or inspiration, and is therefore essential to Orpheus. When she does focus exclusively on Orpheus, he is 'musician' rather than 'poet'. Although she tends to write about the second half of the Orpheus and Eurydice story — Orpheus' emergence from the underworld — the first half, in which Eurydice is bitten by a serpent, expresses itself in her depictions of a serpentine Eurydice.

Inspired victims of Dionysus and Apollo

In Shvarts's self-mythology, poetic inspiration comes at a price.[63] Inspiration is invariably painful, often envisaged as a self-sacrificial act, and frequently brought about through a process that should (and sometimes does) kill the poet. But after this inspired pain, self-sacrifice, or death, Shvarts's poet is more alive than an ordinary mortal. This is why I group such 'inspired victims' together with the katabasists in this chapter: inspiration is figured by Shvarts as a kind of death and rebirth. The link between the inspired victims and the true katabasists is strengthened by the fact that Orpheus is in both camps. But there is a strong connection to the 'celestial bodies', in that the poet is often physically invaded by the inspiring deity — as with Venus and Selene/Luna — and afterwards a connection remains between god and poet.

Shvarts's theme of violent desecration of the individual in the cause of poetry comes from and engages with Pushkin's poem 'Prorok' [Prophet] (1826), in which an angel mutilates the poet so he will spread the word of God. The impact of this single poem should not be underestimated. Not only Shvarts, but also her fellow Leningrad poets, were deeply influenced by 'Prorok',[64] and in the words of Andrew Kahn, 'More than any other single work "Prorok" has shaped the view that poetry occupies a uniquely important place in Russian literature'.[65] 'Prorok', although

---

62   von Zitzewitz, *Poetry and the Leningrad Religious-Philosophical Seminar 1974–1980*, p. 117. 'Bokovoe zrenie pamiati' [The Lateral Vision of Memory] (1985, I.232–33): von Zitzewitz, 'From Underground to Mainstream', in *Twentieth-Century Russian Poetry*, ed. by Hodgson, Shelton, and Smith, pp. 251–52.
63   A typical expression of this comes at the end of the early poem 'Rondo s primes'iu patriotizma' [Rondeau with a Dash of Patriotism] (1969, I.22–24), when she says to her Muse 'усохшие чернила | Развела моею кровью' [you have diluted the dried-up ink | With my own blood].
64   von Zitzewitz, *Poetry and the Leningrad Religious-Philosophical Seminar 1974–1980*, p. 3.
65   Andrew Kahn, *Pushkin's Lyric Intelligence* (Oxford; New York: Oxford University Press, 2008), p. 203.

not overtly classically influenced, assumes a vatic (prophet-poet) posture that is associated with Horace,[66] and therefore very adaptable to classical contexts. Shvarts is also influenced by another Pushkin poem, 'Poet' (1827),[67] in which writing poetry is depicted as a sacrificial act commanded by Apollo: 'Пока не требует поэта | К священной жертве Аполлон' [Until the poet is summoned | To sacred sacrifice by Apollo]. Violent inspiration is therefore especially pronounced when either or both of the gods of poetic inspiration, Apollo and Dionysus, are present.

In her answer to Boileau's philosophy of poetry *L'Art poétique*, 'Podrazhanie Bualo' [Imitation of Boileau] (1971, I.40), Shvarts programmatises the poet's violent mutilation by a god of poetry. (See the Appendix for the full poem.) The poem mimics Boileau's rhyming alexandrine couplets, and is dedicated to El'ga Linetskaia, the Russian translator of *L'Art poétique*, whose translation seminar Shvarts attended in her youth. (III.254) Boileau's opening verse warns that Apollo will be deaf to all but a true poet:

> Si son astre en naissant ne l'a formé poëte,
> Dans son génie étroit il est toujours captif;
> Pour lui Phébus est sourd, et Pégase est rétif.

> [Но, знайте, лишь тому, кто призван быть поэтом,
> Чей гений озарен незримым горним светом,
> Покорствует Пегас и внемлет Аполлон.]

> [If at thy Birth the Stars that rul'd thy Sence
> Shone not with a Poetic Influence:
> In thy strait Genius thou wilt still be bound,
> Find Phoebus deaf, and Pegasus unsound.][68]

Shvarts, elaborating on these lines, gives a warning far more dire than Boileau's to the aspiring poet:

> Но, юный друг, своим считаю долгом
> Предупредить, что Муза схожа с волком,
>
> И если ты спознался с девой страшной,
> То одиночества испробуй суп вчерашний.
>
> Поэт есть глаз, — узнаешь ты потом, —
> Мгновенье связанный с ревущим божеством.
>
> Глаз выдранный — на ниточке кровавой,
> На миг вместивший мира боль и славу.

---

66 Ibid., p. 205.
67 Aleksandr Pushkin, *Izbrannye sochineniia v dvukh tomakh* (Moscow: Khudozhestvennaia literatura, 1978), I, p. 266.
68 Nicolas Boileau-Despréaux, *Œuvres poétiques*, 2 vols (Paris: Imprimerie générale, 1872), I, p. 203; Nicolas Boileau-Despréaux, 'Bualo: poeticheskoe iskusstvo', trans. by E. L. Linetskaia <http://fgpodsobka.narod.ru/poetica.htm> [accessed 29 September 2018]; Nicolas Boileau-Despréaux, *The Art of Poetry Written in French by the Sieur de Boileau; Made English*, trans. by William Soames and John Dryden (London: R. Bentley and S. Magnes, 1683), p. 1.

[But my young friend, I consider it my duty
To warn you: the Muse is like a coyote,

And if you have come to know the dread maiden,
Then try the leftover soup of desolation.

The poet is an eye — you'll learn eventually —
Linked for an instant with a roaring deity.

The eye is torn out — on a thread all gory,
For a moment it contained the world's pain and glory.]

Shvarts's promise is of *pain* to the *inspired* poet, as opposed to Boileau's promise of *mediocrity* to the *uninspired* poet. It is not clear who the poet-mutilating 'roaring deity' is: it could be Apollo, due to his role in *L'Art poétique*, or it could be Dionysus, due to his appearance earlier in 'Podrazhanie Bualo': 'В его разодранном размере, где Дионис живет, | Как будто прыгал и кусался несытый кот' [In his [the poet's] dismembered metre, where Dionysus abides, | It is as if a hungry cat leaps and bites]. Whichever god it is, their dangerousness stems entirely from Shvarts: Boileau's Apollo is at worst merely deaf, while his Bacchus is a merry figure. Dionysus, dismembered by the Titans, here represents the painful disorder (both thematic and metrical) that inspires her frenzied poetry.

The opening of 'Elegiia na rentgenovskii snimok moego cherepa' [Elegy on an X-ray of my Skull] (1973, 1.28–30) represents a poet physically destroyed by contact with Apollo:

Флейтист хвастлив, а Бог неистов —
Он с Марсия живого кожу снял.
И такова судьба земных флейтистов,
И каждому, ревнуя, скажет в срок:
'Ты меду музыки лизнул, но весь ты в тине,
Все тот же грязи ты комок,
И смерти косточка в тебе посередине'.
Был богом света Аполлон,
Но помрачился —
Когда ты, Марсий, вкруг руки
Его от боли вился.
И вот теперь он бог мерцанья

[The Flautist is boastful, and the God frenzied —
He flayed Marsyas alive.
And such is the fate of earthly flautists,
And to each he will jealously say in their turn:
'You have had a lick of the mead of music, but you are wholly in mire,
You are still that selfsame lump of dirt,
And the pip of death is at your core'.
A god of light was Apollo,
But he grew gloomy —
When you, Marsyas, wound round
His hand from pain.
And so now he is a god of glimmering]

Shvarts alludes to Apollo's epithet, Phoebus, or 'shining', and says that after he kills Marsyas he can never be purely light again, but will always contain a measure of darkness. Within the imagery of the X-ray poem, Marsyas and other flautists are Shvarts,[69] the 'смерти косточка' [bone/stone[70] of death] inside them is Shvarts's skull, and the light-and-dark Apollo is the X-ray itself, which strips away the flesh from Shvarts's skull.

Apollo and Dionysus are united in the role of poet-mutilator in 'Krov'iu Motsarta atlasnoi' [With Mozart's satin blood] from *Lestnitsa s dyriavymi ploshchadkami*. Shvarts portrays the gods equally, mirrored within the lines, working in tandem towards a single aim — reforming a human being into a genius capable of receiving their inspiration:

> Аполлона это жилы, это вены Диониса,
> Вживе вживленные в жизнь.
> Аполлон натерся маслом, Дионис натерся соком,
> И схватили человека — тот за шею, тот за мозг,
> Оборвали третье ухо, вырезали третье око,
> Плавят, рвут его как воск,
> Но сияющий, нетленный,
> Равноденственный, блаженный

> [Apollo's are the sinews, the veins are Dionysus's,
> Alive enlivened into life.
> Apollo rubbed himself with oil, Dionysus rubbed himself with juice,
> And they seized a person — this one by the neck, that one by the brain,
> They ripped out a third ear, carved out a third eye,
> They melt and tear him like wax,
> But shining, incorruptible,
> Equinoctial, blessed]

Again, the unnamed victim of the gods is an alter ego of Shvarts; the gods carving out a 'third eye' even makes use of Shvarts's personal mythology of belief/inspiration entering through her forehead — discussed above in connection with Orpheus.

Shvarts portrays Dionysus and Apollo together as equals elsewhere, too. In *Homo Musagetes* the two gods are literally joined together in an embrace, and speak together as well; while in the unpublished *Kinfiia* poem 'Zavistniku' [To the Envier] (1980, BT 89) Dionysus and Apollo join forces to punish a man who has offended Kinfiia. Shvarts's connection of the two gods has its origin in Nietzsche, whose Apollonian/Dionysian polarity was popularised in Russia at the turn of the century by the Symbolists. Viacheslav Ivanov was especially central to disseminating the idea of the two gods as equals and opposites, which he expounded in his book *Dionis i pradionisiistvo* [*Dionysus and Pre-Dionysianism*] (1923). Ivanov even saw the two gods as merged in the figure of Orpheus, calling him 'the two-faced mysterious incarnation of both [Dionysus and Apollo]'.[71] However, despite Shvarts's apparent

---

69 Shvarts herself in later life connected the flayed Marsyas with her (neighbouring) poem about her own skin, 'Nevidimyi okhotnik' [Invisible Hunter] (1975, I.26–27). 7 November 2007, v.181.
70 Translated above as 'pip', since no one English word combines both Russian meanings.
71 Pamela Davidson, 'Divine Service or Idol Worship? Russian Views of Art as Demonic', in

equation of the two gods, Dionysus features much more frequently than Apollo in her poetry.[72] This is probably due to the traditional divide between their two modes of inspiration, which Pamela Davidson articulates:

> Whereas Apollo and the muses confer their gifts on man through a vertical hierarchy of patronage (the artist may invoke them in order to receive their gifts, but may not imitate them), the Dionysian paradigm of inspiration allows man to merge with the god, to enter the state of intoxication which brings about inspiration. The fairly passive and upward-looking hierarchy of receiving a divine gift is replaced by an active descent into chaos.[73]

Shvarts is fascinated by the idea of physically merging with mythical beings (as we have seen throughout this chapter), and also by ideas of intoxication and chaos. The Apollo she gives her reader is a darkened, Dionysian Apollo. Whereas Dionysus needs no darkening — which is why she favours him.

Dionysus is connected with Shvarts's most unconventional alter ego, Svalka, or the rubbish dump. In 'Svalka' [Dump] from *Letnee Morokko* [*Summer Moroque*] (1983, 1.164–76) this repellent aspect of Russian *byt* — the large communal rubbish dump found in the back courtyards of Russian blocks of flats — is not only hymned, but is personified, empowered, and given a voice through poetry. (For the full poem, see the Appendix.) The word 'svalka' is grammatically feminine in Russian, and Shvarts addresses Svalka throughout as if a female poet — this is why I call her 'Svalka' here, and not 'Dump'.

Besides being a female poet, Svalka is marked as an alter ego of Shvarts by being connected with the dismembered Dionysus, since Shvarts had previously used this image to speak about her own poetic style in 'Podrazhanie Bualo'.[74] The first draft reveals that Dionysus was a late addition to the poem: the line that in the printed version reads 'Ты — Дионис, разодранный на части' [You are Dionysus, dismembered into bits] instead reads 'Ты будто мир, разодранный на части' [You are like the world, dismembered into bits]. Her original use of the adjective 'разодранный' [dismembered], which she had already used in 'Podrazhanie Bualo' in connection with Dionysus (discussed above), must have brought to mind Dionysus. The god who was dismembered by the Titans is an apt comparison for the dump, which is composed of many pieces; he is also a more vivid and more human association for Svalka.

Russian Literature and its Demons, ed. by Pamela Davidson, Studies in Slavic Literature, Culture, and Society, 6 (New York, NY; Oxford: Berghahn, 2000), pp. 125–64 (p. 137).
72   Apollo is named in five poems and (probably) alluded to in a further two, including two poems not discussed in this section: 'Pokhorony rifmy' and 'Malen'koe puteshestvie sredi ostrovov i zvezd'. Dionysus is named in thirteen poems, including two unpublished poems not discussed in this section: 'Bogi spiat raskinuv nog[o/i]ruki' [The gods sleep with leg-arms spread] (n.d., ESHA M.0), where Shvarts wishes Dionysus's tiger would roar to dispel boredom, and 'Grustno smotriu ia pod kryl'ia tiazhelye' [I look sadly under the heavy wings] (11 April 1993, ESHA M.2), where Dionysus is connected with the troubled Caucasus region.
73   Davidson, 'Divine Service or Idol Worship?', pp. 134–35.
74   Mirrors, mentioned three times in this 35-line poem, also indicate 'Svalka''s mirroring of Shvarts, as in 'Afrodita uletaet v noch' na subbotu'.

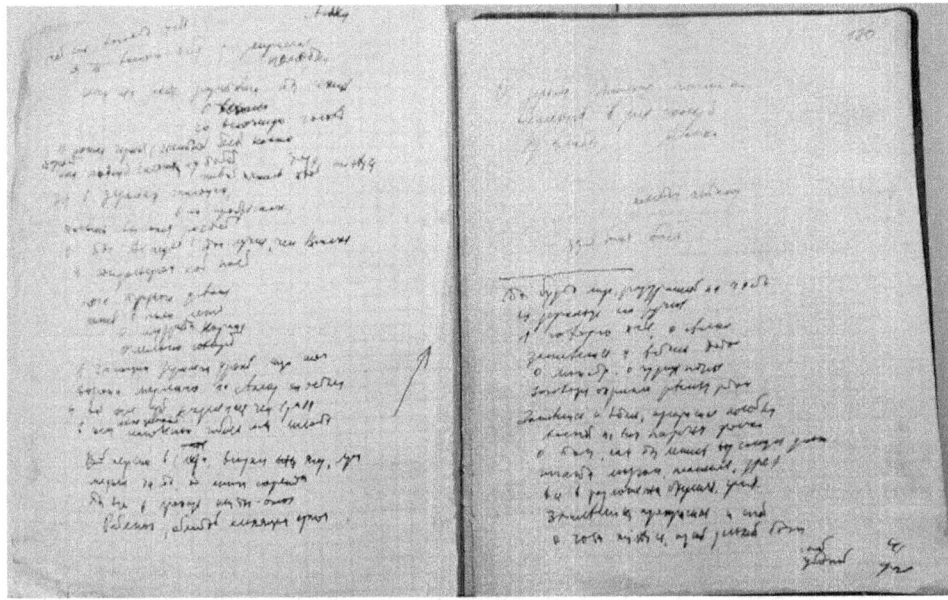

Fig. 2.7. 'Dump', BT 180 (between 5 and 21 July 1983).

Other classical elements of 'Svalka' are in place from the first draft. The poem begins with a classical *recusatio*: 'Нет сил воспеть тебя, прекрасная помойка!' [No, I have not strength to sing your praise, beauteous midden!] And a crow that lands on the dump is anthropomorphised into the Roman dictator Sulla:

> Ворона медленно на свалку опустилась,
> И вот она идет, надменнее чем Сулла,
> И в цепкой лапе гибель или милость.
>
> [A crow has descended slowly upon the dump,
> See, it struts more haughtily than Sulla,
> And in its vice-like claws — death or mercy.]

This suggests the power of authoritarian rulers over poetry, a phenomenon Russia and Rome held in common.

In the last section of the poem, Svalka's decay, literal and graphically described, becomes poetry. By writing an ode to rubbish Shvarts both contradicts[75] and literalises Akhmatova's famous lines in 'Tainy remesla 2' [Secrets of Craft 2] (1940):

> Мне ни к чему одические рати
> [...]
> Когда б вы знали, из какого сора
> Растут стихи.[76]

---

75 Perhaps intentionally: after their ill-fated meeting Shvarts was not a fan of Akhmatova. III.135–36.

76 Anna Akhmatova, *Stikhotvoreniia i poemy* (Moscow: Eksmo, 2008), p. 177.

> [I've no use for odic war hosts
> [...]
> If only you knew from what rubbish
> Poems grow.]

The dump's varied components and the heat of decomposition come together to create her enlightened thought and inspired song.

One of these components, 'гной | Как водку' [Pus like vodka], suggests Dionysus's association with alcohol, and thence with inspiration. This association was present in antiquity:

> Although Dionysus is most commonly thought of as the god of wine and intoxication, he was also the god of tragic art and the protector of theatres (since Greek drama had grown out of the dithyrambic choruses recited at the festival of Dionysus). This allowed the link to be made in his cult between the states of intoxication and inspiration.[77]

Other of Shvarts's poems also connect decay, alcohol, Dionysus, and inspired poetry. 'O nesdannye butylki' [O unreturned bottles] from *Gorbatyi mig* [*Hunchbacked Moment*] (1974, II.71–76) is an ode to empty bottles which Shvarts is returning to the shop for the deposit. As God takes the mingled smells of drunks and transforms it into beauty, hers and the crowd's troubles are similarly transformed into fertile ground for inspired poetry:

> вся тоска уйдет в навоз,
> Чтоб дивный сад на нем возрос
> Для Диониса и для Муз.
>
> [all our anguish will go away into manure,
> So a marvellous garden grows from it
> For Dionysus and the Muses.]

Similarly, *Dva aspekta* [*Two Aspects*] (1979, I.107) contrasts the inevitability of ageing with the immortality of poetry, staging in its two parts[78] the transformation of death and decay into Dionysian poetry:

> В зрелости и разложенья пьянящем соку
> Юным уснешь, а проснешься со смертью в боку
> [...]
> Но хмельные прорастут из меня слова,
> Как из щелей дионисовой лодки — лозы
>
> [In the intoxicating juice of ripeness and decomposition
> You'll fall asleep young and wake up with death in your side
> [...]
> But heady words will grow out of me,
> Like vines out of the cracks of Dionysus's boat]

The poem presents decay and aging as inherent to alcohol; alcoholic language in turn imbues the description of Shvarts's inspired, ecstatic words. *Dva aspekta*, like

---

77 Davidson, 'Divine Service or Idol Worship?', p. 134.
78 It appears from her notebook that the two parts of *Dva aspekta* were written separately, and made into a whole at some point between 24 May and 15 December 1979. BT 48, 57.

'Malen'koe puteshestvie sredi ostrovov i zvezd', draws on the story in the *Homeric Hymn to Dionysus* (VII) of the god's attempted kidnapping by Tyrsenian pirates.[79] In all these poems, as in 'Svalka', Dionysus is a conduit for transforming *byt* into beauty, not only because of his role as god of poetry, but because he is himself flawed — dismembered and reborn.

A Christian tinge enters 'Svalka' in the final line. Shvarts invokes the dump as 'O rosa mystica', after a Catholic miracle, but follows this with 'тебя услышат боги' [the gods will hear you], returning to paganism. This suggests another reason for Shvarts's interest in Dionysus: his connection with Christ. The Christlike Dionysus was a nineteenth-century invention, taken up by Russian Symbolists.[80] Again, Ivanov was the greatest proponent of the Christian Dionysus, calling him 'our barbarian, our Slavic god'; he 'linked Russia's Christian character with its Dionysian roots, finding in the dissolution of self he associated with Dionysus a central feature of the Russian character'.[81] Shvarts writes a Christian Dionysus in many poems. 'Kostroma-Dionis' [Kostroma-Dionysus] (1980, I.114–15) equates the slavic goddess of spring, Kostroma, with Dionysus, calling her 'Славянский тихий Дионис' [Slavic quiet Dionysus]. Dionysus's probable function as a fertility god — he was represented and worshipped in cult by phalli[82] — could be the source of his connection with Easter — the pagan festival of spring, later linked with Christ's death and rebirth. In the course of Shvarts's poem Kostroma dies and is resurrected like Christ, and the poem's three choruses all end with an epithet usually associated with Christ: 'Царь царей' [King of kings]. Poem 6 of *O tom, kto riadom* [*About the One Who's Nearby*] (1981, II.96–101) juxtaposes the cries of grief over Christ's death with the phonally similar bacchanalian ecstatic cries: 'Увы! Эвоэ! Увы!' [Woe! Euhoe! Woe!]. This links Christ's death and rebirth with Dionysus's, and his killing with maenadic frenzy. The section 'Vesnoi mertvye riadom' [In Spring the Dead Are Near] from *Martovskie mertvetsy* [*March Corpses*] (1980, II.102–08) deals with the Leningrad Blockade, when the spring thaw, customarily bringing renewal, uncovered dead bodies. Dionysus replaces Christ in Shvarts's figuring of Lent (the 'Great Fast' in Russian) as the Blockade's starvation: 'И все-таки могучий Дионис, | Обняв за икры Великий Пост' [And yet mighty Dionysus, | Clasping Lent's Great Fast by its calves]. Even *Kinfiia* has a Christlike Dionysus (see chapter 3). By presenting herself as a follower of Dionysus, Shvarts simultaneously affirms her devotion to Christ.

79 Shvarts perhaps has in mind the final line of the *Homeric Hymn to Dionysus* (VII): 'Hail, child of fair-faced Semele! He who forgets you can in no wise order sweet song', since she shows herself creating poetry under the influence of Dionysus. Hesiod, *The Homeric Hymns and Homerica*, trans. by Hugh G. Evelyn-White (London: Heinemann, 1914), p. 433.
80 For example, in Dmitrii Merezhkovskii's novel *Voskresshie bogi: Leonardo da Vinchi* [*Resurrected Gods: Leonardo da Vinci*] (1900); Bernice Glatzer Rosenthal, 'Stages of Nietzscheanism: Merezhkovsky's Intellectual Evolution', in *Nietzsche in Russia*, ed. by Bernice Glatzer Rosenthal (Princeton, NJ; Guildford: Princeton University Press, 1986), pp. 69–93 (p. 82).
81 Judith E. Kalb, *Russia's Rome: Imperial Visions, Messianic Dreams, 1890–1940* (Madison: University of Wisconsin Press, 2008), p. 147.
82 *Masks of Dionysus*, ed. by Thomas H. Carpenter and Christopher A. Faraone (Ithaca; London: Cornell University Press, 1993), p. 1.

Shvarts's perception of poetic inspiration as an act of violence against the poet, requiring self-sacrifice, is evident in all her poems invoking Dionysus or Apollo. Dionysus's capability to take the role of suffering poet, or Christ figure, makes him more appealing to Shvarts than Apollo: Dionysus can be both inspirer of poetry and alter ego.

Pythia

Pythia, the high priestess and oracle of the Temple of Apollo at Delphi, is a frequent figure in Shvarts's poetry, appearing in six poems.[83] But Apollo, the god who inspires the Delphic oracle, is notable in the Pythia poems by his absence. Instead, Shvarts focuses on the physical experience of the inspired woman, without the distraction of the inspiring god. While Pythia is not traditionally a katabasist, she was inspired by underworldly vapours, and another oracle, the Cumaean Sibyl, guides Aeneas into the underworld in the *Aeneid*. These katabasic connections lead Shvarts to imbue her Pythia poems with chthonic imagery, seeing Pythia as both a source of information about the dead, and as close to death herself. Pythia is a very clear-cut alter ego of Shvarts-the-inspired-poet. Shvarts even claimed a real-life similarity with Pythia, saying that she wrote her *Laviniia* cycle 'in the spirit of sacred Dionysian madness, just as Pythia at Delphi in Greece uttered "dark" words'.[84] For Shvarts, Pythian madness is both foundational and essential to poetry:

> Poetry began with sacred madness — with incantations, Pythia's poems — that is, with attempts at obtaining knowledge beyond the reach of reasoning. [...] how beautiful [poetry] used to be, when it would dive into the sea of madness and emerge into the light of reason with a pearl of unreasonable thought in its rapacious teeth![85]

Shvarts even sees Pythia as a poet here rather than an oracle.

Shvarts's first mention of Pythia is in the unpublished poem 'Perekhod cherez Neman i dal'she na Vitebsk' [Crossing of the Neman and on to Vitebsk] (8 May 1976, ESHA M.2). A vision of Napoleon is vouchsafed to her through her 'third eye'. She originally explained her privileged insight into the past by equating poetic inspiration with Pythia's prophesying, but then opted to leave it unexplained: the poem's first title, typed and then crossed out, was 'Pificheskoe' [Pythian]. This title presents Shvarts as a Pythian poet — or the poem as one of her Pythian poems — rather than developing Pythia as an alter ego. Pythia's next appearance in Shvarts's poetry is as the alter ego of her alter ego Kinfiia, in *Kinfiia* II.7 'Na pliazhe v Baii' [On the Beach at Baiae] (1978) — a step closer! When Shvarts herself turns to Pythia as an alter ego, in the late 1980s and early 1990s, the oracle is a perfect bearer for Shvarts's unique brand of irrational associations and inspired suffering.

---

83   Including ones from *Kinfiia* and *Homo Musagetes* — see chapters 3 and 5.
84   Sarah Clovis Bishop, 'In Memoriam: Elena Andreevna Shvarts (17 May 1948–11 March 2010)', *Slavonica*, 16.2 (2010), 112–30 (p. 123).
85   'O bezumii v poezii' [On Madness in Poetry], in *Zapiski na nogtiakh* [*Notes on my Nails*] (n.d., III.270).

More than any other alter ego, Pythia seems to spark thoughts about Shvarts's poetic predecessors, who are figured as Shvarts's forerunners in a line of Pythias.

Shvarts's first inhabitation of Pythia as her alter ego is in 'Pifii' [Pythias] (1988)[86] (see the Appendix for the full poem). She begins by claiming to be a normal human, something she characterises with images of burrowing: through earth, through wood, through time. She qualifies this, saying that sometimes she is one of the prophetesses. There is a significant difference at this point in Shvarts's draft, where she typed line three as 'Но иногда я не могу' [But sometimes I cannot], then crossed out 'не' [not] and wrote in 'и' [too/even] (ESHA M.0). The original version assumes that inspiration is her usual state; the final version is much more humble: 'Но иногда и я могу | Пророчествовать за пророчиц' [But sometimes I, too, can | Prophesy for the prophetesses]. From this point, Shvarts is entirely aligned with the Pythias, and writes in the first-person plural. Who these fellow prophetesses are is a matter for speculation (if they are not taken at face value as simply all the Pythian oracles). In light of Shvarts's later Pythia poems, I interpret them as the canon of female poets before Shvarts, foremost among them Tsvetaeva, who wrote a cycle of poems about the Sibyl. In this light, their tough training, roofless homes, and misfortunes can be read as a comment on the poor lives most (Russian, female) poets live. Apollo is depicted lurking in Pythia's cave, but is not directly named in the poem — instead he is called 'дымный Бог' [a smoky God], referring to the rising vapours through which he inspires his oracle, and 'светлый' [radiant], Shvarts's usual epithet for Apollo, translating 'Phoebus'. 'Pifii' takes a sinister turn in its second half: the prophecies that the Pythias are shown fishing for are about people's deaths; and they know that the world is heading for disaster, but do not care.

The nature of that disaster is (perhaps) revealed in 'Pifiia' [Pythia] (1992, 1.201) (see the Appendix for the full poem). Here Pythia prophesies the impending Judgement Day; her prophecy, complete with dead rising and skies opening, takes up the whole central third of the poem. 'Pifiia' begins with a colloquial address to the oracle from a suppliant asking for knowledge: 'Деушка, деушка' [Mi-iss, Mi-iss]. She is upside-down, feet in the clouds, and head on the ground, spewing out water from the 'темный канал' [dark channel] from which she gets her information about the future. Her position casts her as a conduit from heaven to earth, and the water flowing through her alludes to the Castalian Spring at Delphi; the Castalian spring lay outside Apollo's sanctuary, where Pythia presided, and was used for purification.[87] But Shvarts takes a more sinister view of the spring, here and elsewhere. In *Kinfiia* Shvarts had taken the most deathly associations for the waters of Baiae from the poetry of Propertius to surround Pythia-Kinfiia with an atmosphere of menace. In the 1981 poem 'Zemlia, zemlia, ty esh' liudei' Shvarts had portrayed the Castalian Spring as founded on death:

---

[86] Elena Shvarts, 'Prorochestvovat' za prorochits: neizdannye stikhi', ed. by Pavel Uspenskii and Artem Shelia, *Novyi mir*, 11 (2015), <http://www.nm1925.ru/Archive/Journal6_2015_11/Content/Publication6_6188/Default.aspx> [accessed 4 May 2020].

[87] J. N. Coldstream, 'Greek Temples: Why and Where?', in *Greek Religion and Society*, ed. by P. E. Easterling and J. V. Muir (Cambridge: Cambridge University Press, 1985), pp. 67–97 (p. 96).

> Земля, земля, ты ешь людей,
> Рождая им взамен
> Кастальский ключ
>
> [Earth, earth, you eat people,
> Spawning for them in return
> The Castalian Spring]

And in her 1994 cycle *Homo Musagetes* Shvarts would again strongly link water with Pythia's unspecified malaise. In 'Pifiia' the water inspiring Pythia's speech ultimately kills her:

> Утонула она — потому что тесна
> Водопаду, что в горле спит.
> [...]
> 'Мне тяжело — через воронку
> Переливают океан'.
>
> [She drowned — because she was too tight
> For the waterfall sleeping in her throat.
> [...]
> 'It's hard for me — through a funnel
> They are decanting an ocean'.]

The funnel is a recurring theme in Shvarts's poetry, and may be used knowingly here to establish Pythia as her alter ego.[88] With the drowning of her alter ego Pythia, Shvarts expresses the overwhelming power of poetic inspiration.

The same fatal spring is the focus of 'Kolodets-dub' [Well-Oak] (1994, 1.304), which portrays a hollow oak with a spring welling up through its middle. In the poem's final stanza Shvarts compares the damaged oak to Pythia:

> И я кругами там ходила
> Как кот прозрачный и ученый
> И думала: сей дуб есть образ
> Безумца, пифии, пророка.
>
> [And I walked round in circles there
> Like the transparent and learned cat
> And thought: this oak is the image
> Of madman, Pythia, prophet.]

Placing Pythia in the company of a chained story-telling cat, a madman, and a prophet suggests she is maddened and enslaved by inspiration; this final line retroactively casts 'Kolodets-dub' as Shvarts's view of poetic inspiration. Two fundamental influences are evident in 'Kolodets-dub', and show the sources of Shvarts's portrayal of Pythia in 'Pifii' and 'Pifiia' as well. The first influence is Pushkin. The 'oak' and 'learned cat' allude to Pushkin's epic fairy tale poem *Ruslan*

---

88 In 1977 Shvarts developed the idea that everyone has a 'secret motif' — a single concept that subconsciously guides their life — and gave a paper about this to her private society 'Obez'iana' [Simian]. She writes that 'King-Kong' (Boris Ostanin) co-opted her idea and gave a paper about Shvarts's secret motif — which, he argued, was the funnel. Shvarts, relieved, says funnels are only a 'side-motif' (III.286).

i Liudmila [*Ruslan and Liudmila*], which is narrated by a cat chained to an oak. The final word 'prophet' conjures up Pushkin's 'Prorok', which depicts poetic inspiration as divinely inflicted torture. The second influence is Tsvetaeva. Tsvetaeva also used an oracle as a paradigm for poetic inspiration, and also emphasised her self-sacrifice. Tsvetaeva's cycle *Sivilla* [*Sibyl*] takes the Cumaean oracle from *Metamorphoses* Book 14 and elaborates on Ovid's — or the narrator Orpheus's — depiction of the wrinkled Sibyl, who had been given eternal life, but not eternal youth, by Apollo. In *Sivilla* 1 (1922)[89] Tsvetaeva portrays the Sibyl as a burnt-out tree:

> Сивилла: выжжена, сивилла: ствол.
> Все птицы вымерли, но Бог вошёл.
> Сивилла: выпита, сивилла: сушь.
> Все жилы высохли: ревностен муж!
> Сивилла: выбыла, сивилла: зев
> Доли и гибели! — Древо меж дев.

> [Sibyl: burnt out, sibyl: trunk.
> All the birds died off, but God came in.
> Sibyl: drunk dry, sibyl: desert.
> All the veins shrivelled: jealous the man!
> Sibyl: decreased, sibyl: maw
> Of fate and death! — Tree among maids.]

These lines of Tsvetaeva's have influenced all of Shvarts's Pythia poems. Tsvetaeva's Sibyl as tree motivates Shvarts's statement in 'Pifii' that she is 'Годов дубовых древоточец' [A carpenter moth of the oaken years]. The image, read alongside Tsvetaeva's, suggests Shvarts's mining of Tsvetaeva's Sibyl for her Pythia. Tsvetaeva's view of the Sibyl's open throat as a conduit of doom leads to Shvarts's Pythia vomiting doom-laden water in 'Pifiia'. Shvarts simply makes her Pythia's problem the opposite of Tsvetaeva's Sibyl's: too much water, rather than too little. Tsvetaeva's Sibyl as burnt tree rather than woman prompts Shvarts to see the lightning-struck tree as Pythia in 'Kolodets-dub'. Again, Shvarts has reversed the movement of Tsvetaeva's thought.

Pythia's pain in Shvarts's poems can be traced back to Pushkin's posture of tormented Romantic genius, along with the other inspired victims of Dionysus and Apollo whom Shvarts depicts. But Shvarts's Pythia owes the biggest debt to Tsvetaeva — yet also departs from Tsvetaeva in one key aspect. At first, Olga Peters Hasty's analysis of Tsvetaeva's use of the Sibyl sounds remarkably similar to Shvarts's use of Pythia: 'On the strength of self-surrender the Sibyl finds new existence within herself', an anti-feminist view which Tsvetaeva turns into a mark of 'woman's unarguable ascendancy in the transcendent realm of poetry'.[90] But where Shvarts differs most from Tsvetaeva is that she does not see the oracle as a woman who surrendered her voice to a man (Apollo); to avoid this she deliberately removes Apollo from focus in her Pythia poems and focuses instead on the sacred

---

89 Tsvetaeva, III (1983), 24.
90 Olga Peters Hasty, *Tsvetaeva's Orphic Journeys in the Worlds of the Word* (Evanston, IL: Northwestern University Press, 1996), p. 107.

knowledge that Pythia acquires. Through Pythia Shvarts expresses not only her compulsion to write frenzied poetry, but also her empowerment through the pain inspiration exacts, and her connection to a line of inspired women stretching from Tsvetaeva back to antiquity.

Ariadne

This chapter's final alter ego, Ariadne, is not a katabasist, but an anti-katabasist. In Graeco-Roman myth, Ariadne was known both as the wife of Dionysus and as a Cretan princess who helped the hero Theseus escape from the Minotaur's labyrinth with a thread. It is in this latter aspect that Shvarts invariably depicts Ariadne. She also invariably figures the labyrinth as the underworld and the thread as the (unreliable) connection back to the world of the living. Shvarts, putting herself in Ariadne's place, depicts those on the other end of her thread as katabasists, and herself as alive and abandoned.

'Pis'mo' [Letter] (8 November 1974, ZT 70–71) is dedicated, or addressed, to Nina Perlina. The Dostoevskii scholar had just emigrated to America that year,[91] and Shvarts imagines her disappearance into the West as a form of death:

> Там в долине полусмерти
> Темзой разбавляют Лету.
> Из Римолондона привет,
> Ты пишешь, надо ж, — из Парижа,
> Его на свете вовсе нет,
> Вот Прага есть — она поближе,
> Тебя я, Нина, не увижу,
> А дальних трудно нам любить,
> И Ариадны рвется нить,
> Ее подымешь и завяжешь,
> Она порвется все ж —
> Вот червяка разрезал нож,
> И он живет вдвойне — ты скажешь.
>
> [There in the valley of half-death
> The Thames is diluting the Lethe.
> 'Hello from Romalondon,'
> You write — well, well! — from Paris,
> Which does not even exist,
> Now, Prague exists — it's nearer,
> I won't see you again, Nina,
> It's hard to love at a distance,
> And Ariadne's thread breaks,
> You'll pick it up and tie it,
> It'll break whatever you try —
> 'A worm cut in two by a knife,'
> You'll say, 'gets to live twice.']

Ariadne's thread is not, in Shvarts's view, a reliable lifeline. Even the positive spin that Shvarts puts in Perlina's mouth makes Ariadne's thread a dissected worm. The

---

91 'In Memoriam: Nina Perlina', *Russian and East European Institute*, <https://reei.indiana.edu/news-events/newsletter/archive/Fall-2019/In Memoriam Nina Perlina.html> [accessed 6 May 2020].

West is presented as a generic muddle of real and mythical locations, but by the end of the poem it is firmly the underworld, where Russian émigrés 'по улицам Аида | На машине прокатились' [went for a spin in the car | Through the streets of Hades]. But Shvarts makes a surprise reversal of perspective in the final lines: 'О тень с температурой тридцать шесть, | Для тебя мы тоже тени' [O shade with a temperature of thirty-six, | For you we are also shades]. Shvarts shows she is aware that as Ariadne, holding the thread leading out of the underworld, she could always find herself on the other end of that thread. While 'Pis'mo' gives a quite light-hearted treatment of Ariadne's thread, Shvarts would use it again as a symbol of the — easily broken — connection between life and death in far more tragic contexts.

'Volosovedenie' [Hair-Direction] (1998)[92] imagines there is a voice leading people through life, which Shvarts compares to Ariadne's thread:

> Будто Ариадны нить,
> Долгий змеящийся волос,
> То в Новый Свет, то на Страшный Суд
> Ведет ветвящийся голос.
>
> [Like Ariadne's thread,
> A long serpentine hair,
> The branching voice leads
> To the New World or the Last Judgement.]

In 'Volosovedenie' Ariadne's thread is not only a lifeline. Instead, it diverges — it can take the person following it either to a new life and new possibilities (also America, the setting of the poem), or to death and other ensuing possibilities. 'Volosovedenie' appears in *Solo na raskalennoi trube* [*Solo on a Red-Hot Trumpet*], the collection mourning Shvarts's mother, who died in 1998. Shvarts was extremely close to her mother, and was devastated by her death. The splitting of the thread/hair/voice represents the different paths Shvarts and her mother must now take. The thread/hair/voice is both harmful to those it touches and under threat of being severed:

> Всюду — задушенный нитью шелковый червь,
> Ухо, заклепанное горячим волосом.
> Разве прорежет свету путь
> Сквозь мира колтун тесный
> Молчания острый луч —
> Нож бестелесный.
>
> [Everywhere — the silkworm suffocated by the thread,
> The ear riveted through by the burning hot hair.
> Can it really be that a path for light
> Through the world's tight-matted plait
> Will be cut by silence's sharp ray —
> The incorporeal knife.]

---

[92] Elena Shvarts, 'Na povorote v gefsimaniiu', *Sovremennaia russkaia poeziia*, <http://modernpoetry.ru> [accessed 12 September 2016]; Oleg Rogov, 'Elena Shvarts. Solo na raskalennoi trube: novye stikhotvoreniia', *Volga* 2 (1999), <http://magazines.russ.ru/volga/1999/2/shvarc.html> [accessed 12 September 2016].

Putting aside the pain evident in these lines, the imagery evoking the precarity of Ariadne's thread is remarkably similar to 'Pis'mo': knife, cutting, even a worm. But the harmfulness of this thread/hair/voice is due to the grief that *Solo na raskalennoi trube* explores. For the thread/hair/voice symbolises both poetry — red-hot like the collection's title — and life. For the poet Shvarts, the most salient image for death is silence, which in the final line of 'Volosovedenie' cuts short both the voice of poetry and the thread of life.

Ariadne's thread reappears at a time Shvarts was aware of her own impending death — by then two months away — in her antepenultimate poem 'Korabl' Zhizni unosilsia vdal'' [The Ship of Life scudded into the distance] (early January 2010, v.41). The poem's unusually end-stopped lines convey Shvarts's tiredness and resignation. Here is the poem in full:

> Корабль Жизни уносился вдаль.
> Я с вашего упала корабля.
> Не различить где небо, где земля,
> Где воздух, звезды, череп иль лицо.
> Зачем заветное глотаю я кольцо?
> Мне ничего в себе не сохранить,
> Сгнила в воде и Ариадны нить.
> Птенца самосознанья утопить
> (Но он не хочет исчезать, хоть и устал),
> И вольною волной средь волн уплыть.
> Ах, зубы скалить белые у скал.
> Сверкать сиять в ночи привольно
> И морю не бывает больно.
> Бывает болен Бог? Он ведь боль.
> А ей не больно. И меня уволь.

> [The Ship of Life scudded into the distance.
> I have fallen off the ship — yours, everyone's.
> There's no telling where is sky, where is land,
> Where is air, where stars, a skull or face.
> Why am I swallowing the hallowed ring?
> I cannot keep anything safe inside me,
> Water's rotted even the thread of Ariadne.
> Oh, to drown the chick of self-awareness
> (But though it's tired, it does not want to vanish),
> And float away, a wave, free among the waves.
> Ah, to gnash white teeth at the cliffs.
> To shimmer, to shine in the night, at will,
> And the sea is never hurt or ill.
> Can God be ill, in pain? For He is pain.
> But she is not in pain. Let me go as well.]

'Korabl' Zhizni unosilsia vdal'' does not just use the idea of Ariadne's thread, as 'Pis'mo' and 'Volosovedenie' do, but interacts with the whole story of Ariadne as it is told in Catullus LXIV. The departing ship of the poem's first line is both Shvarts's life leaving her and Theseus's ship sailing away from Ariadne:

> There, staring out from Dia's surf-resounding shore
> And watching Theseus sailing off with his fast fleet,
> Is Ariadne, nursing at heart unmastered passions.
> (Cat. LXIV.52–54, p. 87)

Shvarts's bewildered despair in lines 3–4 echoes Ariadne's hopelessness:

> Every way out is blocked by sea's encircling waves.
> There's no means of escape, no hope. Everything's dumb,
> Everywhere's deserted, everything threatens doom.
> (Cat. LXIV.185–87, p. 91)

The 'hallowed ring' refers to the line 'Я бросил в ночь заветное кольцо' [I threw the hallowed ring into the night] from Aleksandr Blok's poem 'O doblestiakh, o podvigakh, o slave' [Of valour, of feats, of glory] (1908).[93] Retelling Ariadne's abandonment must have made Shvarts think of Blok's poem, in which a woman walks out on the poet, and her own part in continuing the tradition of abandonment poems. In line 7 Shvarts ironises Ariadne's thread, which granted Theseus escape from apparently inevitable death:

> Thence with great renown he walked his way back, safe,
> Directing his bewildered steps with slender thread,
> Lest, while he tried to escape the Labyrinth's meanders,
> The building's inscrutable maze should baffle him.
> (Cat. LXIV.112–15, p. 87)

'Water's rotted even the thread of Ariadne' signals the decay of hope for a way out for both women — Ariadne's due to the sea water all around her, and Shvarts's due to her dying body. Again, as in 'Pis'mo' and 'Volosovedenie', Ariadne's usually life-saving thread symbolises the potential of human life to be cut short. Shvarts's unusual take is informed by the fact that Ariadne's thread is only life-saving for Theseus — Ariadne herself is doomed by her actions, something that Catullus highlights by insetting the backstory of Theseus and the labyrinth within the scene of Ariadne abandoned on the island. Shvarts's life-shortening thread is also informed by the common classical image of the Fates spinning (and cutting) the thread of life, one that Catullus's epyllion explores at great length (LXIV.305–81). Shvarts's enactment of fruitless rage in line 11, 'Ah, to gnash white teeth at the cliffs', repeats and condenses Ariadne's frenzy on the island, and transforms Shvarts into one of the breakers that Ariadne runs into:

> She poured out shrill-edged cries from the depth of her heart,
> And sometimes in her sorrow she clambered up steep cliffs
> From whence to extend her view of the ocean's empty swell;
> Sometimes ran out to meet the restless brine's breakers.
> (Cat. LXIV.125–28, pp. 87–89)

Ariadne, believing she will soon die, appeals to the gods for vengeance with her final words in the poem:

---

93 Aleksandr Blok, *Izbrannaia poeziia/Selected Poems*, ed. by James B. Woodward (London: Bristol Classical Press, 1992), p. 62.

> Be sure you suffer not our grief to go for nothing,
> But with what mind Theseus has left me on my own,
> With such mind, Goddesses, let him doom himself and his.'
>   (Cat. LXIV.199–201, pp. 91–93)

Shvarts's final lines, too, make an appeal to God, but a very different one. She asks whether God can feel pain, and in the final line prays for release from her pain, as 'she' — her mother — was given before her. Ariadne's thread thus connects mother and daughter once more. The prayer for release echoes the plea made by Hamlet in Boris Pasternak's poem 'Gamlet' [Hamlet] (n.d.),[94] in which the poem's 'I' is an actor coming out onto the stage and, Christlike, asking God to be excused playing the part to its fatal end: 'Но сейчас идет другая драма, | И на этот раз меня уволь' [But a different drama's playing out now, | So, just this one time, let me go].[95] Quoting Pasternak (and with him, Shakespeare and the Bible) alongside Catullus, Shvarts again notes her place in a tradition of poems spoken by those about to die. Perhaps citing Catullus, Blok, and Pasternak — works that live on after their creators have died — gave Shvarts some comfort as she wrote about her imminent end.

Shvarts's last classical alter ego, Ariadne holding the thread of life, was used by Shvarts at various stages of her life to conceptualise loss of varying kinds. Finally, Ariadne, abandoned by Theseus/life, is the alter ego Shvarts chooses to help her face death.

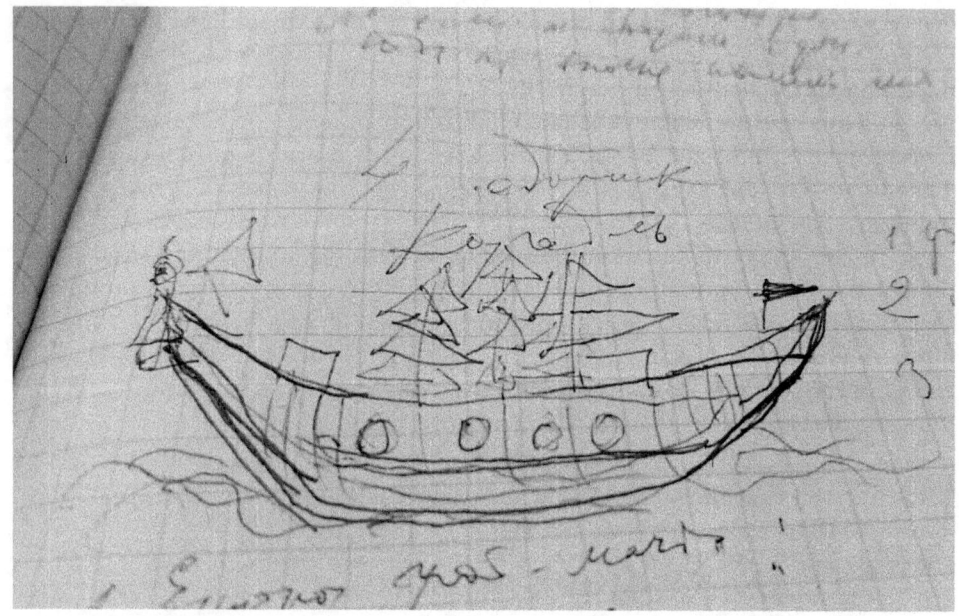

Fig. 2.8. Doodled ship. BT 135 (between 24 January and 17 April 1982).

---

94 *The Heritage of Russian Verse*, ed. by Dimitri Obolensky (Bloomington, IN: Indiana University Press, 1976), pp. 335–36.
95 I am indebted to Katharine Hodgson for this observation, among many others.

Conclusion

Shvarts's classical alter egos are numerous and wide-ranging. This chapter has found Shvarts peeping from behind the mask of Narcissus, Aphrodite/Venus, Selene/Luna, Odysseus, Hades, Persephone, the Dioscuri, Orpheus, Eurydice, Dionysus's and Apollo's victims, Pythia, and Ariadne. The alter egos she chooses show her sustained fascination with Graeco-Roman myth in particular, as well as classical literature by authors such as Ovid, Homer, and Catullus. Her use of classical alter egos constitutes a deliberate placing of herself in an ancient poetic tradition, which she underscores by mediating her receptions through Russian nineteenth- and twentieth-century poets, primarily Pushkin and Tsvetaeva. It is therefore unsurprising that nearly all her classical alter egos reflect on the vocation of poet, something that Shvarts connects with pain and altered states of consciousness. And this is where the true usefulness of the alter ego comes in for Shvarts: inhabiting another persona — besides frequently involving a painful collision of bodies — is a way to achieve a radically altered state of consciousness, and thus to become a true inspired poet.

The next chapter addresses Shvarts's most prominent classical alter ego — Kinfiia. The Kinfiia poems have much in common with the alter egos in this chapter: an exploration of what it is to be a woman, a lover, a drinker, a mortal, and, most importantly, an inspired poet. But as an alter ego Kinfiia is exceptional: she is from a firmly literary rather than a mythical source, and most importantly, unlike all the other alter ego poems, Shvarts is entirely absent as a character, and not even implicitly present as the poet, since Kinfiia *is* the poet, which facilitates almost total identification between Shvarts and her alter ego Kinfiia.

CHAPTER 3

Kinfiia

> Вновь Проперций мой ко мне вернулся —
> Счастие для Кинфии какое!
>
> [My Propertius has returned to me again —
> What luck, what joy for Cynthia!]
>
> E. A. Shvarts, *Kinfiia* R.2, 1980s

The Roman poet Kinfiia is Shvarts's most sustained classical alter ego, 'writing' 27 published poems — and at least six more unpublished poems — over a span of 32 years. She is the star and author of *Kinfiia* (1974, 1978, 1980s, II.5–24), a three-book cycle of poems 'by' the real Roman poet Propertius's probably fictional girlfriend Cynthia.[1] (See the Appendix for the full cycle, the unpublished 'apocrypha', and the 2006 sequel.) Through the cycle, the imperious and impetuous Kinfiia issues orders to her slaves, commits numerous acts of violence, hurls insults and threats, falls in love, watches Bacchic rites, gives out mystic riddles, contemplates the nature of poetic inspiration, justifies her wild behaviour, confronts ageing, challenges gods, bests witches at witchcraft, draws on mythology, conducts affairs, travels away from Rome and back, finds her Propertsii and loses him again. But most importantly, Kinfiia writes — all the poems in the cycle.

The starting point for *Kinfiia* is Sextus Propertius, whose poems are devoted at the outset to his beloved Cynthia — but become less devoted to her as they go along. Propertius published his books of Latin elegies between about 30 and 16 BC under the rule of Augustus, and he was part of the circle of poets (including Virgil and Horace) who wrote under the patronage of Augustus's friend Maecenas.[2] But Propertius is far from the only influence on *Kinfiia*: almost — if not just — as crucial to Shvarts's creation of this alter ego is Gaius Valerius Catullus, who wrote invective epigrams (along with some longer poems) in lyric metres. Catullus lived the generation before Propertius, in the latter years of the Roman Republic, c. 84–54

---

[1] In recognition of the character's distinct Russianness and her distinctness from Propertius's creation, and to distinguish Shvarts's Kinfiia from Propertius's Cynthia, I preserve the Russian spelling of Kinfiia's name throughout the chapter. (Кинфия [Kinfiia] is the slightly more popular of two accepted Cyrillic transliterations for Cynthia — the other being Цинтия [Tsintiia]. A Google search returns 2,580 results for 'кинфия проперций' [kinfiia propertsii] and 2,330 results for 'цинтия проперций' [tsintiia propertsii] [accessed 10 December 2018].) I also call Propertius 'Propertsii' when referring to the character in *Kinfiia* as opposed to the historical person. In the translations in the Appendix I revert to the Latin forms.

[2] Propertius, *Elegies*, trans. by G. P. Goold (Cambridge, MA; London: Harvard University Press, 2006), pp. 1–2.

BC.³ Third in the trio of vital influences on *Kinfiia* is the prolific epigrammatist Marcus Valerius Martialis. Martial's fifteen (at least) books of short, witty poems in the Catullan vein were published *c*. AD 80–104.⁴ *Kinfiia*'s intertextual dialogue with Propertius, Catullus, and Martial, along with other Roman sources, is essential to the believability of the cycle and of its putative Ancient Roman writer, as this chapter will show. Yet *Kinfiia*'s erudition is unobtrusive, fading into the backdrop of the life evoked by Kinfiia. In the words of Barbara Heldt: 'Though the settings and characters are Roman, the language is studiedly contemporary and the emotions universal. [...] She has given Cynthia a living twentieth-century voice and therefore a believable Roman one.'⁵

Knowledge of Ancient Rome and its literature was fundamental to Shvarts's composition of the *Kinfiia* cycle. This chapter uncovers those classical foundations, a task which has been undertaken just once before, with incomplete information: the excellent article on *Kinfiia*'s classical reception by the Russian classicist and friend of Shvarts Dmitrii Panchenko was written before the third book of *Kinfiia*, *Razroznennoe* [*Oddments*], was published. The chapter begins by looking at the origins — both ostensible and real — of Shvarts's 'translations', and analysing the formal construction of the cycle. The next two sections address the cycle's receptions of Roman literature: first Propertius, and then Catullus and others. It then considers Shvarts's subversions of the gender dynamics of Latin love elegy. The penultimate section discovers the Russia behind *Kinfiia*'s Rome, and the woman behind the alter ego. Finally, the chapter turns to the *Kinfiia* 'apocrypha' — poems and fragments from Shvarts's archives that were written from Kinfiia's persona but did not make it into the published cycle; these are analysed and published here for the first time.

I am in no doubt that *Kinfiia* is one of the great works of Russian literature. O'lga Sedakova has called *Kinfiia* 'an achievement of global proportions', and said that the cycle 'eclipses all the famous games at antiquity — both *The Songs of Bilitis* and *Letters to a Roman Friend*'.⁶ Kinfiia even eclipses – in length, commitment to character, and seriousness – its closest Russian forebear, *Rozy Pierii* [*Roses of Pieria*] (1922) by Sofiia Parnok, who ventriloquises Sappho.⁷ As a reworking of classical literature from a female perspective, *Kinfiia* stands alongside — and substantially pre-dates — such works as Margaret Atwood's *The Penelopiad* (2005) and Ursula Le Guin's *Lavinia* (2008). Were *Kinfiia* also in prose and in English, I am sure that it would likewise be ranked as a feminist classic.

3   Catullus, *The Poems of Catullus*, trans. by Guy Lee (Oxford: Oxford University Press, 1991), p. xviii.
4   Martial, *Epigrams*, trans. by D. R Shackleton Bailey, 3 vols (Cambridge, MA; London: Harvard University Press, 1993), I, pp. 2–4.
5   Barbara Heldt, 'The Poetry of Elena Shvarts', *World Literature Today*, 63.3 (1989), 381–83 (p. 382).
6   Olga Sedakova, 'L'Antica Fiamma Elena Shvarts', *Novoe Literaturnoe Obozrenie*, 3 (2010). *Les Chansons de Bilitis* (1894): a pseudotranslation by Pierre Louÿs of the fictional Ancient Greek poet Bilitis; *Pis'ma rimskomu drugu* [*Letters to a Roman Friend*] (1972): a pseudotranslation by Iosif Brodskii of the Roman poet Martial.
7   Amongst other classical and pseudo-classical authors. See Diana Lewis Burgin, *Sophia Parnok: The Life and Work of Russia's Sappho* (New York: NYU Press, 1994), pp. 172–84; Georgina Barker, 'Sofiia Parnok's Sapphic Cycle *Roses of Pieria*: A Commentary' (forthcoming).

Lost and Translated

> Ergo tam doctae nobis periere tabellae,
> scripta quibus pariter tot periere bona!
>
> [So, those very clever tablets of mine are lost;
> how much good writing is lost with them, too!]
> Prop. III.23.1–2

Kinfiia is introduced with a typically Shvartsian paradox:

> Kinfiia is a Roman poetess from the first century BC, the heroine of the elegies of Propertius, famed not only for her talent, but also for her temper. Her poems have not survived to the present day, nevertheless I have endeavoured to translate them into Russian.

This makes *Kinfiia* a pseudotranslation where the author admits she never had access to the supposed originals. Cynthia as a poet has some basis in Propertius's *Elegies*. Propertius presents Cynthia as his '*docta puella*' [learned girl] several times (I.7.11, II.11.6, II.13.11); however, this may be an innuendo [experienced girl].[8] In a few poems Propertius portrays Cynthia as a poet in her own right:

> Phoebus endows you with his songs, and Calliope, nothing loth, with Aonia's lyre (I.2.27–30, p. 45)

> when she attempts songs on the Aeolian lyre, gifted to compose something fit for Aganippe's harp, and when she pits her writings against those of ancient Corinna and deems Erinna's poems no match for her own. (II.3.19–22, p. 113)

In IV.7 we even see Cynthia's poetic skills in action, as Propertius has Cynthia compose her own elegiac epitaph, taking his place as elegiac poet.[9] And in this same poem Propertius addresses the idea of Cynthia being lost along with his poetry, when she asks him to burn the poems he wrote about her, saying 'cease to win praise through me' (IV.7.78, p. 363).

However, Shvarts's paradox covers another, more serious, difficulty: Cynthia was at least partly, if not entirely, fictional. Writing two centuries after Propertius, Apuleius identifies Cynthia as Hostia, granddaughter of the poet Hostius, but his identification is dubious.[10] Cynthia's skills, apparent freedom, and listing alongside famous courtesans (II.6) have led many to believe she was a *meretrix*, or courtesan, in 'real life'.[11] But her meretricious companions are notably literary,[12] one of many metapoetic hints in Propertius's text which indicate that Cynthia is a fictional construct[13] based on generic conventions of love elegy, especially her predecessors

---

[8] Jane Stevenson, *Women Latin Poets: Language, Gender and Authority, from Antiquity to the Eighteenth Century* (Oxford: Oxford University Press, 2005), p. 24.
[9] Barbara L. Flaschenriem, 'Speaking of Women: 'Female Voice' in Propertius', *Helios*, 25.1 (1998), 49–64 (pp. 58–61).
[10] Goold, introduction in Propertius, pp. 8–9.
[11] J. P. Sullivan, *Propertius: A Critical Introduction* (Cambridge: Cambridge University Press, 2010), p. 2.
[12] Alison Keith, *Propertius: Poet of Love and Leisure* (London: Duckworth, 2008), p. 103.
[13] See especially Maria Wyke, 'Written Women: Propertius' Scripta Puella', *The Journal of Roman Studies*, 77 (1987), 47–61.

Catullus's Lesbia, Gallus's Lycoris, and Tibullus's Delia.[14] In the fashion of Latin love poetry, even Cynthia's name is an allusion to another of Propertius's influences, Callimachus: Cynthius was the epithet of Apollo (from Mount Cynthus on Delos where the god was born), the inspirer of Callimachean poetics.[15] So the lost poems that Shvarts translates, and the woman whom Shvarts recreates, never existed.

If not from Cynthia herself, then where did Shvarts get the Roman material for *Kinfiia*? As discussed in chapter 1, Shvarts did have some Latin, but was more likely to work from Russian if possible. Russian translations of all the Latin love poets would have been available for Shvarts to consult.[16] Following a comparison of *Kinfiia* with the available translations, the textual evidence points to Shvarts's major source being a 1963 edition of Catullus, Tibullus (and Sulpicia), and Propertius, edited by Fedor Petrovskii, with Catullus translated by various authors,[17] and Propertius and Tibullus translated by Lev Ostroumov.[18] Kinfiia's claim in 1.1 to be 'переменчивей нравом' [more volatile of temper] echoes Ostroumov's translation 'Как переменчивы все разгневанной женщины клятвы' [How volatile are all an enraged woman's oaths] (Prop. 11.9.35).[19] *Kinfiia* 1.3's 'кельтибера, | Что мочою себе зубы чистит' [Celtiberian, | who cleans his teeth with urine] is close to Solomon Apt's translation

> Но ты — ты кельтибер. А в Кельтиберии
> Уж так заведено — мочою собственной
> Там чистят утром зубы и полощут рот (Cat. xxxix.17–19)[20]
>
> [But you — you are a Celtiberian. And in Celtiberia
> It's their custom — with their own urine
> There in the morning they clean their teeth and rinse their mouths.]

The wording of *Kinfiia* R.2, 'серой окурись' [fumigate yourself with sulphur], is found in Ostroumov's translation: 'Все окурила [...] | Серным коснулась огнем' [She fumigated everything [...] | She touched with sulphurous flame] (Prop. IV.8.83–86).[21] The loanword '*meta*' [turning post] in *Kinfiia* R.3 is probably taken from Ostroumov's transliteration: 'Пусть к этой дальней мете в пене стремится мой конь' [May my horse race towards that far *meta*] (Prop. IV.1.70).[22] Shvarts's

---

14   Keith, p. 104; Maria Wyke, 'Mistress and Metaphor in Augustan Elegy', *Helios*, 16 (1989), 25–47 (pp. 30–31).
15   Wyke, 'Written Women', p. 59.
16   E. V. Sviiasov, *Antichnaia poeziia v russkikh perevodakh XVIII–XX vv.: Bibliograficheskii ukazatel'*, ed. by G. V. Bakhareva (St Petersburg: Dmitrii Bulanin, 1998). Propertius: pp. 351–53, Catullus: pp. 304–15; Ovid: pp. 337–49; Tibullus/Sulpicia: pp. 356–58.
17   Catullus translations by Adrian Piotrovskii, Sergei Shervinskii, Il'ia Sel'vinskii, Sergei Osherov, Solomon Apt, Zinaida Morozkina, Iurii Shul'ts, Fedor Petrovskii.
18   Shvarts's classicist friend Dmitrii Panchenko confirms that this was indeed the edition which Shvarts had in her library. Dmitrii Panchenko, Interview by Georgina Barker, St Petersburg, Russia, 2019.
19   *Valerii Katull, Al'bii Tibull, Sekst Propertsii: perevod s latinskogo*, ed. by Fedor Petrovskii (Moscow: Gosudarstvennoe izdatel'stvo khudozhestvennoi literatury, 1963), p. 305.
20   Ibid., pp. 58–59.
21   Ibid., p. 445.
22   Ibid., p. 417.

idea for her pun in R.6 on 'телки [...] образ' [heifer outfit] must have come from Ostroumov: 'Лживо надела себе телки еловой рога' [Falsely she put on the horns of a spruce heifer] (Prop. III.19.12).²³ These numerous verbal consonances prove that research went into Shvarts's crafting of *Kinfiia*.

Form

> Cynthia, forma potens
> Cynthia, powerful beauty
> Prop. II.5.28

Formally, *Kinfiia* also imitates its Roman models. None of the poems are rhymed, unusually for Shvarts, and extremely unusually for Russian poetry.²⁴ The lack of rhyme is reminiscent of the genre in which this occurs most often, translations of classical poetry.²⁵ The tactic is deliberate: justifying her opinion that rhyme is not essential, Shvarts said 'All ancient poetry is unrhymed'.²⁶ As Heldt notes, *Kinfiia* also uses 'devices of Roman poetry like extended metaphor and alliteration' (e.g. II.2, I.1), such that *Kinfiia* goes 'far beyond mere stylized imitation' of classical poetry.²⁷ But the formal feature that most subtly, pervasively, and indelibly marks *Kinfiia* as classical is its metres. (For a table of *Kinfiia*'s metres, see the Appendix.) The metres of *Kinfiia* are hugely varied, rather than exclusively elegiac — the verse form used in almost all Roman love poetry, consisting of couplets where the first line is a dactylic hexameter and the second line is a dactylic pentameter — which instantly marks the poetry apart from the elegist Propertius, who only wrote elegy, and recalls instead the lyric poet Catullus, who wrote in a variety of metres, including elegiacs.

Before I discuss *Kinfiia*'s classical metres, I must give a picture of *Kinfiia*'s non-classical metres, which are themselves far from standard for Russian poetry of the time. By far the commonest metre in *Kinfiia* is trochaic — where the stress falls on the first of the foot's two syllables — with ten trochaic poems, and two more that mix trochees and dactyls. Trochaic metres are not inherently classical-sounding to the Russian ear, but of the two binary metres they are far less frequently used, especially in the twentieth century.²⁸ Trochees tend to be used in Russian particularly for imitations of folklore,²⁹ and Shvarts is evidently drawing on this connection — all *Kinfiia*'s trochaic poems fall into one or more of the following categories: frenzied,

---

23   Ibid., p. 403.
24   See Barry P. Scherr, *Russian Poetry: Meter, Rhythm, and Rhyme* (Berkeley, CA: University of California Press, 1986), p. 10.
25   Since the eighteenth century, unrhymed verse in Russian has usually been reserved for 'imitations — of Greek and Latin poets (high style) or folk poetry (low style) — or [...] translations', where it signalled poetry that was 'derivative rather than "original"'. Michael Wachtel, *The Development of Russian Verse: Meter and its Meanings* (Cambridge: Cambridge University Press, 1998), p. 60. For example, Parnok chooses to make the majority of the poems in *Rozy Pierii* unrhymed.
26   Nikita Eliseev, '"Triumf" dlia Eleny', *Ekspert Severo-Zapad*, 5 (2004), <https://expert.ru/northwest/2004/05/05no-scult_50671/> [accessed 11 April 2019]. Shvarts is not entirely right here, as rhyme was used very occasionally by ancient writers — as a sort of novelty effect.
27   Heldt, p. 382.
28   Scherr, pp. 69–70.
29   Ibid., p. 70.

magical, religious, metaphysical, folkloric. In their more regular forms, the trochaic poems of *Kinfiia* sound positively incantatory. By contrast with the ten (or twelve) trochaic poems, Shvarts uses the commonest Russian metre — iambics,[30] where the stress falls on the second of the foot's two syllables — just once. Perhaps she allowed herself iambic pentameter in particular because it is the only metre with a tradition of unrhymed poetry in Russia,[31] and therefore somewhat foreign-sounding. Of the non-classical metres besides trochees and iambs, Shvarts has one poem in dolniks, a variable metre where each line has a fixed number of beats but no fixed positions for them; one poem in logaoedics, a metre where feet of various metres mingle in each line; and two poems in no apparent metre: none of these should strike the Russian ear as inalienably Russian. So even the non-classical metres clearly show Shvarts's wish to differentiate *Kinfiia* metrically from modern Russian poetry.

When *Kinfiia*'s poems evoke classical metres they do not strictly follow their rules, being rather 'reminiscences of classical metres'.[32] (It should be noted that Russian poetry imitates classical quantitative, or syllable length-based, metres by the arrangement of stresses in its qualitative, or syllable stress-based, metre.) Nine of *Kinfiia*'s poems display obviously classically derived metres. Throughout the cycle Shvarts makes extensive use of elegiac-type dactylic metres, where (in simplified terms) each foot can be either two long syllables or one long and two short syllables. Sometimes she recreates elegiac hexameters and pentameters very accurately, but never once presents them in the form of the elegiac couplet. This 'elegiac-ish' metre is the second most frequent metre in *Kinfiia*, appearing in five poems; two further poems also use dactyls. Her use of the classical dactylic foot is very unusual: in the decade before the first *Kinfiia* book, only 2 per cent of Russian poetry used dactylic metres.[33] Shvarts's dactyls point clearly to Propertian and Catullan influence (while all Propertius's poems are in elegiacs, elegy is also Catullus's most frequently used metre, featuring in fifty-two poems). Besides elegiacs, two other metres with classical sources appear in *Kinfiia*, each in two poems: hendecasyllables, a metre where every line has eleven syllables; and Sapphics, four-line stanzas consisting of three hendecasyllabic lines then a final five-syllable line (an adonic), made up of a dactyl and a trochee. Both of these metres have ties with Catullus: hendecasyllables were Catullus's second-favourite metre, featuring in forty poems; and although Sapphics inevitably recall their most famous writer — and possible inventor — Sappho, Catullus wrote two poems in Sapphic stanzas (both alluding in some way to Sappho). Metrically, then, *Kinfiia* is very much in the Catullan camp of Roman poetry.

A coherent form can also be discerned in the themes and timeframe of each book. This was noticed by Panchenko, whose schematisation I expand upon here. Passion predominates in the first book (1–4, 6–8), metaphysics in the second (1–5, 7–8), while myth joins the mix in the third (1, 6). The final poem of Book II, Kinfiia's

---

30 Ibid., pp. 44–45, 52.
31 Ibid., p. 53.
32 Dmitrii Panchenko, '"Kinfiia" Eleny Shvarts', *Novoe Literaturnoe Obozrenie*, 103 (2010), <http://magazines.russ.ru/nlo/2010/103/pa22.html> [accessed 4 March 2014].
33 Scherr, p. 96.

dialogue with the Greek philosopher, 'unites the metaphysics of the second book with the psychologism of the first book',[34] while the opening poem of the third book with its theme of memory suggests a reprise, which is consolidated by several more poems about returning (or failing to return) in the rest of the book (2–3, 9–10). Book I begins with a wintry downpour, goes through summer (the long days of 1.5), and ends in September (if 1.7 depicts the Bacchanalia). Book II begins in spring, passes through late summer (the blazing heat of II.7), and ends in May (if Kinfiia shares a birthday with Shvarts). The third book has its midpoint in the autumn/winter flooding, passes through midwinter, perhaps (R.9), and ends with rosy clouds that suggest the imminence of spring. The three *Kinfiia* books thus describe three years (though they may cover a longer period in the heroine's life).

Further specifics of *Kinfiia*'s form will be discussed in the next two sections as they investigate the dialogue that *Kinfiia* (and Kinfiia) strikes up with the Latin love poetry tradition.

Dialogue with Propertius

> furibunda decens
> comely in her fury
> Prop. IV.8.52

Kinfiia can be read as the other half of a dialogue with Propertius, the response that Cynthia never had the opportunity to make. Dialogue occurs within the Propertian references paralleling events, themes, and details from the *Elegies*; within the poems charting Kinfiia's relationship with Propertsii; and within the cycle's overarching narrative. Even in the title Shvarts marks her awareness of *Kinfiia*'s indebtedness to Propertius: Propertius's first poetry book was called in antiquity after its first word, simply, *Cynthia*.[35] Alongside individual poems' dialogue — and at times overt dispute — with Propertius, the three parts of the *Kinfiia* cycle respond to the narrative within the four books of elegies. Propertius's first words, 'Cynthia prima' [Cynthia first], act as a mission statement for the central theme of his first book. Shvarts's first words, 'Дай мне' [Give me], are no less programmatic. They introduce Kinfiia and her personal, practical concerns as the prime focus, with Kinfiia speaking from a position of power, in the imperative; Propertsii is mentioned later in the poem, only in passing and not by name. (Indeed, Kinfiia only once mentions Propertsii by name, in R.2.) Like Propertius, Shvarts moves away from the theme of the elegiac relationship: most of the second book, especially poems 2–6, is conducted without reference to Propertius. Again, like Propertius, Shvarts returns to the elegiac relationship in two poems of the final book, which as a whole is almost as indebted to Propertius as the first. And ultimately, despite the relative unimportance of Propertsii the character in *Kinfiia*, when Propertsii dumps

---

34 Panchenko, '"Kinfiia" Eleny Shvarts'.
35 Propertius calls it this in II.23: 'now that your famous book has made you a legend, and your 'Cynthia' is read all over the forum?' p. 171. The book is also called *Cynthia* by Ovid in *Remedia Amoris* 764, and by Martial in XIV.189.

Kinfiia — in the final poem — his departure from Kinfiia's life seems to spell the end for her poetic cycle, suggesting the vital importance of Propertius the poet to *Kinfiia*'s existence. This section will explore *Kinfiia*'s Propertian influences, poem by poem.

Book I

Kinfiia explodes into life in the first poem, 'K sluzhanke' [To a Slave Girl], with an opening barrage of commands:

> Дай мне мази багровой —
> Ветрянку у губ успокоить,
> Дай, постель подогрев,
> Чемерицы в горячем вине.

> [Give me the crimson ointment
> To soothe the sore on my lip,
> Give me — once you've warmed the bed —
> Hellebore in hot wine.]

Yet Kinfiia's cracked lips and cold bed in these lines allude to Cynthia's appearance as a ghost in IV.7, and have a similar tone to her haranguing of Propertius in that poem:

> I bemoaned the cold empire of my bed. [...] Lethe's water had withered her lips. But it was a living voice and spirit that emerged as her brittle fingers cracked with a snap of her thumb:

> 'Treacherous one [...] Why was my funeral fire not perfumed with spice? Was it then too much to cast hyacinths upon me, no costly gift, and to hallow my grave with wine from a shattered jar? (Prop. IV.7.6–34, pp. 357–59)[36]

Shvarts beginning *Kinfiia* with an allusion to the dead Cynthia opens up an interesting range of interpretative possibilities for the cycle as a whole: perhaps Shvarts is suggesting that her inspiration for the poems came from a Cynthia who is indeed long dead; or that, like Propertius's Cynthia in IV.7 and IV.8, Kinfiia can come back from the grave more alive and feisty than ever before.

Death is a central concern of elegy (the metre was associated with lamentation and funerary inscriptions as well as love), and of all the Latin love elegists, Propertius is the most interested in the theme.[37] So it is very Propertian that the middle of this poem introducing Kinfiia's Rome leaves the city for a gruesome glimpse of Rome's far-off wars:

> Край наш под мокрым застыл одеялом,
> Только там — далеко, в Пиренеях —
>
> На германца идут легионы.

---

36   I am indebted to Donncha O'Rourke for noticing this intertext (and many more).
37   See Robert Maltby, 'Major Themes and Motifs in Propertius' Love Poetry', in *Brill's Companion to Propertius*, ed. by Hans Christian Günther (Leiden; Boston, MA: Brill, 2006), pp. 147–81 (pp. 160–64).

> В ущельях — как мизинец они,
> Что в агонии долго дрожит,
> Когда тело уже омертвело.
>
> [These parts lie congealed under a damp blanket,
> While there — far away, in the Pyrenees —
>
> The legions march against the Germani.
> In the gorges — they're like a little finger
> That twitches in agony long
> After the body has grown stiff in death.]

War is ever-present in both the background and the foreground of Propertius's poetry: in his lifetime Rome underwent one of its bloodiest periods, with constant wars, civil and expansionist, at home and abroad, and Propertius justifies his refusal to participate in those real wars with the elegiac topos of *militia amoris* [love as war]. One of Propertius's many statements of his commitment to love instead of war comes with a description, not unlike Shvarts's, of Roman soldiers battling barbarians:

> care not in what fields the battle is arrayed beneath Marius' standards and Rome beats back Teutonic power, nor where the barbaric Rhine, steeped in Swabian blood, carries mangled bodies downstream in sorrowing waters. For you will sing of garlanded lovers at another's threshold. (Prop. III.3.43–47, p. 229)

Characteristically, Propertius touches upon the subject of war, then turns quickly to lighter, elegiac themes, and Shvarts does likewise: in the following stanza she returns to Kinfiia's personal concerns.

Kinfiia's declaration 'В Риме никто переменчивей нравом | Меня не рождался' [In all Rome none more volatile of temper | Than me has ever been born] corresponds with Propertius's numerous denunciations of Cynthia's fickleness, such as his aphorism 'Cynthia, mighty beauty; Cynthia, flighty slut' (Prop. II.5.28, p. 119). Shvarts may also be perceiving the internal inconsistencies within Cynthia's characterisation: Cynthia is 'endlessly adaptable by the poet because she is a projection of his desires and anxieties, as unstable and slippery as his thoughts', and because she plays a 'foil' to Propertius in his many literary and mythical roles.[38]

It is fitting that in the opening poem of Book I Shvarts uses a dactylic metre of mostly hexameter and pentameter — the metre of elegy. Yet she disguises the familiar uneven form of elegiac couplets by splitting most of the lines across two lines, usually at the caesura, and arranging them into four-line stanzas. So this classical verse looks, for the most part, like regular modern poetry — rather like the clothing of Kinfiia's classical themes in modern Russian.

1.3 'K sluzhanke' [To a Slave Girl] shows Kinfiia enraged with her slave girl, devising punishments for her. Implications of Kinfiia harshly punishing her slaves occur also in *Kinfiia* I.1, II.6, and R.8. While the depiction is motivated more by other Latin poets (see below), this cruelty towards her slaves aligns with the Cynthia

---

[38] Barbara K. Gold, '"But Ariadne Was Never There in the First Place": Finding the Female in Roman Poetry', in *Feminist Theory and the Classics*, ed. by Nancy Sorkin Rabinowitz and Amy Richlin (New York; London: Routledge, 1993), pp. 75–101 (pp. 88–89).

of IV.7.35–38, where she demands that two of her former slaves be tortured to discover who killed her, and IV.8.79–80, where she punishes a slave by having him put up for sale. On the other hand, Cynthia's concern for other of her former slaves in IV.7.43–46, 73–76 demonstrates mutual affection and care between mistress and slaves.

Shvarts's vampiric depiction of Cupid in 1.4 'Kupidonu' [To Cupid] as a 'сосунок крылатый' [wingèd suckler] at Kinfiia's throat, pulling at arrows firmly lodged in her chest, is motivated by Propertius's portrait of Cupid. The god's arrows are stuck in his chest and his veins are drained of blood:

> [In] me still stay his darts, his boyish appearance stays: but he has certainly lost his wings, since nowhere from my breast does he fly away, but at the cost of my blood wages constant war. What pleasure is it for you to lodge in my bloodless veins? For very shame, boy, shoot your arrows elsewhere! (II.12.13–18, p. 137)

But Kinfiia is more successful than Propertius at resisting Cupid's attack: Propertius's heart is still stuck full of arrows in his next poem (II.13.1–2), while at the end of her poem Kinfiia sends the 'мальчик' [little boy] off with a flea in his ear.

In 1.5 'Molodomu poetu' [To a Young Poet] Kinfiia abuses a bad poet. The poem is more Catullan than Propertian (see below), yet it also has a precedent in Propertius. Kinfiia's threat 'на площади людной | Вселится в тебя громовой голос' [in a crowded square | A thunderous voice will possess you] echoes the astrologer Horos's admonishment of Propertius to leave an unpoetic career and instead write small-scale elegiac poetry in the Callimachean vein: 'Apollo dictates a little of his song to you and forbids you to [thunder] speeches in the [crazy forum]' (Prop. IV.2.133–34, p. 321). Shvarts's repetition of the word 'thunder' from Propertius is especially apt, as he is using 'thundering' with reference to Callimachus *Aetia* 1.20 as a shorthand for bad poetry. 1.5 is the first of three poems in *Kinfiia* addressed to a named person (Septimus; 1.6 and II.4 are addressed to Claudia), something that Propertius frequently does.[39]

1.6 'Klavdii' [To Claudia] treats a common elegiac conceit, the *paraclausithyron* [lover's exclusion at the mistress's door], something Propertius frequently alludes to as a cruel occupational hazard.[40] As the poem takes such a distinctively elegiac theme, Shvarts puts it in elegiac metre, although the hexameters and pentameters do not alternate in regular couplets, but at random. Propertius's one *paraclausithyron* treats the theme unconventionally — 1.16 is from the perspective of the door, which complains about Propertius's vigils on its step. Propertius's modification of the motif provides a precedent for Shvarts's own unconventional *paraclausithyron*: she writes it not from the perspective of the excluded lover, usually the elegiac poet, but the woman inside, who in this case *is* the elegiac poet. This sparks a series of role reversals. Kinfiia's would-be lover, waiting by her door, is a gladiator, who is ridiculous in the role of elegiac lover, for which not physical but mental prowess is required:

---

39 Half of all the poems in Book I are addressed to named people (other than Cynthia): 1.1, 6, 22 to Tullus; 1.4 to Bassus; 1.5, 10, 13, 20 to Gallus; 1.7, 9, 12 to Ponticus.
40 For example, 1.5.19–22; 1.18.23–24; II.6.1–2, 37–40.

> Сумерки только падут — в двери мои он стучится,
> Вечер сидит, опираясь на остроблещущий меч.
> Тяжко, с усилием, дышит он через рот и глядит
> Страстно и жалобно вместе...

> [As soon as dusk falls — he comes knocking at my door,
> All evening sits there, leaning on his sharp-shining sword.
> Heavily, strenuously breathing through his mouth, he gazes
> Passionately and plaintively at the same time...]

Propertius mentions gladiators only once in the *Elegies*, but is similarly scornful: 'he will sell his life to eat the foul mash of a gladiator, when to his shame a beard overruns his shaven cheeks' (Prop. IV.8.25–26, p. 367). Kinfiia's lover (presumably Propertius) is not shut outside, but safely inside — though he is scared enough of the gladiator to risk precipitating himself outdoors:

> Чуть гладиатора видит — прыгает прямо в окно.
> [...]
> Люблю, несчастная, я лысого урода,
> Что прячется, как жалкий раб, за дверью

> [Scarcely glimpses the gladiator — straight out the window he jumps.
> [...]
> Wretched me, I love a bald monstrosity
> Who hides like a pitiful slave behind the door.]

Kinfiia's transition from the *paraclausithyron* to fears of losing her looks and thus her suitors to old age —

> Но, подлой, жалко мне его прогнать,
> Когда еще такой полюбит молодец,
> А старости вот-вот они, туманы...

> [But, despicably, I am loath to drive him away —
> When will another such gallant love me again?
> And they're almost upon me, the fogs of age...]

— repeats a transition found in the *Elegies*, when Propertius responds to Cynthia's rejection with a threat:

> Farewell the threshold still tearful at my grievances, and farewell the door, never, in spite of all, shattered by my angry fists!
> May old age oppress you with the burden of the years you have dissembled, and may ugly wrinkles come upon your beauty. [...] Shut out yourself in turn, may you suffer another's haughty scorn. (Prop. III.25.9–15, pp. 303–05)

It appears that Kinfiia is right to fear ageing!

In I.7 Kinfiia goes to watch bacchantes. Propertius compares the sleeping Cynthia to a 'Thracian bacchant[e], exhausted after incessant dances' (Prop. I.3.5, p. 45). And he speaks of a hypothetical woman rushing through the streets 'like a possessed bacchante' (Prop. III.8.14, p. 247). However, he does not explicitly compare any of Cynthia's wild behaviour (her hymning and dancing, or her maenadic fury) to that of bacchantes. Kinfiia's reaction to the bacchantes is surprising — so rowdy elsewhere, here she harms only herself:

> все руки
> Расцарапаны — в крови до локтя...
> [...]
> На себя ты страсть обрушить можешь
>
> [my arms
> Are all scratched — bloodied up to the elbow...
> [...]
> On yourself you can unleash your passion]

Kinfiia's self-harming corresponds with an instance in the *Elegies*: 'Why does a man gash his arms with ritual blades and maim himself at the mad rhythms of the Phrygian piper?' (Prop. II.22.15–16, p. 165). This refers to the cult of Cybele or Cybebe, a mother goddess, whose followers castrated themselves in a parallel gender reversal to that of bacchantes[41] (the parallel is drawn in Catullus LXIII — see below). By not succumbing to the socially sanctioned ecstatic escape from normal gender roles offered by Bacchus, Kinfiia here paradoxically takes on a male role, inflicting suffering on herself like a man driven mad by Cybele rather than a woman driven mad by Bacchus. Propertius's question illustrates his powerlessness not to inflict the pain of love on himself; this suggests that the ending of *Kinfiia* 1.7 may also be a metaphor for love.

Shvarts takes up the Propertian theme of magic in 1.8 'K provintsialke' [To a Provincial Woman]. There are numerous instances of magic in Propertius, in part because he exploits the ambiguity between a poem and a spell (both 'carmen' in Latin) to fashion himself as a 'poet-sorceror'.[42] Cynthia's charms for men are described in ways akin to witchcraft;[43] it is not surprising therefore that Kinfiia becomes a fully fledged witch. Shvarts bases Kinfiia's threats of herbs and spells upon one Propertius poem in particular, where he ascribes malevolent magical powers to the bawd Acanthis: 'if she has brought Colline herbs to the magic trench, standing crops would dissolve into running water. She dared to put spells on the bewitched moon' (Prop. IV.5.11–13, p. 343). Shvarts also seems to have based the effects of Kinfiia's curse on Propertius's gleeful account of Acanthis's death in the same poem.

Shvarts:

> спадешь с лица ты, почернеешь,
> Будешь ты икать и днем и ночью,
> Повар-грек твой будет в суп сморкаться,
> [...]
> Если сделаешь мне что дурное —
> Все равно Юпитер, знай, накажет.

---

41 'Galli', in *Brill's New Pauly: Encyclopaedia of the Ancient World*, ed. by Hubert Cancik and Helmuth Schneider, 15 vols (Leiden: Brill, 2002–09), V (2004), 668–69.

42 James E. G. Zetzel, 'Poetic Baldness and its Cure', *Materiali e discussioni per l'analisi dei testi classici*, 36 (1996), 73–100 (p. 99).

43 Ibid., pp. 93–95.

[your face will shrivel, you'll turn black,
You will hiccup day and night,
Your Greek cook will hawk up in your soup,
[...]
If you do anything bad to me —
Know this: Jupiter will punish you anyway.]

Propertius:

But accept, Queen Venus, in return for your favour a ringdove's throat cut before your altar. I have lived to see the phlegm clotting in her wrinkled throat, the bloody spittle that she coughed up through her decayed teeth, and to see her breathe out her last rank breath on heirloom rags. (Prop. IV.5.65–69, p. 347)

The details differ, but the coincidences of the withered face/neck, the spitting, and the protective deity suggest Propertius's influence. Moreover, Kinfiia's threat that

Даже пьяный негр, матрос просоленный,
В долгой по любви стосковавшийся дороге,
Даже он в постель к тебе не ляжет

[Even a drunk negro, a salty sailor,
Who all voyage long has thirsted for love,
Even he will not get into bed with you]

turns round Acanthis's advice to Cynthia to 'Spurn not [...] the seaman if his gnarled hand carries coin' (Prop. IV.5.49–50, p. 347) — it is the seaman who will spurn the provincial woman. Propertius never mentions black Africans in his *Elegies*, although he does comment on the dark skins of Indians (Prop. IV.3.10). 1.8 'K provintsialke' is not the only time when Kinfiia uses magic: in R.5 she floods Rome through witchcraft.

Book II

The setting of II.1, the Esquiline gardens, a park created by Propertius's patron Maecenas, near which Propertius lived (III.23.24), is in the same area where the jealous Cynthia began a brawl: 'Listen to an incident which last night put to flight the well-watered Esquiline and caused those living near the New Gardens to take to their heels' (Prop. IV.8.1–2, p. 365). Shvarts even incorporates the detail that the gardens are 'aquosas' [watery], taking this to an extreme: 'Все закрыты на просушку Эсквилинские сады' [The Esquiline gardens are all closed to dry out]. The topic of *Kinfiia* II.1 is Dionysus; it is fitting that the phrase 'в чанах сада квасится весна' [in the garden's vats spring is brewing] stems from Propertius's hymn to Bacchus: 'let my vats foam with the purple must' (Prop. III.17.17, p. 281).

II.7 'Na pliazhe v Baii' [On the Beach at Baiae] is in dialogue with Propertius's two poems set in the popular coastal resort of Baiae, I.11 and III.18, a dialogue which is underscored by the poem's mix of quasi-elegiac dactylic metres. Kinfiia's experience of Baiae is at odds with how Propertius imagines it in I.11, where Baiae's corrupting influence becomes the focus of Propertius's jealousy. Shvarts replaces Cynthia's dalliances on the beach with scenes of decay, including a dissected starfish on the sand; rather than love, Kinfiia is given over to the maddening forces of fate and inspired poetry. *Kinfiia* 11.7 is closer in tone to *Elegies* III.18, an elegy to Augustus's nephew Marcellus, who died at Baiae; Shvarts replicates its atmosphere of death and doom, riffing on the infernal associations Propertius gives Baiae's hot waters. Like Marcellus, Kinfiia too succumbs to Baiae's malign waters: her life boils in a cauldron (or is it Baiae's waters?), the Parcae draw in the threads of her life just as fishermen draw in their nets, and Kinfiia, imagining herself their piscine prey, is swept up, flapping her gills for breath. 11.7 'Na pliazhe v Baii' picks up on the malignity that Baiae represents for Propertius in both his Baiae poems.

When Kinfiia compares herself to Pythia, the Delphic oracle, the Baiae landscape in 11.7 blurs with that of Delphi, its caves and vapours, which are unseen yet tangible:

> Я иду — на плечах моих пещера
> Тяжелым плащом повисла,
> И невидимый город Дельфы
> Дышит зловеще.
>
> [I walk; from my shoulders the cave
> Hangs heavy like a cloak,
> And the unseen city Delphi
> Exhales ill omens.]

Although Pythia never appears in Propertius, Pythian Apollo does, and is described in a remarkably similar way to Kinfiia here: '[Pythius/Apollo], wearing a long cloak, plays and sings' (Prop. 11.31/32.16, p. 199). And Kinfiia is under the influence of Apollo: 'Но послушна я веленью бога, | Шьющего стрелой золотые песни' [But I am obedient to the bidding of the god | Who sews golden songs with his arrow]. Apollo is recognisable from his famed shooting, described by Propertius: 'For this feat did Actian Apollo win his temple, that each arrow he launched sank ten ships' (Prop. IV.6.67–68, p. 355). Just as Propertius has Apollo change his bow for a lyre in the following line, in *Kinfiia* 11.7 Apollo's arrows are transformed into the poetry he sends Kinfiia/Pythia.[44]

11.8 'Razgovor' [Conversation] is a philosophical conversation (or argument) between Kinfiia and her Alexandrian slave, whom she asks to impart wisdom to her. This dialogic element is reminiscent of Propertius's exchange with the Babylonian astrologer in IV.1 (although there is none of *Kinfiia*'s back-and-forth in the Propertius). The occasion for the conversation is Kinfiia's birthday, making 11.8 a *genethliacon* [elegiac birthday poem]. It counters Propertius's birthday wishes for Cynthia in III.10: instead of peace and joy and propitious rituals, followed by celebrations and love with Propertius, Kinfiia reacts to her birthday in a more realistic manner for a middle-aged woman, with anxiety about growing old and hope for philosophical comfort. These themes may respond to an underlying 'anxiety' in Propertius's version:

---

44 Panchenko sees a deeper connection between the sun god Apollo and the inspired poet running through the golden imagery of the poem from the beginning, where the sun is covered in golden sores, to the ending, where Kinfiia is a golden fish with golden suns in her blood.

the placing of [lines] 17 and 18 must imply that the loss of *forma* [beauty] will see the fall of Cynthia's *regna* [reign]. [...] The passing of time is inexorable and nothing reminds one more of it than birthdays.[45]

This chimes with Kinfiia's (justified) fear of ageing in 1.6 'Klavdii', stemming from Propertius's threat in III.25 about her ageing (see above).

Razroznennoe [Oddments]

In R.1 'девчонки по-спартански, молча, | Кулаком наотмашь взрослых били' [gals, in Spartan fashion and in silence, | Would beat up the adults with swinging punches]. This references Propertius's poem about Spartan girls:

> O Sparta, I admire [...] the many merits of your training of virgins, for without disrepute a naked girl may engage in physical exercise in the presence of wrestling men, when [...] a dust-soiled woman stands at the end of the course and suffers hurt in the fight with no holds barred: now she binds the glove to her arms that rejoice in its thongs. (Prop. III.14.1–9, pp. 271–73)

Shvarts compresses the twenty-line panegyric to Spartan gender equality to a fleeting simile within a simile.

R.2 shows the other side of Propertius's various poems describing reunion with Cynthia after a night spent drinking and womanising (especially 1.3, II.29, and IV.8). The poem could be the ending of II.29, in which a drunk Propertius, out late at night, is accosted by a group of boys and forcibly dragged back to Cynthia. The poem's opening, 'Вновь Проперций мой ко мне вернулся, | Счастие для Кинфии какое!' [My Propertsii has returned to me again — | What luck, what joy for Kinfiia!], could be sincere or sarcastic. If it is sincere, then its tone echoes Propertius's joy at the opening of the second half of *Elegies* 1.8, when Cynthia decides not to travel to Illyria, and at the opening of II.15, after Propertius has spent the night with Cynthia:

> Here she will stay! Here she is pledged to remain! Let envy burst! I have won: she could not resist my ceaseless prayers. [...] my Cynthia has ceased to travel on an unknown course. (Prop. 1.8.27–30, p. 61)
>
> O happy me! O night that shone for me! And O you darling bed made blessed by my delight! (Prop. II.15.1–2, p. 145)

However, Propertsii's bedraggled state detailed in the following lines suggests that Kinfiia's joy may be feigned. Kinfiia notes Propertsii's shame before her, and apparently misreads it as shame for their tenacious love, rather than his poor behaviour (which is the cause in Propertius's poems). Kinfiia portrays herself as far more patient than Propertius portrays Cynthia. Kinfiia does not harangue him or complain, as her counterpart does:

> 'Has another's scorn then at last brought you to my bed, expelling you from doors closed in your face? For where have you spent the long hours of the night which was due me, you who come, ah me, exhausted, when the stars are driven

---

45 R. O. A. M. Lyne, *Collected Papers on Latin Poetry* (Oxford: Oxford University Press, 2007), p. 29.

from the sky? Oh, may you spend nights like these, you villain, such as you are always compelling poor me to endure! (Prop. 1.3.35–40, p. 47)

Kinfiia does not reject him, as Cynthia once does: 'repelling my kisses with a wave of her hand, [she] tripped forth with loose sandals on her feet' (Prop. II.29.39–40, p. 193). Although Kinfiia does consider it: 'Ах, тебя прогнать отсюда взашей | Так бы мне хотелось' [Ah, how I would like to throw you out | On your ear]. And Kinfiia does not physically attack him, as Cynthia does in reaction to finding Propertius drinking with two courtesans: 'Cynthia [...] hastens back to bruise my face with the back of her hand, marks my neck, drawing blood with toothbites, and especially pokes at my guilty eyes' (Prop. IV.8.63–66, p.369). Kinfiia's restraint may be because Propertsii arrives already 'Исцарапанный, залапанный, помятый' [Scratched, mauled, bedraggled], and generally pitiable. Nevertheless, Kinfiia's reception of her errant lover is based upon this harpy-like Cynthia of IV.8, who:

> fumigated every spot touched by the girls brought in, and mopped the threshold with clean water; she bade me change anew all the oil in the lamps, and thrice with burning sulphur touched my head. (Prop. IV.8.83–86, p. 371)

But Kinfiia, instructing Propertsii to carry out an almost identical purification, is merely mothering:

> Поменяй же тогу, эта в пятнах,
> Залечи царапины, умойся,
> После серой окурись от скверны.
>
> [Go and change your toga, this one's all stained,
> See to your scratches, get washed,
> Then fumigate yourself from the filth with sulphur.]

Yet the role that Kinfiia and Cynthia play in *Kinfiia* R.2 and *Elegies* IV.8 is the same: both are women wronged by their man, whom they both ultimately decide to forgive.

R.3 flaunts Kinfiia's disregard of Propertius's frequent imprecations against women enhancing their appearance through artificial means: he admonishes Cynthia: 'In hell below may many an ill befall that girl who stupidly dyes her hair with a false colour!' (Prop. II.18.27–28, p. 155) 'Propertius stands alone among the poets of his day in his praise of the *fulva coma* [ginger hair] and his opposition to the *flava coma* [...], or artificially colored "golden" hair, which was the fashion of the time.'[46] Shvarts highlights his hypocrisy, as Kinfiia uses the same substance that Propertius depicts himself using: 'Я хочу достать шафранной краски | Для волос' [I want to get saffron dye | For my hair] | 'let Cilician saffron drench my locks' (Prop. IV.6.74, p. 355). There is a further irony: whilst Kinfiia says 'Рыжей стать хочу' [I want to become ginger], Propertius states that Cynthia 'has ginger hair' (Prop. II.2.5) — perhaps Shvarts is suggesting that the 'natural' hair Propertius admired was, in fact, dyed. At the end of the poem Kinfiia characterises her fluctuating whims with a common Roman metaphor:

---

46 Jesse Benedict Carter, *Selections from the Roman Elegiac Poets* (Boston: D. C. Heath & Company, 1909), p. 181.

> О желанья, вы — скороходы,
> Что, сменяясь, жизнь влекут
> К мете заветной.
> Вы — погонщики, вы и кони...
>
> [O wishes, you are seven-league boots,
> Which, taking turns, drag life along
> Towards the ultimate *meta*.
> You are both jockey and horses...]

Propertius uses *metae* [turning posts] twice metaphorically (and once literally: III.14.7). At II.25.21–26 he writes:

> You, too, credulous one, who put on airs because your love is at the full, no woman can be relied upon for long. [...] Does any man claim the prize with the race unfinished, before his chariot's axle has grazed the turning-post [*metam*] a seventh time? (p. 177)

And at IV.1.69–70 he writes: 'I shall sing of rites and deities and ancient names of places: this is the goal [*metas*] to which my foaming steed must press' (p. 315). Shvarts reverses Propertius's meaning on both counts: making *metae* stand for the end of the race of life (as they often do in Latin literature) instead of the successful completion of a relationship or a poetic work, she puts women's whims in the driving seat — the same female fickleness that Propertius says will impede a man's attainment of his goal (II.25) and that he eschews as poetic material in favour of an epic goal (IV.1).

R.4 'K Morfeiu' [To Morpheus] deals with dreams, a concern of Cynthia's, who goes 'to tell her dreams to chaste Vesta, in case they were dreams to bring her harm or me' (Prop. II.29.27–28, p. 193). Kinfiia takes the matter further than Cynthia's consultation, personally warning Morpheus not to send her bad dreams... or else. Propertius is also concerned about Cynthia having bad dreams: 'I feared lest some nightmare be bringing you fantastic terrors, and a phantom lover forcing you to yield to him against your will' (Prop. 1.3.29–30, p. 47). Kinfiia likewise accuses Morpheus of sending a rapist to a Vestal virgin in her sleep — perhaps prompted by Propertius's mention of Vesta in conjunction with harmful dreams in II.29.

Kinfiia's flooding of Rome through witchcraft in R.5 suggests the power that witches supposedly had to influence the moon — especially with its final lines:

> Я плыла в водоворотах,
> Души по волнам босые
> Пробегали и носили
> Низко палки чадных звезд,
> При высоком полнолуньи...
>
> [I swam amidst the whirlpools,
> Spirits ran barefoot over the waves
> And carried held low
> Their torch-sticks of fuming stars
> Beneath a high full moon...]

There are multiple parallels between these lines and a section of Propertius's first elegy, which briefly invokes witches: 'you, whose practice it is to lure the Moon down from the sky and to propitiate spirits over the magic fire [...] the power of summoning ghosts and stars with Thessalian spells' (1.1.19–24, p. 41). (See also above on *Kinfiia* 1.8 'K provintsialke'.)

In R.6 Shvarts reverses a mythical exemplum that Propertius is fond of using to illustrate women's wantonness: Pasiphaë. Pasiphaë is the penultimate in a host of sinful women to whom Propertius compares Cynthia in the spirit of excusing her infidelities: 'Once was the wife of mighty Minos, so they say, seduced by the snow-white form of a glowering bull' (Prop. II.31/32.57–58, p. 205). When the dead Cynthia divides famous women in the underworld into the virtuous and the sinful, the latter are represented by 'the Cretan queen whose guile contrived the wooden monstrosity of a cow' (Prop. IV.7.57–58, p. 361). But Shvarts's particular polemic is with Propertius's use of Pasiphaë to demonstrate that women are more lustful than men:

> You are constantly reproaching me with men's lust: take it from me, lust commands women even more. [...] Witness is she who suffered the disdain of a Cretan bull and put on the false horns of a timber cow' (Prop. III.19.1–12, p. 287)

Kinfiia's poem is the retort, as she takes the figure of Pasiphaë and uses her to represent not a woman made irrational by passion, but a predatory and calculating man:

> Кинется ль она быку на шею?
> Нет, пылая, ждет она, терпит.
> Кто в любви терпелив
>
> [Does she throw herself headlong at the bull?
> No: aflame, she waits, she endures.
> He who bides his time in love]

Kinfiia's Pasiphaë symbolises male guile, and, what is more, she is modelled on Propertius. Shvarts incorporates Propertius's complaint about the expense of bribing his mistress's slaves.

Propertius:

> Does any free-born man give bribes to another's slave to carry a message to his mistress [...]? How expensively does a night of joy come round but once in the whole year! (Prop. II.23.3–11, p. 169)

Shvarts:

> кто служанок подкупит
> Всех до единой,
> [...]
> Сердца его не измеришь, вечно
> Будет расчетлив.
>
> [who bribes your slave girls,
> Every last one,
> [...]
> You cannot ever gauge his heart, he will be
> Eternally calculating.]

Shvarts rightly notes Propertius's monetary calculation in wooing a woman, and translates that into emotional calculation once the woman is wooed.

Propertius complains frequently of Cynthia's infidelities — for example, 'Is it right, Cynthia, for your name to be a byword throughout Rome and for you to flaunt a life of shame?' (Prop. II.5.1–2, p. 117). In R.7 Shvarts again gives the other side of this quarrel — in an elegiac-ish mix of dactylic metres to underscore the response to Propertius — showing Kinfiia's lack of pleasure, even pain, in behaviour Propertius perceives as frivolous:

> Что меня бросило в объятья Диомида?
> [...]
> От нелюбви за ночь
> Стерся как будто и пол.
>
> [What threw me into the arms of Diomedes?
> [...]
> In the course of the night, even our sexes
> Seemed to rub away, from lack of love.]

Kinfiia's loveless sex with the soldier, which turns them into fighting circus wolves by the end, draws on Propertius's frequent depiction of love as war (the elegiac topos *militia amoris*). Besides its condemnation of Cynthia's promiscuity, *Elegies* II.5 also contains a depiction of animals fighting that transitions into a violent travesty of elegiac lovemaking:

> It is not only the bull that strikes his foe with curved horns, but even the injured sheep turns upon an aggressor. I shall not tear the clothes from your perjured body, nor let my anger shatter your locked door, nor bring myself in my rage to pull at your plaited hair, nor hurt you with brutal thumbs. (Prop. II.5.19–24, pp. 117–19)

This may have inspired the *militia amoris* of *Kinfiia* R.7, as may Propertius's poem about his and Cynthia's violent fights and lovemaking:

> I enjoyed the lamplight brawl we had last night and all the abuse of your frenzied tongue. But I dare you: come, tear my hair and scratch my face with your pretty nails [...] Let rivals see the wounds I have sustained in neck-bites: let bruises on me show that I have had my girl with me. I want either to suffer in love or hear that you are suffering. (Prop. III.8.1–23, p. 247)

Propertius theorises that anger is a sign of love; Kinfiia in R.7 seems to disagree. Propertius concludes with a message to the man Cynthia has gone off with: 'If you have now been offered the chance of stealing a night, it is not because she loves you, but because she is vexed with me' (Prop. III.8.39–40, p. 249). This perhaps answers Kinfiia's question at the beginning of the poem: what threw her into another man's arms.

Kinfiia ends with Propertsii bidding Kinfiia farewell. R.10 takes themes of parting from various elegies by Propertius. It is similar to III.21 in both circumstance — Propertius running away from Cynthia to seek distraction from the pain of love — and tone: 'you, sweetheart, however you have treated me, farewell!' (Prop. III.21.16, p. 293). In both III.21 and I.17 — another escape from Cynthia — Propertius imagines his own death; Propertsii's letter to Kinfiia imagines her death:

> Пусть твое некогда столь любимое тело,
> [...]
> Станет пеплом
> В золоте костра погребального

[May your body, formerly so beloved,
[...]
Turn to ashes
In the gold of a funeral pyre]

Propertius depicts Cynthia's death as reality in iv.7, and in this last *Kinfiia* poem, as in the first, Shvarts draws on his depiction of Cynthia's ghost: 'a pale shade vanquishes and escapes the pyre [...] her dress was charred at the side, and the fire had gnawed at the familiar beryl on her finger' (Prop. iv.7.2–9, p. 357). When Propertsii says he will join the legions, Kinfiia detects the lie. For one, the threat is belied by Propertius's own poems, which often flaunt their unwarlike nature, and the elegiac poet's replacement of war with love; indeed, in iii.12 he remonstrates with a friend for leaving his girlfriend to go off to fight, as Propertsii has threatened to do here. But the threat is conclusively belied by the tablets the letter is written on: 'Пахнут устрицами таблички, | Жареным вепрем, вином сицилийским, духами' [The tablets smell of oysters, | Roasted wild boar, Sicilian wine, perfume]. Propertius's writing tablets are the subject of *Elegies* iii.23; in the first line he calls them '*doctae*' [learned/experienced] — just like Cynthia! — and then claims that he has taught them to speak for themselves: 'They had by now learned how to mollify girls in my absence, and in my absence utter some persuasive phrases' (Prop. iii.23.5–6, p. 299). It serves Propertsii right that in this final poem they betray him to Kinfiia by contradicting his written words — just as Kinfiia herself, who learned speech from Propertius (through Shvarts), has contradicted Propertius's *Elegies* with her own, independent poetic voice. Kinfiia also demonstrates her financial independence in the poem's final lines. In one elegy Propertius tells the reader that Cynthia 'is always sending me to the ocean to look for pearls' (ii.16.17, p. 149) and complains that any man can buy her affections with presents. But Kinfiia, newly single, buys her own pearls.

The fact that Propertsii's departure ends the cycle suggests that, although the poems present him as almost entirely extraneous, he is essential to Kinfiia's poetry, perhaps due to Kinfiia and Shvarts's dependence upon Propertius for Cynthia's existence. Propertius's move away from Cynthia did not entail the end of his poetry: he renounces her at the end of Book iii to continue to greater, more epic themes in Book iv; kills her off and brings her back as a ghost in iv.7 and larger than life in iv.8; and closes the collection in iv.11 with an epigraph in the voice of an altogether different woman, Cornelia, an exemplary Roman matron. While Propertius's collection ends on this apparent non sequitur, Shvarts's is circular, returning to the themes of the first poem in the final poem: military issues far from Rome, and its weather, which has progressed from storms to pearly pink clouds, signifying

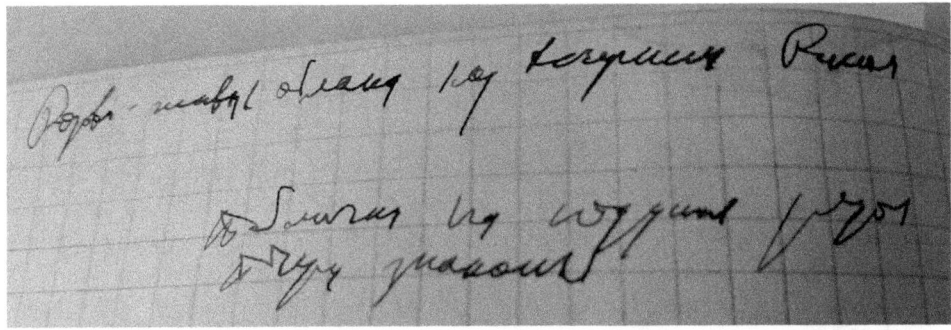

Fig. 3.1. 'Rosy-hued clouds', BT 137 (between 24 January and 17 April 1982).

Kinfiia's final state of peace.[47] This echoes the elemental calm which represents the apparent closure of Propertius and Cynthia's textual relationship near the end of Book III: 'after being shipwrecked in a very Aegean sea of passion […] my garlanded ship has reached harbour' (Prop. III.24.11–15, p. 303).

Conclusion

Specific influence from 38 separate Propertian elegies can be detected in *Kinfiia*.[48] The elegies Shvarts drew on most for her characterisation of Kinfiia are IV.7 and IV.8, each of which she references in four *Kinfiia* poems. Shvarts's repeated use of IV.7 and IV.8 is unsurprising, as these are the poems where Cynthia is most strongly characterised by Propertius, and where, almost uniquely in the *Elegies*, Cynthia is given direct speech. (See below for more discussion of Cynthia's voice.) Both the other elegies in which Cynthia speaks, I.3 and II.29, are referenced in multiple *Kinfiia* poems: thrice and twice, respectively. Of the other elegies that Shvarts references more than once, four focus on Cynthia, depicting her as fickle, wanton, violent, beautiful yet subject to age (II.5, 31/32, III.8, III.25); of the three that do not focus on Cynthia (III.14, IV.1, IV.6), one depicts active and unrestrained women, like Cynthia, and the other two deal with poetic practice, a topic of interest to the poets Shvarts and Kinfiia. While Propertius is undoubtedly the most important influence on *Kinfiia*, other Latin poets went into the mix too — which the following section will explore.

---

47 An early draft of *Kinfiia* R.10 shows that Shvarts wrote the pink clouds first; the distant military issues are present in a different form; and she makes a point of Propertsii not venturing out to sea. See the Appendix for a transcription and a translation.
48 I.1, 3, 8, 11, 16, 17; II.2, 5, 9, 12, 15, 16, 18, 22, 23, 25, 29, 31/32, 34 (see below); III.3, 8, 10, 12, 14, 17, 18, 19, 21, 23, 24, 25; IV.1, 2, 5, 6, 7, 8.

Dialogue with Catullus and Other Classical Writers

> Passer mortuus est
> The sparrow is dead
> Cat. III.3

Propertius is, in Panchenko's words, 'too rhetorical, and in places even insipid' to be *Kinfiia*'s sole classical influence. It is to Catullus that Panchenko attributes *Kinfiia*'s 'seething passion'.[49] And it is true that Catullus is foremost among *Kinfiia*'s non-Propertian classical influences — he is even named in the cycle — and his invective style is the source for a lot of Kinfiia's verbal bite. However, Catullus is not the only invective poet in *Kinfiia*'s literary 'genetics': the catty first-century epigrammatist Martial is arguably as influential on *Kinfiia* as Catullus, with his younger contemporary, the acerbic second-century satirist Juvenal (Decimus Iunius Iuvenalis), and the Augustan poet Horace (Quintus Horatius Flaccus) in his satirist guise bringing up the rear. Many of the realia of Roman life also come from these poets. The most famous Latin love poet is of course also represented in *Kinfiia*'s DNA: Ovid (Publius Ovidius Naso). The only female Latin love elegist, Sulpicia, is also present, although very little of her work survives for Shvarts to draw on. Much of *Kinfiia*'s metaphysics stems from the fourth-century BC Athenian philosopher Plato — *Kinfiia*'s only major Greek influence, and the only other author besides Propertius and Catullus named. Minor Greek influences are Euripides, Homer, and Sappho — if she is counted separately from Catullus's Sapphic imitations. This section will explore *Kinfiia*'s non-Propertian classical influences, poem by poem.

Book I

A prominent reference to Kinfiia's non-Propertian forebears comes in the first poem, 'K sluzhanke'. The reference bears implications for poetic speech — who, traditionally, has been allowed it, and who not — and ushers in Kinfiia's new rules about who may speak in her poetry.

> Все верещит попугай —
> Жалкого жалкий подарок,
> Задуши его быстро, рабыня.
> Тельце зеленое после в слезах поплывет,
> Буду тебя проклинать, но сейчас задуши поскорее.
>
> [The parrot keeps jabbering —
> Pitiful present of a pitiful man,
> Strangle him quickly, slave girl.
> The little green body will swim in tears after,
> I shall curse you, but now strangle him quick as you can.]

This reference is to two famous deaths of pet birds in Latin love poetry: Lesbia's sparrow and Corinna's parrot. Lesbia's sparrow has a short but glorious career, going from life to death in Catullus's second and third poems; Catullus depicts Lesbia playing with the sparrow in a sexualised manner, such that the bird comes to take

---

49   Panchenko, '"Kinfiia" Eleny Shvarts'.

the place of the poet-lover:

> Nor would he ever leave her lap
> But hopping around, this way, that way,
> Kept cheeping to his lady alone. (Cat. III.9–11, p. 5)

The sparrow has even been read as a metaphor for Catullus's penis.[50] Ovid likewise uses the speaking bird as a metaphor for the poet himself — his over-the-top eulogy for the parrot concludes with an epitaph 'spoken by' the parrot itself: 'YOU MAY JUDGE FROM MY VERY MONUMENT MY MISTRESS LOVED ME WELL. | I HAD A MOUTH WAS SKILLED IN SPEECH BEYOND A BIRD' (*Amores* II.6.61–62).[51] Kinfiia's ire is provoked when the parrot begins to speak — the reverse of Corinna's reaction to her parrot/poet — and she literally has it stifled. Kinfiia's silencing of the bird who in Latin love poetry represents the poet sends a powerful programmatic message: she will not allow herself to be ventriloquised or spoken over by Propertius or Catullus or any other (male, canonical) poet. Kinfiia's action also constitutes a rejection of the behaviour expected of the mistress in Latin love poetry. Catullus's poem on the death of Lesbia's sparrow ends 'my girl's | Eyelids are swollen red with crying' (III.17–18, p. 5). Shvarts gives a nod to this with 'The little green body will swim in tears after' — but it is she who orders its death.

The hellebore that Kinfiia requests in the first stanza of 1.1 was an ancient cure for madness — featuring as such in Horace *Satires* II.3.82 and *Epistles* II.2.137, and Martial IX.94 — perhaps a hint about Kinfiia's mental state!

The pouring rain that never disfigures Propertius's Rome is conspicuous in Martial's depictions of the reality of Roman life:

> The grapes are drenched, lashed by continual showers. Innkeeper, you cannot sell wine unwatered, even if you wished. (Mart. 1.56, p. 81)

> I sent your runner back to you at midday, Rufus, and I imagine he was wet through when he brought my verses, for the sky happened to be pouring with torrential rain. (Mart. III.100.1–3, p. 259)

Kinfiia's statement at the end of 1.1 that 'today no one [...] will leave the house' is evidently untrue; her ability to weather the storm indoors perhaps points to her high status and wealth.

Kinfiia's attack on her father in 1.2 is not quite unparalleled in Latin poetry, as Panchenko believes.[52] Horace gives two instances of parenticide: as an example of madness — 'When you strangle your wife and poison your mother, are you sound in head?' (*Satires* II.3.131–32, p. 165); and as a joke — 'Henceforth if anyone with unholy hand chokes the aged throat of [their parent], let [them] eat garlic, a plant more deadly than hemlock' (*Epodes* III.1–3, pp. 277–79). But Shvarts draws the gory

---

50 Arguments for and against given by Julia T. Dyson Hejduk, 'The Lesbia Poems', in *A Companion to Catullus*, ed. by Marilyn B. Skinner (Malden, MA: Blackwell, 2007), pp. 254–75 (p. 257).
51 Ovid, *Heroides; Amores*, ed. by G. P. Goold, trans. by Grant Showerman (Cambridge, MA; London: Harvard University Press, 1977), p. 403.
52 Panchenko, '"Kinfiia" Eleny Shvarts'. Panchenko brings Catullus's disrespect of his elders in poem V as a rare, slightly similar example.

details of the manner of Kinfiia's father's death from other Roman writers. First Kinfiia throws her father to moray eels to be eaten alive — a punishment used by Vedius Pollio, an equestrian and favourite of Augustus — which was cited as an example of unacceptable cruelty by Roman historians.[53] Then she imagines her father's death in the circus:

> лев в цирке
> Дожевывает его печень.
> [...]
> тигр вылизал даже пар от крови
>
> [a lion in the circus
> Chews on the last of his liver.
> [...]
> a tiger had licked up even the steam from his blood]

Martial has a whole book of epigrams celebrating the new Colosseum, in which lions (*Spectacles* 8, 12, 17, 21, 26, 32) and tigers (*Spectacles* 21) appear — but the death that most resembles Kinfiia's father's is inflicted by a bear: 'His lacerated limbs lived on, dripping gore, and in all his body, body there was none' (*Spectacles* 9).

Shvarts flaunts *Kinfiia*'s Catullan influence in 1.3 'K sluzhanke' [To a Slave Girl]. Kinfiia upbraids her slave girl for hurting her by stepping on her shadow, and threatens to 'Выдать замуж за кельтибера, | Что мочою себе зубы чистит' [Marry you off to a Celtiberian | Who cleans his teeth with urine]. This detail is taken from Catullus's invective poems XXXVII and XXXIX in which he attacks the Celtiberian Egnatius, who is trying to take his place in Lesbia's affections:

> A son of rabbit-ridden Celtiberia,
> Egnatius, whom a shady beard upgrades
> And teeth rubbed down with Iberian urine.
>   (Cat. XXXVII.18–20, p. 39)

> Because Egnatius has white shiny teeth
> He's always grinning.
> [...]
> But you're Celtiberian and in Celtiberia
> Everyone uses his own pee each morning
> For rubbing down his teeth and his red gums.
> So the more highly polished your teeth are
> The more the piddle you are proved to have drunk.
>   (Cat. XXXIX.1–21, p. 41)

Two lines later, Kinfiia says 'Катулла я твердила' [I was reciting Catullus] — implying that Kinfiia got the idea for the punishment from what she was reading. There are more metaliterary twists... Propertius says Catullus's Lesbia is the model for Cynthia's behaviour: 'Lesbia has already done all this before her with impunity: Lesbia's follower is surely less to blame' (Prop. II.32.45–46, p. 203). Ovid, too,

---

53   Pliny, *Natural History: Books 8-11*, trans. by H. Rackham (London: Heinemann, 1940), pp. 212–15 (IX.39); Lucius Annaeus Seneca, *Moral Essays*, trans. by John William Basore, 3 vols (London; Cambridge, MA: Heinemann, 1928), I, pp. 348–49, 408–09 (*De ira* III.40; *De clementia* I.18).

tells girls to learn how to behave by reading love poetry, including Propertius (*Ars Amatoria* III.333). Shvarts follows these precedents by having Kinfiia copy her behaviour from Catullus. The next poem but one begins with Propertius warning a rival: 'When alone, I am even jealous of my shadow, a thing without substance' (Prop. II.34.19, pp. 209–11). *Kinfiia* 1.3 echoes this treatment of the shadow as a semi-physical entity: 'тень моя ее дубленой кожи — | [...] болимей и нежней' [my shadow is more sensitive and tender — | [...] than her leathery hide]. At the end of this poem Propertius positions himself as a successor to Catullus: 'such themes the verse of wanton Catullus also sang, which made Lesbia better known than Helen herself [...] Yea, Cynthia glorified in the pages of Propertius shall live, if Fame consent to rank me with bards like these' (Prop. II.34.87–94, p. 217). So Shvarts's reference to Catullus in *Kinfiia* 1.3 encompasses references to Catullus by Propertius.

The shadow of Kinfiia's ringlet — which her slave girl 'к полу придавила | Своей ножищей' [ground into the floor | with [her] hoof], hurting Kinfiia and eliciting threats of punishment — is the descendant (or the shadow!) of two such ringlets in Martial and Juvenal:

> A single ringlet out of the whole circle of hair had gone amiss, fixed insecurely with an unsteady pin. Lalage punished this misdeed with the mirror in which she had seen it, and Plecusa fell smitten, victim of the cruel tresses. (Mart. II.66.1–4, pp. 171–73)

> unlucky Psecas will be arranging her hair with her own strands torn, with her shoulders and her breasts stripped bare. 'Why is this curl sticking up?' The bullhide strap is the immediate punishment for the wicked crime of the twisting ringlet. (Juv. VI.490–93, p. 281)

Both Martial and Juvenal refer back to Catullus's Lesbia and Propertius's Cynthia. Martial asks for a beloved like Lesbia or Cynthia to inspire his poetry (Mart. VIII.73), while Juvenal chooses Cynthia and Lesbia to begin his catalogue of bad women in satire VI: '[Chastity] was nothing like *you*, Cynthia, or *you* with your bright eyes marred by the death of your sparrow' (Juv. VI.7–8, p. 235). So they too, as well as the love poets, are useful models for Shvarts/Kinfiia.

In *Kinfiia* 1.3 Shvarts steps knowingly into the intertextual morass of Latin poetry. She shows Kinfiia learning elegiac modes of behaviour by reading Catullus, as Propertius, Ovid, Martial, and Juvenal all do — just as Shvarts herself learned to write as Kinfiia by reading Latin poetry.

1.4 'Kupidonu' is in Sapphics (fairly regular ones, but not in the usual 3-long-lines-1-short-line pattern), a metre Propertius, the poem's major reference, never used, but which Catullus used twice. This is the first of *Kinfiia*'s two poems in Sapphics, both of which use the famous love metre to voice anti-love sentiments. Shvarts's inspiration for her ironic usage of Sapphics is surely Catullus, who in poem XI uses Sapphics ironically, to send a rude message to Lesbia (who was named after Sappho) about her promiscuity:

> Farewell and long life with her adulterers,
> Three hundred together, whom hugging she holds,
> Loving none truly but again and again
> Rupturing all's groins.
>   (Cat. XI.17–20, p. 13)

Kinfiia's ironic Sapphics declare her freedom from love, with which Sappho's poetry is associated. Kinfiia's brusque tone, too, is similar to Catullus XI. Her statement that she has fallen out of love, yet is pained by this — 'Хоть и разлюбишь — проститься больно' [Though we fall out of love — parting is painful] — is close to the message of Catullus's final stanza:

> And let her not as before expect my love,
> Which by her fault has fallen like a flower
> On the meadow's margin after a passing
> Ploughshare has touched it.
>   (Cat. XI.21–24, p. 13)

Since her Kinfiia is also based on Lesbia, via this intertext Shvarts gives the other side of Catullus's monologue about Lesbia, as she has done with Propertius and Cynthia. Shvarts's graphic description of the physical pain of love also has much in common with Catullus's other Sapphic poem, LI, which adapts Sappho XXXI, listing the uncomfortable symptoms the poet experiences at the sight of their beloved. Kinfiia's mention of her throat, where Cupid has stubbornly leant, connects with Catullus's 'my tongue's paralysed' (Cat. LI.9, p. 51). The implication is that Kinfiia was enthralled like Catullus/Sappho, and likewise lost her (poetic) voice as a result. But in I.4 Kinfiia is healing and once more master of herself, saying to Cupid: 'больше мне не хозяин' [you're my master no more].

Kinfiia I.5 'Molodomu poetu' is an invective against a certain Septimus:

> Чего ты, Септим, пристал к Музе?
> Зря гнусавишь, зря ручонками машешь,
> Такт отбивая.
>
> [Why, Septimus, did you harass the Muse?
> In vain you elocute, in vain you flail your arms
> Beating out the time.]

Criticism of bad poets is a major theme of Roman invective poetry. Shvarts references Horace's disapproval of those who 'recite their writings in the middle of the Forum' (*Satires* I.4.74–75, p. 55), which he thinks is in bad taste, when Kinfiia threatens Septimus that 'на площади людной | Вселится в тебя громовой голос' [amidst a crowded square | A thunderous voice will possess you], forcing him to declare the foolishness of his recitations in the Forum, in an ironic reiteration of his former behaviour. Martial, too, has many epigrams on the theme (e.g. IV.41, IX.83, XII.63), and even backhandedly praises a bad poet for not making others listen to his work: 'Although you make two hundred verses every day, Varus, you never recite. You are a fool, and you are no fool' (Mart. VIII.20, p. 171). But the major inspiration of I.5 is Catullus's frequent castigation of bad poets.[54] Catullus reviles the 'curse of

---

54 While there is no Septimus in Catullus, there is a Septimius (XLV) — who is not, however, a poet, bad or otherwise.

our time, appalling poets' (Cat. XIV.23, p. 17). He muses on a clever man's lack of talent for poetry:

> Suffenus
> Is a charming person, witty and urbane;
> Besides, his verse production is enormous –
> [...]
> But when you read them, that nice urbane man
> Suffenus now seems a mere clodhopper
> (Cat. XXII.1–10, p. 23).

And he plans to burn

> Volusius' *Annals*, paper crap,
> [...]
> the worst poet's choicest
> Work.
> (Cat. XXXVI.1–7, p. 37)

Shvarts evokes Septimus's ill-judged attempts at poetry as physical harassment of the Muses: 'Не дергай Музу за подол больше' [Don't go tugging at the Muse's skirts any more], and the proclamation she threatens to force him to make emphasises this unwanted physical contact still further: 'Раз сдернул я туфлю с Музы, | Раз оцарапал я ей лодыжку' [Once I pulled the Muse's shoe off, | Once I scratched her ankle]. This physicality is surely drawn from Catullus's epigram in which a presumptuous poet tries to make contact with the Muses, who instead make rather more painful contact with him: 'Tool tries to scale the Mount of Pipla: | Muses with pitchforks throw him down' (Cat. CV, p. 141). Shvarts incorporates this literal superiority of the Muses to the poet, who touches — and by implication, can only reach — their skirt hems, shoes, and ankles; perhaps being struck down with pitchforks is the divine punishment Kinfiia urges him to avoid: 'Чтоб гнев богини мимо пронесся' [So the goddess's anger might pass over]. The connection between *Kinfiia* 1.5 and Catullus is underscored by 1.5's metre, which is mostly hendecasyllables, the metre of both the invective poems XIV and XXXVI.

1.6 'Klavdii' may have been inspired by Juvenal's account in satire VI about a woman leaving her husband and children for a gladiator:

> But what were the good looks and youthfulness that enthralled Eppia and set her on fire? What did she see in him to make her put up with being called a gladiator's groupie? After all, her darling Sergius had already started shaving his throat and with his gashed arm had hopes of retirement. Besides, his face was really disfigured: there was a furrow chafed by his helmet, an enormous lump right on his nose, and the nasty condition of a constantly weeping eye. But he was a gladiator. That's what makes them into Hyacinthuses. [...] It's the steel that they're in love with. (Juv. VI.103–12, p. 243)

Shvarts contradicts every element: Kinfiia's gladiator is good-looking while her lover is ugly, yet Kinfiia still prefers her lover; Kinfiia's gladiator's scars ennoble him rather than disfiguring him, and he is beautiful in his own right; his sword is part of what makes him a figure of fun for Kinfiia, rather than adding to his attraction. The only element not contradicted is that Kinfiia's gladiator, like Juvenal's, is young but starting to get too old for the arena, and thinking of retirement. When Kinfiia characterises her chance to have a fling with a younger man as 'Как сытый волк и на зиму овца' [Like a sated wolf wanting a sheep for the winter] she repeats a formula put by Horace into the mouth of a disgusting old woman trying to seduce him: 'You run away from me like a lamb frightened by fierce wolves' (*Epodes* XIII.25–26, p. 301). The reference to a poem where the horrors of old age are graphically explored underscores Kinfiia's fear of ageing.

Kinfiia's experience of not becoming a bacchante in 1.7 has much in common with Catullus's poem about Attis becoming a *gallus* (eunuch follower of the goddess Cybele). Kinfiia self-harms, like Attis.

Shvarts:

> все руки
> Расцарапаны — в крови до локтя...
> [...]
> На себя ты страсть обрушить можешь
>
> [my arms
> Are all scratched — bloodied up to the elbow...
> [...]
> On yourself you can unleash your passion]

Catullus:

> He tore off with a sharp flint the burden of his groin.
>   (Cat. LXIII.5, p. 75)

Kinfiia and Attis both want to join the bacchantes (or maenads), but are outsiders.

Shvarts:

> Как я вам завидую, вакханки,
> [...]
> Как-то раз в сторонке я стояла
>
> [How I envy you, bacchantes,
> [...]
> One time I stood on the sidelines]

Catullus:

> Where ivy-bearing Maenads violently toss their heads
> [...]
> Thither it is our duty to speed in leaping dance.'
> Soon as false female Attis had sung her companions this.
>   (Cat. LXIII.23–27, p. 77)

Kinfiia compares the bacchantes to wild mares, while Attis is compared to an 'untamed heifer' (Cat. LXIII.33, p. 77). Both Kinfiia and Attis discover their injuries once the madness has passed:

Shvarts:

> А домой пришла — смотрю — все руки
> Расцарапаны

>   [But when I get home — I see — my arms
>   Are all scratched]

Catullus:

>   So, after gentle rest-time, from frenzied madness free,
>   When Attis' self went over in thought what she had done
>   And in her mind saw clearly where, without what, she was.
>   (Cat. LXIII.44–46, p. 77)

Panchenko has identified the episode in which Kinfiia watches the bacchantes tear apart a live bull — 'Вы быка живого растерзали | И, давясь, его сжирали мясо' [You tore a live bull to pieces | And, jostling, gorged yourselves on his meat] — as stemming from Innokentii Annenskii's translation of Euripides' *Bacchae*, lines 743–46:

>   Свирепые быки [...]
>   теперь лежат,
>   Поверженные тьмою рук девичьих.
>   Быстрее кожу с мяса там сдирали[55]
>
>   [Ferocious bulls [...]
>   now lie,
>   Subjugated by a myriad of maidens' hands.
>   They stripped the skin from the meat there faster]

As Panchenko notes, Euripides' is the most vivid description of bacchantes in the classical tradition, so perhaps Shvarts was led to Annenskii's translation after finding only passing mentions of bacchantes in Propertius and Catullus.

The witchcraft threatened by Kinfiia in 1.8 may have been motivated by Horace's vivid depiction of witches in epodes V and XVII and satire 1.8, alongside Propertius's witches. Its title, 'K provintsialke', suggests the poem was influenced by Catullus XLIII, which insults a provincial girl:

>   Greetings, girl with no mini nose
>   Nor pretty foot nor dark eyes
>   Nor long fingers nor dry mouth
>   Nor altogether felicitous tongue,
>   Friend of the bankrupt from Formiae.
>   And does the Province call you pretty?
>   (Cat. XLIII.1–6, pp. 43–45)

The disfiguring diseases with which Kinfiia threatens to curse the provincial woman make her sexually repulsive:

>   Даже пьяный негр, матрос просоленный,
>   В долгой по любви стосковавшийся дороге,
>   Даже он в постель к тебе не ляжет.
>
>   [Even a drunk negro, a salty sailor,
>   Who all voyage long has thirsted for love,
>   Even he will not get into bed with you.]

---

55 Quoted in Panchenko, '"Kinfiia" Eleny Shvarts'.

This echoes Catullus LXIX, which informs Rufus that he cannot entice women to sleep with him because he is too smelly:

> You should not wonder, Rufus, why no woman
> Wants to lay her soft thigh under you
> [...]
> You feed a fierce goat down in Arm-Pit Valley.
>   (Cat. LXIX.1–6, p. 123)

Catullus mentions black-skinned people: 'I am none too keen to wish to please you, Caesar, | Nor to know if you're a white man or a black' (Cat. XCIII, p. 135);[56] while a black slave is a sex object in an epigram by Martial: 'Canius enjoys a sombre Ethiop' (Mart. VII.87.2, p. 143).[57] Kinfiia's additional threat to the provincial woman — 'залечит тебя твой хваленый | Врач-египтянин' [you will be physicked by your vaunted | Egyptian doctor] — chimes with Martial's low opinion of doctors — as quacks, torturers, and killers (e.g. I.47, X.77) — one held by most Romans about medics, who were predominantly foreign (usually Greek).[58]

Book II

Kinfiia II.1 is set inside the Esquiline gardens. Horace describes their transformation from paupers' burial ground: 'To-day one may live on a wholesome Esquiline, and stroll on the sunny Rampart where of late one sadly looked out on ground ghastly with bleaching bones' (*Satires* I.8.14–16, p. 97). Shvarts shows her awareness of the land's previous use, as the whole poem is about death. Horace goes on to present a scene of grotesque witchcraft that Shvarts could have transformed into *Kinfiia* II.1's more serious and mystical scene of Dionysus's rebirth.

II.3 centres on an image that stems from Plato. Kinfiia compares her friend's life 'в глуши' [in the backwoods], far from Rome, with her life in Rome, far from the rest of the universe. She writes:

> А далёко — в господской вилле
> Музыка, свет и пенье.
> Мы, как жертвенные ягнята,
> В щели видим отблеск и отзвук
> И дрожим, что вот рукой грубой
> Дверь откроется резко настежь...
>
> [But far off — in the masters' villa
> There is music, light, and song.
> Through a crack, like sacrificial lambs, we
> See the reflection and hear the echo,
> And tremble, lest of a sudden some rude hand
> Should brusquely throw the door wide open...]

In his Allegory of the Cave Plato writes:

---

56 While this is proverbial (Cat., p. 180), it still constitutes a reference to black people.
57 Alternatively, the 'Aethiope' may be a fish: Michael Hendry, 'Martial's Gloomy Ethiopian (7.87)', *Curculio*, 38 (2017), 1.
58 M. J. Mans, 'Humour, Health and Disease in Martial', *Akroterion*, 39 (1994), 105–20 (pp. 112–15).

'Imagine people as it were in an underground dwelling like a cave with a long wide entrance facing the light along the whole length of the cave. They have been there since childhood shackled by the legs and the neck, so that they remain in the same spot facing only forward, unable to turn their heads right round because of the chains. There is light from a fire burning from above a long way behind them, and between the fire and the prisoners there is a path leading upward across which you should imagine there is a low wall built, just as puppeteers have a screen in front of the audience above which they present their entertainments.'

[...]

'Now imagine people carrying props of all kinds along this wall above the top of it

[...]

'And what if the prison chamber were to throw back echoes from the wall in front whenever any of the passersby spoke; do you think they would think this was anything but the passing shadows speaking?'

[...]

'what people in this situation would consider the real world would be nothing other than the shadows of the objects making them.'

[...]

'Now think about setting them free [...] Whenever anyone was freed and suddenly made to stand up, look around, walk, and look up toward the light, it would be painful doing all this.' (*Republic* VII.514a–515d)[59]

Shvarts turns Plato's cave entrance into a crack — either in a door or in the sky; his prisoners into sacrificial lambs; and his puppeteers into revellers — either Roman nobles or gods. At the end she vividly imagines what would happen if the door (or sky) were opened, just as Plato vividly imagines the prisoners' feelings upon being forced out of their cave. All of Shvarts's changes give Plato's hypothetical situation a Christian, apocalyptic tinge, but confirm his point that our perception of reality is only partial.

In II.4 'Klavdii — posle poseshcheniia bol'noi babki' [To Claudia, after Visiting My Sick Granny] Kinfiia calls her aged relative a 'Жирно-сухим насекомым' [greasy, dry insect]. Martial has an invective epigram directed against an old woman who has 'the bosom of a grasshopper and the leg and complexion of an ant' (Mart. III.93, p. 253). The two poems are mostly at odds — Shvarts's revulsion is mixed with sadness and love, while Martial's revulsion is mixed with mockery and cruelty — but Shvarts may have got her inspiration from him. The poem's addressee, Claudia — also the addressee of 1.6 — shares her name with the addressee(s)/protagonist(s) of three of Martial's epigrams (IV.13, VII.60, XI.53).

Kinfiia II.5 is a poem entirely about poetry, which never once alludes directly to poetry. It figures the process of writing poetry and presenting it to readers as gathering multicoloured stones and setting them out in a pub. The entire poem is in very correct dactylic hexameter and pentameter lines, which alternate in groups of three, unlike — yet very like — elegy's couplets. Martial has an epigram in which he compares precious stones to poetry:

---

59   Plato, *Republic*, trans. by Jeffrey Henderson, 2 vols (Cambridge, MA: Harvard University Press, 2013), II, pp. 107–11.

> My friend Stella, Severus, turns sardonyxes, emeralds, diamonds, jaspers on a single finger joint. You will find many gems on his fingers, more in his poetry; hence, methinks, is his hand adorned. (Mart. v.11, pp. 337–39)

The connection with Martial is strengthened by the fact that Martial's epigram is also in elegiacs, and that Shvarts's poem is also an epigram. There is an interesting coincidence between 11.5 and Posidippus's collection of epigrams *Lithika* [*On Stones*]. Each epigram in *Lithika* is an *ecphrasis* [description of a visual artwork] of a rock, which can also be read metapoetically as a metaphor for a poem.[60] However, *Lithika* was published for the first time in modernity in 2001, so could not have been a source for *Kinfiia*.[61]

11.6 shows Kinfiia hosting dinner parties for her clients, at which she throws soup over one boy, throws a statue at a client, and attacks her guests with a weapon. Client service — and the disappointing dinner parties that tended to go with it — is the subject matter of many of Martial's epigrams, although such a scenario never occurs. It does occur, however, in Juvenal, where the poor wine served by the patron to his clients starts a food- and crockery-fight (Juv. v.24–29).

The fish caught by fishermen in 11.7 'Na pliazhe v Baii' may have been influenced by Martial's epigram warning a fisherman not to catch Baiae's sacred fish (IV.30).

In both its philosophical discussion of the nature of the soul and its dialogic structure *Kinfiia* 11.8 resembles a Platonic dialogue. Indeed, in earlier *samizdat* publications it was titled 'Dialog s Grekom' [Dialogue with a Greek].[62] At the beginning of the poem Kinfiia tells the Greek that she bought him so he 'Помогал мне понимать Платона' [Would help me to understand Plato], flagging up the poem's major reference. Although 11.8 pastiches a Socratic dialogue, it does not follow the Socratic method of facilitating the emergence of knowledge, since Kinfiia's slave attempts to impart knowledge to her.[63] Possible Platonic sources for 11.8's discussion of the shifting colours of Kinfiia's soul include Plato's dialogues about the soul, *Phaedo*, *Phaedrus* 245c–249d, and *Republic*, and his discourse on colours in *Timaeus* 67c–68d — although none of Plato's theories about souls or colours appear to have been specifically incorporated by Shvarts; the Platonic influence is more general. Slaves are rare interlocutors in Plato; an exception is *Meno*, in which a slave boy has a speaking role (82b–85b). Horace's satire 11.7 is a dialogue with a slave; the slave even reminds Horace how much he cost him (11.7.43), the question Kinfiia asks her slave in the opening line. But Horace's slave is given far more opportunity to talk than Kinfiia's slave, and far more licence, since it is Saturnalia, when masters and slaves would switch roles. Finally, Kinfiia's uncelebratory attitude to her birthday in 11.8, 'Razgovor', may echo Sulpicia's similar subversion of the elegiac convention

---

60   David Schur, 'A Garland of Stones: Hellenistic *Lithika* as Reflections on Poetic Transformation', in *Labored in Papyrus Leaves: Perspectives on an Epigram Collection Attributed to Posidippus (p. Mil Vogl. Viii 309)*, ed. by Benjamin Acosta-Hughes, Manuel Baumbach, and Elizabeth Kosmetatou (Washington, D.C.: Center for Hellenic Studies, 2004), pp. 118–22.
61   Acosta-Hughes, Baumbach, and Kosmetatou, 'Introduction', in *Labored in Papyrus Leaves*, pp. 1–7 (p. 2).
62   Elena Shvarts, 'Poemy' (Bremen), p. 60, Forschungsstelle Osteuropa, FSO 01–265 Pazuchin K35.
63   I am indebted to Elena Cagnoli Fiecconi for this observation, among others.

of the *genethliacon*, as she "de'-celebrates her own birthday':[64] 'My hated birthday is come, to be passed in sorrow and vexation | Off in the country — and without my Cerinthus' (Sulpicia II.1–2).[65]

Razroznennoe [Oddments]

R.1 views Kinfiia's former selves as if they were ghosts, and her present self as if a reincarnation of her past selves:

> В хижину вошла и огляделась:
> Будто привиденья увидала –
> В том углу однажды я рыдала,
> В том молилась...
> [...]
> Но душа бы искрой убегала
> От одной — в другую — до живущей,
> До меня
>
> [I walked into the hut and looked about me:
> It seemed I was seeing ghosts —
> In that corner I sobbed one time,
> In that one I prayed...
> [...]
> But the soul, flying spark-like, would flee
> From one — to another — until it found life,
> Until [...] me]

This is an unusual take on the Pythagorean concept of metempsychosis, or transmigration of souls, something Shvarts wrote about in her story *Vzryvy i gomunkuly* [*Explosions and Homunculi*] (1979, IV.32–64, p. 51). Metempsychosis is articulated in a form closest to *Kinfiia* R.1 by Ovid:

> why do you dread the Styx, the shades and empty names [...]? [...] Our souls are deathless, and ever, when they have left their former seat, do they live in new abodes and dwell in the bodies that have received them. [...] The spirit wanders, comes now here, now there, and occupies whatever frame it pleases. (*Met.* xv.154–59)[66]

R.1 ends with 'город после изверженья | Равнодушно-дикого вулкана' [a city after the eruption | Of an indifferent and savage volcano]. Martial deals with the AD 79 eruption of Vesuvius and its destruction of Pompeii and Herculaneum: 'This is Vesuvius [...] This was Venus' dwelling, [...] this spot the name of Hercules made famous. All lies sunk in flames and drear ashes' (IV.44. 1–7, p. 293).

R.3 sees Kinfiia going to court with a neighbour for a piece of land. Martial has many epigrams in which he or others go to court; in one he sues his neighbour

---

64 Lyne, p. 354.
65 Albius Tibullus, Lygdamus, and Sulpicia, *The Complete Poems of Tibullus*, trans. by Rodney G. Dennis and Michael C. J. Putnam (Berkeley; Los Angeles; London: University of California Press, 2012), p. 123.
66 Ovid, *Metamorphoses*, trans. by Frank Justus Miller, 2 vols (Cambridge, MA: Harvard University Press, 1977), II, pp. 375–77.

for stealing his goats (vi.19). Juvenal vituperates the greed for more land: 'You like extending your boundaries, and the neighbouring cornfield looks bigger and better. This too you buy up, along with the vineyards and the hill pale with a mass of olive trees' (xiv.142–44, p. 469). Kinfiia suddenly stops wanting the land, and wants something else; the poem turns into a discourse on whimfulness. Horace attacks the whimfulness of modern Romans in epistle 1.1.82–105, and, in assessing it as a form of madness, diagnoses Kinfiia's malaise: 'when my judgement is at strife with itself scorns what it craved, asks again for what it lately cast aside' (1.1.97–98, p. 259). *Kinfiia* R.3 concludes by comparing whims to jockey and horses, and the *meta* [turning-post] to the end of the race of life. Memorialising a dead charioteer, Martial plays upon the hackneyed Roman metaphor: 'So soon you yoke black horses. The goal [*meta*], ever quickly gained by your hastening car — your life's goal too' (x.50.6–8, p. 365).

R.4 'K Morfeiu' is in hendecasyllables, a metre characteristic of Catullus (and when she noticeably breaks metre in the penultimate line, it is for effect: Kinfiia wilfully staying awake past bedtime).

The apocalyptic flood of R.5, when 'Затопило Рим и мир' [Drowned is Rome and the Globe], recalls Jupiter's flooding of the world in Ovid *Metamorphoses* 1. Shvarts's use of the significant and commonly used Russian palindrome 'рим и мир' [Rome and the globe] allows her to extend the flood of Rome to the whole world very easily. Kinfiia's characterisation of herself as 'птицерыбой' [a birdfish] flying underwater is reminiscent of Ovid's list of contradictory objects in the water during Jupiter's flood, particularly 'fish caught in the elm-tree's top' and 'dolphins [...] brushing against the high branches' (*Met.* 1.296, 302–03).[67] Kinfiia's witchcraft is apparently the cause of the flood; the focus on the moon in the last line is reminiscent of the connection which Horace, as well as Propertius, makes between witches and the moon (*Epodes* xvii.78, *Satires* 1.8.21, 35).

R.6, which takes the story of Pasiphaë as its starting point, draws not only on Propertius, but also on Ovid, who treats the story of Pasiphaë in far greater depth. In *Ars Amatoria* 1.289–326 Ovid uses Pasiphaë to illustrate the same point as Propertius, which *Kinfiia* R.6 debates, that women are as lustful and deceitful as men. Ovid emphasises, as Propertius does not, Pasiphaë's hope to attract the bull with her beauty: 'What gain to thee, Pasiphaë, to wear thy purple gowns? that lover of thine recks not of any splendour. [...] Nay, believe thy mirror when it tells thee thou art no heifer' (*Ars Am.* 1.303–07).[68] Shvarts echoes Ovid's Pasiphaë's vanity with the pun on 'телка' [heifer/attractive woman] and the fact that the cow costume is made of leather rather than wood:

> телки
> Сделай образ и недавней укрой
> Содранной шкурой

---

67 Ibid., I, p. 23.
68 Ovid, *The Art of Love, and Other Poems*, ed. by G. P. Goold, trans. by J. H. Mozley (Cambridge, MA; London: Harvard University Press, 2004), pp. 33–35.

[make me a heifer
Outfit, from a recent hide]

Most tellingly, Ovid precedes his Pasiphaë story by promising to tell men — who are the addressees of *Ars Amatoria* I and II — how to catch women, and writes: 'all women can be caught; spread but your nets and you will catch them' (*Ars Am.* 1.269–70, p. 31). And he follows the Pasiphaë story with similar advice to Propertius's — only without the bribery — to 'know the handmaid of the woman you would win' and perhaps even 'seduce the maid herself' (*Ars Am.* 1.351, 375, pp. 37, 39). This is like Kinfiia's lover's tactics in R.6:

кто служанок подкупит
Всех до единой,

Кто, пути к тебе торя, — с подругой твоею
Шашни затеет — чтобы ты ревновала,
Чтобы ты вернее попалась
Ловцу в сети

[He who [...] bribes your slave girls,
Every last one,

He who, beating a path to you, contrives a
Dalliance with your friend, so you'll be jealous,
So that you fall all the more surely into
The hunter's net]

Shvarts, then, combined Ovid's *Ars Amatoria* with Propertius III.19 and II.23 in writing *Kinfiia* R.6.

R.6 is in clearly demarcated (if somewhat irregular) Sapphic stanzas. As with 1.4, Shvarts is playing with the generic expectations raised by the Sapphic metre: she writes a non-love poem in an amatory metre that draws attention to the incongruity of the content. This tactic is the same as the tactic used by Catullus in poem XI, where his Sapphics are an ironic commentary on Lesbia's promiscuity; Shvarts's Sapphics are an ironic commentary on the deviousness of lovers. The poem is like its duplicitous occupants — housed within a form that conceals its intent and belies its nature.

The name of Kinfiia's unloved soldier lover in R.7, 'Diomid' [Diomedes], must refer to the Homeric hero Diomedes, one of the most ferocious Greek warriors in the *Iliad*, and the rival lover in Chaucer/Shakespeare's *Troilus and Cressida*.

The slave whom Kinfiia orders to throw her cats out of the house in R.8 is named Priscus, a name that Martial uses frequently. A gladiator called Priscus is given his wooden sword (honourable discharge; freedom) from the arena in *Spectacles* 31, chiming to some extent with Shvarts's description of Kinfiia's Priscus as 'старый воин' [old campaigner]. The name is also chosen for its Latin meaning ('former', 'ancient', 'old-fashioned') and for its Russian associations with jumping or rushing (*priskok*, jump; *priskakat'*, to come galloping) — suggesting how the aged Priscus will 'jump' to Kinfiia's orders.

In R.9 Kinfiia mentions poultry being sent to eat on festival days; Martial describes this Roman custom in epigrams IX.54–55.

The luxury goods that Propertsii's writing tablets smell of in R.10 — oysters, boar, wine, and perfume — are all found in Martial's epigram on a man with an expensively fed fever: 'It dines on mushrooms, oysters, udder, boar. It often gets drunk on Setine, often on Falernian, and drinks Caecuban only through snow water. It reclines wreathed in roses and black with pomade' (XII.17.4–7, p. 103). Martial also has an epigram about a woman who loves her pearls more than anything (VIII.81), making pearls an apt consolation for Kinfiia after being dumped.

Conclusion

Despite the cycle's deep indebtedness to Propertius, *Kinfiia* has more of a Catullan than a Propertian tone, due to its realism, its physicality, which is more often violent or unpleasant than erotic (something not only Catullan but also typically Shvartsian), its frequent use of invective, and its mix of metres. Catullus is also named, as we have seen, in such a way as to acknowledge him as a vital poetic influence on Kinfiia/Shvarts. Yet for sheer number and extent of *Kinfiia* poems where I have detected a particular poet's influence, Catullus is put in the shade by Martial: Catullus has eight poems,[69] nearly all in Book I, whereas Martial has thirteen,[70] spread through all three books. Martial even overtakes Propertius as an influence in the least Propertian of the three books, Book II. Unsurprisingly, this metaphysical book is the one in which Plato appears.[71] Ovidian influence is present in the first and third books,[72] but, oddly, more from Ovid's hexameter works (epic and didactic) than his love elegy. Horatian influence appears in all three books, but only from his satirical writings — the *Odes* will not come into their own until *Homo Musagetes*.[73] A little Juvenalian influence is present in all three books.[74] Sulpician influence is only found in Book II (for more on Sulpicia, see below).[75]

Kinfiia's allusivity is fundamental to its credentials as a work of Roman poetry. In Latin love elegy each successive poet displays their debt to their predecessors through imitation and innovation. The first Latin love elegist[76] Catullus pays homage mostly to Greek influences: Callimachus, from whom stems his polished, nugatory aesthetic; and Sappho, whom he famously adapts in LI (and probably XI). Sulpicia, the next, apparently refers to both Catullus and Callimachus.[77] Propertius references, directly and indirectly, Catullus, Gallus (credited as the first love elegist, although only a few lines of his survive), Sulpicia,[78] Callimachus, and even Horace.[79] Ovid, belated to love elegy, draws upon and subverts all his predecessors.

69 Catullus: *Kinfiia* I.1, 3, 4, 5, 7, 8; R.4, 6.
70 Martial: *Kinfiia* I.1, 2, 3, 5, 8; II.4, 5, 7; R.1, 3, 8, 9, 10.
71 Plato: *Kinfiia* II.3, 8.
72 Ovid: *Kinfiia* I.1, 3; R.1, 5, 6.
73 Horace: *Kinfiia* I.1, 2, 5, 6, 8; II.1, 8; R.3, 5.
74 Juvenal: *Kinfiia* I.3, 6; II.6; R.3.
75 Sulpicia: *Kinfiia* II.8.
76 Though neither exclusively elegist nor love poet.
77 Carol U. Merriam, 'Sulpicia and the Art of Literary Allusion: [Tibullus] 3.13', in *Women Poets in Ancient Greece and Rome*, ed. by Ellen Greene (Norman: University of Oklahoma Press, 2005), p. 161.
78 Lyne, p. 350.
79 Keith, p. 65.

Shvarts's appropriation of — and departure from — a panoply of Roman poets heightens the authenticity of Kinfiia's poetry.

A Woman's Voice

> texisse pudori
> quam nudasse alicui sit mihi fama magis.
> to have covered it up, rather than laid it bare
> to all and sundry, would be a reputation more to my shame.
> Sulp. 1.1.1–2

In the Contents of her 1978 *samizdat* collection *Orchestra* Shvarts compares its poems to parts of the orchestra. Unsurprisingly, *Kinfiia* is 'голос' [voice].[80] This section explores how Shvarts's assertion of Kinfiia's voice interacts with literary tradition, which denies women a voice of their own (especially a permanent, written voice), and with feminist literary counter-tradition, which combats that denial.

Just a scripta puella*?*

The double paradox with which Shvarts opens *Kinfiia* — translating lost poetry that never existed — exposes a fundamental void at the heart of Latin love elegy: the woman's voice. Elegiac women, although fundamental to the poetry written about them by men, are 'silenced'; Barbara K. Gold gives a list of the many techniques through which elegiac women (amongst others) are silenced, so as to be 'deprived of any official means of expression, excluded from male constructions of meaning and experience, and [...] made to serve as signs or vehicles of the discourse in which they are inscribed'.[81]

In the *Elegies* Propertius as good as tells his reader that Cynthia's actions and words are not her own: she is merely a 'scripta puella' [written girl] (II.10.8), created and manipulated by the poet. Moreover, while the *Monobiblos* [first book] gives a fairly realistic portrayal of Cynthia, from the beginning of Book II Propertius makes it clear that Cynthia was only ever a literary construct,[82] and she is gradually displaced from the centre of his poetry through Books II and III. As Maria Wyke concludes, Cynthia's

> name, physical features, and psychological characteristics shaped a woman who should not be read as external to the elegiac text, but as its embodiment. Even Cynthia's apparently rebellious and uncontrollable attributes reveal her to be a written woman (a *scripta puella*, 2.10.8). She is the subject-matter of a Callimachean poetic practice, her author's creation, and a commodity of exchange between the Augustan elegist and the literary market-place.[83]

---

80 Elena Shvarts, *Orchestra* (Moscow/St Petersburg, 1978), p. 87, ESHA M.
81 Barbara K. Gold, 'The Natural and Unnatural Silence of Women in the Elegies of Propertius', *Antichthon*, 41 (2007), 54–72 (p. 57).
82 Wyke, 'Written Women', pp. 47–48.
83 Maria Wyke, *The Roman Mistress: Ancient and Modern Representations* (Oxford: Oxford University Press, 2002), p. 160.

Even Cynthia's learnedness (see above), which motivated Shvarts's adoption of Cynthia as a persona, is intended to reflect upon the attributes of Propertius's writing: 'The *docta puella* operates not as a potential judge or rival in the field of poetic composition but as the embodiment of her author's learned subject-matter.'[84] So why does Shvarts choose such an unreal, contingent, two-dimensional figure as her Roman persona? One answer is that Shvarts wanted to lift the two-dimensional Cynthia into three dimensions as Kinfiia. Another answer is that Cynthia is not entirely two-dimensional, after all.

Unlike other Latin love poets (with the exception of Ovid in the *Heroides*), Propertius does convey at least the illusion of a female voice. Cynthia is given speech, at length, in four poems: 1.3, where she wakes up and berates Propertius for staying out all night, shattering his prior representation of her as a mythical heroine; II.29, where she wakes up and berates Propertius for spying on her; IV.7, where her ghost chastises Propertius for his faithlessness after her death, and gives instructions about the treatment of her slaves and her grave; and IV.8, where she sets out her terms for forgiving Propertius, having caught him *in flagrante* with two other women. The speech assigned to Cynthia in IV.7 and IV.8 is part of Book IV's turn away from the hegemony of the male elegiac lover, and towards other narrative voices, including various women.[85] And the fact that Propertius gives Cynthia speech as early as 1.3 shows a sustained 'fascination with feminine subjectivity'.[86] Although these instances of Cynthia speaking are few, far between, and not straightforward, they nevertheless constitute a 'space' for marginal voices. Gold sees such 'space' as particular to elegy, characterised by

> an uneasiness in the representation of gender for both the author and reader, where the language seems to have more potentiality to be interpreted from many different perspectives, where the marginalized characters seem to be trying to 'speak', and where there are border challengings (voices speaking against the text).[87]

Cynthia has not only speech, but even elegiac writing. She dictates a two-line elegiac epitaph for Propertius to have inscribed on her grave (similar to the parrot's self-composed epitaph in Ovid's *Amores* II.6): 'HERE IN TIBUR'S SOIL LIES GOLDEN CYNTHIA: | FRESH GLORY, ANIO, IS ADDED TO THY BANKS' (IV.7.85–86, p. 363). As Barbara Flaschenriem notes, Cynthia's composition of her own memorial 'points to the difference between the poet's representations of the female and the stories that she herself might wish to tell'.[88] It is this implied 'difference' from the man's writing, this elegiac 'space' for the woman's perspective, which Shvarts exploits to write as Kinfiia.

---

84 Ibid., pp. 171–72.
85 Ibid., p. 102.
86 Flaschenriem, p. 49.
87 Gold, '"But Ariadne Was Never There"', in *Feminist Theory and the Classics*, ed. by Rabinowitz and Richlin, p. 84.
88 Flaschenriem, p. 63.

The missing Sulpicia?

Yet as my analysis of *Kinfiia*'s classical intertexts (above) shows, Shvarts makes little apparent use of the only real female voice from Latin love elegy, Sulpicia.[89] Sulpicia actually did what Shvarts's Kinfiia purports to do:

> a *puella*, rather than being silenced, actively speaks her own desire and, rather than being written, writes herself into Augustan love poetry. The female narrator [...] appropriates many of the discursive strategies employed by the male *ego* in the poems of Propertius, Tibullus, and Ovid.[90]

Sulpicia's absence may be because Shvarts had not read Sulpicia, or because there is so little of Sulpicia's poetry extant (and what remains is subsumed into the *Corpus Tibullianum*). Or it may be because Sulpicia presents herself as independent-minded whilst in a position of dependence, and not as an elegiac *domina* [mistress], whose extremes of behaviour are so evident in Kinfiia:

> Sulpicia is not represented in any of these poems as an abjectly lovelorn damsel [...] for a man, taking up a position of abjection (however sincerely) is not to lose his social status and dignity. Sulpicia insists on her control over the relationship, where her male counterparts insist on their lack of it. She is thus not imitating Tibullus or Propertius, and she is most certainly not playing at being Cynthia or Delia, since she makes no claim to be either sexually libertarian or even socially independent.[91]

For example, in Sulpicia's second poem she complains that her uncle and guardian Messalla is taking her to the country against her wishes; in the following poem she expresses relief that he has relented and allowed her to stay in the city. She has little influence over either decision.

But if not an intertext, Sulpicia may be a model — or a counter-model — for Kinfiia. In the second poem Kinfiia stages a series of violent murders of her father, which are only revealed to be imaginary towards the end — even up to the penultimate word, 'не' [not], Kinfiia's father appears to be in real danger. And before she begins her attacks, Kinfiia ensures that the reader is in no doubt as to his identity — writing the word 'father' three times in different forms in the first stanza. Kinfiia's imagined assaults on her father, a figure who in Roman society was the ultimate authority in the life of an unmarried woman, may be a reaction against the position of dependency shown by Sulpicia: Kinfiia literally attacks the patriarchy.

Subverting elegy's gender subversion

The sort of violent cruelty Kinfiia imagines in 1.2 is unusually masculine, and entirely unlike Cynthia's typical cruelties. The violence of 1.2 is part of a triad of violent poems that open the collection, sitting between 1.1 in which Kinfiia orders her parrot strangled, and 1.3 in which Kinfiia persecutes her slave girl over a trivial

---

89 There is one possible Sulpician intertext in *Kinfiia* 11.8.
90 Wyke, *The Roman Mistress*, pp. 163–64.
91 Stevenson, p. 41.

offence.[92] Shvarts's opening display of Kinfiia's propensity for violence echoes the abnormal and unstable power dynamics that are central to Latin love elegy. Elegy's fundamental conceit is a subversion of traditional Roman gender roles: the male poet is enslaved to his *domina*.[93] This is a particularly transgressive situation for a society in which sex was seen as a hierarchical, gendered act: of masculine, dominant penetrator vs feminine, submissive penetrated.[94] According to Gold, in the *Elegies*

> Propertius [...] put[s] himself into play as the feminine and himself fill[s] the space that has been created in the text for 'woman'. Propertius removes from Cynthia traits that would have been traditionally ascribed to females such as devotion, submissiveness, loyalty, subservience, passivity, and procreativity, and he appropriates them for himself. [...] Cynthia, on the other hand, has attributes that are a mimesis of the values recognized in the classical tradition by and for the male: she is demanding, faithless, hard-hearted, domineering, self-absorbed, and interested in competition and rivalry.[95]

Wyke sees the gender subversion of the characters reflected within the metapoetics of Propertius's *Elegies*:

> Propertian elegy [...] is engendered as masculine in its discursive mastery over the female object of its erotics and poetics, but engenders itself as effeminate in its association with softness, submissiveness, and impotence, and as feminine especially in its self-critique and its interrogation of Roman gender and sexuality.[96]

But *Kinfiia* even upsets the gender balance of Latin elegy. Whereas traditionally the mistress is written by the apparently servile male poet, who therefore ultimately controls her actions and voice, Kinfiia, as the putative poet, takes back that control. Her freedom is even greater than that of Propertius, as she is both poet and *domina*.

Kinfiia's dual role from Latin love elegy is behind the opening poems' contradictory depiction of Kinfiia as both powerful and vulnerable, hard and soft. The first four poems of *Kinfiia* Book 1 can thus be seen as programmatic poems establishing Kinfiia's position relative to the gender play of Propertius. The last in this series of programmatic poems, 1.4 'Kupidonu', demonstrates Kinfiia's transcendence of elegy's gender roles: Kinfiia informs Cupid that he is no longer her master, and contemptuously dismisses him at the end. Kinfiia's refusal to participate in elegiac love slavery [*servitium amoris*] is in stark contrast with Propertius's assessment of his servitude to Cupid in the opening of Book 1:

> Cynthia first with her eyes ensnared me, poor wretch, that had previously been untouched by desire. It was then that Love made me lower my looks of

---

92 However, it should be noted that the reader does not see Kinfiia's threats of violence carried out, and in each case Kinfiia simultaneously presents herself as in some way vulnerable: grief-ridden (1.1), merciful (1.2), and sensitive (1.3).
93 Wyke, *The Roman Mistress*, pp. 32–45.
94 Ibid., p. 166.
95 Gold, '"But Ariadne Was Never There"', in *Feminist Theory and the Classics*, ed. by Rabinowitz and Richlin, pp. 91–92.
96 Wyke, *The Roman Mistress*, p. 189.

stubborn pride and trod my head beneath his feet, until the villain taught me to shun decent girls and to lead the life of a ne'er-do-well. (1.1.1–6, p. 39)

By ridding herself of the tyranny of love, the chain that binds the male Roman poets to their mistresses, Kinfiia prevails in this power dynamic as well. Thus she is in a dominant position in all three major power battles in Latin love elegy: between man and woman; beloved (mistress) and lover (slave); and writer and subject.

Textual bonding

Intertextuality establishes a bond between the later author and the author whom they cite, especially when the citation is overt. This kind of 'textual bonding' is usually conducted between men, due to the overwhelming maleness of the literary canon, especially from antiquity; yet women, too, have 'a small and precious group of auctrices' whom they can cite, and who also go all the way back to antiquity.[97] One of the earliest instances of textual bonding between women is found in the work of Louise Labé, who invokes Sappho in her *Elegy* 1 (1555): 'The lyre he gave me once chanted the verse of love on Lesbos, in the olden times; now, in the same way, it will sing of mine.'[98] Labé assumes 'expressive power through the agency of her female predecessor'; other female writers since the Renaissance have followed suit.[99]

A related kind of textual bonding is that between female writers and mythical women, whose untold/male-lensed stories they intuit/retell from a female perspective. The first female writer to do this (as far as we know) is Sappho, who in fragment XVI relates Helen's elopement with Paris sympathetically, unlike the theme's treatment in other (male-authored) classical literature. Feminist retellings of the lives of fictional classical women have proliferated in the twentieth and twenty-first centuries, with a veritable glut in the past few years, apparently tracking feminism's resurgences in society. I can list the following anglophone feminist retellings of classical stories in poetry: Laura Riding, 'Poems of Mythical Occasion' in *Collected Poems* (1938);[100] H. D., *Helen in Egypt* (1961);[101] Adrienne Rich, *Snapshots of a Daughter-in Law* (1963);[102] Margaret Atwood, *Circe/Mud*

---

97 Stevenson, p. 23.
98 Annie Finch, in Louise Labé, *Complete Poetry and Prose: A Bilingual Edition*, ed. by Deborah Lesko Baker, trans. by Annie Finch (Chicago: University of Chicago Press, 2006), p. 153.
99 Deborah Lesko Baker, in Labé, pp. 134, 236 n. 3.
100 Riding has six short classical retellings here: 'Chloe Or...' (probably pairing the Chloe of *Daphnis and Chloe* with the biblical Lilith as modern women), 'Lucrece and Nara' (probably about Lucretia), 'Goat and Amalthea', 'As Well as Any Other' (featuring Erato), and the pair of poems about Helen of Troy, 'Helen's Burning' (which casts Riding as Cassandra) and 'Helen's Faces'.
101 As well as the epic poem *Helen in Egypt*, H.D. has seven poems/cycles that read as feminist retellings of classical myth (among many classically receptive poems) in *Collected Poems 1912–1944*: *Eurydice* (1917), 'Orion Dead' (spoken by Artemis, 1914), *Demeter* (1921), 'She Contrasts with Herself Hippolyta' and 'She Rebukes Hippolyta' (1921), 'At Ithaca' (written from the perspective of Penelope, 1924), and *Calypso* (1938).
102 Rich has five short classical retellings: the titular cycle, which contains two (Catullus/Sappho, and Corinna: see below), 'Euryclea's Tale' (1958), 'Antinoüs: The Diaries' (1959), and 'Always the Same' (1962).

(1974);[103] Judith Kazantzis, *The Wicked Queen* (1980);[104] Michelene Wandor, *Gardens of Eden* (1984);[105] Carol Ann Duffy, *The World's Wife* (1999);[106] Myra Schneider, 'Eurydice's Version' (2008).[107] To these I can add the following anglophone feminist retellings of classical stories in novels: Riding, *A Trojan Ending* (1937); Atwood, *The Penelopiad* (2005); Ursula Le Guin, *Lavinia* (2008); Emily Hauser, *For the Most Beautiful* (2016), *For the Winner* (2018), and *For the Immortal* (2019); Natalie Haynes, *The Children of Jocasta* (2017) and *A Thousand Ships* (2019); Pat Barker, *The Silence of the Girls* (2018); Madeline Miller, *Circe* (2018).[108] It is noticeable that among a slew of feminist Helens, Eurydices, Circes, Demeters, Penelopes, etc., Shvarts is alone in retelling the story of Cynthia — if not quite alone in recovering the voice of a classical female writer. It is also noticeable that Shvarts was ahead of the curve with *Kinfiia* (1974 onwards). But it is a work written in the same year as the first book of *Kinfiia* that is closest to *Kinfiia* in its conception: Atwood's twenty-four-poem cycle *Circe/Mud*, which does not centre on the known events of Circe's story but departs from Homer to give Circe her own voice. Yet it should also be noted that, unlike Atwood and most of the other authors listed above, Shvarts did not set out to create a feminist retelling — although she has undoubtedly created one — since she was in no way politically feminist.

Shvarts's Kinfiia sits midway between these two strains of classical textual bonding: she is neither real writer nor mythical woman, but in between. It is vital to Shvarts that Cynthia be a poet; yet rather than choosing a real classical female poet, such as Sappho or Sulpicia, Shvarts has (mostly) invented one. This is perhaps because both these real poets still have a voice through their extant poems; neither Sappho nor Sulpicia needs to be recovered or 'translated'. Whereas the works of the male Latin love poets are full of unheard, implied, and ventriloquised female voices, such that — in Flaschenriem's words — elegy 'often gives the impression of presenting only one side of a provocative dialogue'.[109]

To conclude this section I will discuss three interventions into elegy's 'provocative dialogue' that may have directly influenced Shvarts's choice to textually bond with Cynthia.

The first is a counter-influence rather than an influence: Iosif Brodskii's 'Anno Domini' (1968).[110] Brodskii wrote the poem six years before Shvarts began *Kinfiia*,

---

103 As well as the cycle *Circe/Mud*, Atwood also has one short classical retelling: 'Siren Song'.
104 Kazantzis has three mid-length classical retellings: 'Circe', 'The Queen Clytemnestra', and 'Persephone'.
105 Wandor has four short classical retellings: 'Antigone 1', 'Antigone 2', 'Antigone 3', and 'Myth' (featuring bacchantes, Orpheus, Eurydice, Deianira, and Heracles).
106 Duffy has twelve short classical retellings: 'Thetis', 'Mrs Midas', 'Mrs Tiresias', 'Mrs Aesop', 'Mrs Sisyphus', 'Medusa', 'Circe', 'Pygmalion's Bride', 'Mrs Icarus', 'Eurydice', 'Penelope', and 'Demeter'.
107 Schneider's mid-length retelling of the Orpheus and Eurydice story is in *Circling the Core*.
108 In French prose, I am also aware of: Monique Wittig, *Le Corps lesbien* (1973); Luce Irigaray, *Speculum* (1974); Hélène Cixous, *Le Rire de la Méduse* (1975).
109 Flaschenriem, p. 49.
110 Iosif Brodskii, *Chast' rechi: izbrannye stikhotvoreniia* (St Petersburg: Azbuka-klassika, 2009), pp. 83–85.

so Shvarts would almost certainly have read it. 'Anno Domini' is apparently written from the point of view of Propertius, but is focalised through an unnamed Governor for much of it. Although Cynthia and her son — invented, like much of Shvarts's version of Cynthia — feature in the poem, they are barely characterised, and are present only to signify Brodskii's former lover Marina Basmanova and their son Andrei (born in 1967[111]), and also Mary and Jesus:

> чужие господа
> у Цинтии в гостях над колыбелью
>   склоняются, как новые волхвы.
>
> [gentlemen, strangers,
> guests of Cynthia's, are leaning
>   over the cradle, like new Magi.]

Even Propertius and the Governor, the apparent foci of the poem, are really vehicles for the emotions and experiences of Brodskii himself:

> И я, писатель, повидавший свет,
> [...]
> думаю о сходстве наших бед:
> его не хочет видеть Император,
> меня — мой сын и Цинтия.
>
> [And I, a writer, who has seen the world,
> [...]
> think about the similarity of our troubles:
> him [the Governor] — the Emperor does not want to see him,
> me — my son and Cynthia.]

There is a lot for Shvarts to react against in Brodskii's self-pitying and misogynist poem, since it makes Cynthia less fully characterised and more symbolic than even in Propertius's *Elegies*. According to the criteria laid out by Gold — deprivation of expression; exclusion from constructions of meaning/experience; transformation into symbols/vehicles of discourse — Brodskii's Cynthia is silenced on all fronts.

The second possible influence is 'Snapshots of a Daughter-in-Law' (1958–60) by feminist poet and essayist Adrienne Rich, which gives an acute critique of just such male silencing of female voices. It is, however, a moot point whether Shvarts had access to Rich's poetry.[112] In poem VI of 'Snapshots of a Daughter-in-Law' Rich makes the point — as Jan Montefiore summarises — that 'male poets' image of Woman 'negates everything [the woman writer] is about' [Rich], not only because it does not fit her experience, but because of its usual connotations of uncreative

---

111 Keith Gessen, 'The Gift: Joseph Brodsky and the Fortunes of Misfortune', *The New Yorker*, 23 May 2011, <http://www.newyorker.com/arts/critics/atlarge/2011/05/23/110523crat_atlarge_gessen?currentPage=all> [accessed 16 July 2014].
112 The copy currently in the National Library of Russia was published after *Kinfiia* 1: *Adrienne Rich's Poetry* (New York: Norton, 1975): IK 2000-3/537, https://primo.nlr.ru/primo-explore/fulldisplay?docid=07NLR_LMS002142354&context=L&vid=07NLR_VU1&lang=en_US&search_scope=default_scope&adaptor=Local%20Search%20Engine&tab=default_tab&query=lsr24,contains,adrienne%20rich&offset=0 [accessed 16 June 2020].

passivity'.[113] Rich does this by first quoting and then departing from a male poet's view[114] of the Ancient Greek poet Corinna:

> When to her lute Corinna sings
> neither words nor music are her own,
> only the long hair dipping over her cheek, only the song
> of silk against her knees
> and these
> adjusted in reflections of an eye.[115]

Rich's poem says that the male construct of Corinna does not compose, but is important merely for her effect on the man viewing her (and that prompted mostly by her appearance). Montefiore writes:

> for Rich to designate the woman idealized in song as 'Corinna' is a highly appropriate irony, for it is the name of an Ancient Greek woman poet whose works have disappeared even more completely than Sappho's. 'Corinna' thus stands for the double exclusion of women from poetry: by omission and by (mis)representation.[116]

In Shvarts's construction, Cynthia is in the same category as Corinna: a poet whose poetry is lost and who has been ventriloquised by a male poet. But here Shvarts's apoliticism comes into play: because Shvarts has no feminist point to make, unlike Rich she does not highlight 'the alienation experienced by a woman poet encountering a tradition full of Corinnas',[117] but instead simply 'solves' the problem with her 'translations'. Indeed, the fact that no original poems of Cynthia's survive is artistically freeing for Shvarts.

The third possible influence for Shvarts's inhabitation of Cynthia is Dorothy Parker's 'From a Letter from Lesbia' (1931). Parker gives Catullus's mistress, Lesbia, a voice that is not dissimilar to the voice which Shvarts gives to Propertius's mistress, Cynthia — critical, querulous, vituperative:

> ...So, praise the gods, Catullus is away!
> And let me tend you this advice, my dear:
> Take any lover that you will, or may,
> Except a poet. All of them are queer.
>
> It's just the same — a quarrel or a kiss
> Is but a tune to play upon his pipe.
> He's always hymning that or wailing this;
> Myself, I much prefer the business type.
>
> That thing he wrote, the time the sparrow died –
> (Oh, most unpleasant — gloomy, tedious words!)
> I called it sweet, and made believe I cried;

---

113 Jan Montefiore, *Feminism and Poetry: Language, Experience, Identity in Women's Writing* (London: Pandora, 1987), p. 27.
114 Thomas Campion, 'When to her lute Corinna sings' (c. 1601).
115 Adrienne Rich, *Snapshots of a Daughter-in-Law* (London: Chatto & Windus/The Hogarth Press, 1970), p. 23.
116 Montefiore, p. 28.
117 Ibid.

> The stupid fool! I've always hated birds...[118]

Parker's Lesbia even expresses dislike of her pet bird, something Shvarts's Kinfiia takes a step further. However, it is crucial to Shvarts's textual bonding with Cynthia that Kinfiia is a poet, whereas Catullus himself never calls Lesbia a poet or *docta*, as Propertius does Cynthia, and Parker's Lesbia actually disparages poets and poetry.

Conclusion

In *Kinfiia*, Kinfiia's independent, authentic persona (albeit imagined by Shvarts) is foremost. Cynthia, who in the original poems acts mostly as a catalyst for Propertius's rather self-involved poetry — although she does at times speak with an apparently independent voice — gains an authentic voice and agency as Kinfiia. Shvarts has fully fleshed out Propertius's somewhat meagre representation of a female poet. Shvarts thus ensures that her Kinfiia outdoes Propertius's Cynthia: no longer a written girl, Kinfiia is a writing woman.

Kinfiia's Rome or Shvarts's Russia?

> 'dicite, quo portu clausa puella meast?'
> 'tell me, in what port is my girl shut away?'
> Prop. 1.8.24

Despite Shvarts's extensive use of Latin poetry, *Kinfiia* is not totally immersed in its Roman context. Occasionally, Shvarts uses a word or a reference that causes the reader to glimpse Russia behind the façade of Rome, or Shvarts behind the mask of Cynthia. The following section explores how Kinfiia grows from being a translation of Cynthia to become an alter ego of Shvarts.

Anachronisms

Anachronisms are rare in *Kinfiia*, and well disguised, but when the reader notices them, they disrupt the ancient setting. One anachronism that crops up in 1.5 is probably a mistake: Septimus pleads for his 'таблички и грифель' [tablets and slate-pencil/lead] to be hidden, whereas a Roman poet would have written on a wax tablet with a stylus.[119] Otherwise, Shvarts's anachronisms mostly seem deliberate, for effect.

Several poems in *Kinfiia* anachronistically reference Christianity behind a semblance of paganism. The most Christian of all the *Kinfiia* poems is the one explicitly concerned with pagan religion: II.1. It depicts the ritualistic death and rebirth of Dionysus Zagreus. Though set at the Dionysia, on the spring equinox, the name Shvarts invents for the rites, 'Диониса ночь' [Dionysus's Eve], is intentionally redolent of another solar festival — Midsummer — called in Russian 'Иванова ночь' [St John's Eve]. This sets up the poem's Christianised depiction of Dionysus, linking him with John the Baptist's associations with water and rebirth, as well

---

118 Dorothy Parker, *Dorothy Parker* (New York: Viking Press, 1954), p. 452.
119 My translation accordingly corrects 'slate-pencil/lead' to 'stylus'.

with St John's Eve's reputation for magical mischief. But Shvarts has her sights on a greater Christian figure: by setting Dionysus's rebirth at the spring equinox, she conflates the pagan god with Jesus, whose resurrection is celebrated at Easter — around the spring equinox.

At the end of the poem she exhorts the reader to join the god in death and resurrection — an eminently Christian message, with overtones of Judgement Day:

> Умирай же вместе с богом,
> [...]
> Ты воскреснешь чистым, юным — воскресит тебя Загрей.

> [Die together with the god,
> [...]
> You will rise from the grave pure, young — Zagreus will resurrect you.]

Shvarts's source for Zagreus, the Christlike Dionysus, is not classical: the identification of Zagreus with Dionysus is a nineteenth/twentieth-century scholarly invention.[120] However, it was enthusiastically accepted by Russian Symbolists, especially Viacheslav Ivanov, whose understanding of Dionysus as offering dissolution of self — the Christian ideal of *sobornost'* [spiritual togetherness][121] — evidently influenced *Kinfiia* II.1. The poem is full of images of dissolving and mixing of bodies; *sobornost'* is most clearly indicated with the line 'Я забвенью, полусмерти научусь у Диониса' [I shall learn oblivion, half-death from Dionysus]. (See chapter 2 for more of Shvarts's Christian Dionysuses.) The next Christian poem, II.3, opens with perhaps the most glaring anachronism of all: 'Саратоге дальней' [remote Saratoga] — impossibly remote for Ancient Romans, since Saratoga is a native-American place name. The poem dwells on the gods'/God's power over human lives: the gods/God are 'далёко — в господской вилле' [far off — in the masters' villa], while people — compared to 'жертвенные ягнята' [sacrificial lambs], a Christian image — are 'На дальнем дворе вселенной' [In the remote backyard of the universe]. The 'backyard' alludes to the Christian view of the insignificance of earthly power — even Rome's.[122] Finally, *Kinfiia* R.9 may allude to Christmas:

> битая птица
> К нам иногда прилетает
> На праздник

> [on occasion [...]
> A plucked bird flies in for a festival]

The Christian irruptions into *Kinfiia* align Kinfiia with another of Shvarts's poetic personae, Lavinia, who lives in a nunnery that similarly mingles faiths — although these faiths are predominantly Christian.

R.1 appears to make an anachronistic — if still classical — reference to the eruption of Vesuvius in 79 AD (*c.* eighty years after Propertius's death):

---

120 Radcliffe Edmonds, 'Tearing Apart the Zagreus Myth: A Few Disparaging Remarks on Orphism and Original Sin', *Classical Antiquity*, 18.1 (1999), 35–73 (p. 37, nn. 6, 66).
121 Bernice Glatzer Rosenthal, 'Introduction', in *Nietzsche in Russia*, ed. by Bernice Glatzer Rosenthal (Princeton, NJ; Guildford: Princeton University Press, 1986), pp. 3–48 (p. 21).
122 Panchenko, '"Kinfiia" Eleny Shvarts'.

> Оставляя позади все толпы
> Тающих, одетых, неодетых,
> Гневных, и веселых, и печальных —
> Будто город после изверженья
> Равнодушно-дикого вулкана.

> [Leaving behind all the crowds of
> Phantoms — fading, clothed, unclothed,
> Wrathful, and merry, and sorrowing —
> Like a city after the eruption
> Of an indifferent and savage volcano.]

The 'phantoms' frozen in various attitudes are reminiscent of the body-cavities discovered by archaeologists at Pompeii.

The most cleverly encoded anachronism appears in the final poem, R.10. At first glance, the anachronism appears to be classical, like the Vesuvius/Pompeii reference above. Propertsii (presumably) threatens to join the Fifth Legion, signified by a literal translation of its Gaulish name, Alauda, 'lark'.[123] The Fifth Legion was made up of barbarian Gauls,[124] so is equivalent to the French Foreign Legion: 'Записываюсь центурионом | В легион Жаворонка' [I shall sign up as a centurion | In the Gaulish Foreign Legion]. This anachronism is a joke shared only between Shvarts and the modern reader.

Such unobtrusive anachronisms sideline Kinfiia, consigning her to the past, while Shvarts and the reader engage in a direct, unmediated communication. This is why there are so few anachronisms in the cycle as a whole.

Anachorisms

Anachorisms reveal the hand of Shvarts more frequently. 'Anachorism' is my coinage for an inconsistency of place (rather than time): from the Greek χώρα [space/place/country]. Every so often in *Kinfiia* a word or phrase will occur that is so fundamentally Russian that it causes the illusion of Ancient Rome to fracture momentarily, and to blur with the author's reality, modern Russia. Such instances occur throughout the collection, and although the use of modern Russian words is unavoidable in poetry that aims to give the impression of the voice of a real Roman woman translated into Russian, certain of them intentionally disrupt the authenticity of the picture.

The implied scene in *Kinfiia* 1.1 of Kinfiia looking out of a window in a block of flats onto the rainy street is highly anachoristic, as Panchenko points out, since although Romans did get rain and did live in flats, they did not have glazed windows with views onto the street. The rain and the flat with a window are, however, typical of 'Another city, northern, famed for its bad weather' — St Petersburg.[125] Throughout the cycle Shvarts evokes the typically damp St Petersburg by waterlogging Rome.

---

123 M. C. Bishop, 'Legio V Alaudae and the Crested Lark', *Journal of Roman Military Equipment Studies*, 1 (1990), 161–64 (p. 161).
124 Hans Delbruck, *History of the Art of War*, trans. by Walter J. Renfroe, Jr., 4 vols (Lincoln, NB and London: University of Nebraska Press, 1990), I, p. 526.
125 Panchenko, '"Kinfiia" Eleny Shvarts'.

In 1.2 the anachorism is Kinfiia's diction. The first stanza is full of slang and folksy modes of speech: 'мол' [like], 'этак' [that], 'папаша' [Daddy]. The final stanza repeats the word 'тыща' [thou/ton], a slang contraction of тысяча [thousand]. By giving Kinfiia and her father modern Russian speech, Shvarts reflects the dysfunctional and violent relationship within a Roman family back onto the relationships within Russian families.

Food is the anachorism in 1.3. Shvarts treats mackerel as a delicacy: Kinfiia's slave girl carries the fish 'на золоченом блюде' [on a gilt platter], and it is given the epithet 'благородною' [noble]. In Rome, mackerel was seen as meagre, pauper's fare (e.g. Mart. XI.27; Juv. XIV.132). In a Russian city like St Petersburg fish is prized.

The most glaring anachorism occurs in 1.7. Kinfiia addresses bacchantes: 'Кобылицами несетесь вы степными' [You gallop like mares on the steppe]. 'Steppe' relocates the bacchantes to the wilds of Russia — as more suitable for them than civilised Rome. The line refers to Aleksandr Blok's 'степная кобылица' [steppe mare] from *Na pole Kulikovom* [*On Kulikovo Field*] (1908).[126] In *Na pole Kulikovom* Blok connected the defeat of Mamai's Mongol-Tatars by Prince Dmitrii Donskoi for Rus' at the battle of Kulikovo in 1380 with contemporary Russian events.[127] The steppe mare appears twice in the cycle's first poem — she even 'Несется' [gallops] like Shvarts's mares — and herds of steppe mares are mentioned in the fourth poem. The significance of Shvarts's citation of Blok is clarified by Irene Masing-Delic's analysis of Blok's mare:

> the steppe mare offers a both feminized and 'Asianized' (nomadic) version of two other equestrian images of Russia and her people: Peter's 'fiery steed' in Pushkin's *The Bronze Rider* (1833)[128] and Gogol's swift troika flying across the wide expanses of endless Russia ([...] *Dead Souls*, 1842), both of them images of Russia's historical progress through space and time [...]. Blok's mysterious mare, as unstoppable as a Tatar arrow, is a harbinger of popular revolutions.[129]

The feminising, Asianising, and revolutionary associations brought by Blok's *Na pole Kulikovom* to the bacchantes are singularly appropriate: the maddened female followers of Dionysus are the focus of Shvarts's major classical source for 1.7, Euripides' *Bacchae* (a tragedy which plays with gender in multiple other ways, too); in the *Bacchae* Dionysus travels from Asia to exact vengeance on Thebes through his power to madden women, who as bacchantes kill the Theban king, in a revolution of sorts. More than this, through her citing of Blok Shvarts connects the bacchantes' unleashing of passions with a fundamentally Russian unruliness. Yet Kinfiia is unable to participate in the bacchantes' Russian revolt, since her temperament, reflecting Shvarts's poetic persona, inclines her to self-sacrifice rather than sacrifice.

---

126 Aleksandr Blok, *Izbrannaia poeziia/Selected Poems*, ed. by James B. Woodward (London: Bristol Classical Press, 1992), pp. 73–78. I am indebted to Josephine von Zitzewitz for this observation, among many others.
127 The Russo-Japanese War of 1904–05 and the Revolution of 1905: Irene Masing-Delic, *Exotic Moscow under Western Eyes* (Boston, MA: Academic Studies Press, 2016), pp. 130–31.
128 A poem that Shvarts will anachoristically evoke in *Kinfiia* R.5.
129 Masing-Delic, p. 136.

II.1 contains the eminently Roman detail of the gardens on the Esquiline Hill created by Propertius's patron Maecenas: 'Все закрыты на просушку Эсквилинские сады' [The Esquiline gardens are all closed to dry out]. Yet even these are Petersburgified, as Panchenko notes: 'the practice of closing gardens to allow them to dry out in the spring following a snowy winter points to another city entirely'.[130]

Food is once again anachoristic in II.6, where Kinfiia is eating soup — not a typical Roman food, but a typical Russian one.

In R.2 Propertsii turns up at Kinfiia's house in a state, drunk and battered after a fight. Kinfiia reacts with typical Russian diction and in a typical Russian manner, veering swiftly from anger to mothering:

> Ах, тебя прогнать отсюда взáшей
> Так бы мне хотелось [...]
> Поменяй же тогу, эта в пятнах,
> Залечи царапины, умойся
>
> [Ah, how I'd like to throw you out
> On your ear [...]
> Go and change your toga, this one's all stained,
> see to your scratches, get washed]

The poem's final line — 'Видно, уж судьба моя такая...' [Apparently, such is my fate...] — is a phrase from the Russian folk songs 'Letiat utki' [Ducks Are Flying] and 'Ne brani menia rodnaia' [Do Not Scold Me, Dear Mother], in which the singer is ill-treated by her beloved but accepts it as a good Russian woman should. There is irony in this, as Kinfiia is far from the devoted, chaste girl who would normally sing such a song, but it fits the context of a woman wronged by her man, which is the part that Kinfiia — and Cynthia too: see above — is playing at this point. Kinfiia's fatalistic tone, unlike Cynthia's fieriness, is also typically Russian.

In R.5 evil witches cause Rome to be submerged under a flood of apocalyptic proportions: 'Город бьет волна сырая, | Заливает Рим и мир' [The dank tide [...] batters the city, | Floods Rome and the Globe]. Shvarts accentuates the connection with oft-flooded St Petersburg by invoking a famous Russian intertext: Pushkin's *Mednyi vsadnik* [*Bronze Horseman*] (1833/37), a narrative poem about the floods caused by Peter's hubris in founding St Petersburg on the Neva. The poems have many elements in common. Both floods have malign motivation behind them. The tide is evoked with almost identical wording by Shvarts: 'встает волна' [the wave is rising], and Pushkin: 'Вставали волны' [the waves were rising].[131] Both heroes are mad: Kinfiia has a 'глаз безумный' [mad eye], while Pushkin calls Evgenii 'Безумец' [Madman] thrice.[132] *Kinfiia*'s 'ведьмы злые' [evil witches] and 'волны в окна бьются' [waves are beating at the windows] echo Pushkin's 'злые волны, | Как воры, лезут в окна' [evil waves, | Like thieves, creep through

---

130 Panchenko, '"Kinfiia" Eleny Shvarts'.
131 Aleksandr Pushkin, *Izbrannye sochineniia v dvukh tomakh* (Moscow: Khudozhestvennaia literatura, 1978), I, p. 615.
132 Ibid., I, pp. 619–20.

the windows].¹³³ The parallel is heightened by the classical grandeur of flooded Petersburg, as Shvarts's 'Затопило площадь, форум' [Drowned is the Square, the Forum] brings to mind not only Rome, but also the flooded square where Evgenii climbs a column to survive; 'площадь' [square] occurs four times in Pushkin's account of Evgenii's flight from the flood and the Bronze Horseman.¹³⁴ Kinfiia's whispered prayer — 'Зашептала — Дионисе!' [Whispered — 'Dionysus!'] — parallels Evgenii's whispered threat against his tormentor Peter: 'Шепнул он [...] — | "Ужо тебе!.."' [He whispered [...] | 'I'll get you!'].¹³⁵ However, where Pushkin's Evgenii drowns, Kinfiia swims.

R.6 combines myth with modern Russian slang to create a pun:

> Сделай, мастер, мне, — Пасифая Дедалу
> Быстро шепчет, — ну, постарайся, телки
> Сделай образ

> ['Master, make me,' Pasiphaë to Daedalus
> Whispers quickly, 'please, try to make me a heifer
> Outfit]

The word 'тёлка' [heifer] is slang for an attractive woman, thus also translating as 'make me the image of a babe'.

R.7 depicts Kinfiia and her lover as circus wolves. While wolves are often the 'bad guy' in Russian folklore, Rome's foundation myth meant wolves were revered, and were about the only dangerous animal exempt from appearing in circus games.¹³⁶

Anachorisms can be discerned in approximately a third of *Kinfiia*'s poems. Some are simply slips, a result of Shvarts extrapolating an Ancient Rome from the basis of Soviet Leningrad. Others are deliberate, and Shvarts uses these deliberate anachorisms to make Ancient Rome comment upon modern Leningrad, and to bring Kinfiia closer to her as an alter ego.

Biographical coincidences

Just as Shvarts puts a lot of St Petersburg in her Rome, she puts a lot of herself in her Roman poetess persona. In her introduction to *Kinfiia*, 'Neobiazatel'nye poiasneniia' [Optional Explanations], Shvarts suggests that when she is writing as Kinfiia, she is still writing about herself, just in different (more interesting) circumstances: 'to transport your life from seventies Russia to, like, Ancient Rome — everything becomes funnier and prettier'.¹³⁷ The theatrical metaphor with which she describes writing from personae, 'speaking from under a mask', echoes Kinfiia's simile for the bacchantes' frenzy in 1.7: 'И съезжали набок ваши лица, | Будто бы с плохих актеров маски' [And your faces slipped down on one side,

---

133 Ibid., I, p. 614.
134 Ibid., I, pp. 614, 619–20.
135 Ibid., I, p. 619.
136 Mika Rissanen, 'Was There a Taboo on Killing Wolves in Rome?', *Quaderni Urbinati di Cultura Classica*, 107 (2014), 125–47.
137 Elena Shvarts, '"Mundus Imaginalis": neobiazatel'nye poiasneniia', *Vavilon* (2001), <http://www.vavilon.ru/texts/shvarts1-6.html> [accessed 12 September 2016].

| Like masks on bad actors].¹³⁸ Kinfiia's inability to relinquish control and join the bacchantes in I.7 can be seen as a metatextual comment on the fact that Kinfiia must not lose her mask — without it she would no longer be Kinfiia, but Shvarts. Kinfiia's association of Dionysus and masks with the theatre also recalls Shvarts's close personal connection with the theatre. In 'Neobiazatel'nye poiasneniia' Shvarts goes on to say: 'I used Ancient Rome as something like maids' quarters or a kitchen — for gossip and settling scores'. *Kinfiia* is therefore full of references to incidents from Shvarts's life and the Leningrad underground scene — some of which I have succeeded in decoding.

In I.6 'Klavdii' Kinfiia writes to her friend about a besotted gladiator. The gladiator is 'целомудренный, честный, смуглый, огромный, печальный' [chaste, honest, swarthy, huge, sorrowful] with 'глаз оленьих' [doe eyes] and 'мощных темных рук' [powerful dark hands], but Kinfiia does not return his affection. The gladiator has a real-life prototype: Sergei Lerner, who was a bodybuilder.¹³⁹ Shvarts's description of Lerner in her prose piece 'Sergei' agrees in many respects with Kinfiia's depiction of the gladiator: Sergei has an expression of 'defencelessness, simple-heartedness', he has a 'huge body', in his eyes there is 'either suffering or the expectation of suffering' (ESHA D.proza, p. 1). The gladiator's heavy mouth-breathing even has an analogue in 'Sergei': 'Sometimes he breathes like a fish, thrown out on the sand — open-mouthed'. In 'Sergei' Shvarts also compares Lerner to a classical figure, though a different one: Hercules. I.6 'Klavdii' is a perfect example of the veiled gossip that Shvarts says was the point of *Kinfiia*. However, in this case the Roman setting failed to disguise the reality. Shvarts writes in her diary about what happened when Lerner read *Kinfiia*:

> Sergei, on reading *Kinfiia*, which I had long kept hidden, recognised himself — and it's quite offensive, and what's more, cruder than how it was in real life — and said: 'An artist has the right.' (v.210)

II.4 'Klavdii — posle poseshcheniia bol'noi babki' relates Kinfiia's distress on seeing her grandmother, once 'Столбом, подпирающим мирозданье' [The pillar propping up all Creation], so helpless. It probably refers to Shvarts's great aunt — in Russian, 'двоюродная бабушка' [grandmother once removed] — Berta; Shvarts writes 'she was grandmother, father, and nanny to me' (III.200). Berta lived with Shvarts almost all her life, helped her mother bring her up, and died in 1980,¹⁴⁰ two years after II.4 was written.

II.8 'Razgovor' is a philosophical exchange between Kinfiia and her Greek slave, in which she orders him to explain the meaning of time, ageing, and mortality to

---

138   The bacchantes' masklike faces also draw on Dionysus's association with masks: 'The mask was Dionysus' favourite attribute, not only an accessory that recalled his involvement with and patronage of the theatre but a metaphor for his own character, so much so that he was often worshipped in the form of a mask.' *Role Models in the Roman World: Identity and Assimilation*, ed. by Sinclair Bell and Inge Lyse Hansen, Memoirs of the American Academy in Rome, 7 (Ann Arbor: University of Michigan Press, 2008), pp. 238–39.
139   Kirill Kozyrev, 'Razreshenie postavit' perevod stikhotvoreniia Eleny Andreevny', 23 August 2018.
140   Kirill Kozyrev, 'Ot publikatora', *NLO*, 115 (2012), <http://magazines.russ.ru/nlo/2012/115/kk25.html> [accessed 3 March 2014].

FIG. 3.2. Sergei Lerner. Photograph courtesy of Kirill Kozyrev.

Fig. 3.3. Shvarts and Murka. Photograph courtesy of Kirill Kozyrev.

her, because it is the eve of her fortieth birthday. The poem was written in the year Shvarts turned thirty, a milestone which evidently induced Kinfiia's own musings.

Both Shvarts and Kinfiia are notorious for their brawling. In II.6 Kinfiia justifies herself for scalding a boy with soup, throwing a bust of Brutus at a client, and attacking guests with a pike, while in R.1 Kinfiia compares her younger selves to 'девчонки' [gals], who 'по-спартански, молча, | Кулаком наотмашь взрослых били' [in Spartan fashion and in silence, | Would beat up the adults with swinging punches]. Shvarts herself writes about throwing food at people in her youth (III.219–20), while her friend Ol'ga Martynova recounts a bar brawl in which Shvarts was the leading and most successful participant, and justifies the numerous occasions when Shvarts threw things at people: 'If she threw a bottle at someone, spat at them, threw wine over them — then they deserved it'.[141] Shvarts even accidentally hospitalised one of her friends when she hit him in the face with a bottle (III.287).

Kinfiia is a cat-lover: in R.8 she has a house full of cats. Shvarts also loved animals, and had four pets in her lifetime — three dogs and a cat — but she loved dogs best ('Liubov'' [Love], III.243).

Shvarts suggests that, despite the great difference between her persona and

---

141 Ol'ga Martynova, 'S nebes v nakazan'e na zemliu poverzhennyi', *Novaia kamera khraneniia* (2010), <http://www.newkamera.de/martynova/omartynova13.html> [accessed 28 February 2014].

herself, writing from a persona allows her to most truly be herself: 'it is so good sometimes to run as far as possible away from yourself, in order to more surely return' ('Neobiazatel'nye poiasneniia'). This would make the Roman poetess a more lifelike portrait of Shvarts than her poems written from her own persona — a claim supported by the numerous biographical coincidences between Shvarts and Kinfiia.

Poetic coincidences

Some of the most telling connections between Shvarts and Kinfiia appear in Shvarts's other poetry. Shvarts even mentions Kinfiia in one poem, 'Chem byla i chem stala' [What I Was and What I Have Become], part of her life-summary cycle *Stikhi o Gore-Zloschast'e i beskonechnom schast'e byt' mechennoi Bozh'ei rukoi* [*Poems on Grief-Ill-Fortune and the Endless Joy of Being Marked by God's Hand*] (2004, III.81–85). The poem, Shvarts's response to the burning of her flat earlier that year, attempts to recover past themes and personae — including the Chinese vixen, Arno Tsart, and Lavinia — fragments of herself otherwise lost in the flames. Kinfiia is top of the list of identities to be recovered: she is the poem's first line, 'Была римской поэтессой' [I was a Roman *poetess*]. This section examines the overlaps between Kinfiia and Shvarts's other personae.

The Kinfiia of 1.4 reacts to Cupid's attack in a similar way to the Shvarts of 'Afrodita uletaet v noch' na subbotu' [Aphrodite Flies off at the End of Friday Night], written four years after *Kinfiia* I (see chapter 2). Kinfiia tells Cupid the wound from his arrow has healed, while Shvarts tells Cupid that his arrows, albeit effective that night, would be useless by morning. Cupid is patronisingly called 'мальчик' [boy] in both poems. So Kinfiia is in the mix of poets whom Shvarts cites in 'Afrodita uletaet v noch' na subbotu'.

The violence and unpleasantness of sexual love implied in 1.4 is expressed more fully in R.7 especially — Kinfiia's night with Diomedes — and also features in 1.6 'Klavdii', R.2, R.4 'K Morfeiu', and R.6. Erotics are virtually always tinged with violence in Shvarts's poetry. Violence accompanies almost all of Shvarts's interactions with the goddess of love, Aphrodite/Venus (see chapter 2). Violent eros reaches its apogee in the cycle *Grubymi sredstvami ne dostich' blazhenstva* [*Rough Methods Won't Get You Bliss*] (1978, II.90–95), the subtitle of which — 'horror eroticus' — says it all.

Dionysian rites are the subject of two *Kinfiia* poems, 1.7 and II.1, and Kinfiia invokes Dionysus in R.5. Dionysus occurs repeatedly in Shvarts's poetry as a dark source of inspiration (see chapters 2 and 5). Shvarts's Dionysus is consistently dangerous, and the Dionysus of *Kinfiia* is no exception, even though in Propertius Bacchus is an overwhelmingly benign god. Kinfiia's departure from Propertius is underscored by their use of different names for the god of intoxication: in Propertius he goes exclusively by the Roman name Bacchus, and in *Kinfiia* always by the Greek name Dionysus — although she does call his followers 'bacchantes' rather than 'maenads'.

Pythia is another connection between Shvarts and Kinfiia. Kinfiia compares herself to Pythia in II.7 'Na pliazhe v Baii':

> Вечно бледной пифией в лихорадке
> Вдыхать испарения злые
> И вцепляться в невидимое, как собака
> В кус вцепляется, головой мотая...
>
> [To be perpetually a pale pythia, fevered,
> Breathing in baleful vapours
> And grabbing on to the unseen, just as a dog
> Grabs on to a scrap and shakes its head...]

This ominous depiction of Pythia as a model of poetic inspiration is similar to those in Shvarts's later Pythian poems 'Pifii' [Pythias] (1988), 'Pifiia' [Pythia] (1992), 'Kolodets-dub' [Well-Oak] (1994), and *Homo Musagetes* VI 'Pifiia' [Pythia] (1994) (see chapters 2 and 5). It is interesting that Kinfiia took Pythia as an alter ego first — and Shvarts followed suit.

In R.1 Kinfiia imagines her life so far, her past up to the present moment, as a 'свалка' [rubbish dump]. Her use of this precise word for her former selves connects Kinfiia with another alter ego of Shvarts: Svalka the rubbish dump, who, in the eponymous 'Svalka' [Dump] (1983: around the same time as *Kinfiia Razroznennoe*), stands up and sings like an inspired poet (see chapter 2).

In R.3 Kinfiia states: 'Рыжей стать хочу — лисицей в поле' [I want to become ginger — like a fox in the field]; dyeing her hair in disregard of Propertius highlights Kinfiia's changefulness, perversity, and wilfulness, which she has in common with Shvarts. The fox alludes to one of Shvarts's alter egos, which is itself within an alter ego: the Chinese fox invented by the Estonian poet invented by Shvarts in *Sochineniia Arno Tsarta* [Collected Works of Arno Tsart] (1981–84: around the same time as *Kinfiia Razroznennoe*). Here Shvarts connects Kinfiia's changefulness with her own.

Finally, there are also some connections between Kinfiia and Shvarts's most famous and prolific alter ego, the nun Lavinia, from *Trudy i dni Lavinii, monakhini iz ordena obrezaniia serdtsa* [The Works and Days of Lavinia, a Nun from the Order of the Circumcision of the Heart] (1984, II.165–221). Kinfiia's repetitions of the word 'pity' and its derivatives — in 1.1 'K sluzhanke': 'Жалкого жалкий подарок' [Pitiful present of a pitiful man], and R.2:

> только жалко
> Бедную сестрицу ту — любвишку,
> Жалкую
>
> [only I feel sorry
> For that poor little sister, love,
> In a pitiful state]

are echoed by Lavinia in 43 'Ognennyi urok' [Fiery Lesson]: 'Все плакалась и хныкала и ныла | Про жалкую и к жалкому любовь' [I kept crying and snivelling and mewling | About my pitiful love for a pitiful man]. In *Laviniia* 29 an old demon tells Lavinia 'Вы ловитесь на то же, что и все: | Вино, амур, ням-ням, немного славы' [You are hooked on the same things as everyone else: | Wine, cupid, yum-yum, a little glory]. Not only are these aspirations particularly Propertian/Kinfiian, the word 'amur' [cupid/love] appears also in *Kinfiia* 1.6 'Klavdii'. And when in R.4 'K Morfeiu' Kinfiia accuses Morpheus of sending 'Весталке в сон развратника' [a Vestal virgin a debaucher in her sleep], she speaks from the experience of her fellow alter ego, who in *Laviniia* 25 'Soblaznitel'' [Seducer] is visited by an incubus: 'Как ляжешь на ночь не молясь, — то вдруг | Приляжет рядом бес — как бы супруг' [When you go to bed without praying — then suddenly | A demon will lie down beside you — like a husband]. The nun Lavinia is the Christian equivalent of the Vestal, and the incubus is the Christian equivalent of the debaucher. Lavinia is closest to Kinfiia when she is emphasising her human side, open to temptation and sin; equally, Kinfiia is closest to Lavinia when she is emphasising her compassion and self-sacrifice (caring for Propertsii in R.2).

Conclusion

The multiple similarities between *Kinfiia* and Shvarts's other poetry mark Kinfiia indelibly as Shvarts's creation. The anachronisms contribute to this, especially the unclassical Christian tinge of many of the *Kinfiia* poems, while the russifying and Petersburgifying anachorisms and the biographical coincidences with Shvarts's own life contribute still further. But it is Kinfiia's similarities with and even references to Shvarts's other alter egos — Aphrodite, Dionysus, Pythia, Svalka, the Chinese vixen, and Lavinia — that give her the strongest 'family resemblance' to Shvarts's oeuvre, and compete with her classical 'DNA'.

The Apocrypha

> versus,
> ure mihi
> the poems,
> burn them for me
> Prop. IV.7.77–78

In this final section I discuss the group of ten surviving poems which I designate the *Kinfiia* apocrypha: poems that were apparently intended for inclusion in the cycle, but did not make the final cut. (See the Appendix for transcriptions and translations of the apocrypha.) Because Shvarts for whatever reason did not want these poems to stand alongside those in the three *Kinfiia* books, I also keep them separate. However, the apocrypha share many of the same qualities as the poems discussed in the rest of this chapter, as this section will show. They come from two sources: the notebook in Shvarts's Bremen archive (BT), and Shvarts's St Petersburg archive. The former are datable, the latter not (unless Shvarts dated them herself). I first explain why I ascribe the poems to *Kinfiia* and hypothesise why they were rejected from the published cycle. Then I explore the poems' classical influences, as for the published *Kinfiia* cycle.

'Chernyi, kak veslo Kharona, griaznyi' [Black, like Charon's paddle, dirty] (1978, ESHA M.2, M.atom) is found in two archival versions and two provisional positions in *Kinfiia*, II.5 and R.3, which dates its first version to the same time as Book II. It was possibly rejected for being too critical of Propertius's poetry.

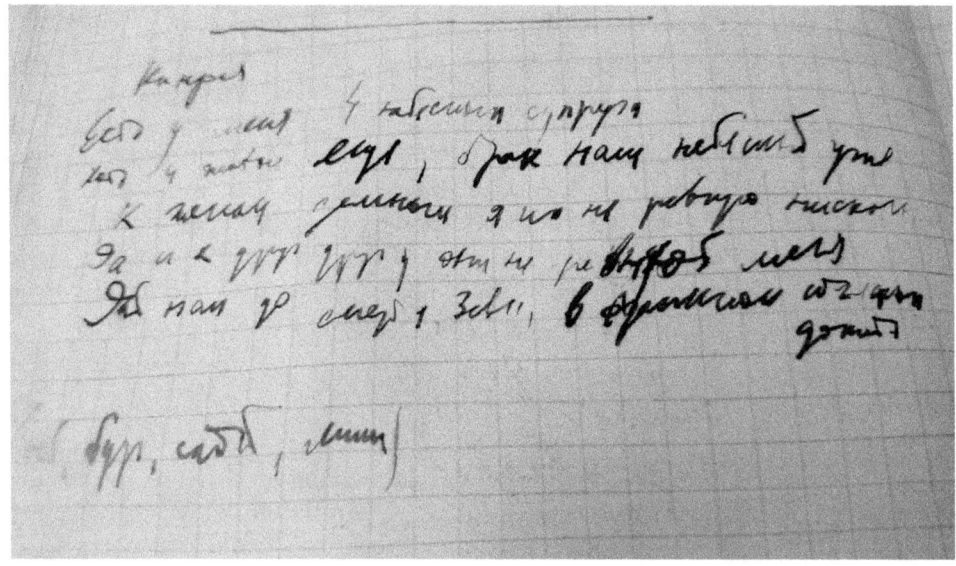

FIG. 3.4. 'I have 4 heavenly husbands', BT 30 (27 December 1978?).

'Est' u menia 4 nebesnykh supruga' [I have 4 heavenly husbands] (27 December 1978?, BT 30) appears to be unfinished, and is about Kinfiia's otherworldly polygamy. In keeping with its date, it is closer in tone to the poems of Book II, but was probably rejected for being too silly.

'Zavistniku' [To the Envier] (between 24 and 28 September 1980, BT 89) is another of Kinfiia's witchcraft poems, like I.8 and R.5, and was probably rejected for being too similar to these.

'Gor' — ká | ia ty liu — | bov" [Bit — tér | are you | love] (28 September 1980, ESHA S)[142] was originally titled 'Iz Kinfii' [From Cynthia], but was ultimately published as the first poem of *Dva stikhotvoreniia na osobyi raspev* [Two Poems to a Special Chant] (I.150–51) from Shvarts's own persona. 'Gor' — ká | ia ty liu — | bov" was possibly poached from *Kinfiia* as it has no apparent classical references, except perhaps 'богов' [gods] at the end.

The pair of poems 'Tsirtseia' [Circe] and 'Pasifaia' [Pasiphaë] (1983, ESHA M.2) are not labelled as *Kinfiia*, but are together with other *Kinfiia* papers, and are very much in keeping with the tone and themes of *Razroznennoe*. They were probably rejected as too similar to *Kinfiia* R.6.

The poem 'povsiu[d]u v dvorakh stoiali polennitsy' [everywhere stacks, all round the courtyards] (n.d., ESHA M.2) is also not labelled as *Kinfiia*, but it has a classical setting and is together with other *Kinfiia* papers in the archive. It is unfinished, and was probably rejected because it has little narrative direction.

'Ty opiat' o Tite rech' zavodish'' [Yet again you turn to talk of Titus] (n.d., ESHA M.atom), titled 'Kinf', is also unfinished, but in theme and tone could fit in any of the *Kinfiia* books. It may have been rejected because of its homophobia.

---

142 'Gor'kaia ty' is also listed as a *Kinfiia* poem in BT 92 (January 1981).

'Iz vosp. Kinf.' [From Kinf.'s Mem.] (n.d., ESHA M.atom) may be complete, and tonally seems to fit with the third book. It was possibly rejected for being too obviously biographical.

Finally, 'Akh esli b vse zhili tak druzhno' [Ah, if only everyone could live as harmoniously] (1974?, ESHA M.atom) may be complete, is not labelled as *Kinfiia*, but is together with other *Kinfiia* papers, and treats the most classical of topics — the Latin language. Since it views Latin from a modern perspective, the poem cannot be properly ascribed to *Kinfiia*, and I analyse it in chapter 1 instead; however, 'Akh esli b vse zhili tak druzhno' is compelling evidence for Shvarts's deep engagement with Latin literature in the original during her writing of *Kinfiia*.

Dialogue with Propertius and other classical writers

'Chernyi, kak veslo Kharona, griaznyi' begins by attacking Propertsii (presumably) for his dirty appearance, like *Kinfiia* R.2, perhaps drawing on the same sources for his disarray (Propertius II.29, IV.8). The tone of Kinfiia's invective is, however, Catullan, and Catullus may be the source for Propertsii's foulness. Among those Catullus attacks for their dirtiness is Victius:

> Of you, if of anyone, stinking Victius, can be said
> What's said to windbags and the absurd.
> With a tongue like that you could, if you should have occasion,
> Lick arseholes and farm-labourers' boots.
> If you wish to lose us all altogether, Victius,
> Just open your mouth; you'll be altogether successful.
> (Cat. XCVIII, p. 137)

Catullus's invective linking unclean body with unclean utterance, particularly his focus on the tongue, is reminiscent of 'Chernyi, kak veslo Kharona, griaznyi', in which Propertsii has first a 'языке липком' [sticky tongue] then a 'языке скользком' [slippery tongue].

Comparing Propertsii to Charon's oar suggests that Propertsii has killed Kinfiia with his poetry (given Charon's job as ferryman for the dead).[143] Kinfiia berates Propertsii for his inaccurate depiction of her:

> И не страшно тебе на языке липком
> Искаженное мое носить подобье,
> Будто статую варварской работы –
> В пятнах и с отбитым напрочь мозгом?
>
> [And aren't you scared to carry my likeness
> On your sticky tongue — distorted,
> Like a statue of barbarian workmanship,
> Stained and with brains knocked clean out?]

Propertius often writes of how Cynthia's appearance inspires his verse — most notably, in the first poem of Book II: 'If I have seen her step forth dazzling in Coan silks, a whole book will emerge from the Coan garment' (Prop. II.1.4–5,

---

143 Charon is mentioned twice by Propertius (III.18.31, IV.11.7), although not by name.

p. 103). Shvarts understands that Propertius's greatest interest is in Cynthia's looks — so here Kinfiia refuses the fame that comes from her objectification in poetry, rather than from her own learned poetry. And Propertius does literally objectify Cynthia — in places he conflates the girl with the written work, for example: 'your "Cynthia" is read all over the forum' (Prop. II.23/24.2, p. 171). Kinfiia picks up on the objectification of women in Propertius's poetry by calling the poetic Cynthia a statue. Propertius never makes such a comparison himself — although he makes a statue the narrator of *Elegies* IV.2. Martial does, however: he warns a girl to stay still like a picture or statue so as not to ruin her looks by speaking (XI.102) — a warning Kinfiia is arguably disregarding here.[144] In an interpretation of 'Chernyi, kak veslo Kharona, griaznyi' opened up by Martial's self-objectification as his own poetry scroll, 'handsome with bosses and cedar oil' (Mart. VIII.61.4, p. 207), Kinfiia dishes out the same treatment to Propertsii when she describes him as 'Жиром нечистым налит от пят до макушки' [Soaked in foul grease from head to toe]. In the final line Kinfiia orders Propertsii to stop writing about her: 'Выплюнь и позабудь мое имя' [Spit out my name and forget it]. This order could be read as a vitriolic rephrasing of Cynthia's posthumous request to Propertius: 'As for the poems you composed in my honour, burn them, I pray: cease to win praise through me' (Prop. IV.7.77–78). Although 'Chernyi, kak veslo Kharona, griaznyi' is a short poem, in it Shvarts reacts to many classical influences — angrily.

'Est' u menia 4 nebesnykh supruga' is in *Kinfiia*'s classic Propertian metre: elegiac-ish — dactylic hexameter and pentameter, but not in couplets. However, the god whom Kinfiia calls upon, Zeus, is distinctly unPropertian, a Greek god rather than Roman.

'Zavistniku' gives a detailed depiction of witchcraft:

> Аполлон [...]
> в котел тебя кинет кипящий
> Фессалийской прожорливой ведьмы
> Где ты будешь вариться рядом
> Со смердящей жабой лопаткой
> Разложившимся глазом спрута
> Превратишься в мазь и колдунья
> Тебя вмажет в свои морщины

> [Apollo, he'll [...]
> chuck you into a gluttonous
> Thessalian witch's bubbling cauldron
> Where you will be boiled alongside
> A pongy toad, a shoulder blade,
> An octopus's putrefied eyeball
> You'll turn into ointment and the hag
> Will rub you into her wrinkles]

Witchcraft is a very Propertian topic. He shows notorious witches brewing potions in cauldrons (Prop. II.1.51–54) and a god throwing him into a cauldron: 'Venus

---

144 Martial also has two epigrams where a sculpture speaks in the first person — XIV.176, a mask of a German, and XIV.178, a statue of Hercules.

seized me and roasted me in her cruel cauldron' (Prop. III.24.13, p. 303). The witch Acanthis in IV.5 is the very definition of a wrinkled hag. He even lists a toad as a magic ingredient (Prop. III.6.27). One of the other ingredients, the 'putrefied eyeball', is reminiscent of the fate planned by Horace's witches for a boy they captured: 'when his eyeballs had finally rotted away from staring at the forbidden food, his dried-up marrow and liver should be cut out and used as a love charm' (*Epodes* v.37–40, p. 283). This is the only poem in which Kinfiia specifies that witchcraft is Thessalian, the region of Thessaly being renowned in antiquity for its witches; Propertius mentions Thessalian witches three times (1.1.24, 1.5.6, III.24.10). But if Propertius was not source enough for Shvarts on the antics of Thessalian witches, there are extensive depictions of Thessaly's witches in Apuleius's *Metamorphoses*, making ointments like the witch does in 'Zavistniku': in Book II witches steal body parts to be magic supplies; in Book III the witch Pamphile concocts a love potion with a lengthy list of ingredients, including parts from corpses (III.17–18), smears herself in magic ointment to turn into a bird (III.21), and the protagonist Lucius smears himself in another of Pamphile's ointments and turns himself into an ass, kick-starting his adventures (III.24). But Shvarts's Thessalian witch's ointment is imagined not as metamorphic, but rather anachronistically as an anti-ageing cream!

In the pair of poems 'Tsirtseia' and 'Pasifaia' Kinfiia (presumably) gives her take on two classical examples of female vice, Circe and Pasiphaë.

Circe features very briefly in Propertius's summary of the *Odyssey*: 'the deceit of Circe' (Prop. III.12.27, p. 265). Shvarts has drawn not on Propertius but on the *Odyssey* itself — but making major changes. In the first line she implicitly contrasts herself/Kinfiia with Odysseus: 'И я была в Цирцеиных садах' [I, too, have been in the gardens of Circe]; this was written in the same year that Shvarts had first taken Odysseus as her alter ego in 'Malen'koe puteshestvie sredi ostrovov i zvezd' [A Little Journey among Islands and Stars] (March 1983) (see chapter 2). Shvarts's Circe's 'стадо' [flock] contains hogs, cats, and donkeys; whereas Homer's Circe is accompanied by bewitched wolves and lions (*Odyssey* x.212–13). The animals' circus-like behaviour in 'Tsirtseia' may be motivated by Circe's animals' unnatural, dog-like behaviour in Homer (*Odyssey* x.216–19). Circe is sexualised by Homer — she offers herself to Odysseus for sex (*Odyssey* x.333–35); but Shvarts anachronously turns her into a whip-wielding, dominatrix-like 'одалиска' [odalisque]. The poem's punchline — 'так легко (досада!) | Вы превращаетесь в свиней' [it was | So easy (how disappointing!) | For all you guys to turn into pigs] — is supported by Homer's account of Odysseus's men foolishly succumbing to Circe's trick (*Odyssey* x.231–40). Shvarts's double-entendre ('all men are pigs') does not seem to be present in Homer, but similar readings of Circe's swine as an allegory for debauchery have been common from antiquity onwards.[145]

---

[145] Greta Hawes, 'Circean Enchantments and the Transformations of Allegory', in *A Handbook to the Reception of Classical Mythology*, ed. by Vanda Zajko and Helena Hoyle (Chichester; Malden, MA: Wiley-Blackwell, 2017), pp. 123–38.

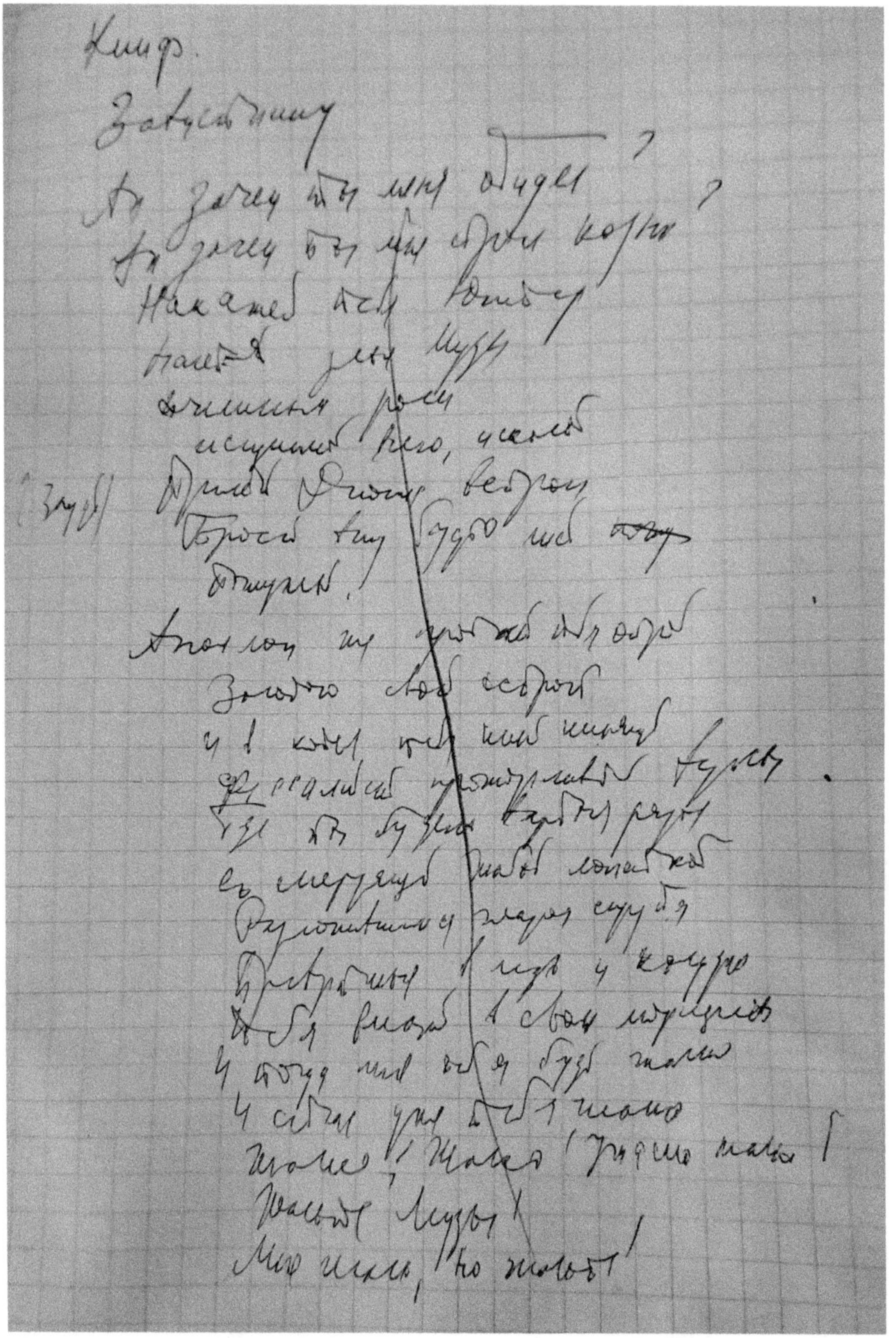

FIG. 3.5. 'To the Envier', BT 89 (between 24 and 28 September 1980).

'Pasifaia' treats the same topic as *Kinfiia* R.6 (see above), but whereas R.6 argues with Propertius's and Ovid's demonstrations using Pasiphaë that women are more lustful than men, 'Pasifaia' exaggerates Pasiphaë's lust, confirming the ancient writers' view: 'Похоть злая — на века' [Evil lust to last down the ages]. The biblical word Shvarts uses for 'lust', *pokhot'*, sounds very judgemental.

It is unclear what the subject of the unfinished 'povsiu[d]u v dvorakh stoiali polennitsy' is, but it features the offspring of Pasiphaë's lust for the bull:

> таким лабиринтом змеились дворы
> в них было не[л]ьзя не поймать Минотавра
> с детским лицом ~~минотавр~~
> в перешитом пальтишке
>
> [the courtyards snaked about so labyrinthinely
> you couldn't not catch a Minotaur in them
> ~~a minotaur~~ one with a child's face
> in a little rehemmed coat]

Shvarts's depiction of the Minotaur as a poor child rather than the conventional fierce monster reminds the reader that Pasiphaë gave birth to him like a normal baby. 'povsiu[d]u v dvorakh stoiali polennitsy' is next to 'Pasifaia' in the archive, so the poem may have been conceived by Shvarts as a sort of sequel.

'Ty opiat' o Tite rech'' zavodish'' is an invective against a man whom Kinfiia had loved, and Titus, with whom she says he is in love:

> Ты опять о Тите речь заводишь
> ты влюблен в него — мне эт[о] ясно
> хоть ты не похож на мужеложца
>
> [Yet again you turn to talk of Titus
> you're in love with him — it's obvious to me,
> although you don't seem like a sodomite]

Love or sex between men is a theme peculiarly absent from Propertius, who is the most heterosexual of the Latin love poets — his one elegy treating homosexual love at any length is 1.20; II.4 and II.34 mention it briefly.[146] But Catullus and Martial, in particular, wrote many invective poems attacking men who allow themselves to play the passive role in sex — whether with boys or men or women. Both poets also wrote many love poems to boys. Shvarts's terminology here — the word *muzhelozhets* [sodomite; literally, 'man who lies with a man'], which is in a Christian, archaic, legal register — would encompass both these categories of men-who-have-sex-with-men, which for these poets were entirely different. This is because Ancient Roman ideas of sexuality revolved not so much around gender, but around power and the phallus: penetrator vs penetrated. The former — typically male, free, and adult — was elevated above the latter — typically female, a slave, and/or a youth.[147] Martial has just one epigram aimed against a male couple who

---

[146] Jennifer Ingleheart, '"Greek" Love at Rome: Propertius 1.20 and the Reception of Hellenistic Verse', *Eugesta*, 5 (2015), 124–53 (pp. 125–26).
[147] Craig A. Williams, *Roman Homosexuality: Ideologies of Masculinity in Classical Antiquity* (Oxford; New York: Oxford University Press, 1999), pp. 3–13. Williams notes that Greek pederasty was never wholly naturalised in Rome.

are explicitly adult: 'Bearded Callistratus married rugged Afer in the usual form in which a virgin marries a husband' (Mart. XII.42.1–2, p. 125). Martial's mockery of the men's incongruous manliness may have prompted Shvarts's description of Titus as 'Темной сливой полежалой | тронутой гнилью' [A dark plum, past its best, | touched by mould]. Epigram XII.42 is not among the many epigrams excised from the 1968 Russian translation of Martial on 'moral grounds', so Shvarts could have accessed it — at least, in a bowdlerised form.[148]

Shvarts's voice in the apocrypha

'Chernyi, kak veslo Kharona, griaznyi' is the clearest statement of Shvarts's dissatisfaction with Propertius's depiction of Cynthia, and hence of her reasons for writing Cynthia's own side of the story. Saying that Propertius's Cynthia has her 'отбитым напрочь мозгом' [brains knocked clean out] is especially damning.

'Zavistniku' has multiple connections with the rest of Shvarts's oeuvre: the bee-like Muses return in *Homo Musagetes*, as does the pairing of Dionysus and Apollo (see chapters 2 and 5). 'Zavistniku' ends with a riff on the characteristically Kinfiian repetition of the word 'pitiful':

> Жалко! Жалко! Ужасно жалко!
> Жальте Музы!
> Мне жаль, но жальте!
>
> [Pitiful! Pitiful! Terribly pitiful!
> Prick him, Muses!
> It's a pity, but prick him!]

This Kinfiian repetition, which also occurs in the other apocryphal poems 'Chernyi, kak veslo Kharona, griaznyi' and 'Gor' — ká | ia ty liu — | bov'', is connected with Shvarts's other alter ego Lavinia as well (see above). The fact that Shvarts could take the poem 'Gor' — ká | ia ty liu — | bov'', which she originally wrote from Kinfiia's persona, and publish it unchanged as her own poem, is a powerful argument for the essential identity of the two personae, Kinfiia and Shvarts. Indeed, the final lines 'боль, | Что во юдоли цветет' [pain | That flowers in this vale] have a Christian tinge that is associated with Shvarts's poetry more generally.

But the closest tie from Kinfiia to Shvarts in the apocrypha comes in 'Iz vosp. Kinf.'. Kinfiia's authorship is confirmed not only by the title, which states that the event described in the poem is from Kinfiia's memory/reminiscences, but also by the metre, which is her characteristic quasi-elegiacs. The poem opens with a quote from the Bible: 'женское обыкновенное' [the custom of women], the phrase Rachel used in Genesis 31:35 to say she was menstruating. The poem's account of Kinfiia's first period aligns in most salient points with Shvarts's account of her own first period in 'Komarovo' (III.329–36), from the collection *Istinnye proisshestviia moei zhizni* [*True Events of my Life*].

---

148 *Mark Valerii Martsial: Epigrammy*, ed. and trans. by Fedor Petrovskii (Moscow: Khudozhestvennaia literatura, 1968).

'Komarovo':

> my women's custom started. [...] It was full moon [...] I couldn't tear my eyes away from [the moon] [...] I saw the stain spreading over the sheet, black in the moonlight, and I felt a strange excitement, liberation, and sweet horror. (III.330)

'Iz vosp. Kinf.':

> было тогда полнолунье
> цепко светила луна
> не отвести зрачок
> нравится ей
> в темном крови кольце
> отражаться.
> казалось ~~ей~~ страшно ~~ужас ее объял~~ ей было
> ~~обеим.:~~ ~~больше че~~ . Было мне жутче
>
> [it was then full moon
> the moon shone tenaciously
> can't tear the pupil away
> she likes
> to be reflected
> in the dark ring of blood.
> it seemed ~~to her~~ *she was* afraid ~~horror seized her~~
> ~~to both of us.:~~ ~~more tha~~ . *I was more horrified*]

The major difference is in their levels of fear: Shvarts portrays herself as only slightly afraid; Kinfiia as very afraid. The poem expresses the same 'связь' [connection] between her blood and the moon that Shvarts felt as a child (III.331) through Kinfiia and the moon's joint feeling of fear/horror; Shvarts clearly took pains to express this, as the multiple corrections on this line show. (See chapter 2 for discussion of the moon as Shvarts's alter ego.) The same logical leap between starting menstruation and losing virginity is implied in both the biographical story and the poem:

'Komarovo':

> Someone's mum called mine and said: 'Your daughter has become a woman.' Mama was frightened at first.

'Iz vosp. Kinf.':

> так испугалась тогда
> своего же родимого тела
> и обещала себя
> в брачную жертву луне
>
> [then I was so frightened
> by my own body
> and I promised myself
> as a nuptial sacrifice to the moon]

In both accounts of first menstruation Shvarts turns a mundane occurrence into a mystic event that inextricably links herself/Kinfiia with the moon, but when writing as Kinfiia the emotions and mysticism are heightened.

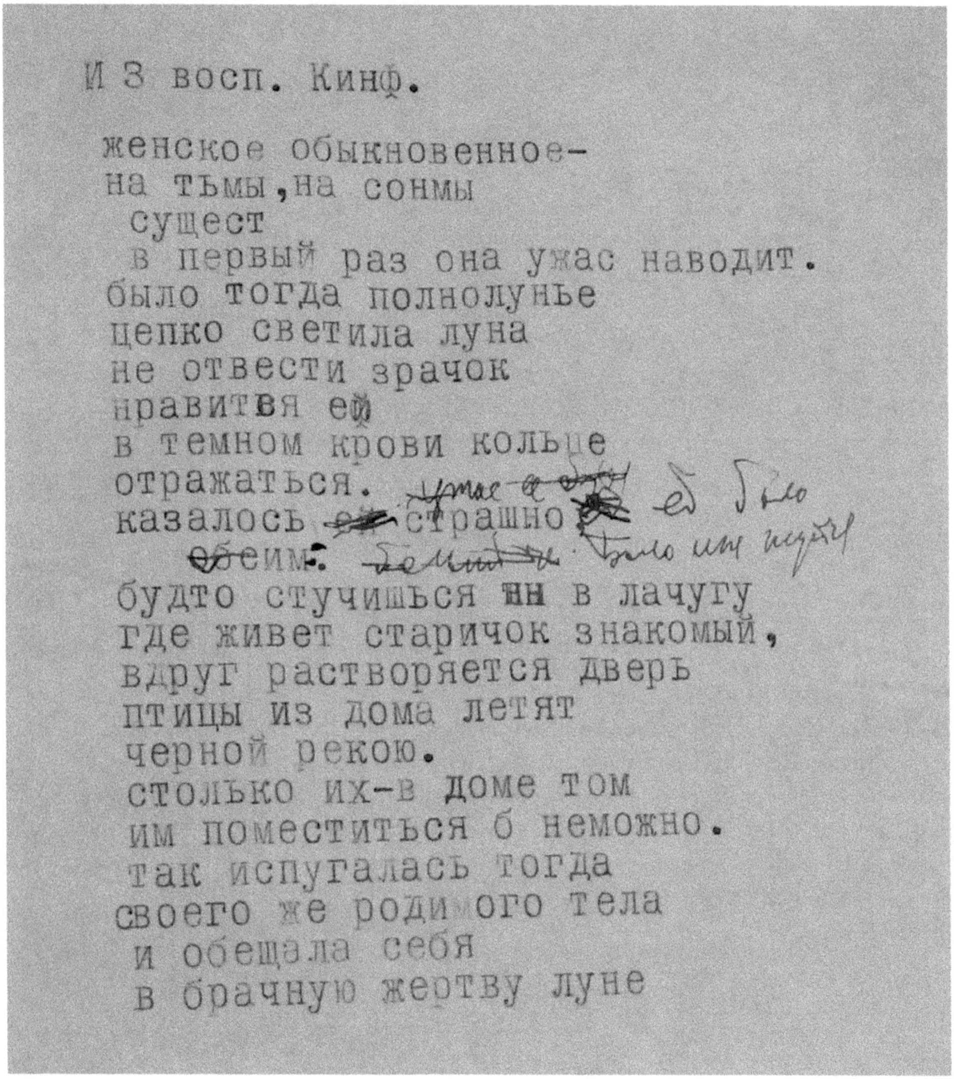

> И З восп. Кинф.
>
> женское обыкновенное-
> на тьмы, на сонмы
>   сущест
>   в первый раз она ужас наводит.
> было тогда полнолунье
> цепко светила луна
> не отвести зрачок
> нравитвя ей
> в темном крови кольце
> отражаться.
> казалось страшно
> обеим.
> будто стучишься нн в лачугу
> где живет старичок знакомый,
> вдруг растворяется дверь
> птицы из дома летят
> черной рекою.
> столько их-в доме том
> им поместиться б неможно.
> так испугалась тогда
> своего же родимого тела
>   и обещала себя
>   в брачную жертву луне

Fig. 3.6. 'the custom of women'. ESHA M.atom.

Conclusion

The apocrypha make fewer references, overall, to classical literature than the *Kinfiia* books do, and this may have been a contributing factor in their exclusion from the cycle. However, there is still extensive dialogue with Propertius, and the influence of Catullus and Martial is very evident, particularly in Kinfiia's invectives. Horace, Ovid, and Homer return as sources from *Kinfiia*. The only source not found in *Kinfiia* — new to the apocrypha — is Apuleius. Like *Kinfiia*, the apocrypha assert an independent female voice for Kinfiia, and that voice has much in common with Shvarts's own persona.

The End?

> solvimus arma
> we laid down our arms
> Prop. iv.8.88

Kinfiia drew on a huge range of classical sources as well as Shvarts's own poetic idiom and life experiences to create a rounded and believable Roman voice, as this chapter has shown. And *Kinfiia* was perhaps Shvarts's greatest poetic success. *Kinfiia* has been translated to the stage: the three books, plus two of Shvarts's more Kinfiian poems[149] and 'Zhaloba Kinfii' [Cynthia's Complaint] (2006), form a one-woman show starring Tat'iana Morozova that premiered in 2008 (v.188) and was still being performed in 2020.[150]

Kinfiia was hailed by Sedakova as a work that put Shvarts among poets whose words transcend their lifetimes:

> Тихого мальчика в сад тихий садовник ведет:
> — Видишь розы мои? это Гораций. А это —
> возле фиалок Сафо — Кинфия, тайна и мак.[151]
>
> [A quiet gardener leads a quiet boy into a garden:
> 'See my roses? That one is Horace. And that one –
> Next to Sappho's violets — is Cynthia, mystery and poppy.']

The secret to *Kinfiia*'s success is, to my mind, its authenticity: despite being a pseudotranslation, it is rooted in classical literature just like the works it is inspired by; and despite being about an ancient Roman, it conveys the experiences of a modern Russian more vividly and truthfully than poetry without a persona could. Kinfiia would not leave Shvarts after she wrote the final *Kinfiia* book, but would continue decades later to colour her view of both Rome and Russia, as we will see in the next chapter.

---

149 'Kak stydno starit'sia' [How shameful ageing is] (1994, I.302); 'Ia znaiu, chego ia khotela' [I know what I wanted] from *Lestnitsa s dyriavymi ploshchadkami* [*Staircase with Holey Landings*] (January–February 1978, I.74).

150 '"KINFIIA" 14 fev v 21:35', *VKontakte* (2020), <https://vk.com/event191088171> [accessed 29 June 2020].

151 Sedakova.

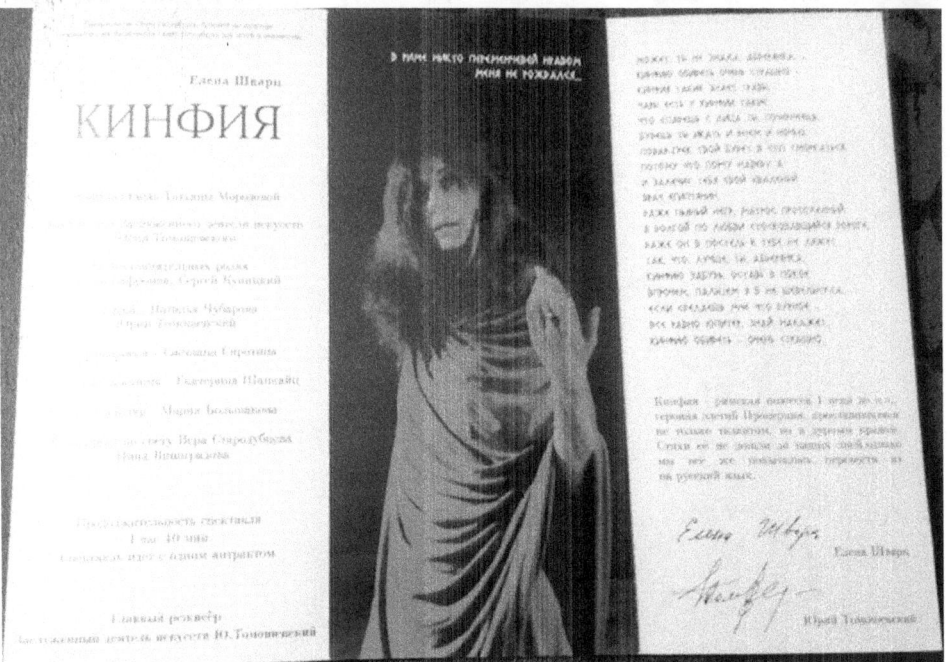

Fig. 3.7. *Kinfiia* play programme, Studio of Iurii Tomoshevskii, 2008. ESHA M.

CHAPTER 4

Rome

> Меня, как сухую ветвь,
> К Риму долго несла река
> [I was carried, like a dry branch,
> Long by the river to Rome]
>
> E. A. Shvarts, 'Vospominanie o Rime'
>   [Remembering Rome], 6 March 2009

From her earliest to her latest poems, Rome occupies a central position in Shvarts's conception of the world. The idea of Rome's centrality becomes more pronounced as Shvarts recognises similarities between Rome and her beloved St Petersburg, as the USSR undergoes a decline and collapse like that of the Roman Empire, and as she finally gets to know the city in real life that had so long intrigued her in the abstract. Following on from chapter 3's exploration of Kinfiia's Rome, this chapter looks at Shvarts's other receptions of Rome. It investigates how Ancient Rome connects with Shvarts's ideas about history, St Petersburg, empire, architecture, Christianity, and mortality. Whereas *Kinfiia* drew most on Roman literature and largely ignored Roman history, the poems analysed in this chapter are very aware of Rome's history. The first two sections show how Shvarts uses key events as foci for her idiosyncratic view of history and as comparison points with Russian history. As in *Kinfiia*, Shvarts consistently conflates Rome with St Petersburg, a conflation that is partly motivated by the 500-year-old myth of Russia/Moscow as the Third Rome. Next the chapter discusses the poems written during the winter Shvarts spent in Rome, and how the reality of the modern city influenced her view of Ancient Rome. The final section marks the return of Kinfiia, and addresses the memory of Rome in Shvarts's late poems, where the ancient city represents decay and loss. Moving more or less chronologically, this chapter charts the constants and the changes in Shvarts's view of the Eternal City.

1963–1996: The Russianness of Rome

There is evidence of Shvarts's long-standing interest in Rome in one of her earliest poems, written when she was just fifteen: 'Monolog lodki' [The Boat's Monologue] (1963, v.227). (See the Appendix for the full poem.) The poem was not published in her lifetime, but features in a typewritten stapled booklet of early poems signed with her childhood/informal name, 'Lena Shvarts', and a letter sent to her mentor and 'first reader' Iuliia Berezhnova.

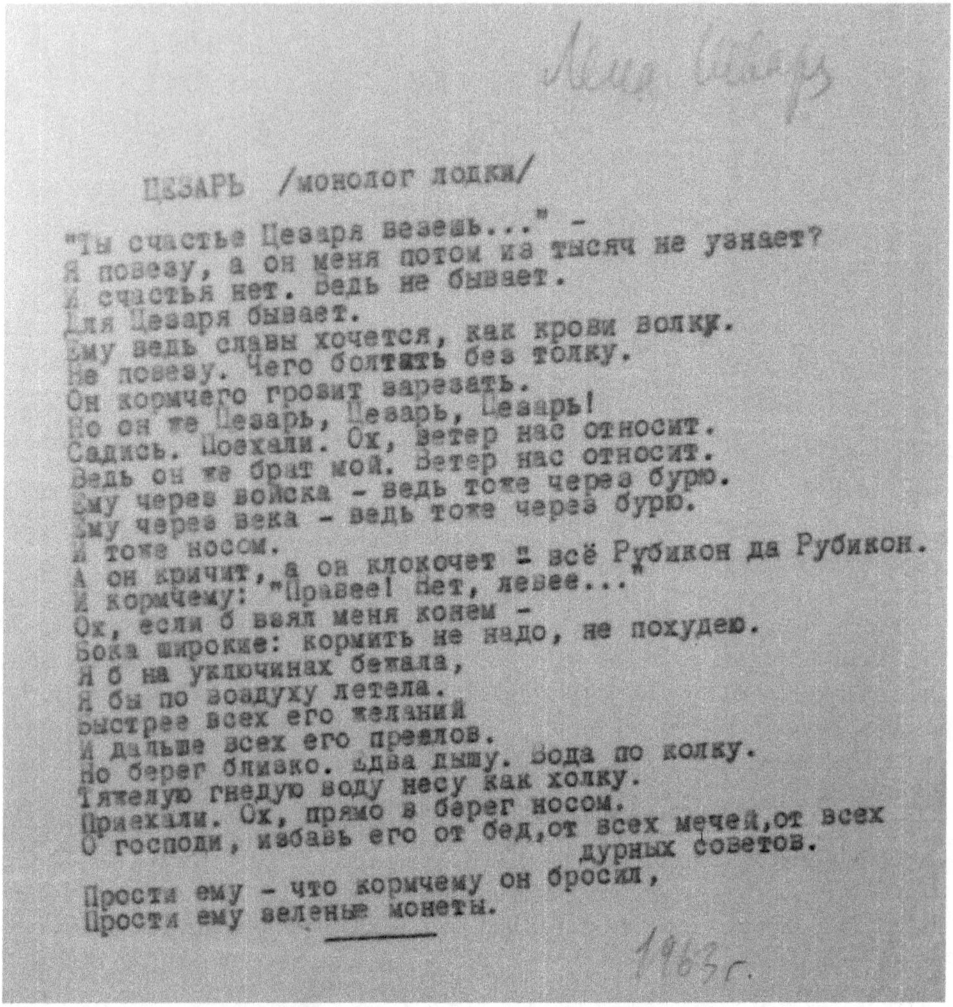

> ЦЕЗАРЬ /монолог лодки/
>
> "Ты счастье Цезаря везешь..." —
> Я повезу, а он меня потом из тысяч не узнает?
> И счастья нет. Ведь не бывает.
> Для Цезаря бывает.
> Ему ведь славы хочется, как крови волку.
> Не повезу. Чего болтать без толку.
> Он кормчего грозит зарезать.
> Но он же Цезарь, Цезарь, Цезарь!
> Садись. Поехали. Ох, ветер нас относит.
> Ведь он же брат мой. Ветер нас относит.
> Ему через войска — ведь тоже через бурю.
> Ему через века — ведь тоже через бурю.
> И тоже носом.
> А он кричит, а он клокочет — всё Рубикон да Рубикон.
> И кормчему: "Правее! Нет, левее..."
> Ох, если б взял меня конем —
> Бока широкие: кормить не надо, не похудею.
> Я б на уключинах бегала,
> Я бы по воздуху летела.
> Быстрее всех его желаний
> И дальше всех его предков.
> Но берег близко. Едва дышу. Вода по холку.
> Тяжелую гнедую воду несу как холку.
> Приехали. Ох, прямо в берег носом.
> О господи, избавь его от бед, от всех мечей, от всех
>   дурных советов.
>
> Прости ему — что кормчему он бросил,
> Прости ему зеленые монеты.
>
> 1963 г.

FIG. 4.1. 'Caesar (The Boat's Monologue)', 1963. ESHA J.

'Monolog lodki' recreates one of the most famous moments of Roman history — Julius Caesar's crossing of the Rubicon. Her interest in the subject seems to have been aroused by Sergei Iurskii's performance of (most likely) a monologue — influencing the title of 'Monolog lodki' — from Shakespeare's *Julius Caesar*, which she watched from backstage on 5 February 1963:

> Serezha read 'Caesar' for the first time. He came out in a black cloak and said something terrible and beautiful. Then he looked straight at me and loudly and haughtily spoke directly to me — something about Cassius. I answered with my pupils and white face. Thank god I'm not in love with him any more. (v.326)

Typically, in her poem Shvarts takes an atypical view of her Roman subject. Shvarts writes from the perspective of the boat carrying Caesar across the river.

She disregards the facts of the Rubicon crossing — that it was only a shallow river, which Caesar and his legion crossed on horseback and on foot[1] — so the boat would have been both superfluous and too small. None of the conventional elements are present — rather than uttering the famous words 'alea iacta est', Julius Caesar's words as reported by the boat are unmemorable and banal: 'всё Рубикон да Рубикон. | И кормчему: "Правее, нет, левее!.."' [Rubicon this, Rubicon that. | And to the helmsman: 'Right a bit, no, left!...'].[2] Nor does Shvarts pay any attention to the momentous consequences of Caesar's crossing of the Rubicon, precipitating the Roman Empire into civil war and ending the Republic — although there are some hints of Caesar's impending death and future fame. Her focus is on the emotions at work. The poem shows the influence of Caesar's charisma, as the boat first refuses to carry him, only relenting when Caesar threatens to kill the helmsman, but then begins to identify with Caesar, calling Caesar 'брат мой' [my brother], and describing the general's progression through battles and through history as 'тоже через бурю. | И тоже носом' [sailing through storms. | And also nose-first]. This comparison of Caesar's nose to the prow of a boat may be a joke about his famously big nose. In the course of identifying with Caesar, the boat begins to anthropomorphise itself, yearning to serve Caesar as his horse. In early versions (a deleted couplet after line 21) the boat is even tired out by the journey: 'Но берег близко. Едва дышу. Вода по колку. | Тяжелую гнедую воду несу как холку' [But the bank's close. Can hardly breathe. Water up to my rowlocks.[3] | I carry the heavy chestnut-coloured water like withers]. Finally, the boat asks God to protect and forgive Caesar — a possibly anachronous prayer[4] that makes the boat sound suddenly quite Russian. 'Monolog lodki' is, almost literally, an underdog's view of history, written in a first-person style that powerfully aligns the boat's perspective with both Shvarts and the reader.

A decade later, in her mature poetry, Shvarts comes as close as ever she can to setting out her views on the nature of history with 'Rasprodazha biblioteki istorika' [Sale of a Historian's Library] (1970s, 1.13–15). The historian of the title, whose perspective the poet and reader share, walks along his books into history, inhabiting various historical moments and figures, each for a stanza or less. Of the identifiable historical figures (Jesus, Francis of Assisi, Mary Queen of Scots,[5] Charlotte Corday, Marat, Socrates, Nero, Caligula, Cleopatra, Peter the Great, Paul I), it is notable that over a third of them are classical: Shvarts clearly thinks of classical antiquity as

1   John Warrington, *Everyman's Classical Dictionary: 800 B.C.–A.D. 337* (London: J. M. Dent, 1961), p. 446; Tom Holland, *Rubicon: The Triumph and Tragedy of the Roman Republic* (London: Hachette UK, 2011), pp. xix–xxi.
2   In an early version of the poem, Caesar talks about 'Геликон да Рубикон' [Helicon this, Rubicon that] — which may be a slip of the pen. 'Iuliia Aleksandrovna, milaia' (14.8.63?), ESHA J.
3   Or thole pegs, which go through the gunwales: so a twist on the English phrase 'full to the gunwales'; Shvarts probably intended it to sound anthropomorphised, like the Russian phrase 'по колено' [knee-deep]; 'rowlocks' hopefully conveys some of this anthropomorphisation.
4   Seeing as the majority religions of the first century BC were pagan.
5   Catriona Kelly identifies the queen about to be beheaded as Marie Antoinette, but her gaze previously fixed on the south leads me to conclude that she is actually the Scottish queen who schemed to take over England. Catriona Kelly, *A History of Russian Women's Writing, 1820–1992* (Oxford: Clarendon Press, 1994), p. 415.

particularly 'historical'. I quote the classical stanzas 12–14:

> Повсюду центр мира — страшный луч
> В моем мизинце и в зрачке Сократа,
> В трамвае, на луне, в разрыве мокрых туч
> И в животе разодранном солдата.
>
> Где в огненной розе поет Нерон
> И перед зеркалом строит рожи,
> Где в Луну Калигула так влюблен,
> Что плачет и просит спуститься на ложе.
>
> Где Клеопатра, ночной мотылек,
> С россыпью звезд на крылах своих нежных,
> Флот деревянный — магнит уволок,
> Дикий, он тянет — что не железо.
>
> [Everywhere is the centre of the world — the terrible ray
> In my little finger and in Socrates' eye,
> On the tram, on the moon, in the rupture of damp clouds
> And in the lacerated stomach of a soldier.
>
> Where Nero sings within a fiery rose
> And pulls faces in front of a mirror,
> Where Caligula is so in love with Luna
> That he cries and asks her to descend to his couch.
>
> Where Cleopatra is, a night-time moth,
> With a smattering of stars on her tender wings,
> The fleet, wooden — a magnet stole it,
> Cruel, it draws to itself — all that is not iron.]

Shvarts states that every moment and place in history is 'the centre of the world', and gives a few examples of apparently insignificant moments to back this up. But all the moments are prefaced by 'ray', which (as discussed in chapter 2) represents inspiration for Shvarts. As such, these incidents are not in fact insignificant — especially as one of them involves Socrates, perhaps the world's most influential philosopher. And Shvarts further undermines her position in the ensuing stanzas, as she presents a group of rulers from Roman history at moments that really did change the course of world history: Nero during the Fire of Rome,[6] mad Caligula, and Cleopatra at the Battle of Actium.[7] The magnet that destroys Cleopatra's (and Antony's) fleet could be construed either as Augustus, who was the literal destroyer of Cleopatra's ships at Actium, or as the imperial power of Rome, or as the more nebulous force of history behind the victor. The notes accompanying the *samizdat* edition of 'Rasprodazha biblioteki istorika' state that 'history presents like a long chain of repetitions — rebirths'.[8] This confirms Ol'ga Sedakova's opinion

---

6   Her comical interpretation of Nero would alter some thirty years later, after her own close encounter with fire (see below).
7   Shvarts had 'Шекспир — отрывок из Ант и Клео' [Shakespeare — excerpt from Ant and Cleo] on her to-memorise list. 'Lists: Vyuchit' liuboe iz sleduiushchikh stikhotvorenii. Rasskazat' o', ESHA D.
8   *Exercitus Exorcitans* (St Petersburg, 1979), p. 105, ESHA M.

that 'despite her exhaustive knowledge of history', Shvarts saw history not as 'the movement of particular political or social impetuses' but as 'a series of reincarnations, metempsychoses'.[9]

Her cyclical view of history makes Shvarts an inevitable adherent of the Third Rome myth, which sees Rome's religious and imperial authority reincarnated first in Byzantium and then in the capital of Russia through *translatio imperii* — the transfer of global dominance from one state to another.[10] The Third Rome idea in its original formulation of *c.* 1523–24 goes as follows:

> вся христианская царства приидоша в конец и снидошася во едино царство нашего государя, по пророческим книгам, то есть *Ромеиское* царство: два убо Рима падоша, а третий стоит, а четвертому не быти.[11]

> [all Christian kingdoms have come to an end and converged into the single kingdom of our sovereign, as per the prophetic books, which is the *Roman* kingdom; for two Romes have fallen, but the third stands, and a fourth is not to be.]

The Pskovian monk Filofei wrote these words seventy years after the fall of Byzantium when Muscovy was emerging from under the Tatar Yoke as an independent state; his intention in employing the medieval concept of *translatio imperii* was — in Nina Sinitsyna's expert analysis — to establish the right of the Russian Orthodox Church to govern itself.[12] Indeed, the phrase the 'Third Rome' was first used officially to mean the 'Tsardom of Great Russia' at the inauguration of the Moscow Patriarchate in 1589.[13] The formula that is remembered in Russia today — 'Moscow is the Third Rome' — does not appear in any of Filofei's[14] epistles, and all the evidence points to Filofei intending 'Rome' to mean not only the city but also Roman Catholicism, and the 'Third Rome' to mean not only Moscow but also Russia and Russian Orthodoxy.[15] But this multivalence led Russians to apply messianic, political, and imperial senses to Filofei's idea — along with the religious and apocalyptic senses that he intended — after the myth came to light again in the late nineteenth century.[16] It likewise allowed Shvarts to have

---

9   Nina-Inna Tkachenko, '"I ves' sostav moi budet napoen stradan'ia svetom..." Interv'iu s O. A. Sedakovoi v pamiat' poetessy Eleny Shvarts', *Gazeta KIFA* (2010), <http://gazetakifa.ru/content/view/3454/38/> [accessed 25 April 2019].
10 Stephen L. Baehr, 'From History to National Myth: *Translatio Imperii* in Eighteenth-Century Russia', *Russian Review*, 37.1 (1978), 1–13 (p. 1).
11 Epistle to M. G. Munekhin, in V. V. Kolesov, 'Biblioteka literatury Drevnei Rusi, tom 9: Poslaniia startsa Filofeia', *Elektronnye publikatsii Instituta russkoi literatury (Pushkinskogo Doma) RAN*, 2006 <http://lib.pushkinskijdom.ru/Default.aspx?tabid=5105#> [accessed 10 August 2020].
12 Nina Vasil'evna Sinitsyna, *Tretii Rim: Istoki i evoliutsiia russkoi srednevekovoi kontseptsii (XV–XVI vv.)* (Moscow: Indrik, 1998), p. 324.
13 Ibid., p. 11.
14 Three epistles attributed to Filofei express the idea 'Moscow is the Third Rome'; authorship of the other two is disputed: A. L. Gol'dberg, 'Tri "poslaniia Filofeia" (Opyt tekstologicheskogo analiza)', *Trudy otdela drevnerusskoi literatury*, 29 (1974), 68–97; Andrey Korenevskiy, 'Kem i kogda byla "izobretena" teoriia "Moskva — Tretii Rim"?', *Ab Imperio*, 1–2 (2001), 87–124; Sinitsyna, p. 325.
15 Sinitsyna, pp. 324–25, 243.
16 Ibid., pp. 10, 327 (the 'prophetic books' Filofei mentions are the Book of Daniel about the

her own take on the Third Rome, connecting it with Petersburg, not Moscow, and with the Roman Empire, not the Roman Church. Shvarts's use of the Third Rome is not only idiosyncratic, it is muted, and — in all but one case — entirely implicit. Nevertheless, I argue that the historic linking of the course of Roman history with that of Russian history is a motivating factor and a subtext of Shvarts's pre-2001 Roman poems, especially those concerned with history, politics, and the ending of empires.

And so 'Rasprodazha biblioteki istorika' segues from Roman history to Russian history without a pause, as if following the course of *translatio imperii* directly from the first Rome to the third. The first of the two Tsars who feature after the two Caesars, in the stanza following Cleopatra, is Peter the Great, pictured in the act of founding St Petersburg:

> Ах, он всех — он даже Петра любил,
> Что Россию разрезал вдоль,
> Черной икрой мужиков мостовые мостил,
> Но душ не поймал их, вертких, как моль.
>
> [Ah, he [the historian] loved them all — even Peter,
> Who cut Russia in two, from end to end,
> Paved the pavements with black peasant caviar,
> But could not catch their souls, nimble as moths.]

This segue demonstrates that for Shvarts, Petersburg is indelibly associated with Rome since its founding, when Peter forced a European form onto a piece of contested Slavic/Scandinavian swampland. The implicit brutalities of the Julio-Claudian emperors give way to the explicit brutalities of Peter the Great. The peasants killed while building Petersburg are affined with Cleopatra, as both are called by different words for 'moth'. Given the Third Rome context implied by Shvarts's segue, one of Peter's brutalities she may have in mind is his secularisation of Russia, which went hand in hand with Westernisation[17] — making Peter simultaneously a Romanising and an anti-Third Rome tsar. But the escape of the peasants' souls indicates that Peter's Westernisation of Russia is only surface-deep, and that the religious Third Rome endured under Petersburg's neoclassical façade.

Shvarts would return to the theme of the Russianness underlying Petersburg's Western façade, but with her sympathies decidedly on the opposite side. 'Gde my?' [Where Are We?], the second poem in the pessimistic cycle *Chernaia paskha* [*Black Easter*] (1974, II.77–83), opens with an episode of domestic violence, which prompts the exploration of Petersburg's true nature in the second half of the poem. Shvarts expresses her disillusionment upon discovering that St Petersburg is no longer an island of Western civilisation:

---

end of the world; this is why there will be no fourth Rome), 13 (Filofei's works were published in *Pravoslavnyi sobesednik* [*Orthodox Interlocutor*], 1861–63).

17 Peter replaced the Patriarchate with the Holy Synod, subjugating the Church to the state. Andreas Schönle and Andrei Zorin, *On the Periphery of Europe, 1762–1825: The Self-Invention of the Russian Elite* (DeKalb, IL: Northern Illinois University Press, 2018), pp. 100–03.

> Я думала — не я одна, —
> Что Петербург, нам родина — особая страна,
> Он — запад, вброшенный в восток,
> И окружен, и одинок,
> [...]
> Но рухнула духовная стена —
> Россия хлынула — дурна, темна, пьяна.
> Где ж родина? И поняла я вдруг:
> Давно Россиею затоплен Петербург.
> [...]
> О Парадиз!
>
> [I thought — not just me —
> That Petersburg, our homeland, was a special country,
> It was west, flung into the east,
> And surrounded, and lonely,
> [...]
> But the spiritual wall collapsed —
> Russia gushed in — bad, dark, drunk.
> Where is our homeland? And I suddenly understood:
> Petersburg was swamped by Russia long ago.
> [...]
> O Paradise!]

'Gde my?' pits the explicitly Western and implicitly classical and literary civilisation of St Petersburg against the explicitly non-European barbarism of Russia. Her use of the word 'затоплен' [drowned, flooded, swamped] to describe the influx of Russia into Petersburg is not coincidental: it connects Russianness and barbarism with the swampland Petersburg is built on and the floods that regularly assail it. The barrier that used to prevent Russia from overwhelming Petersburg is a 'spiritual wall', which — the rest of the poem makes clear — is made up of culture. Rather than being religious, as the word 'spiritual' would imply, this culture is primarily literary,[18] 'Western in essence',[19] and therefore grounded in classical tradition. The classical, Petrine associations come to the fore a dozen lines later, when Shvarts addresses Petersburg with the same word Peter the Great often used to describe his city, 'Парадиз' [Paradise].[20] It is a markedly un-Russian word, transliterated from post-classical Latin; Russian has its own native word for 'paradise', 'рай', which is much more common. The Latinate word suggests St Petersburg's neoclassicism, and Peter's westernising imperialism, both modelled on Rome.[21] Through comparison

---

18   Shvarts's prioritising of literary culture is made evident by the poem's allusivity: Heldt calls 'Gde my?' a continuation of 'the long Gogolian-Dostoevskian literary tradition in an elegiac variant associated with Anna Akhmatova'. Barbara Heldt, 'The Poetry of Elena Shvarts', *World Literature Today*, 63.3 (1989), 381–83.
19   Josephine von Zitzewitz, 'From Underground to Mainstream: The Case of Elena Shvarts', in *Twentieth-Century Russian Poetry: Reinventing the Canon*, ed. by Katharine Hodgson, Joanne Shelton, and Alexandra Smith (Cambridge: Open Book Publishers, 2017), pp. 225–63 (p. 233).
20   Baehr, p. 9 n. 31.
21   Eighteenth-century responses to Peter's new city included comparisons of Petersburg to Rome: 'Подобен Риму стал среди счастливых дней' [It became like Rome during happy days]

with 'Rasprodazha biblioteki istorika', we can see Shvarts aligning St Petersburg with the First, imperial, classical Rome against the Third, religious, innately Russian Rome — as Peter had originally done — and, likewise, ultimately losing. Shvarts would again call St Petersburg 'Парадиз' [Paradise] in a similar context of fallen perfection in 'Kak eta ulitsa zovetsia — ty na doshchechke prochitai' [What this street is called — you can read it off the sign] (1982, I.135). Her use of the Latinate, Petrine 'Paradise' as the final word[22] serves to answer the riddle at the beginning, when she refuses to name 'этот город' [this city], calling it simply 'мой рай, потерянный мой рай' [my paradise, my lost paradise].[23] These two poems show how much the classicised façade and history of Petersburg define her city for Shvarts.

Petersburg's neoclassical form seems always to move Shvarts to thoughts of decline. In 'Dostoevskii i Pleshcheev v Pavlovskom parke' [Dostoevskii and Pleshcheev in Pavlovsk Park], from the 'evolutionary-alchemical' cycle *Kh'iumbi* [*Humbe*] (1982, II.125–33), Fedor Dostoevskii is walking in a Petersburg park, where 'Римских цезарей печальных жирный мрамор представляет' [Greasy marble presents sad Roman Caesars]. Although the classical statues are depicted as repulsive and pitiable, Shvarts merges them with the Russian writers. Delirious, Dostoevskii says: 'Вот Нерон. Я был Нероном. | И еще я буду, буду' [Here's Nero. I was Nero. | And I shall be again, I shall]. Unlike his most famous character, Raskol'nikov's, delusion of becoming a Napoleon, as a writer Dostoevskii identifies with an emperor who considered himself an artist. 'Dostoevskii i Pleshcheev v Pavlovskom parke' reworks in a minor way the central idea of 'Gde my?': whereas 'Gde my?' uses Dostoevskii's creation Raskol'nikov to exemplify the Russianness underlying Petersburg's Western façade, 'Dostoevskii i Pleshcheev v Pavlovskom parke' has Dostoevskii recognise Petersburg's classical features as part of his being.

Thanks to *perestroika*, in 1989 Shvarts was permitted to travel abroad for the first time.[24] She visited England first, and later West Germany and the German Democratic Republic.[25] 'Dva nadgrobiia' [Two Headstones] (1990) in *Stikhi o Germanii* [*Poems about Germany*] (I.224–30) tells the story behind a Roman tomb in Oppidum Ubiorum — modern-day Cologne — then switches the scene to a new gravestone, also in Cologne. (See the Appendix for the full poem.) The two headstones are connected not only by their location, but by the fact that the people they memorialise both died in a foreign country. 'Dva nadgrobiia' is highly personal — its second headstone is Lena Vargaftik's, the wife of Shvarts's friend

(Ippolit Bogdanovich, 1773?). Mikhail Sinel'nikov, *Peterburg, Petrograd, Leningrad v russkoi poezii* (St Petersburg; Moscow: Limbus Press, 2013), p. 33.

22   The final three lines of 'Kak eta ulitsa zovetsia — ty na doshchechke prochitai', including the word 'Paradise', were added after the first draft (BT 136–37).

23   The other answer to Shvarts's riddle is in the opening line's echo of Petersburg poet Mandel'shtam's 'Eto kakaia ulitsa?' [What street is this?] (1935) (although he wrote his poem from and about Voronezh).

24   Michael March, in Sarah Clovis Bishop, 'In Memoriam: Elena Andreevna Shvarts (17 May 1948–11 March 2010)', *Slavonica*, 16.2 (2010), 112–30 (p. 124).

25   Her German travels took in (at least) Cologne, East Berlin, and Weimar. 'Primechaniia k stikham o Germanii', ESHA D.

Fig. 4.2. Tomb of Poblicius (from Teretina, Veteran of the 5th Legion), c. AD 40, Römisch-Germanisches Museum, Cologne, 2012. Photograph by Carole Raddato. Published on Wikimedia Commons.

and fellow poet Igor' Burikhin[26] — yet the poem also bears great national and historical significance. Ol'ga Martynova has called 'Dva nadgrobiia' a 'seismogram' for its prescience about the fate of the USSR.[27] 'Dva nadgrobiia''s first headstone is the tomb of Poblicius, which stands three-stories-high in Cologne's Romano-Germanic Museum.

The magnificence of Poblicius's tomb occasions the promise Shvarts has Poblicius's soldiers make to him on his death-bed:

> — Поблиций, — говорят ему солдаты, —
> Мы тебе воздвигнем такое надгробье —
> Выше ворот, что твой Цезарь.
> Посредине ты в полный рост, со свитком
> Стихов любимых,
> Чтоб они были с тобою и в смерти.
> А мы останемся у твоей могилы,
> Никуда не пойдем отсюда –
> Потому что Империя наша крошится,
> Как засохший хлеб,
> Как гнилая палка. —

> ['Poblicius,' the soldiers say to him,
> 'We will build you such a headstone —
> Higher than the gates your Caesar built.
> In the middle — you, life-size, with a scroll
> Of your favourite poems,
> So they will be with you even in death.
> And we will stay by your tomb,
> We won't budge from this spot –
> Because our Empire is crumbling
> Like stale bread,
> Like a rotten stick.']

Shvarts can hardly fail to comment on the tomb's enormous height, or the life-size statue of Poblicius within the monument, but she even notes the scroll in the statue's hand, and imagines it contains poems, a touch that brings Poblicius closer to her. The soldiers go on to say 'our Empire is crumbling'. This was hardly the case in AD 40, when Poblicius's tomb was built: although Rome had probably its most insane emperor, Caligula, at the time, the Roman Empire had at least a century and a half of expansion, stability, and prosperity ahead. But Shvarts needs Rome to be crumbling in order to make the leap from juxtaposing the two headstones to likening the two empires they represent. She parallels a crumbly Rome with a crumbly USSR:

> За спиной оседает, как снежная баба,
> Империя наша.
> Нету Рима, но нету Германии тоже.

---

26 Ibid.
27 Ol'ga Martynova, 'V lesu pod kel'nom', *Novaia kamera khraneniia* <http://www.newkamera.de/martynova/omartynova12.html> [accessed 30 April 2015].

> [Behind us our empire founders
> Like a snowman.
> There's no Rome, but there's no Germany, either.]

The incipient crumbling of her native empire could be felt best, she said, in Germany: 'The death of our [empire] was not obvious yet, but it was there, in Germany, that you could feel it "foundering behind your back".'[28] At Christmas 1989 Shvarts observed the Germans crossing freely through the Brandenburg Gate in the Berlin Wall[29] — a little over a month since the borders had opened and demolition of the Wall begun. By 1990, when Shvarts wrote 'Dva nadgrobiia', the GDR had ceased to exist, and the Soviet Union was indeed soon to go the same way, a year later, in 1991. 'Dva nadgrobiia' connects the small-scale, inevitable deaths of people with the large-scale, but equally inevitable, deaths of empires.

Two poems written in 1996, after the USSR had ceased to exist, again draw the comparison between the falls of the Roman and Soviet empires; one of these contains the only explicit reference to the Third Rome myth in Shvarts's oeuvre. Both the poems appear in a collection which Andrei Anpilov called Shvarts's 'poetic response to the current total collapse — national, governmental, confessional, aesthetic'.[30] Its oxymoronic title, *Zapadno-vostochnyi veter* [*West-East Wind*], points to the theme of power shifts between East and West, which is pertinent to both the Soviet Union's collapse and the *translatio imperii* inherent in the Third Rome myth.[31]

The first[32] of her two Roman responses to the recent collapse occurs in 'Glava 7. Prodolzhenie (eshche bolee bessviaznoe)' [Chapter 7. Continuation (Even More Incoherent)] of the multifaith cycle *Preryvistaia povest' o kommunal'noi kvartire* [*Discontinuous Story about a Communal Flat*] (1996, II.153–64). The cycle is arranged like a play, and the stage directions assign this section to Shvarts's persona, 'Я' [*I*]:

> Вода превратилась в пламень,
> Мы заперты и горим.
> Храм наш давно сгорел,
> Ныне сгорает Рим.
>
> [Water has turned to flame,
> We are sealed in and we burn.
> Our temple burned down long ago,
> Now Rome is burning down.]

The 'Rome' of this poem is evidently the Third Rome. Since the cycle as a whole is set in Petersburg — what is more, the temple seems analogous to the 'spiritual wall' of 'Gde my?' (i.e., Petersburg's culture) — yet again Shvarts is applying the Third Rome myth to her home city. But there is a new development: this reference to Rome appears in the middle of an apocalyptic speech that otherwise revolves around biblical imagery — the story of Noah's Ark — within a cycle that

---

28   Shvarts, 'Primechaniia k stikham o Germanii'.
29   She also saw an announcement of Nicolae Ceauşescu's execution. Shvarts, 'Primechaniia k stikham o Germanii'.
30   Andrei Anpilov, 'Svetlo-iarostnaia tochka', *NLO*, 35 (1999), 362–72 (p. 363).
31   The title also alludes to Goethe's collection *West-östlicher Divan* [*West-Eastern Diwan*].
32   I discuss the poems in the order they appear in the collection.

is explicitly religious. So Rome burning down apparently predicts an impending apocalypse in post-Soviet Petersburg (which indeed occurs in the cycle's final poem). With this, Shvarts takes Filofei's original formulation 'for two Romes have fallen, but the third stands, and a fourth is not to be' and interprets the fall of the USSR as a herald of the apocalypse.

The second of her two Roman responses to the recent collapse is 'Stambul ne pal, ne pal Konstantinopol'' [Istanbul did not fall, nor did Constantinople] (1996, 1.324). (See the Appendix for the full poem.) In the poem's opening lines Shvarts openly references the *translatio imperii* from the Second Rome to the Third:

> Стамбул не пал, не пал Константинополь,
> А с грохотом расшибся третий Рим,
> На дне морей, под изумрудной коркой
> В его развалинах, в золе горим.

> [Istanbul did not fall, nor did Constantinople,
> But the Third Rome came crashing down,
> On the bottom of seas, under an emerald crust
> In its ruins, in its ashes we burn.]

In this way Shvarts talks about contemporary Russia entirely by way of the Third Rome; she goes on to lament what she saw as her narrowed travel opportunities following the Soviet Union's fragmentation in terms that could apply equally in modern, medieval, or ancient times: 'Проливов не видать, теперь уж это ясно, | На что они? На что мне Рим?' [I shan't see the gulfs, that is now quite clear, | Why should I want them? Why should I want Rome?]. This Rome clearly refers to the same political collapse as 'Glava 7. Prodolzhenie (eshche bolee bessviaznoe)': Shvarts repeats 'горим' [we burn] from that poem. But here she mobilises the myth in an over-the-top way, so much so that it reads as tongue-in-cheek, especially given the poem's extreme descent into self-pity by the end. 'Stambul ne pal, ne pal Konstantinopol'' is purposely historically perverse. Two empires had to fall for Russia to become the 'Third Rome': the Western Roman Empire, headed by Rome, then the Eastern Roman (Byzantine) Empire, headed by Constantinople (formerly Byzantium). Shvarts disregards this, as well as the fact that Istanbul and Constantinople are the same city, which changed names precisely because of its fall to the Ottoman Turks. Her focus is not on the exact history of imperial collapses, but on her emotions: for Shvarts, the fall of Istanbul/Constantinople is so insignificant compared to the collapse of the USSR, by which she has been personally affected, that it may as well not have happened. The opening line is therefore an emotional (and maybe ironic) hyperbole. When Shvarts responds to current events via the Third Rome myth in 'Stambul ne pal, ne pal Konstantinopol'', she is raising her sights from 'Petersburg-as-Rome' to 'Russia-as-Rome' — like Filofei's intention; yet she returns to seeing the Third Rome not as a religious concept, but primarily as a political and cultural one.

Shvarts's 1996 Third Rome poems participate in a wider trend: Sinitsyna reports that the Third Rome myth resurfaced in the Russian media in the late 1990s[33] —

---

33 Sinitsyna, p. 9.

no doubt triggered by the dual phenomenon of the Soviet Union's collapse and the ending of the century, which always brings apocalyptic ideas to light. The ending of empires and apocalyptic thinking is the spark for both 'Glava 7. Prodolzhenie (eshche bolee bessviaznoe)' and 'Stambul ne pal, ne pal Konstantinopol'', but she takes her Third Rome in different directions in these two poems: one Petersburg-based and religious, the other Russia-wide and political. She would return to the conflagration a decade later as she felt the loss of Rome-as-Petersburg.

Shvarts puts an idiosyncratic and personal slant on all her interactions with Roman history in her pre-2001 poems. She reveals her belief that a precursor for Russian history can be found in Ancient Rome. The neoclassicism of St Petersburg, in particular, makes Shvarts see the city as a Rome sadly in decline. Finally, Shvarts finds in the Third Rome myth an appropriate response to the disintegration and chaotic end of the USSR. Throughout, Rome is a guiding mark for comparisons, a centre point in history.

2001–2002: The Reality of Rome

Living in the USSR, Shvarts loved Italy from afar, studied its culture and language, and thought that she would never have the chance to visit it (v.170). She even used the word 'Римолондон' [Romalondon] to characterise a generic West that was so remote as to be like the underworld (in 'Pis'mo' [Letter] (1974, ZT 70–71): see chapter 2). However, the break-up of the Soviet Union and a fellowship from the Brodsky Fund allowed Shvarts to spend the winter of 2001–02 in Rome.[34] Her *Rimskaia tetrad'* [Roman Notebook] (2002, III.43–51) chronicles her time there in eleven poems.[35] The importance of Rome's classical past to Shvarts's perception of the real city is evidenced by the fact that nine of the *Rimskaia tetrad'*'s eleven poems invoke Ancient Rome — for comparison, just four poems invoke religion. The dedicatee of the *Rimskaia tetrad'* is Ol'ga Martynova, a friend of Shvarts who visited her in Rome and later wrote some recollections of their time together there.[36] Martynova writes how Shvarts staged her first sight of the ruins of the Roman Forum for maximum dramatic effect:

> suddenly we came out into the place where the view opens out from the Capitoline Hill onto the Forum Romanum — Lena, who like an experienced director had prepared that entrance of Ancient Rome onto the stage, saw my astonished face, knew the performance had been a hit, and laughed.[37]

Shvarts's interests in Rome were many and diverse, as Martynova recounts:

---

34 'Elena Shvarts — Joseph Brodsky', *Joseph Brodsky Fellowship Fund*, <http://www.josephbrodsky.org/fellow13> [accessed 22 January 2019]. Part of the funding came from the University of Bologna, where she also stayed some of the time. (v.49)
35 Five more poems, sometimes included in the *Rimskaia tetrad'*, chart her visits to other Italian cities (Florence, Venice, and Bologna) and Gogol''s visit to Rome, <http://www.newkamera.de/roma.html>.
36 Martynova also dedicated her own cycle of *Rimskie stikhi* [Roman Poems] to Shvarts.
37 Ol'ga Martynova, 'S nebes v nakazan'e na zemliu poverzhennyi', *Novaia kamera khraneniia* (2010), <http://www.newkamera.de/martynova/omartynova13.html> [accessed 28 February 2014].

Fig. 4.3. Ol'ga Martynova and Elena Shvarts by the Roman Forum, November 2001. Published on Novaia kamera khraneniia.³⁸

> Lena learned Rome very quickly and knew everything. Where so-and-so lived, where such-and-such obelisk was, where such-and-such fountain was, which Russian poets had spat off which cupola onto which spot. [...] Besides the Christian antiquities, she particularly loved the Roman Baroque.³⁹

Even though the majority of the poems in the *Rimskaia tetrad'* return at some point to classical Rome, they usually reach antiquity via another period of Rome's existence, testifying to the diversity of Shvarts's Rome.

The cycle's first two poems are religious in theme, and contain only fleeting classical references. In poem 1, 'Vospominanie o freske Fra Beato Andzheliko "Kreshchenie" pri vide golovy Ioanna Krestitelia v Rime' [Remembering Fra Beato Angelico's 'Baptism' Fresco upon Seeing the Head of John the Baptist in Rome], Shvarts describes the preserved head of John the Baptist as like 'lapis niger'. Martynova recounts how she and Shvarts 'walked all round the Roman Forum in search of the black stone (Lapis Niger — as legend has it, Romulus was killed there), but for some reason however much we tried we could not find it'.⁴⁰ So in this poem Shvarts finds Romulus's stone elsewhere, in a relic of another murder,

---

38 Ol'ga Martynova and Elena Shvarts, '"Khrustia, rastsvetaet zvezda Aventina..." (vstrecha Ol'gi Martynovoi i Eleny Shvarts v Rime, stikhi i fotografii)', Novaia kamera khraneniia <http://www.newkamera.de/roma.html> [accessed 24 January 2019].
39 Martynova, 'S nebes v nakazan'e na zemliu poverzhennyi'.
40 Ibid.

of significance to a Christian rather than a classical foundation myth. In poem 2, 'Ploshchad' Mal'tiiskikh rytsarei v Rime' [Knights of Malta Square in Rome], Shvarts describes the classical architectural decorations around her: 'Факелы, урны, Медузы' [Torches, urns, Medusas]. Both these references are to tangible details, and both — a scientific Latin name and neoclassical style — are remnants of antiquity rather than specific to Ancient Rome.

It is only in the fourth poem of the *Rimskaia tetrad'* that Shvarts delves into Rome's classical past. 'Circo Massimo' conveys Shvarts's sense that in Rome antiquity is only just under the surface. (See the Appendix for the full poem.) 'Circo Massimo' begins firmly in the present, with the Circus Maximus's modern Italian name in the title and line 2, and Shvarts on a 'автобус' [bus] in line 1. But as Shvarts contemplates the ruined Circus Maximus, the poem gradually immerses itself in the past. She imagines the Circus as a living creature, and the broken *meta*, or turning-post, in its arena as a broken vertebra in its spine: 'Днём он дремлет, сохнет позвоночник | С сломанной навек метой' [By day it slumbers, its agèd spine — | With *meta* broken forever — gets parched]. The Circus's depiction as a broken creature echoes Mandel'shtam's poem 'Vek' [The Age] (1922),[41] in which he laments the twentieth century's violent break from classical culture: 'Но разбит твой позвоночник, | Мой прекрасный жалкий век!' [But your spine is broken, | My beautiful pitiful age!]. It also echoes Shvarts's earlier use of *meta* to represent the end of the race of life in *Kinfiia* R.3. Shvarts imagines the Circus trying to continue its original function at night in its broken and darkened state, with ghostlike chariots bound never to reach the *meta*. The chariots' crashes, in which the charioteers die from broken collarbones, mirror the condition of the Circus. She addresses a poisoned Caesar, and in the penultimate line urges him: 'Чашу цирка поднимать не надо' [You do not have to raise the circus cup]. This image of the Circus as a cup filled with poison, held by Caesar, echoes Shvarts's first impression of the Circus as elderly and water-filled: 'в седой арене | Стынет тьмы зацветшая вода' [The icy water of darkness | Stagnating in the grey-haired arena]. In the final line Shvarts spells out the equivalence: 'Там отрава — будущее там' [There lies poison — the future lies there]. It is the inevitable ruin the future brings — and has already brought to the Circus Maximus, Roman emperors, and the Roman Empire as a whole — that is the real poison.

Shvarts explores a similar idea of modern Rome being built on a dead Ancient Rome in poem 5, 'Ten' u fontana na P'iatstsa del' Popolo' [Shade by a Fountain on the Piazza del Popolo]. Shvarts washes her bleeding finger in one of the four lion fountains in the middle of the square. This prompts her to muse on what lies below the neoclassical architecture:

> Капли крови развела в фонтане
> Возле морды мраморного львёнка,
> Чтоб она умчалась в водостоки,
> В кровные и тёмные болота,

---

41   Osip Mandel'shtam, *Sochineniia v dvukh tomakh*, ed. by A. D. Mikhailov and P. M. Nerler (Moscow: Khudozhestvennaia literatura, 1990), I, pp. 145–46.

> На которых мир стоит и дышит
> (И уже так долго, очень долго),
> Я дивилась — кровь моя живая,
> Шёлковая, алая, родная,
> Так мгновенно унеслась к потокам,
> И так скоро к смерти приложилась.
>
> [I diluted the drops of blood in the fountain
> Beside the muzzle of the marble lion cub,
> So it would whirl away into the drains,
> Into the bloody and dingy swamps,
> On which the world stands and breathes
> (And for so long already, so very long),
> I marvelled — my living blood,
> Silky, scarlet, mine,
> So instantaneously sped off to the streams,
> And so quickly attached itself to death.]

While the poem makes no direct reference to Ancient Rome, Shvarts's thoughts about the importance of drains in general as the foundations of the world must apply to Rome's drains in particular, which were established in antiquity, and which have popularly been seen as the foundations of the Roman Empire.[42] The swampy underside of Rome is also connected with Ancient Rome by association with the previous poem, in which 'заболоченн[ая] вод[а]' [swampy water] represents the Circus's ancient history. Finally, the merging of Shvarts's blood with the Ancient Roman groundwater is figured as a merging with death, which repeats 'Circo Massimo''s conceit of Ancient Rome having been killed by the future, or Shvarts's present.

Poem 6, 'Rim kak budto varvar-gladiator' [Rome like a barbarian-gladiator] again views Rome in terms of death: her residence in and love for the city is figured as a defeat or capture, with death its result. (See the Appendix for the full poem.) Shvarts is a gladiator defeated — captured — by the gladiator Rome in the Circus: 'Рим как будто варвар-гладиатор | Цепь накинул на меня стальную' [Rome like a barbarian-gladiator | Threw a chain of steel over me]. She expresses

---

42   See, e.g., Monty Python's 'What have the Romans ever done for us?' scene in *Life of Brian*, in which waterworks are the first Roman contributions mentioned, and 3/9 items in the final list:

> 'REG: [...] And what have they ever given us in return?!
> XERXES: The aqueduct?
> REG: What?
> XERXES: The aqueduct.
> REG: Oh. Yeah, yeah. They did give us that. Uh, that's true. Yeah.
> COMMANDO #3: And the sanitation.
> LORETTA: Oh, yeah, the sanitation, Reg. Remember what the city used to be like?
> [...]
> REG: All right, but apart from the sanitation, the medicine, education, wine, public order, irrigation, roads, a fresh water system, and public health, what have the Romans ever done for us?'

Monty Python, 'Life of Brian Script — Scene 10: Before the Romans Things Were Smelly', *Another Bleedin' Monty Python Website*, <http://montypython.50webs.com/scripts/Life_of_Brian/10.htm> [accessed 23 January 2019].

her willingness to die — that is, remain in Rome — but the crowd wish her to live — that is, continue her life in St Petersburg. Her love for Rome is presented as a dangerous, powerful force; the alternative, her native city, is less compelling, and more feared, as it is described sibilantly as 'северное страшное сиянье' [frightful northern light]. Her return is made seemingly without her volition, as she is turned into a 'самолётную снежинку' [airborne snowflake] and thrown back to the frozen north. Already at the mid-point of the cycle, Shvarts is imagining the impact her time in Rome will have on her after her return home.

Poem 7, 'Sluchai u pamiatnika Dzhordano Bruno' [Incident by the Monument to Giordano Bruno] again focuses on a historical death, although of a Christian rather than a classical figure. After Shvarts is hit on the head by a football, classical 'Фурии' [Furies] are among the beings that admonish her not to wander over the site of the 'saint''s execution.[43]

Another mundane event becomes an occasion to muse on Rome's position at the centre of history in poem 9, 'Zabastovka elektrikov v Rime' [Electricians' Strike in Rome]. (See the Appendix for the full poem.) When the — presumably electrical — workings of the fountains go wrong, Shvarts imagines that their grinding is because 'вместо них крутилась, | Скрипя и плача, мира ось' [revolving there, in their place, | Grating and groaning, was the world's axis]. For her, the world literally revolves around Rome. In the darkened city the moon is suddenly prominent; Shvarts personifies her as 'Luna' and then 'Selene', as she has done before (see chapter 2). In the final stanza Shvarts explores, seriously yet whimsically, the freight Rome carries as the Eternal City. The removal of modernity's electric light allows Rome to be its ancient self:

> Тьма нежная и неживая —
> Живых и мёртвых клей и связь.
> Вдруг вечный мрак и вечный город
> Облобызались, расходясь.
>
> [Dark, you are gentle and inanimate —
> Glue and bond of the living and dead.
> Suddenly eternal gloom and eternal city
> Kissed as they parted.]

As in 'Circo Massimo' and 'Ten' u fontana na P'iatstsa del' Popolo', darkness allows Rome's ancient past to come into the present. When the electricity comes back on the illusion of antiquity ends, as does the poem.

Poem 10, 'U Panteona' [At the Pantheon] addresses another Ancient Roman building. The Pantheon's round side is compared to 'гиганта мощный череп' [a giant's potent skull]. Shvarts elaborates on this comparison with a definitely classical reference later in the poem, when, already inside 'глубь его чела' [the depths of its brow], she says the hole in the centre of the Pantheon's roof is 'Будто голый глаз циклопа' [Like the naked eye of a cyclops]. Given that this hole is technically called an oculus [eye], Shvarts's observation is both apt and unoriginal.

---

43 Shvarts calls the philosopher/scientist a saint even though he was burned alive by the Catholic Church rather than canonised.

The final poem of the *Rimskaia tetrad'*, 'Sad villy Medichi' [Medici Villa Garden], is written retrospectively, in the past tense, as a farewell to Rome. The poem's opening conveys Shvarts's wonder at living in such a historic spot:

> В центре Рима, в центре мира
> В тёмном я жила саду.
> [...]
> И стеной Аврелиана
> Этот сад был огражден.
> Здесь ее ломали готы,
> Здесь они врывались в Рим,
> То есть это место крови.

[In the centre of Rome, in the centre of the globe
I lived in a dark garden.
[...]
And by the Aurelian walls
That garden was enclosed.
Here the walls were ruptured by goths,
Here they burst into Rome,
So this is a place of blood.]

She uses the common and significant Russian palindrome 'рим и мир' [Rome and the globe] — like *urbi et orbi* — to convey how being in Rome makes her feel at the centre of everything. Shvarts has used this palindrome before, in *Kinfiia* R.5, and will use it again, in 'Blagodarenie' [Thanksgiving]. As the last of many poems in the *Rimskaia tetrad'* that express her feeling of Rome's centrality, this potentially glib line reads as entirely sincere. The Goths' sack of Rome is felt as a violation of Shvarts's own sanctuary in the here and now — not simply a fact of history. She hears the knocking of the Goths' sledgehammers in the night — or is it 'Фердинанд, Атилла, Гоголь?' [Ferdinando, Atilla [*sic*], Gogol'?]. The people she imagines knocking on her wall are: Ferdinando de' Medici, the villa's founder; Attila the Hun, who never actually reached Rome in his invasion (Shvarts is confusing him with Alaric, who invaded Rome through the villa's wall, a mistake she makes in her diary also (v.52); and Nikolai Gogol', who lived nearby in a house on the Spanish Steps, and about whom Shvarts thought constantly while in Rome (v.53). Shvarts also suspects a statue of a dead boy that was on a tomb in the garden. Another statue from the Villa Medici garden enters the poem near the end, in a way calculated to break the spell of Rome. This is Dea Roma, the tutelary goddess and personification of Rome. Yet Shvarts does not view her as Roman; instead Dea Roma reminds her rather incongruously of a quintessentially Soviet Russian figure: 'похожая на колхозницу статуя богини Рима' [the statue of the goddess of Rome who looks like a *kolkhoznitsa* [female collective farmer]]. Dea Roma's muscularity, plumpness, and broad shoulders do bear a resemblance to the ideal women of (neoclassical-influenced) Socialist Realist art. The connection from Ancient Rome back to Soviet Russia at the close of the cycle is a timely reminder of Shvarts's return to St Petersburg.

Fig. 4.4. Dea Roma, Giardini di Villa Medici, Rome, 2013. Photograph by Sailko. Published on Wikimedia Commons.

Unlike her pre-2001 evocations of Rome, the poems of the *Rimskaia tetrad'* are highly textured with details from Shvarts's lived experience of Rome. Yet even when she has discovered the real, modern city, Rome remains at the centre of history — perhaps because the tangible remains of its illustrious past are so omnipresent there. Indeed, in the *Rimskaia tetrad'* Rome's long history seems to weigh on Shvarts viscerally, and beneath its touristic view of Rome's art and architecture the cycle is obsessed with death. Death lurks especially in Rome's classical past, ready to well up with the dark. The morbid side of the *Rimskaia tetrad'* may not be due entirely to Ancient Rome: Shvarts admits to unhappiness and loneliness during her time there, and a sense of belatedness (v.49) — probably because her mother, who had died three years before, could not rejoice in her success or visit the city with her.

2006–2009: The Loss of Rome

There is a surprising absence in the *Rimskaia tetrad'* — Kinfiia. Shvarts does not allude to her Roman alter ego once in either her Roman poems or her Roman diary. Why did Shvarts not write from Kinfiia's perspective when she was in Rome? Martynova, seeing Kinfiia in the person of Shvarts in Rome, hits upon a possible reason:

> Lena in Rome — hurtling black lightning, God's sparrow. Self-willed belle-poetess, Kinfiia. I was present at the return of Kinfiia to Rome. In a black coat with a red scarf, with eyes permanently focused on her own inner life, which managed nonetheless to notice all Rome's trivial details.[44]

When confronted with the tangible reality of Rome, Shvarts's personal perspective was all-consuming; there was no need and no space for alter egos.

But four years after her stay in Rome, and after a two-decade hiatus, Shvarts did return to Kinfiia, in 'Zhaloba Kinfii' [Cynthia's Complaint] (2006, III.140–41).[45] (See the Appendix for the full poem.) The poem is divided into three parts:[46] the first seems to be a quotation of Kinfiia's complaint; the second a parallel complaint by Shvarts; and the third an address by Shvarts to Kinfiia. But there are so many cross-overs between these sections that any one of them can be read as written by or about either Shvarts or Kinfiia. 'Zhaloba Kinfii' has an atemporal quality: at times the poet is distanced from events, both temporally and stoically; at others, the poet is corporally very present, but not within her own persona; and references to people and objects from various eras mean that the setting remains unclear. 'Zhaloba Kinfii' exists simultaneously on the two planes of Ancient Rome and contemporary Russia to an even greater extent than *Kinfiia*.

The poem begins with a conflagration: 'Чем виноват соловей — что в эпоху лесного пожара | Довелось ему сгинуть в огне?' [Is the nightingale to blame, if

---

44 Martynova, 'S nebes v nakazan'e na zemliu poverzhennyi'.
45 Elsewhere titled 'Zhaloba rimlianina' [A Roman's Complaint]. Elena Shvarts, 'Stikhi', *Novaia kamera khraneniia*, <http://www.newkamera.de/shwarz/escwarz_08.html> [accessed 8 September 2016].
46 The manuscript evidence shows the three parts were written at different times. 'Zhaloba rimlianina' (St Petersburg, 2006), ESHA S.

in the epoch of forest fire | It chances to perish in the flame?]. The word 'epoch' turns the 'forest fire' from a literal occurrence into a metaphor for socio-political disruption, a metaphor which embraces the entire first stanza. A few lines later, the phrase 'Варваров новых язык' [The tongue of new barbarians] suggests that Kinfiia is lamenting the sack of Rome. The trees amidst which the nightingale lives become Kinfiia's writings, and the nightingale therefore is Kinfiia:

> Видеть, как свитки родимых деревьев
> В пепел сухой обратились —
> Будто и не было вовсе.
> [...]
> Разве мне жаль было б жалкое тело покинуть,
> Если б душа моя в свитках родимых жила?
>
> [To see the scrolls of its native trees
> Turn to dry ashes —
> As if they had never been at all.
> [...]
> Would I be loath to quit this pitiful body,
> If my soul lived on in its native scrolls?]

This chimes with the 'loss' of Cynthia's poems which Shvarts records at the very beginning of *Kinfiia*; it may also refer to Cynthia's ghost commanding Propertius to burn his poems about her (Prop. IV.7.77–78). Either this Kinfiia does not know of Shvarts's 'translation' of Cynthia's lost works, or she does not deem it 'native' enough. The fire that begins 'Zhaloba Kinfii' also brings to mind the fire that destroyed Shvarts's own papers in 2004 — and Kinfiia's previous appearance was in a poem commemorating the losses from that fire, 'Chem byla i chem stala' [What I Was and What I Have Become] (2004, III.81–85). So Shvarts had already connected Kinfiia and her writings with destruction by fire. Moreover, Russia-as-Rome had previously burned down in two poems from a decade before 'Zhaloba Kinfii': 'Stambul ne pal, ne pal Konstantinopol'' and 'Glava 7. Prodolzhenie (eshche bolee bessviaznoe)'. Since then, Shvarts had also lived in the spot where the real sack of Rome began: 'Sad villy Medichi' [Medici Villa Garden]. So the metaphorical conflagration in Kinfiia's complaint signifies multiple events: Cynthia's lost poems, Shvarts's lost possessions, the fall of the USSR, and the sack of Rome.

At first the second section seems to be in the same location as the first: 'С жалобой этою римской свою я свивала | Сидя в развалинах римских в слезах' [Together with this Roman complaint I span out my own, | Sitting in the Roman ruins in tears], but then it abruptly relocates the reader to modernity: 'В городе сняли трамвай' [In the city they've taken up the tram tracks]. This temporal transition is characteristic of Propertius Book IV, especially elegies 1 and 4, which compare the contemporary city of Rome with the rural site it once was — but Propertius's temporal transitions imply progress rather than decline.[47] The modern city is not Rome but St Petersburg: the tram was a symbol of St Petersburg, especially since Nikolai Gumilev's poem 'Zabludivshiisia tramvai' [The

---

47   The transition also reverses the one in 'Circo Massimo', which goes from a modern bus, to ancient ruins, to ghosts of antiquity.

Runastray Tram] (1919) and the Blockade, when it was the only form of transport that ran in the city.[48] Shvarts even connected the tram with her personal poetics in 'Podrazhanie Bualo' [Imitation of Boileau] (1971, see chapter 2). But trams began to be removed from Petersburg in the late 1990s,[49] to which Shvarts responds 'Не на чем в рай укатиться' [There's nothing to trundle off to paradise on] — her urban and poetic paradise is being dismantled. Alaric, the king of the Goths who sacked Rome in AD 410,[50] becomes a vulgar New Russian: 'Новый Аларих ведет войско джипов своих' [New Alaric leads the war host of his jeeps].[51] The sack of Rome decried in the first section is reread in the second as a decline of art:

> Варваров новых язык
> [...]
> Седою бедною мышкой
> Искусство в норку забилось,
> Быстро поэзия сдохла
> Будто и не жила.
>
> [The tongue of new barbarians
> [...]
> Poor grey mouse
> Art hid cowering in a burrow,
> Poetry quickly dropped dead
> As if it had never lived.]

The artistic decline is equally the one which took place in Europe in the Dark Ages following the fall of Rome, and the one taking place in Russia following the reinstatement of capitalism, when poetry went from a matter of vital (censorship-worthy) importance to an (unprofitable) irrelevance.

In the third and final section a transition from Rome to now and from second person to first person blurs the identity of the addressee and the locale of the lament:

> Римлянка, плач твой напрасен —
> Через века возродится многое, пусть изменясь.
> Ныне ж всё кажется мне безвозвратным
>
> [Roman woman, your weeping is in vain —
> In centuries to come much will revive, albeit in altered forms.
> Right now, though, everything seems irrevocable,
> [...] to my eyes].

The poem ends in destruction that both mirrors the destruction of Rome and Russia lamented throughout the poem, and acknowledges the artificiality of the setting:

> лучше —
> Хрупкий стеклянный поэзии город
> Грубо о землю разбить.

48 Kirill Kozyrev, Interview by Georgina Barker, St Petersburg, Russia, 2019.
49 Ibid.
50 'Alaricus', in *Brill's New Pauly: Encyclopaedia of the Ancient World*, ed. by Hubert Cancik and Helmuth Schneider, 15 vols (Leiden: Brill, 2002–09), I (2002), 423–24.
51 In the draft version the jeeps were originally 'БМВ' [BMWs]. 'Zhaloba rimlianina', ESHA S.

> [better
> To dash this brittle glass city of poetry
> Roughly to the ground.]

The glass city of poetry is not only the St Petersburg/Rome which Shvarts has built in this poem and others, but the real St Petersburg written about by so many poets. Calling St Petersburg 'city of poetry' is a reminder of Leningrad's status in the 1970s and early 1980s as the undisputed capital of unofficial poetry; the shattering of this city conveys the rapid end of poetry's importance in the late 1980s. Ostensibly a lament for the sack of Rome, 'Zhaloba Kinfii' really responds to the passing of the cultured Russia Shvarts knew. The 'Roman woman' is both Kinfiia and Shvarts.

Why did Shvarts return to Kinfiia after her time in Rome, if not during it? Her inhabitation of her Roman alter ego to complain about the state of affairs in noughties Russia is similar to her use of the Third Rome myth to complain about the state of affairs in nineties Russia. But whereas the Third Rome is apt to express the ending of empires, in 'Zhaloba Kinfii' the ending is of culture. The Roman poetess is perfect for expressing the personal ramifications on a poet whose society has largely moved on from poetry.

Another Roman poem written the same year reacts to a real conflagration: the fire that partially destroyed the Izmailovskii Cathedral. In 'Smotriu na goriashchii sobor' [I Watch the Burning Cathedral] (25 August 2006, III.131–32) Shvarts states 'И зловещего Нерона | Мне открылась правота' [And sinister Nero's | Rightness was revealed to me]. She is imagining Nero at the Fire of Rome, not as the ridiculous figure of 'Rasprodazha biblioteki istorika', but as a true artist who understood 'fire as a kind of art' (v.152). Beauty, Shvarts writes in both the poem and the short prose piece 'Pravota Nerona' [The Rightness of Nero] (v.152) which accompanies her diary entry for the same day, is only enhanced by transience. Shvarts ends 'Smotriu na goriashchii sobor' with her feeling that Ancient Rome had suddenly intruded upon her familiar St Petersburg:

> И стоит теперь наш храм
> Как античная руина,
> Будто к дому подошел
> Призрак Рима.
>
> [And our temple now stands
> Like an ancient ruin,
> Like the ghost of Rome
> Just walked up to our home.]

Once again, the Rome that Shvarts remembers is the ruined ancient city.

Shvarts's next group of Roman poems, written in the last year of her life, reflect on the lasting significance that visiting the city had for her.

'Vospominanie o Rime' [Remembering Rome] (6 March 2009, v.30) opens with an image expressing the fatedness of her visit to Rome: 'Меня, как сухую ветвь, | К Риму долго несла река' [I was carried, like a dry branch, | Long by the river to Rome]. (See the Appendix for the full poem.) These lines acknowledge what a long time it took her to finally reach a place she had been thinking about her whole life. The floating branch image parallels the image at the end of 'Rim kak budto varvar-gladiator', when Shvarts is carried in the opposite direction, from Rome to St Petersburg, as a snowflake on the wind. The lines also recall the opening lines of the fifth of Akhmatova's *Severnye elegii* [*Northern Elegies*]: 'Меня, как реку, | Суровая эпоха повернула' [I was turned, like a river, | From my course by a harsh era] (1945).[52] In contrast to Shvarts's poem, Akhmatova's laments the cities she has never known; the elegy may have occurred to Shvarts because the same restrictive political system stopped her, too, from travelling in her youth. Shvarts casts herself as Romulus or Remus: she is revived after her journey 'чуть отпив | Древле волчьего молока [with a small sip | Of the ancient wolf's milk]. Drinking the wolf's milk makes her one of the Romans, who, she says, drink it from infancy from the she-wolf that hangs over Rome, its stomach blue and fathomless like the sky. Next she depicts herself wandering about under this sky: her intensive explorations during her winter in Rome. 'Vospominanie o Rime' concludes: 'Обломок жизни моей | Прилепился к руинам Рима.' [A fragment of my life | Stuck to the ruins of Rome.] Shvarts's life is fragmented by her contact with the fragmentary remains of antiquity. This happened 'незримо' [imperceptibly]; it is only in retrospect, when considering her life from the vantage point of death, that Shvarts realises the deep effect Ancient Rome has had on her.

'Vospominanie o reanimatsii s vidom na Nevy techen'e' [Remembering Resuscitation with a View of the Neva Flowing By] (2 November 2009, v.38) takes place in the hospital where Shvarts had an operation, the Military-Medical Academy,[53] with Shvarts lying in a wheeled hospital bed looking out of the window onto the Neva. She imagines her bed being swept into the river, which briefly turns into the Tiber: 'Я в ней как будто Ромул утопала, | А вместо Рема ёрзала беда' [I was drowning in it like Romulus, | And misfortune was wriggling instead of Remus]. This conflates St Petersburg and Rome, as Shvarts has done elsewhere many times. It also repeats motifs from 'Vospominanie o Rime': the river carrying Shvarts to Rome, and Shvarts as Romulus or Remus. In Roman legend, the twins' usurper uncle Amulius ordered the baby Romulus and Remus to be drowned, but a servant saved their lives by placing them in the Tiber in a basket. Their survival stands for Shvarts's 'resuscitation' — the word can also be read as 'reanimation' — or recovery from her operation. The fact that Shvarts sees herself as Romulus rather than Remus, and that the baby wriggling is 'misfortune' rather than Remus, may allude to Remus's future death, as only Romulus will live to found Rome; this could be due to the fact that she herself has evaded death for now. At the end of the poem Shvarts is taken from the river to return to her body — but is not sure that she really can reinhabit her body. The poem's thematic doubling — past and present, life and death, self and other, Romulus and Remus, Petersburg and Rome — expresses Shvarts's alienation from herself and life. 'Vospominanie o reanimatsii s vidom na Nevy techen'e' is a precursor to 'Korabl' zhizni unosilsia vdal'' [The Ship of Life scudded into the distance], where the dying Shvarts is lost at sea (see chapter 2).

52   Anna Akhmatova, *Stikhotvoreniia i poemy* (Moscow: Eksmo, 2008), pp. 280–81.
53   Sarah Clovis Bishop, 'Harmonious Disharmony: Elena Shvarts's *Trudy i Dni Lavinii, Monakhini iz Ordena Obrezaniia Serdtsa*', *The Slavic and East European Journal*, 56.2 (2012), 213–31 (p. 229).

Shvarts's last remembrance of Rome comes in 'Blagodarenie' [Thanksgiving] (6 October 2009, v.219). (See the Appendix for the full text.) It is more of a prayer than a poem, and indeed Shvarts called it 'a non-literary composition'.[54] The central of its nine lines of thanks for her life reads: 'За то, что видела Рим и мир и Иерусалим' [Because I saw Rome and the globe and Jerusalem]. Once again, at the end of her life as at its beginning, she places Rome at the centre of her conception of what is important in a varied world and her own varied life.

The sense of loss and endings compels Shvarts to return to writing about Rome. The first of her post-Rome poems is prompted by national decline and personal loss, the second by a scene of destruction, while the last three are prompted by Shvarts's awareness of her impending death. This tallies with the death that Shvarts found lurking in Rome's classical past throughout her *Rimskaia tetrad'*, but it also brings her back to her enduring impression of Rome as being at the centre of things, and confirms her sense of Rome remaining within her — and a part of herself remaining in Rome — after her time in the city.

Conclusion

Rome has held a central place in Shvarts's poetry, not only in the *Kinfiia* poems, but also in poems written from her own persona, from childhood up to her death. The Third Rome myth is a major factor in the immediacy, personal significance, and Russianness of Shvarts's Rome. So is the fact that Shvarts's Rome is imbued with St Petersburg literary tradition; she cites the Petersburg writers Gogol', Mandel'shtam, and Akhmatova in connection with her Rome. Shvarts's time in Rome had a lasting impact on her; the poems she wrote from Rome and afterwards confirm that it was Ancient Rome in particular that captivated her. Even before she visited Rome and 'a fragment of her life stuck to its ruins', her idea of Ancient Rome as being 'funnier and prettier' than reality has begun to tarnish. This, too, is in large part due to the Third Rome myth: Rome's imperial connotations and the fall of its empire become applied to Russia when the USSR dissolves and plunges Shvarts's poetry into irrelevancy. Eventually, Rome, though still beloved, comes to exemplify decline and the ravages of time. And it is this classical antiquity in decline that we meet in the final chapter, which explores Shvarts's second major classical cycle, *Homo Musagetes*.

---

54   Martynova, 'S nebes v nakazan'e na zemliu poverzhennyi'.

CHAPTER 5

Homo Musagetes: Human, Leader of the Muses

Не тяните меня, Музы, в хоровод
Do not pull me, Muses, into the circle dance
E. A. Shvarts, *Khomo Musaget* [*Homo Musagetes*], 1994

The nine Muses are dancing into the deepening winter of 1994 towards St Petersburg — towards the poet Elena Shvarts, whom they call to join their dance. This is the scenario of *Khomo musaget*[1] [*Homo Musagetes/Human, Leader of the Muses*] (November 1994, II.63–70). (See the Appendix for the full cycle.) The cycle opens with an epigraph taken from Horace's *Odes*: 'Vester, Camenae, vester...' [Yours, Camenae, yours...]. Thus begins an intertextual dialogue with Horace, conducted by Shvarts via diffuse and often tangential allusions to Horace's *Odes*. Quintus Horatius Flaccus wrote his four books of odes between *c.* 30 and 13 BC, under the patronage of Maecenas, and later, Augustus himself.[2] While the *Odes* are far from Horace's only celebrated works, or even definitive of his style or themes (he also published *Epodes* and *Satires* in the invective vein, and *Epistles* in the philosophical vein), his poems in lyric metres extolling good living and friendship, the successes of the Augustan era, Stoic virtues, and the glory of poetic inspiration are what Horace is most remembered for. While *Homo Musagetes* does not contain any concretely identifiable references to specific moments from the *Odes*, beyond its epigraph, Shvarts mobilises an array of Horatian elements — including the seasons, wine, inspiration, bees, the number nine, the figures Apollo, Dionysus, and Orpheus, and the Muses themselves. But the Horatian theme that Shvarts most responds to in *Homo Musagetes* is the theme for which he is most remembered: that all things — except, perhaps, poetry — pass and are subject to time and fortune. This chapter explores the Horatian reception underlying the plot of *Homo Musagetes* and asks what are the implications of Shvarts's use of Horace to the world-view encapsulated in the cycle.

---

1   As *Khomo musaget* is a retransliteration of a Cyrillic transliteration from Latin, I refer to the cycle in its original Latin as *Homo Musagetes*.
2   Horace, *Odes and Epodes*, trans. by Niall Rudd (Cambridge, MA; London: Harvard University Press, 2004), pp. 3–9.

Horace in Russia

Shvarts's love of Horace's poetry is on record. In an interview she picked out Horace as her example of classical literature: 'Horace, whom I love so much'.[3] Ol'ga Sedakova states that Shvarts 'loved to read and reread Horace'.[4] Shvarts had a small bilingual Latin–Russian edition of Horace in her library (*Izbrannaia Lirika*, Akademiia, 1936).[5] In one poem Shvarts even depicts herself reading Horace in the original:

> Потом я в ванне до свету лежу.
> Курю табак турецкий, оду
> Горация с трудом перевожу,
> И часто мой словарь ныряет в воду.
>
> [Then I lie in the bath 'til daybreak.
> I smoke Turkish tobacco, translate
> an ode of Horace's with difficulty,
> And often my dictionary dives into the water.]

The poem, 'Vremiaprovozhden'e' [Passing Time] (January 1981, 1.120) is about Shvarts's wait for (Horatian) inspiration, and is dedicated to the classicist Dmitrii Panchenko, who had become friends with Shvarts the previous year, and had written an article about *Kinfiia*.[6] But despite Shvarts's love of Horace, overall Horace appears infrequently in Shvarts's poetry. Even her Roman cycle *Kinfiia* contains relatively few Horatian allusions. *Dve satiry v dukhe Goratsiia* [*Two Satires in the Spirit of Horace*] (1978, 1.64–68) are, as advertised, only 'in the spirit' of Horace, containing no direct Horatian references.[7] Outside Shvarts's poetry, Horace features in her essay 'I-tszin' [*I Ching*] (n/d, IV.321–22). Having recounted her narrow escape from being killed by a tree, and before coming to a quintessentially Horatian

---

3   Nikita Eliseev, '"Triumf" dlia Eleny', *Ekspert Severo-Zapad*, 5 (2004), <https://expert.ru/northwest/2004/05/05no-scult_50671/> [accessed 11 April 2019].
4   Nina-Inna Tkachenko, '"I ves' sostav moi budet napoen stradan'ia svetom..." Interv'iu s O. A. Sedakovoi v pamiat' poetessy Eleny Shvarts', *Gazeta KIFA* (2010), <http://gazetakifa.ru/content/view/3454/38/> [accessed 25 April 2019].
5   Dmitrii Panchenko, Interview by Georgina Barker, St Petersburg, Russia, 2019. The 1936 bilingual edition contains only selected poems, and *Homo Musagetes*' epigraph ode (III.4) is not among them, so Shvarts must have used another, Latin-only copy of Horace.
6   *The Blue Lagoon Anthology of Modern Russian Poetry*, ed. by Konstantin Kuzminskii and Grigorii Kovalev (Newtonville, MA: Oriental Research Partners, 1980–86), 2B (1985). <http://kkk-bluelagoon.ru/tom2b/shvarts.htm> [accessed 11 April 2019]. Besides their shared interest in Classics, 'Vremiaprovozhden'e' recalls a conversation Panchenko and Shvarts had about the Inquisition. Panchenko.
7   The reference to Horace in the title was itself a late addition; *samizdat* editions title the pair of poems simply 'Vecherinka i Spiriticheskii seans' [Party and Séance]: Elena Shvarts, 'Stikhi, Poemy' (Bremen; Leningrad, 1980), p. 79, Forschungsstelle Osteuropa, FSO 01-265 Pazuchin K35. The poems' main classical reference, to the Cynics Crates and Hipparchia, does not stem from Horace, who writes little about Cynicism (Horace uses Cynicism as a negative example in *Epistles* 1.17, and, arguably, *Satires* 1.2). The séance has a — probably incidental — parallel with *Satires* II.5, which parodies Odysseus's conversation with the spirit Tiresias. Another small incidental parallel is between 'выпывает штрафную бутылку' [drinks a forfeit bottle] and 'ludus erat culpa potare magistra' [there was a drinking game with a forfeit as MC] (*Satires* II.2.123).

conclusion about a poet foreseeing immortality for his poetry, Shvarts quotes not from Horace's ode II.13, where he relates his experience of narrowly escaping being crushed by a falling tree, or from one of his many odes about poetic immortality, but from ode I.11: '«Nefas» — говорил Гораций — «недолжно, неблагочестиво» гадать' ['Nefas', said Horace, it is 'improper, impious' to divine the future]. Thus, Shvarts uses Horace to subtly bind together the essay's themes of divination, near-death by falling tree, and the immortality of poetry, and to align herself just as subtly with Horace and his biography.

Horace has been an influential presence in Russian literature since the eighteenth century,[8] when Antiokh Kantemir, Vasilii Trediakovskii, Mikhailo Lomonosov, and Gavrila Derzhavin first translated and imitated Horace in Russian.[9] When Derzhavin evoked Horace's countryside odes and epodes in the poem 'Evgeniiu. Zhizn' Zvanskaia' [To Evgenii. Life at Zvanka] (1807),[10] he was the first Russian poet to receive Horace in a manner akin to Shvarts's idiosyncratic reception, intertwining 'the high style and the evocation of antiquity [...] with everyday events of Russian life, a combination that contradicted the aesthetic norms of classicism.'[11] But the most famous and enduringly influential rendition of Horace in Russian literature is Pushkin's imitation of ode III.30 'Exegi monumentum', 'Pamiatnik' [Monument] (1836), which had already been imitated by Lomonosov and Derzhavin, among others.[12] Andrew Kahn writes that 'Pushkin turned to Horace in the knowledge of the poem's general importance in European literary culture and its status in Russia', and that therefore Pushkin's 'most blatant assertion of originality', 'Pamiatnik', is based on 'one of the most intertextual tributes to imitation'.[13] Ever since 'Pamiatnik', Russian writers have wanted to write themselves into the tradition established by Pushkin of claiming originality through reception of Horace and Pushkin simultaneously.[14] *Homo Musagetes* engages specifically with the Russian Horatian tradition. Like Russia's favourite work by Horace, ode III.30, the cycle looks ahead from a late stage in the poet's career to her death. Like Pushkin, Shvarts balances Horatian imitation with constantly reasserted freedom and originality. Like Lomonosov, Derzhavin, and Pushkin, Shvarts brings together Horatian antiquity and contemporary Russia.[15] And like Pushkin and subsequent Russian poets, she mediates her reception of Horace through other Russian poets, most notably Osip Mandel'shtam and Aleksandr Blok.

8   Zara Martirosova Torlone, *Vergil in Russia: National Identity and Classical Reception* (Oxford: Oxford University Press, 2014), p. 4.
9   Zara Martirosova Torlone, *Russia and the Classics: Poetry's Foreign Muse* (London: Duckworth, 2009), pp. 25–26, 49, 35.
10 Charles Byrd, 'Thunder Imagery and the Turn against Horace in Derzhavin's "Evgeniyu. Zhizn' Zvanskaya" (1807)', in *Russian Literature and the Classics*, ed. by Peter I. Barta, David H. J. Larmour, and Paul Allen Miller (Amsterdam: Harwood Academic, 1996), pp. 13–34 (p. 16); Torlone, *Russia and the Classics*, p. 35.
11 Torlone, *Russia and the Classics*, pp. 35–36.
12 Andrew Kahn, *Pushkin's Lyric Intelligence* (Oxford; New York: Oxford University Press, 2008), pp. 82–83.
13 Kahn, p. 83.
14 Torlone, *Russia and the Classics*, p. 234 n. 142.
15 Ibid., p. 49.

The reasons behind Shvarts's connecting of Horace with Mandel'shtam are obscure, but fathomable. While Mandel'shtam's poetry is replete with classical references, he wrote no direct receptions of Horace, although he did write a cryptic reception of 'Pamiatnik'.[16] Mandel'shtam may have come so forcibly to Shvarts's mind while writing poetry inspired by Horace because of the two poets' shared Hellenism. Indeed, when Shvarts imagines Russian poetry achieving an equivalent place on the world stage to classical poetry, she writes: 'Mandel'shtam would become like Horace' (III.275). Another possible connection is between the word 'Camenae', the Italian Muses whom Horace invokes, and the title of Mandel'shtam's famous first poetry collection, *Kamen'* [*Stone*] (1913). Mandel'shtam may also have been on Shvarts's mind during the turbulent and depressing 1990s due to the troubled and ultimately tragic circumstances of his poetic career, which took him from acclaim in pre-revolutionary St Petersburg to poverty after the 1917 Revolution, followed by exile in Voronezh and then death in a Stalinist GULag. But it is the Mandel'shtam poems that Shvarts cites in *Homo Musagetes* which provide the strongest connection back to Horace. They all belong to his 'Tauride poems' — a group of poems written during his time in Crimea in 1917–20, inspired by the region's classical history.[17] The five poems Shvarts references — 'Cherepakha' [Tortoiseshell] (1919), 'Kogda Psikheia-zhizn' spuskaetsia k teniam' [When Psyche-life descends to the shades] (1920), 'Lastochka' [The Swallow] (1920), 'Voz'mi na radost' iz moikh ladonei' [Take from my palms to your delight] (1920), and 'Chut' mertsaet prizrachnaia stsena' [The phantom scenery shimmers slightly] (1920)[18] — feature a complex of overlapping Hellenistic images that revolve around the Muses and the underworld, and thus fit well with the tenor of Shvarts's Horatian reception in *Homo Musagetes*.

Blok's major connection with Horace is that he translated ode II.20 (the 'swan metamorphosis' ode), an important ode for Shvarts's Horatian reception in *Homo Musagetes*, as well as I.11 (the 'carpe diem' [pluck the day] ode). But it is Blok's entirely un-Horatian cycle *Dvenadtsat'* [*Twelve*] (1918) — which Shvarts first read aged ten (V.265) — in which twelve Red Guardsmen march through the snowstorm of post-revolutionary Petrograd, that is the single most important overarching intertext for *Homo Musagetes* after Horace's *Odes*. *Dvenadtsat'*'s influence can be felt from the very beginning of *Homo Musagetes*: both cycles open with a snowstorm in Petersburg, both cycles' protagonists are a group of beings progressing through winter's storms towards their goal, and both cycles have a significant number of poems (Shvarts's nine and Blok's twelve). But there are few direct verbal parallels, and only occasional parallels in imagery. Instead, the parallels between *Homo Musagetes* and *Dvenadtsat'* are in the cycles' dramatic movement. Both poets were writing these cycles in the aftermath of a major overturning of Russia's political order — the 1917 October Revolution and the 1991 dissolution of the Soviet Union.

---

16   Roman Voitekhovich, 'Dopolneniia k interpretatsii stikhotvoreniia O. Mandel'shtama "Da, ia lezhu v zemle, gubami shevelia…"', *Toronto Slavic Quarterly*, 13 (2005), <http://sites.utoronto.ca/tsq/13/vojtehovich13.shtml> [accessed 26 February 2019].
17   Iurii Levin, 'Zametki o "krymsko-ellinskikh" stikhakh O. Mandel'shtama', in *Mandel'shtam i antichnost'*, ed. by Oleg Lekmanov (Moscow: Radiks, 1995), pp. 77–103 (p. 77).
18   Osip Mandel'shtam, *Sochineniia v dvukh tomakh*, ed. by A. D. Mikhailov and P. M. Nerler (Moscow: Khudozhestvennaia literatura, 1990), I, pp. 125, 130, 130–31, 131, 132.

Shvarts seems to have turned to Blok for a model of how to respond to revolution with something lacking in both Horace and Mandel'shtam: Dionysian frenzy, which she sees as essential to poetry. Blok's *Dvenadtsat'* evokes the 'Dionysian wind' transforming Russia, and links it to Christianity after the example of Viacheslav Ivanov.[19] (See chapter 2 for discussions of Dionysus and Ivanov.) When Shvarts puts the pagan Muses in place of Blok's Red Guardsmen at the heart of the snowstorm of change, she implies continuity between the pagan/Christian/Soviet world orders — but as in Blok's poem (the ultimate meaning of which is elusive) the reader could see either cataclysm or rebirth in the revolution overturning the classical Muses.

Title

The title *Homo Musagetes* takes the epithet usually given to Apollo, 'Musagetes', or 'leader of the Muses',[20] and applies it instead to 'man', 'homo'. In the surviving drafts, the title arrives relatively late: the original title, *Muzy zimoi* [*Muses in Winter*], becomes the subtitle.[21] In one draft, Shvarts translates *Homo Musagetes* as 'человек — водитель муз' [human/person — leader of muses],[22] rendering the Latin 'homo' [man/human] genderlessly as 'human'. The 'homo musagetes' of the title is presumably Shvarts — on the face of it a bold claim for her poetic abilities. The claim is corroborated both on a textual and a narrative level, as Shvarts marshals the Muses within her poetry, and the Shvarts persona within the cycle draws the Muses to herself, albeit unwillingly.

Horace often depicts Apollo Musagetes, who is recognisable as the god of poetry rather than the bow. Apollo Musagetes tends to appear in the context of Horace's pride in his own identity as a Latin, specifically Apulian, poet, and therefore in conjunction with the Latin Muses, the Camenae. He presents 'Phoebus acceptusque novem Camenis' [Phoebus, dear to the nine Camenae] (*Carmen Saeculare* l. 62) — in other words, Apollo Musagetes.[23] He connects Apollo's leadership of the Muses with his own status as an inspired poet: 'Phoebus, minstrel-teacher of the clear-voiced Thalia, you who wash your hair in Xanthus' stream, protect the glory of the Daunian [Apulian] Muse [Camena]' (IV.6.25–28, pp. 237–39).[24] And the ode from which Shvarts's epigraph is taken features both Apulia (III.4.6–20) and Apollo Musagetes: 'he who washes his untied hair in the pure stream of Castalia, [...] the god of Delos and Patara: Apollo' (III.4.60–64, p. 157).[25]

Horace's appropriation of Apollo Musagetes for himself and his native region is repeated by Shvarts in her cycle, starting with her transliteration of his epithet into

---

19 Judith E. Kalb, *Russia's Rome: Imperial Visions, Messianic Dreams, 1890–1940* (Madison: University of Wisconsin Press, 2008), pp. 106–28.
20 Alex Hardie, 'Etymologising the Muse', *Materiali e discussioni per l'analisi dei testi classici*, 62 (2009), 9–57 (p. 48).
21 'Khomo musaget [1]' (1994), p. 1, ESHA P.
22 'Khomo musaget [2]' (1994), p. 1, ESHA P.
23 Michael C. J. Putnam, *Horace's Carmen Saeculare: Ritual Magic and the Poet's Art* (New Haven, CT; London: Yale University Press, 2000), pp. 87–88.
24 Michael C. J. Putnam, *Artifices of Eternity: Horace's Fourth Book of Odes* (Ithaca, NY and London: Cornell University Press, 1996), pp. 120–21.
25 John F. Miller, 'Horace's Pindaric Apollo (Odes 3.4.60–64)', *The Classical Quarterly*, n.s., 48.2 (1998), 545–52 (p. 551).

Cyrillic for the title. By transliterating the Latin rather than translating it, Shvarts creates nonsensical Russian: 'хомо'/'khomo' seems to be Shvarts's neologism, while 'мусагет'/'musaget' was pre-existent but rare.[26] The unnatural-sounding Russified Latin expresses the uncomfortable collision within the cycle of the classical world of the Muses with Shvarts's Russia. But she goes further, replacing Apollo with a 'human', thus giving the first indication of the demise of the pagan gods that becomes evident as the cycle progresses.

Subtitle

Homo Musagetes' subtitle '*Зимние Музы*' [*Winter Muses*] (which was originally its title) pairs a seemingly incompatible adjective and noun: the general image of a Muse is minimally clad, at home in balmy Mediterranean countries, and throughout the cycle Shvarts makes apparent how ill-suited the Muses are to Russia, constantly pairing their light clothing and bare feet with freezing conditions. Other Russian poets have imagined the Muses in the Russian winter before: Mandel'shtam, in 'Chut' mertsaet prizrachnaia stsena' (see below) — though Mandel'shtam is not interested in exploring the consequences, as Shvarts does; and Georgii Adamovich, in 'Eshche i zhavoronkov khor' [Still even the larks' choir] (1921) — Adamovich's nine Muses turn round and leave because it is too cold. Winter is not a natural element for Horace, either. He consistently speaks of love, life, and death in seasoned terms, linking youth and love with spring and greenery, and old age and death with winter and snow.[27] In seven odes which describe or mention winter, only one, 1.9, describes a winter which is entrenched; all of the others describe winters which are passing: four (1.4, 1.11, IV.7, IV.12) are about spring or fleeting seasons, one is historical (1.2), and one (II.10) is metaphorical. Horace deeply dislikes winter: he speaks of 'ugly winters' (II.10.15, p. 115), and the entrenched winter of 1.9 is to be combatted by staying indoors, lighting fires, drinking wine, and leaving everything to the gods. Most crucially, Horace links the end of winter with the coming of song and dance: 'the meadows are no longer white with hoar frost. Now Cytherean Venus leads the dancers as the moon hangs overhead, and the lovely Graces, hand in hand with the Nymphs, beat the ground with one foot after the other' (1.4.4–7, p. 33). Shvarts's winter is ever deepening, unrelenting, and unending — no place for Horatian Muses, but they dance into it nevertheless.

The subtitle points to the fact that the nine Muses, the classical embodiments of inspiration, are the protagonists of the cycle. Sedakova has noted that Shvarts, unlike her contemporaries, often appealed to the Muse (or Muses), and that for Shvarts the Muse was 'an irrefutable reality. She used to describe her own muse:

---

26 In a footnote to the seventh poem she cites Goethe's 'Die Musageten', which may be her original source for the word. Other possible sources include Igor' Stravinskii's ballet 'Apollon musagète', or the Russian Symbolist publishing house *Musaget*.

27 Brian Arkins, 'The Cruel Joke of Venus: Horace as Love Poet', in *Horace 2000: A Celebration: Essays for the Bimillennium*, ed. by Niall Rudd (London: Duckworth, 1993), pp. 106–19 (p. 110); Steele Commager, *The Odes of Horace: A Critical Study* (New Haven: Yale University Press, 1962), p. 268.

she has a fox's step, she's a fat maiden with a holdall over her shoulder'.[28] But this is the Muse singular, whom Shvarts indeed mentions in many poems.[29] The nine Muses rarely appear outside *Homo Musagetes*, despite the fact that she was interested in them from an early age — when she was fourteen or fifteen she listed all nine and their functions in a notebook.[30] The Muses feature as comic figures in the short note 'Ded Mazai i Muzy' [Grandpa Mazai and the Muses] (n/d, III.266), where they replace the hares from Nikolai Nekrasov's original story, in an idea for a poem that Shvarts says she will never write: 'when the muses have become exhausted [from swimming], they need grandpa Mazai to go round the bay of barrenness and gather them up: crying Euterpe, yelping Erato, howling Calliope'. The pathetic Muses here illustrate the feeling of writer's block. A decade on from *Homo Musagetes*, the Muses figure prominently in the poem 'Podzemnyi ogon'' [Subterranean Fire] (14 January 2005, III.110–11):

> Вниз — не вверх, — подсказали мне Музы.
> Восемь. Урания (дева небесная)
> На галактических светах,
> На холодных бенгальских
> Унеслася туда, где гуляют кометы.
> Остальные спустились в нутро,
> Где и Муз и людей переплавит ядро.
> [...]
> Музы, сказали вы мне:
> Там, в ядре, там, в огне, выход есть, оркестровая яма, раек,
> славный рай.

> ['Down — not up' — the Muses advised me.
> Eight. Urania (heavenly maiden)
> Sped off on the cold,
> Bengali, galactic lights
> To where the comets hang out.
> The others went down into the interior
> Where both Muses and people are smelted by the core.
> [...]
> Muses, you told me:
> There, in the core, there, in the fire, is an exit, an orchestra pit, a
> gods, glorious paradise.]

Here the Muses — all except the Muse of astronomy, who appropriately flies off into Space — descend into the Earth's core in an imagining of death that is also a metaphor for inspiration complete with all the trappings of a theatre. The only other appearance of the Muses in Shvarts's poetry is in the unpublished poem

---

28   Tkachenko.
29   'Rondo s primes'iu patriotizma' [Rondeau with a Dash of Patriotism] (1969, I.22–24), 'Podrazhanie Bualo' [Imitation of Boileau] (1971, I.40), *Gorbatyi mig* [Hunchbacked Moment] (1974, II.71–76), 'V bolezni — Navarin' [In Sickness — Navarin] (1974, ZT 72–73), *Kinfiia* I.5 'Molodomu poetu' [To a Young Poet] (1974, II.9), *Grubymi sredstvami ne dostich' blazhenstva* [Rough Methods Won't Get You Bliss] (1978, II.90–95), 'Zimniaia Florentsiia s kholma' [Wintry Florence from a Hill] (2002, III.38).
30   See Fig. 1.10. ESHA J.VT 94.

'Zavistniku' [To the Envier] (between 24 and 28 September 1980, BT 89), from the *Kinfiia* apocrypha.

So, given their scanty representation elsewhere in Shvarts's oeuvre, why do the Muses take centre stage in *Homo Musagetes*? The answer is simple: because the Muses are central to Horace's *Odes*.

Epigraph

The Latin epigraph 'Vester, Camenae, vester...' [Yours, Camenae, yours...] is from Horace *Odes* III.4.21, and Shvarts attributes it, also in Latin, to 'Horatius'. In a footnote she gives a translation: 'Я ваш, Музы, я ваш...' [I am yours, Muses, yours...]. Whereas all the available Russian translations retain 'Camenae', translating the phrase 'Я ваш, Камены, ваш...' [I am yours, Camenae, yours...],[31] Shvarts substitutes the more familiar 'Muses' for the more literal 'Camenae'.[32] This is not for fear of the rare word 'Камены' [Camenae] not being understood, since she uses it in poem III; her adaptation turns specifically Italian Muses[33] into general Muses, transferrable to a Russian poet.

The epigraph signals the significance of ode III.4 in motivating *Homo Musagetes*. Ode III.4 is one of six Roman Odes which open *Odes* Book III in a more elevated style and serious tone. In the Roman Odes Horace takes on the guise of *sacerdos Musarum* [priest of the Muses] (III.1.3), a guise which, in Steele Commager's words, draws on 'dusty beliefs about the poet's privileged status', through which

> Horace invests his calling with something of the antique dignity that it possessed for a Hesiod or a Pindar. He consciously dons the robes of a *sacer vates* [sacred prophet-poet], asserting his right to speak as from the holy grove, carried along by an ecstatic vision.[34]

This vatic Horace of the Roman Odes would have appealed greatly to Shvarts's view of herself as an inspired poet in the Pushkinian prophetic mould (itself influenced by Horace — see chapter 2). Shvarts chooses ode III.4 out of all the Roman Odes because it is in this ode that Horace makes the 'fullest statement of his devotion to the muses'.[35]

Horace's imaginary inspired travels in the lines following the epigraph culminate in Scythia:

> Yours, Camenae, yours, I am raised
> into the high Sabine Hills,

---

31 Goratsii, *Sobranie sochinenii*, ed. by S. V. Chistobaev (St Petersburg: Biograficheskii institut 'Studiia biografika', 1993), p. 110; Goratsii, *Ody. Epody. Satiry. Poslaniia*, ed. by M. L. Gasparov (Moscow: Izdatel'stvo 'Khudozhestvennaia literatura', 1970), p. 134; Goratsii, *Ody*, trans. by N. I. Shaternikov (Moscow: Izdatel'stvo 'Khudozhestvennaia literatura', 1935), p. 94.
32 She changed her mind more than once about this decision: in the first surviving draft she has crossed out the typewritten 'Музы' [Muses] and written in 'Камены' [Camenae]. 'Khomo musaget [1]', p. 1, ESHA P.
33 'Muses', in *Brill's New Pauly: Encyclopaedia of the Ancient World*, ed. by Hubert Cancik and Helmuth Schneider, 15 vols (Leiden: Brill, 2002–09), IX (2006), 322–25.
34 Commager, p. 207.
35 Ibid., p. 17.

> [...]
> As long as you are with me, gladly
> [...]
> I shall see the quiver-bearing Geloni,
> and, unharmed, the Scythian stream.
> (III.4.21–36; my translation)

Shvarts surely also chose her epigraph due to the prominence of ancient Russia in these lines. When she decided to bring the Muses to Russia she may even have taken her cue from this journey.

However, the epigraph is not a straightforward homage or acknowledgement of a source. In the poems that ensue, Shvarts will question and contradict many elements of ode III.4 — such as Horace's vatic pose, his wish for the Muses' company, and his claim that they can make Scythia safe — rendering her quotation of ode III.4 multiply ironic.

Scythia vs Hyperborea

Scythia is the destination that Horace names in the epigraph ode, III.4. Yet the only ancient Russian location named in *Homo Musagetes* (VII) is Hyperborea, which instead features in ode II.20 (see below: poem VII). The real Scythia and the fictional Hyperborea have been muddled and merged since antiquity. When searching for their place on the Graeco-Roman world map, Russians enthusiastically adopted and conflated Scythia and Hyperborea as 'Ancient Russia'. This section summarises the qualities ascribed to Scythia and Hyperborea in antiquity, gives an overview of Scythia vs Hyperborea in Russian literature, and ascertains which place has most influenced the setting of *Homo Musagetes*.

There was much disagreement in antiquity as to the location and disposition of Hyperborea and Scythia. Before Herodotus, Scythia was proverbial in Ancient Greece for its extreme distance from civilisation, its unbearable cold, its people's nomadism, and its liminality — being in both Europe and Asia.[36] Herodotus's *Histories* IV complicated this picture, showing that Scythia was a varied territory inhabited by various peoples, not all of them exclusively nomadic.[37] Later historians ennobled the Scythians — as early Greek writers, including Homer, had also done — and chose to view them as milk-drinkers rather than cannibals.[38] Hyperborea was even further north of the Graeco-Roman 'centre' of civilisation. Unlike the Scythians, the Hyperboreans were depicted in antiquity as fortunate, godlike, extremely long-lived, and connected to Apollo: Pindar describes the 'blissful and toilfree existence of the Hyperboreans', 'their constant dances and songs' (*Pythian* X),[39] and Pausanias conveys the legend that Hyperboreans founded the Delphic

---

36 François Hartog, *The Mirror of Herodotus: The Representation of the Other in the Writing of History* (Berkeley; London: University of California Press, 1988), pp. 12, 28, 193, 30.
37 Ibid., pp. 13–14, 194–99.
38 James S. Romm, *The Edges of the Earth in Ancient Thought: Geography, Exploration, and Fiction* (Princeton, NJ: Princeton University Press, 1992), pp. 45–47.
39 Maria Pavlou, 'Pindar Olympian 3: Mapping Acragas on the Periphery of the Earth', *The Classical Quarterly*, n.s., 60.2 (2010), 313–26 (p. 322).

oracle.[40] Far from the inclemency of Scythia, Hyperborea was '*huper boreas*, "beyond the North Wind"' — 'beyond the source of the cool, rainy weather which descends on Greece during winter months', in 'a "pocket" of climatic tranquillity'.[41] Horace mentions trans-Danubian peoples — Hyperboreans, Scythians, Geloni, Getae, or Massagetae — in thirteen poems, often in combination.[42] Horace refers to these trans-Danubian peoples quite loosely and inconsistently,[43] generally intending to convey remoteness, exoticism, hostility, and the expanse of Roman dominion.

Russia's literary tug-of-war between Hyperborea and Scythia has, overall, gone the way of the Scythian team. The evidence for Hyperborea begins marginally earlier. Nikolai Karamzin identified the Hyperboreans' territory as northern Russia in his *Istoriia Gosudarstva Rossiiskago* [*History of the Russian State*] (1816–17). This identification was embraced a century later by the Acmeist poets, who named one of their journals *Giperborei*.[44] However, the evidence for Scythia is more weighty, both in quantity and in prominence. Pushkin used his exile in southern Russia — which he repeatedly calls Scythia — as a point of contact between him and the exiled Ovid in 'K Ovidiiu' [To Ovid] (1821). Then the translator of the *Iliad* Nikolai Gnedich unequivocally identified as a Scythian in his poem 'Inostrantsam gostiam moim' [To My Foreign Guests] (1824). And the two most famous twentieth-century parallels between Russians and ancient peoples are with Scythians: Aleksandr Blok's poem 'Skify' [Scythians] (1918) and Marina Tsvetaeva's cycle *Skifskie* [*Scythian Poems*] (1923). Finally, just the year after *Homo Musagetes*, in his essay 'Letter to Horace' (1995) Iosif Brodskii has his Hyperborean-Scythian cake and eats it too. Brodskii mentions all but one of the Horatian Russian tribes — 'we were Geloni, Getae, Budini, etc.'[45] — but settles on Hyperborea, which he designates part of Scythia, as his ancestry: 'northern Scythia — Hyperborea to you'.[46]

Shvarts never refers to Scythia in her poetry. She refers to Hyperborea in three poems (including *Homo Musagetes*), in all three associating Hyperborea with St Petersburg. In 'Zver'-tsvetok' [Animal-Flower] (1978, 1.96) Shvarts transforms herself into a flower, giving herself a Latin botanical name based on her own:

> Напишут в травнике — elena arborea,
> Во льдистой водится она гиперборее
> В садах кирпичных, в каменной траве.
>
> [At the herbalist they'll write — *Elena arborea*,
> It's endemic to icy Hyperborea,
> Typically found in brick gardens, in stony grass.]

---

40 Romm, pp. 60–62.
41 Ibid., p. 65.
42 I.19, 35; II.9, 11, 20; III.4, 8, 10, 24; *Carmen Saeculare*; IV.5, 14, 15.
43 R. G. M. Nisbet and Margaret Hubbard, *A Commentary on Horace: Odes, Book I* (Oxford: Clarendon Press, 1970), p. xxxiv.
44 Alexandra Smith, *The Song of the Mocking Bird: Pushkin in the Work of Marina Tsvetaeva* (Bern, Berlin, New York: Peter Lang, 1994), p. 99.
45 Joseph Brodsky, *On Grief and Reason: Essays* (London: Penguin, 1995), p. 430. Brodskii even corrects Horace for generically calling one of these tribes 'Scythians': p. 429.
46 Brodsky, p. 432.

This pairs Hyperborea with Latin, characterises the place through cold, and brings its mystical connotations into conflict with a real cityscape, all of which she does again and more extensively in *Homo Musagetes*. She equates St Petersburg with Hyperborea more explicitly — but not from her own persona — at the start of 'Arno Tsart''s fantastical cycle about a Taoist alchemist, *Vtoroe puteshestvie lisy na severo-zapad* [*The Fox's Second Journey to the North-West*] (1981–84, II.48–60). She writes: 'Я живу теперь в Санкт-Петербурге | (Городок такой гиперборейский)' [I currently live in St Petersburg | (Such a Hyperborean little city)]. This aside implies that Hyperborea's mystical qualities have transferred to its equally northerly successor. Within 'Hyperborea', in *Homo Musagetes* and elsewhere, Shvarts incorporates qualities of both Hyperborea and Scythia. From Hyperborea: unearthliness, association with death, religiosity, connection with Apollo and Pythia. And from Scythia: liminality, hostility, inclemency, unending winter. From both: extreme northerliness and mysterious non-Europeanness. These are essentially the same qualities that Horace aims to suggest when he mentions Scythians or Hyperboreans.

Form

In her other major classically receptive work, *Kinfiia*, Shvarts used a variety of metres that imitated classical metres, both elegiac and lyric, and significantly eschewed rhyme throughout. Because in *Homo Musagetes* she is writing from her own persona, rather than as a Roman poet, she does not take such pains to mark its poems formally as classical: the majority of the poems in *Homo Musagetes* are rhymed to an extent, and in iambics, the commonest Russian metre. This indicates that *Homo Musagetes* is departing from Horace, rather than imitating him. However, one classical metre is notable by its presence in three poems (II, VII, and VIII): Sapphics — four-line stanzas consisting of three hendecasyllabic (eleven-syllable) lines then a final five-syllable line (an adonic) made up of a dactyl and a trochee. Shvarts had used Sapphics in *Kinfiia* to point to Catullus (pointing to Sappho), but here her allusion is different. Sapphics are the second most common of the thirteen metres employed by Horace in the *Odes*, after Alcaics, so Shvarts's Sapphics put *Homo Musagetes* into a Horatian mode. But by using Sapphics, Shvarts is pointing not only — not even primarily — to Horace, but to Sappho, who is an unspoken absence throughout *Homo Musagetes*.

The nine poems in Shvarts's cycle equal the number of classical Muses, who were first catalogued by Hesiod in the *Theogony*:[47]

> the Muses sang, who have their mansions on Olympus, the nine daughters born of great Zeus, Clio (Glorifying) and Euterpe (Well Delighting) and Thalia (Blooming) and Melpomene (Singing) and Terpsichore (Delighting in Dance) and Erato (Lovely) and Polymnia (Many Hymning) and Ourania (Heavenly), and Calliope (Beautiful Voiced) — she is the greatest of them all.[48]

Whilst some of the Muses' spheres of artistic influence are indicated within their

---

47 Hardie, p. 9.
48 Hesiod, *Theogony; Works and Days; Testimonia*, trans. by Glenn W. Most (Cambridge, MA: Harvard University Press, 2018), p. 9.

names, the assignation of specific genres to each Muse was begun somewhat unsystematically by the Greek lyric poets,[49] and only rigidified in late antiquity.[50] According to Robin Nisbet, Margaret Hubbard and Niall Rudd, by Horace's time poets could 'already play with the idea that different Muses had different provinces', but 'the assignment of provinces was still vague';[51] so Horace rarely differentiates his Muses by genre,[52] instead following his Greek predecessors in 'indifference': he 'sometimes speaks vaguely of "the Muse" [...] and sometimes of a particular Muse'.[53] But Shvarts is informed by the later categorisation of the Muses, and many of the nine poems correspond thematically with individual Muses' purviews. In my analyses of the poems I assign each one an appropriate Muse.

Nine is a significant number in *Homo Musagetes*. The word 'nine' echoes through the cycle, occurring four times from the fourth poem onwards; 'ten' appears instead in the first two poems. The number nine was also programmatic for Horace in his *Odes*. He opens Book I with nine Parade Odes, all in different metres; he then repeats a metre — Sapphics — in 1.10, before bringing in yet another new metre in 1.11 after this 'false closure', thus — as J. S. C. Eidinow writes — 'enacting within his collection [...] his prospective addition to the canonical nine'.[54] Shvarts's comparable repetition of Sapphics, alongside the cycle's insistence on 'nine', is connected with Sappho's status in antiquity not only as one of the nine lyric poets, but as the tenth Muse.

I

The first poem starts with Shvarts looking out of the window of her Petersburg flat at the weather itself dancing — 'Ветер подъемлет кругами' [The wind, circling, rises] — which then merges with the circle dance of the unseen Muses. The Muses have drawn the elements into their dance. The first poem is therefore under the aegis of Terpsichore, the Muse of dancing. The theme of dancing sets up the cycle's central conflict of youth and age, antiquity and modernity. Dancing is a frequent theme of the *Odes*, associated by Horace with youth: 'do not say no to sweet love and dancing, while you are still a lad' (1.9.15–16, p. 43). Yet this first poem of *Homo Musagetes* establishes an aged poet, who by Horatian logic does not want to dance.

Although Shvarts implies in the first stanza that she is both moved and flattered by the Muses' visit, in the second stanza she refuses to join them:

---

49 Hardie, p. 30.
50 Richard F. Thomas, ed., *Horace: Odes Book IV; and Carmen Saeculare* (Cambridge: Cambridge University Press, 2011), p. 123.
51 Nisbet and Hubbard, *A Commentary on Horace I*, p. 283.
52 R. G. M. Nisbet and Niall Rudd, *A Commentary on Horace: Odes, Book III* (Oxford: Oxford University Press, 2004), p. 377.
53 Nisbet and Hubbard, *A Commentary on Horace I*, p. 282.
54 J. S. C. Eidinow, 'Horace: Critics, Canons and Canonicity,' in *Perceptions of Horace: A Roman Poet and his Readers*, ed. by L. B. T. Houghton and Maria Wyke (Cambridge; New York: Cambridge University Press, 2009), pp. 80–95 (p. 92).

> Не тяните меня, Музы, в хоровод,
> Я устала, я сотлела.
> Не во что ногою топнуть —
> Под ногами топлый плот.
> Я уже вам не десятый,
> И уже не мой черед.
>
> [Do not pull me, Muses, into the circle dance,
> I'm tired, I'm burnt out.
> There's nothing to tap my feet on —
> Underfoot is a sodden, sinking raft.
> I am no longer your tenth,
> And it is no longer my turn.]

Shvarts's refusal to dance seems to be worded as a counter to Horace's exhortation to dance: 'Now let us thump the ground with unfettered feet!' (1.37.1–2, p. 93). Her rejection of the Muses' inspiration is a classic *recusatio* (refusal to write what is expected of the poet). Horace opens *Odes* IV with a similar *recusatio*:

> Are you making war again, Venus, after so long a truce? Have mercy, I beg you, I *beg* you! I am not the man I was in the reign of Cinara the Good. Stop, o cruel mother of sweet Desires, stop driving one who after nearly fifty years is now too hardened to answer your soft commands. (IV.1.1–7, p. 219)

Love, rather than dancing, is the metaphor Horace chooses to symbolise his return to lyric after a long hiatus. But both Shvarts and Horace ask to be excused on the basis of old age.

The first poem of Blok's *Dvenadtsat'* also foregrounds wind and the instability of the ground under people's feet: 'Ветер, ветер! | На ногах не стоит человек.' [The wind, the wind! | Impossible to stay on your feet.][55] This literal elemental instability is a metaphor for the chaos of revolution, and Shvarts takes it up in an even more metaphorical form. The middle section of *Dvenadtsat'* 1 contains the voices of a number of people who reject the revolution brought by the Red Guard — an old woman, a bourgeois, a writer, a priest. Though not a *recusatio*, these voices parallel Shvarts's dissent.

References to two Mandel'shtam poems underscore the unusual nature of Shvarts's refusal of a place among the Muses. Shvarts's position in the opening lines — 'Ветер шумит за стеклами, | Вид на задний двор' [Wind whistles outwith windowpanes | Overlooking the rear courtyard] — echoes the position of the Muse Melpomene in the first stanza of Mandel'shtam's 'Chut' mertsaet prizrachnaia stsena':

> Захлестнула щелком Мельпомена
> Окна храмины своей.
> [...]
> На дворе мороз трещит,

---

55 Aleksandr Blok, 'Twelve', trans. by Maria Carlson, p. 1, <https://kuscholarworks.ku.edu/bitstream/handle/1808/6598/BlokTwelve_RusEngTxt.pdf?sequence=1&isAllowed=y> [accessed 22 February 2019].

[...]
И горячий снег хрустит.

[Melpomene has lashed the windows
Of her dwelling with silk.
[...]
In the courtyard frost is crackling
[...]
And burning snow[56] is crunching.]

Shvarts taking the place of a Muse is ironic, since that is precisely what she refuses to do here. The Muses' circle dance alludes to Mandel'shtam's poem 'Cherepakha', which begins 'На каменных отрогах Пиэрии | Водили музы первый хоровод' [On the stony spurs of Pieria | The Muses led the first circle dance]. In her *recusatio* Shvarts specifies that she does not want to be the Muses' *tenth*. In antiquity Sappho was reputed to be the tenth Muse; Plato is quoted as writing: 'Some say there are nine Muses: how careless! Look — Sappho of Lesbos is the tenth!'[57] Sappho appears in 'Cherepakha', and Mandel'shtam's lines about her have a similar focus on dancing feet and the surface being danced on: 'Бежит весна топтать луга Эллады, | Обула Сафо пестрый сапожок' [Spring runs to trample the meadows of Hellas, | Sappho has donned her motley boot]. So the position Shvarts refuses — knowingly, as later poems will show — is that of the most prominent ancient female poet. These two Mandel'shtam poems continue to resonate through Shvarts's cycle. 'Cherepakha' is particularly important: in it Mandel'shtam longs 'for a golden age of humanity, now irretrievably lost',[58] a loss which is palpable in *Homo Musagetes* too. But while Mandel'shtam looks back to the spring of world culture, Shvarts sets her poem in its winter, turning his images to decay.

The third stanza brings a sudden *locus amoenus* ('pleasant place' — a description of an idyllic landscape): 'Пахнет льдом, вином и мятой, | Травы горные в росе' [Scent of ice, wine, and mint, | Mountain grasses in the dew]. This total dislocation from the windy back courtyard of the first stanza represents the powerful temptation that the Muses exert on Shvarts's mind. Horace describes just such a *locus amoenus* whilst invoking Calliope in *Homo Musagetes*' epigraph ode: 'a sacred grove, through which delightful streams and breezes wander' (III.4.6–8, p. 153). Shvarts's list of 'ice, wine, and mint' adapts two similar lists by Mandel'shtam, selectively replacing items with phonetically similar ones. One is from 'Cherepakha': 'мед, вино и молоко' [honey, wine, and milk]. The other is from 'Voz'mi na radost' iz moikh ladonei': 'время, медуница, мята' [time, honeysuckle,[59] mint]. Crucially, the items replaced (honey, milk, time, honeysuckle) are either redolent of Mediterranean warmth or of bees, and Shvarts's addition (ice) is redolent of Russian cold. Both Mandel'shtam poems referenced here involve bees: the list in 'Voz'mi na radost' iz moikh ladonei'

---

56   Mandel'shtam's 'burning snow' is reminiscent of the hot/cold oppositions that Shvarts consistently associates with her Muses.
57   *Greek Lyric*, 1: *Sappho, Alcaeus*, ed. by David A. Campbell (Cambridge, MA; London: Harvard University Press, 1982), p. 48 (Plato, *Anth. Pal.* IX.506).
58   Taranovsky, p. 84.
59   Literally 'lungwort', but chosen for the name's association with honey.

is of bees' food, while in 'Cherepakha' Mandel'shtam compares the Muses and their circle dance to bees: 'Чтобы, как пчелы, лирники слепые | Нам подарили ионийский мед' [So that, like bees, blind lyrists | Would gift us Ionian honey]. In the light of the bees that feature in *Homo Musagetes* III and v, this double bee connection and Shvarts's replacement of 'honey' with 'ice' becomes significant: her bees will dispense not honey-like but ice-like inspiration.

The *locus amoenus* is followed by a reference to Aphrodite, possibly motivated by the appearance of Venus in Horace's *recusatio*. The connection with Aphrodite is pointed out by Shvarts in a footnote:

Вертишейкою распятой**
Закружили в колесе.
** Вертишейку, распятую в колесе, приносили в жертву Афродите.

[A crucified wryneck**
Has been spun in a wheel.
** Wrynecks, crucified on a wheel, used to be brought as a sacrifice to Aphrodite.]

Love is a prominent Horatian theme that is almost entirely absent from *Homo Musagetes*, and where it does appear, like the reference to Aphrodite here, it is conflated with death. The wryneck love charm is ominous: the nymph Iynx, who reputedly invented the charm, ended up being turned into a wryneck herself, and in another version she and her sisters enter a music contest with the Muses and are transformed for their hubris.[60] The rather strange couplet may respond to Mandel'shtam's reference to a 'колесо' [wheel] in the final line of 'Cherepakha', and to the line earlier in the poem 'На свадьбу всех передушили кур' [For the wedding all the chickens have been strangled]. Most importantly, the word 'crucified' introduces the suggestion of a pagan/Christian clash, which is reinforced by Shvarts's instruction to the Muses in the poem's final line: 'Позовите Бога вы' [Call ye upon God instead].

The description of the dancing Muses in the penultimate stanza emphasises their colour and energy, but more so their dangerous, hypnotic power:

Музы кружатся, как бусы
Разноцветные, — пестрей!
И одна из них как прорубь,
А другая как Орфей.
И одна из них как морфий,
А другая как Морфей.
И одна как сон тягучий,
А другая — сноп огней.

[The Muses spin, like beads
Multicoloured — yet more motley!
And one of them is like a hole in the ice,
Yet another is like Orpheus.

---

60 W. Geoffrey Arnott, *Ancient Birds from A to Z* (London and New York: Routledge, 2007), pp. 118–19.

And one of them is like morphine,
Yet another is like Morpheus.
And one of them is like clinging sleep,
Yet another is a shaft of lights.]

The description of the Muses evokes figures who appear elsewhere in the cycle and Shvarts's other poetry, either directly — as with Orpheus (see poem IV and chapter 2) and Morpheus (see chapter 3) — or indirectly: the ice-hole is like Pythia, whom Shvarts consistently characterises as a water conduit (see poem VI and chapter 2), and the shaft of lights (or 'fires') is like Eurydice, whom Shvarts often characterises as a fire-creature (see chapter 2). The comparisons connect the Muses with poetry, hypnosis, and heat versus cold. At the end of the first stanza the Muses' singing and dancing seems to create heat, despite their unsuitable footwear:

Но поднимается жар
И разгорается хор,
Легких сандалий лепет

[But the heat is rising
And the choir igniting,
Light sandals' lisping blether]

The following poems pitch the Muses' persuasive poetic power and heat against Shvarts's will and the cold Russian winter.

II

The second poem belongs to Calliope, the Muse of epic and leader of the Muses, since Calliope herself appears at the end of the poem: 'С первою порошей, по ледку босая | С черно-красным камнем первая бредет' [With the first dusting of snow, barefoot over frost, | With her black-red stone the first goes wandering]. The connection with epic is underscored by the fact that the poem is mostly in hexameter lines (albeit not dactylic). The focus on a single Muse parallels Blok's focus on a single Red Guardsman, Van'ka, in *Dvenadtsat'* II. Again, the barefoot Muse is out of place in the winter's first snow, and instead of playing or singing living music she carries a stone. She is depicted very differently by Horace in the epigraph ode: 'Descend from heaven, Queen Calliope, and come, sing a lengthy song with the pipe or, if you prefer, with your clear voice alone, or with the strings and lyre of Phoebus' (III.4.1–4, p. 153). Yet poem II does open with an acclamation to the Muses that similarly calls on them to make music, albeit more informally than Horace: 'Музы! Девушки! Зима уж навалилась. | Снег под кожею — где флейта, где тимпан?' [Muses! Ladies! The winter really has closed in. | Snow under the skin — where's the flute, where's the timpani?].

A poet should not have to ask the Muses why they are not playing. It becomes clear in the next lines that the Muses are not responding properly to the acclamation:

С верткою поземкой вы впервой явились
С углями в ладонях... или заблудились?
Сгинули, как Пан?

[It was with the twisting blizzard you first appeared
With coals in your palms... or have you lost your way?
Vamoosed, like Pan?]

Already in the second poem the plans the Muses initiated in the first poem are going awry. The coals come from Pushkin's 'Prorok' [Prophet], a poem that underpins Shvarts's conception of poetic inspiration (see chapter 2). In 'Prorok' an angel places a burning coal in the poet's chest to inspire him with God's word:

> И он мне грудь рассек мечом,
> И сердце трепетное вынул,
> И угль, пылающий огнем,
> Во грудь отверстую водвинул.[61]

[And he split my chest with his sword,
And pulled out my trembling heart,
And pushed a coal, blazing with fire,
Into my rent-open chest.]

Shvarts's reference to this graphic metaphor for inspiration tells the reader that the Muses, like Pushkin's angel, are seeking to force inspiration upon a poet. But Pushkin's angel has no trouble finding and inspiring his poet — unlike Shvarts's Muses. The snow under the Muses' skin and the blizzard in which they have got lost suggest the cause of the Muses' trouble: winter.

In the second stanza, Pan's disappearance, ominously for the Muses, resolves into his death: 'Моряки-эгейцы на недвижном море | Услыхали голос: — Умер Пан!' [The Aegean sailors on the becalmed sea | Heard a voice: 'Pan is Dead!']. The story of Pan's death comes from Plutarch's *On the Obsolescence of Oracles*, related specifically as an instance of a god dying.[62] But Shvarts's source is Elizabeth Barrett Browning's poem 'The Dead Pan'.[63] In each of the three subsequent lines Shvarts compresses a section of 'The Dead Pan'. 'Вздох слетел с вершины, солнце побелело' [A breath dropped from the mountain top, the sun turned pale] reworks Barrett Browning's relation of the original pronouncement in stanza 24:

> When a cry more loud than wind,
> Rose up, deepened, and swept sunward,
> From the pilèd Dark behind;
> And the sun shrank and grew pale,
> Breathed against by the great wail, —
> 'Pan, Pan is dead.'

'В мареве Олимп пропал' [In a haze Olympus fell] paraphrases Barrett Browning's

---

61 Aleksandr Pushkin, *Izbrannye sochineniia v dvukh tomakh* (Moscow: Khudozhestvennaia literatura, 1978), I, p. 256.
62 Plutarch, *Moralia: Volume V*, trans. by Frank Cole Babbitt (London: Heinemann; New York: G. P. Putnam's Sons, 1936), p. 401.
63 Elizabeth Barrett Browning, *The Poetical Works of Elizabeth Barrett Browning*, 6 vols (London: Smith, Elder & Co, 1890), III, pp. 280–93. I have been unable to ascertain if a translation of 'The Dead Pan' was available in Russia when Shvarts wrote *Homo Musagetes* in 1994, but as this was after Shvarts began to travel abroad, she could have gained access to Barrett Browning in English, if not in Russian.

description of the dead gods on Olympus in stanza 4:

> Or lie crushed your stagnant corses
> Where the silver spheres roll on,
> Stung to life by centric forces
> Thrown like rays out from the sun? —
> While the smoke of your old altars
> Is the shroud that round you welters?
> Great Pan is dead.

'Только Музы живы' [Only the Muses are alive] responds to Barrett Browning's description of the Muses' reaction in stanza 12:

> Ha, Apollo! floats his golden
> Hair all mist-like where he stands,
> While the Muses hang enfolding
> Knee and foot with faint wild hands?

Shvarts leaves as subtext the connection that Barrett Browning makes overtly — between Pan and Christ, whose death kills the 'false' pagan gods. The gods' deaths may explain why Calliope seems lost and aimless. It is in this poem that the demise of the pagan gods, implicit in the cycle's title, is first addressed. This parallels the Red Guard's intention to kill religion in *Dvenadtsat'* 11: 'Пальнем-ка пулей в Святую Русь' [Let's put a bullet into Holy Russia].[64]

The final stanza begins 'Только Музы живы' [Only the Muses are alive] — out of the pagan gods they are the only ones left. The Muses' quest for a tenth member is then repeated from the first poem: 'им десятый нужен | В разноцветный их и пьяный хоровод' [they need a tenth | To join their multicoloured, drunken circle dance]. This poem's focus on the first Muse's search for a tenth Muse (traditionally Sappho) is the reason why it is laid out in Sapphic stanzas. Furthermore, poem II is in the same position within the cycle as the first of Horace's *Odes* in Sapphics, ode 1.2.

III

The third poem is Erato's, the Muse of lyric and erotic poetry: a bee, a Horatian motif characteristic of lyric poetry, appears here for the first time, and love is mentioned for the only time, paralleling the focus on the doomed love between Van'ka and Kat'ka in *Dvenadtsat'* IV.

The poem begins with a libation to the Muses in the winter snow:

> Вот выпал первый снег.
> Багровое вино
> В сугробы возливая,
> Чтобы почтить озябших Муз
> И дикие стихи
> На свечке сожигая

---

64 Blok, p. 4.

> [So, the first snow has fallen.
> Libating blood-red wine
> Onto the snowdrifts
> To honour the frozen Muses
> And burning wild poems
> Over a candle]

Shvarts libating the Muses suggests a softening of her attitude towards them, a possible acceptance of their inspiration, which seems to be forthcoming in poem IV. Her offerings to the Muses are wine and poetry. Wine is prominent elsewhere in *Homo Musagetes*: Shvarts associates the scent of wine with the coming of the Muses in poem I, and poem IV begins and ends in a wine-cup. Many of Horace's odes involve wine, frequently in contexts pertinent to Shvarts's situation in *Homo Musagetes*. Odes I.19, I.31, III.8, and III.18 all depict wine as part of a sacrifice to the gods. Odes I.9 (the Soracte ode) and I.11 (the 'carpe diem' [pluck the day] ode) both portray wine-drinking as an antidote to winter and advancing time. In I.9 wine stands for Horace's acceptance of mortality: as Commager puts it, 'To drink wine while confronting Soracte is to seize the present, though remaining aware of its briefness'.[65] Shvarts inverts Horace's usage, since she uses the wine to challenge death. Ode I.31 is most similar to Shvarts's libation, with Horace asking for poetry in his old age:

> What boon does the bard ask of the newly consecrated Apollo? What does he pray for as he pours a libation of new wine from the bowl? [...] may I have an old age that is not lacking in dignity or bereft of music. (I.31.1–3, 19–20, p. 81)

Shvarts may also have taken the poem-burning from I.16, in which Horace invites his addressee to burn his invective poetry — albeit not in sacrifice.

The first stanza ends with an unHoratian use of a Horatian image: 'Я Смерти говорю: | Пчелой в тебя вопьюсь.' [I say to Death: | As a bee I will suck of thee.] This alludes to Horace's 'Pindaric' ode, where he also compares himself to a bee:

> I, in manner and method like a Matine bee that with incessant toil sips the lovely thyme around the woods and riverbanks of well-watered Tibur, fashion in a small way my painstaking songs. (IV.2.27–32, p. 223)

But Shvarts's bee is most unlike Horace's bee. Shvarts distorts the significance of the Horatian bee — its aesthetic of humble poetic industry, its connection with (Pindaric) poetic inspiration, and its acknowledgement of Horace's indebtedness to his Greek poetic predecessors — into a communion with Death.[66] The reason for this is what the bee represented in ancient poetry, and what this represents to Shvarts in *Homo Musagetes*. Rachel Carlson explains:

---

65   Steele Commager, 'The Function of Wine in Horace's Odes', in *Horace: Odes and Epodes*, ed. by Michèle Lowrie (Oxford: Oxford University Press, 2009), pp. 33–49 (p. 40).
66   It is interesting to note (but probably not a factor in Shvarts's deathly bees) that bees were traditionally associated with death in antiquity — because of their appearance from out of the ground and caves, and because of their heavenly honey, which was used in rituals. Rachel D. Carlson, 'The Honey Bee and Apian Imagery in Classical Literature' (PhD thesis, University of Washington, 2015), pp. 20–34.

> The equation of the sweetness of song with the sweetness of honey was common in both Greece and Rome [...] The stem for honey (μελι-) appears throughout early Greek poetry, in words used to describe the poetic craft.⁶⁷

Horace's bee comes from the fifth-century BC Greek poet Pindar, who compares his poems to bees: 'the finest of victory hymns | flit like a bee from one theme to another' (*Pythian* X.53–54).⁶⁸ In myths about Pindar (and certain other ancient poets), as a child he was fed honey by bees, turning him into a poet of divinely inspired, honey-sweet songs.⁶⁹ Shvarts was aware of Pindar's connection with bees. She concludes her discourse on poetry 'Poetika zhivogo' [Poetics of the Alive] (1996, IV.272–75) with her own version of the ancient story about how Pindar became a poet:

> Once Pindar fell asleep on Mount Helicon, where the Muses live, and turned into a hive, out of his mouth there flew bees. On waking, he started to compose poems. When I wake up, poems will fly out in all directions, like bees, buzzing and playing, and they will completely replace me.

Not only is her account of the Pindaric myth far more physically disruptive than ancient accounts — the bees actually take over Pindar's body — but her bees are themselves equated with poems (as in Pindar's *Pythian* x), which then take her place just as they took over Pindar's body. Shvarts's transformation into a bee in *Homo Musagetes* III is therefore a sign that, through her acceptance of the Muses, she is becoming a Horatian/Pindaric poet. However, the Shvarts-bee feeds on death because the source of her inspiration — classical lyric poetry — is from a dead world, even if the Muses do not know this yet.

The other source for Shvarts's deathly bees in poem III and V is Mandel'shtam's 'Voz'mi na radost' iz moikh ladonei', which Shvarts quoted in poem I (see above). Mandel'shtam's bees are connected with death from the start: they are 'пчелы Персефоны' [bees of Persephone],⁷⁰ and he calls kisses 'Мохнатые, как маленькие пчёлы | Что умирают, вылетев из улья' [Fuzzy, like little bees, | That die once flown from the hive]. These dying bee-kisses are reminiscent of Shvarts's Death-sucking bee.⁷¹ The bees of *Homo Musagetes* will be discussed further below when they return, even more deathly, in poem V.

In the middle stanza Shvarts anthropomorphises death:

> О, как она бывает рада,
> Когда ее встречают
> [...]
> как любовника: и с трепетом в очах,
> И сладострастьем нетерпенья.

---

67   Ibid., p. 43.
68   Pindar, *Olympian Odes, Pythian Odes*, trans. by William H. Race (Cambridge, MA: Harvard University Press, 2015), p. 375.
69   Carlson, p. 43.
70   'Greek sources (e.g., Hesychius, *Scholia* to Pindar, *Pythian*, IV, 60) report that bees were sacred to Persephone and that they were her initiates (*mystides*).' Victor Terras, 'Classical Motives in the Poetry of Osip Mandel'štam', *The Slavic and East European Journal*, 10.3 (1966), 251–67 (p. 267 n. 73).
71   For analysis of the bee theme in Mandel'shtam, see Kiril Taranovsky, *Essays on Mandel'štam* (Cambridge, MA: Harvard University Press, 1976), pp. 83–114.

> [Oh, how happy she is
> When she is met
> [...]
> as a lover: with tremulousness in their eyes,
> And concupiscent impatience.]

This echoes and alters Horace's anthropomorphisation of death: 'Pale Death knocks with impartial foot on the poor man's cottage and the rich man's castle' (1.4.13–14, p. 33). This ode, like Shvarts's, links death with winter and includes wine and love — but concludes, unlike Shvarts's, that death precludes these latter pleasures.

The final stanza confirms the death of the gods alluded to in the previous poem, and explores the consequences:

> Все боги умерли,
> Оне одне остались.
> Они и в смерть перелетают —
> Как захотят летят они,
> Горя вкруг древа мирового
> Как новогодние огни.
>
> [All the gods were dead,
> They alone were left.
> The others — even unto death they flit —
> Flying howsoever they will,
> Burning round the world tree
> Like so many New Year's lights.]

The Muses have lost their world. Death or obsolescence seem to be the only options left to pagan deities. But the final couplet is replete with imagery from Christianised paganism: the world tree from Slavic (as well as Indo-European) folk belief[72] becomes a Christmas tree (or the secular, communist version, a New Year's tree). This ending of poem III suggests the eventual resolution to the Muses' problem, and the cycle's plot — the pagan Muses' capitulation to modern Christianity.

IV

The fourth poem opens in the style of sympotic lyric with the command to mix wine for the poet:

> Снега насыпьте в красный
> Стакан с тяжелым вином,
> Может быть, я забудусь
> Горько-утешным сном.
>
> [Sprinkle some snow into a red
> Cup with some heavy wine,
> And perhaps I will find oblivion
> In a bitter-consoling dream.]

This makes the poem Euterpe's, the Muse of lyric poetry. The mixing of wine may

---

72 Linda J. Ivanits, *Russian Folk Belief* (Armonk, NY; London: M. E. Sharpe, 1989), p. 30.

come from the *Odes*: 'quench the cups of burning Falernian with water from the stream that's flowing by' (II.11.19–20, p. 117). Particularly similar is the use of natural water: in Horace, a stream, and in Shvarts, snow. When Shvarts wishes for oblivion through wine, she echoes a wish that Horace expresses in this ode and many others; once Horace even gives wine the epithet 'oblivioso' [oblivium-bringing] (II.7.21). Even more significant for Shvarts's wine-mixing is the ode in which Horace counts the measures of wine by the number of Muses: 'Cups are mixed appropriately with three or nine ladles. The inspired poet who loves the odd-numbered Muses will ask for three times three ladles' (III.19.11–15, p. 191). Appropriately, the first appearance of the important word 'девять' [nine], referring to the Muses, comes after the return of the wine-mixing motif in poem IV's final stanza. Horace goes on to say 'insanire iuvat' [going mad is delightful] (III.19.18), a sentiment Shvarts likewise expresses: 'Счастье [...] | В исступленно-строгом бреду.' [Happiness [...] — | It is in ecstatic-strict delirium]. The rest of poem IV, between the wine-mixing introduction and conclusion, is the poetic madness Shvarts experiences as a result of drinking such Horatian, Dionysian wine.

The core of poem IV concerns the archetypal lyric poet, Orpheus. Here Orpheus becomes Shvarts's alter ego, as he has been many times before (see chapter 2), through various very physical interactions between Shvarts and Orpheus's head.[73] Shvarts hopes to dream of Orpheus's severed head; she sails in it like a sailor in a boat. This is Orpheus's second appearance in *Homo Musagetes*, after poem I; his prominence in the cycle is due to his close connection with the Muses — Orpheus's mother was the Muse Calliope.[74] Viacheslav Ivanov even identified Orpheus as 'Мусагет' [Musagetes] in his essay 'Orfei' [Orpheus] (1912).[75] Orpheus likewise appears twice in the *Odes*, in I.12 and I.24, both times following an acclamation to a Muse (Clio and Melpomene). Horace alludes to Orpheus's provenance: 'by his mother's art he checked the rapid course of rivers and the swift winds' (I.12.9–10, pp. 45–47). He also alludes to Orpheus's failure to overcome death by bringing Eurydice back to life, a failure that is central to Shvarts's depiction of Orpheus here and elsewhere: 'What if you [Virgil] could play more charmingly than Thracian Orpheus the lyre that was once heeded by the trees? Would blood return to the empty wraith [...]?' (I.24.13–15, pp. 69–71). Yet despite these limited similarities, Horace's Orpheus is significantly different from Shvarts's Orpheus: both times Horace depicts Orpheus as the poet who can move trees with his song, rather than the man dismembered by maenads. The disembodied head of Shvarts's poem again reflects Shvarts's reception of Horace as a dead poet.[76]

---

73 This is similar to physical intrusions into Shvarts's head by her alter egos Luna/Selene and Venus/Aphrodite (see chapter 2).
74 Nisbet and Hubbard, *A Commentary on Horace I*, p. 148.
75 Ivanov wrote 'Orfei' for the *Musaget* publishing house. V. I. Ivanov, *Sobranie sochinenii*, 4 vols (Brussels: Foyer Oriental Chrétien, 1971–87), III (1979). I am indebted to Pamela Davidson for this observation, among many others.
76 I am indebted to Calum Maciver for this observation, among many others.

The stanzas either side of her voyage in Orpheus's head-boat show its effect on Shvarts:

> Как ее колотило
> Солью, и тьмой, и волной!
> Как она небо корила
> Черным своим языком
> И ослепляла звезды
> Бездонным пустым зрачком.
> [...]
> С тех пор, как я прикоснулась
> К разодранному рту,
> Я падаю тяжким камнем
> В соленую пустоту.
> С тех пор, как я посмотрела
> Глазами в глаза голове,
> Я стала выродком, нищим,
> Слепою, сестрой сове.

> [How it was pounded
> By the salt, and the dark, and the waves!
> How it reproached the heavens
> With its black tongue
> And blinded the stars
> With bottomless empty pupils.
> [...]
> Ever since I touched
> That dismembered mouth
> I have been a heavy stone falling
> Into salty emptiness.
> Ever since I looked
> The head in the eyes
> I am become degenerate, indigent,
> Sightless, a sister to the owls.]

Shvarts herself takes on characteristics of the severed head. She turns into a stone: a round object like the head. She falls into 'salty emptiness': salty like the sea in which the head floats and empty like the head's pupils. She becomes 'sightless': like the stars blinded by the head's pupils, and like those 'bottomless empty pupils' themselves. Shvarts's voyage in Orpheus's head is thus a (terrifying) metaphor for inspiration, as she loses herself in the head of the archetypal poet.

Shvarts's most important source for her Orpheus is Tsvetaeva, a poet who is particularly influential on Shvarts's view of inspiration (see especially chapter 2). Tsvetaeva's poem 'Tak plyli: golova i lira' [So they floated: head and lyre] (1921)[77] presents the same disembodied Orpheus as Shvarts's. I quote the beginning and end of Tsvetaeva's six-stanza poem:

---

77 Marina Tsvetaeva, *Stikhotvoreniia i poemy v piati tomakh* (New York: Russica publishers, 1980–90), II (1982), 137.

> Так плыли: голова и лира,
> Вниз, в отступающую даль.
> И лира уверяла: мира!
> А губы повторяли: жаль!
>
> Крово-серебряный, серебро-
> Кровавый след двойной лия,
> Вдоль обмирающего Гебра —
> Брат нежный мой, сестра моя!
> [...]
> Так, к острову тому, где слаще
> Чем где-либо — лжёт соловей...
>
> Где осиянные останки?
> Волна солёная — ответь!
> Простоволосой лесбиянки
> Быть может вытянула сеть? —
>
> [So they floated: head and lyre,
> Down, into receding distance.
> So the lyre intoned: 'world!'
> And the lips reiterated: 'pity!'
>
> Spilling a blood-silvery,
> Silver-bloody double trail
> Along numb-struck Hebrus —
> Tender brother mine, sister mine!
> [...]
> So, to that island, where sweeter
> Than anywhere are the nightingale's lies...
>
> Where are the illumined remains?
> Salty wave — reply!
> Perhaps the bareheaded Lesbian
> Has pulled in her net? —]

There are multiple consonances between the two poems: the words 'плыли' [floated/sailed], 'голова' [head], 'сестра' [sister], 'Волна' [wave], and 'солёная' [salty] all have direct correspondences in Shvarts; paralleled less directly are Tsvetaeva's focus on Orpheus's lips, the appearance of a bird — a nightingale in Tsvetaeva, an owl in Shvarts — and Tsvetaeva's use of hyphenated compound adjectives and verbal echoes. But there are two crucial differences between the poems. The first is Orpheus's lyre, which in Tsvetaeva has equal billing with Orpheus's head, but in Shvarts is totally absent. Shvarts's absolute focus on the head allows it to be present, in various forms, at all stages of poem IV. The second is Sappho, who at the end of Tsvetaeva's poem provides a hopeful glimpse of a future for Orphic poetry, but who is absent from Shvarts's poem. This ties in with the narrative of *Homo Musagetes*, in which Sappho is a conspicuous absence. Sappho's absence also makes Shvarts's version of the Orpheus myth far bleaker than Tsvetaeva's.

The metaphor of Shvarts's sailing in Orpheus's head as inspiration is supported by the appearance of the gods of poetic inspiration Dionysus and Apollo. Unlike

Horace,[78] Shvarts habitually pairs the two gods (see chapter 2, and the *Kinfiia* apocrypha), a pairing which she takes to an extreme here — Dionysus and Apollo are virtually one being: they fly 'обнявшись' [embraced], and say Orpheus loves them both. The gods represent the danger of inspiration, foreshadowed by Shvarts's opening reference to Horace's maddening/inspiring wine. Horace acknowledges the danger of Bacchic inspiration in odes II.19 and III.25; the latter is especially relevant to *Homo Musagetes*, as it shows a maenad looking out at Hebrus, the river down which Orpheus's head floats, and snowy Thrace, which was associated with Dionysus[79] and next to Scythia.

The last stanza returns to the wine mixing of the beginning. Through repetition and the bloodlike potential of the wine, Shvarts transforms the earlier red cup into her own severed head: 'Вмешайте в вино мне снегу, | Насыпьте в череп льду' [Mix my wine with snow, | Sprinkle some ice into my skull].[80] She thus completes her merging with Orpheus as her alter ego. As well as this, the poem's severed heads parallel Kat'ka's cut neck in *Dvenadtsat'* v (which presages her death in the next poem), and aligns Shvarts with Kat'ka herself, an alignment that will be repeated in *Homo Musagetes* v.

The final couplet shows the Muses in the falling snow, reminding the reader that they are still approaching, despite their apparent absence from poem IV: 'Кружатся девять незримых | В снегопадных столбах звеня' [The nine are wheeling unseen, | Amidst flurries of snowy columns they chime]. The snow forms into a semblance of a building, with the Muses as bells inside it. The bells — the instrument particularly associated with Russian worship — make the snow-building a Russian Orthodox church: another encounter between the pagan Muses and Christianity.

V

The fifth and central poem revolves around two prominent Horatian references. The second of these is stars — making Urania, Muse of astronomy, the Muse of poem v. The first is bees. These bees, while still derived from the industrious Pindaric bee of Horace's ode IV.2, are more numerous and more threatening than the Shvarts-bee of poem III. Moreover, they are now frozen:

Мохнато-белых пчел
[...]
Я отличу легко
От хладных настоящих.
У этих из-под белизны
Косится темный глаз блестящий

---

78 Horace only depicts Dionysus and Apollo together five times, as compared to seventeen individual appearances; one of these instances is in the same ode as Orpheus, I.12.
79 Nisbet and Rudd, p. 304.
80 This is one of many poems in which Shvarts displays her fascination with skulls, and her connection of skulls with inspiration. See the analysis of 'Elegiia na rentgenovskii snimok moego cherepa' [Elegy on an X-ray of my Skull] (1973, I.28–30) in chapter 2, and also Shvarts's prose piece 'Gabala' [Kapala] (1996, III.319–24).

И жальца острые ресниц
Нацелены на предстоящих.

[Fuzzy white bees
[...] —
I can tell them easily
Apart from these frosty ones.
From under their whiteness, these
Squint with a dark, glittering eye,
And the sharp stings of their eyelashes
Are pointed at whoever's in their sights.]

The bees' cold state suggests that they bring death — perhaps the same death that the bee sucked in poem III. There are classical precedents for such violent, threatening bees: in Homer's *Iliad* troops are compared to bees (II.87–93), and in Virgil's *Georgics* two swarms engage in human-like battle (IV.67–90).[81] But the key to understanding the cold bees lies, again, in bees' ancient association with poetry. The Muses were associated with bees because of the connection between honey and poetry,[82] and the first-century BC Roman author Varro called bees 'volucres musarum' [birds of the Muses] (*De Re Rustica* III.16.7).[83] And indeed, in the second stanza it becomes clear that the bees are actually the Muses, when Shvarts addresses the bees as 'Музы' [Muses]. This is not the first time that Shvarts has depicted the Muses as bees. In 'Zavistniku' Kinfiia threatens someone with the Muses' wrath, in the form of bees:

Налетят злые Музы
Пчелиным роем
искусают всего, исколют
[...]
Жальте Музы!
Мне жаль, но жальте!

[Ireful Muses will swoop down
As a swarm of bees
and sting and prick you all over
[...]
Prick him, Muses!
It's a pity, but prick him!]

As in *Homo Musagetes*, Shvarts emphasises the bee-Muses' stings, and even plays on the ironic similarity between the Russian for 'pity' (*zhalko/zhalet'*) and 'sting' (*zhalo/zhalit'*). But there is a crucial difference. In 'Zavistniku' the bee-Muses are under Kinfiia's command, attacking her enemy. In *Homo Musagetes* the bee-Muses are coming for Shvarts.

---

81   Calum A. Maciver, 'Representative Bees in Quintus Smyrnaeus' *Posthomerica*', *Classical Philology*, 107.1 (2012), 53–69 (p. 55); Carlson, pp. 97–100.
82   Carlson, p. 45 n. 123. See also p. 56. The honey connection extended to prophecy, too — Pythia was called the 'Delphic bee' by Pindar (*Pythian* IV.60). Carlson, p. 44.
83   Nicholas Horsfall, 'Bees in Elysium', *Vergilius*, 56 (2010), 39–45 (p. 42).

The bee-Muses bring Dionysian inspiration: 'Тебя оплетает хмельная, | Ледяная, в слезах, лоза' [You are entwined | By a heady, freezing, tear-dewed vine]. Shvarts again alludes to the *Homeric Hymn to Dionysus* (VII) (see chapter 2). Dionysus's vine, imbued with the bees' cold, entangles the reader like the Tyrsenian pirates.

Despite the dread the bee-Muses inspire, inspiration is unavoidable, and it strikes Shvarts — literally — in the final couplet: 'Девять звезд каменистых, | Кружась, ударяют в виски' [Nine stony stars, | Spinning, strike me in the temples]. This blow reverses Horace's programmatic final couplet of his first ode, in which he calls upon the Muses for inspiration and his readers to rank him with his predecessors, the Greek lyric poets, through a metaphorical catasterism (placing among the stars):

> As for me, the ivy crown, the reward of poetic brows, puts me in the company of the gods above [...] provided Euterpe does not cease to pipe and Polyhymnia does not refuse to tune the Lesbian lyre. But if you rank me among the lyric bards of Greece, I shall soar aloft and strike the stars with my head. (1.1.29–36, p. 25)

Instead of raising her head to strike the stars like Horace, Shvarts — using the same, violent verb as Horace — is struck by them against her will. Shvarts's stars are also her Muses: she conflates them via a pun on the Russian words 'каменистый' (*kamenistyi*) [stony] and 'Камены' (*Kameny*) [Camenae].[84] This also parallels *Dvenadtsat'* VI: a jealous Red Guardsman shoots Kat'ka in the head. In part due to the violent influence of Blok, Shvarts's Muses are far more down-to-earth (literally), dangerous, and unwished-for than Horace's.

Shvarts's inversion of Horace's catasterism as the tenth lyric poet reflects her reluctance — stated from the start of *Homo Musagetes* — to become the tenth Muse, as well as the tenth lyric poet. The canon of nine lyric poets was selected at the Library of Alexandria in the early second century BC, 150 years before Horace began his *Odes*. As Denis Feeney notes, for Horace, the list of canonical lyricists

> was closed, fixed forever, as proclaimed in an epigram which was probably written around 100 BC, where the nine are named in nine lines and hailed as the ones who constitute 'the beginning and final boundary [...] of the whole of lyric'.[85]

But for Shvarts, the canon had already expanded once to admit Corinna as the tenth lyric poet.[86] Here, like in poem I, it is not only Horace's position that she is refusing, but that of a prominent ancient female poet. By analogy with Russia, her reluctance to take the place of Sappho (the tenth Muse) or Corinna (the tenth lyric poet) could be understood as unwillingness to follow Russia's most famous female poets, Anna Akhmatova and Marina Tsvetaeva, into the Russian poetic canon.

Horace's invocation of both Euterpe, the lyric Muse, and Polyhymnia, whose name means 'many hymns/odes', signals that he aims to combine the many songs

---

84 A translation retaining the pun might read 'petrean' and 'Pierian'.
85 Denis Feeney, 'Horace and the Greek Lyric Poets', in *Horace*, ed. by Lowrie, pp. 202–31 (p. 202).
86 Ibid.

of his Greek predecessors to create his own lyric poetry. This, in his first ode, is Horace's most explicit statement of his *receptive* poetic programme. Shvarts's reception of this moment may be read as an acknowledgement that her inspiration to write *Homo Musagetes* is inextricably tied up with her reception of her poetic predecessors, just like her primary source, Horace's *Odes*.

VI

The sixth poem, 'Pifiia' [Pythia], presents the reader with a pathetic, hiccupping, and deranged Pythia. As this is as comic as the cycle gets, this is the poem of Thalia, the comic Muse. Thalia was initially intended to *be* the hiccupping woman: poem VI was originally titled 'Taliia' [Thalia].[87] Thalia appears once in the *Odes*: 'Phoebus, minstrel-teacher of the clear-voiced Thalia' (IV.6.25–26, p. 237). Pythia also appears once, by implication: 'nor the resident in Pytho's shrine [Apollo] [...] has such a shattering effect on the minds of his priests' (I.16.5–6, p. 57). This double connection to Apollo may answer the question at the end of the poem as to why Pythia (or Thalia) is hiccupping uncontrollably: ' — Да что же с ей такое? | Иль умер кто у ней?' [What on earth's the matter with her? | Has there been a death in the family?]. Her hiccupping derangement may be due to the absence (death) of Apollo, upon whom Pythia and the Muses traditionally depend. Her hiccups could be yet another sign of the demise of the pagan gods. Pythia's distress and the 'death in the family' also parallels *Dvenadtsat'* VII: the Red Guardsman Petrukha's despondency at having murdered Kat'ka, whom he loved.

The other possible answer for why Pythia is hiccupping lies elsewhere in Shvarts's oeuvre, where more than once Shvarts takes Pythia as her alter ego (see chapter 2), and depicts the oracle as an inspired poet, whose inspiration, figured repeatedly as water, can prove fatal to her. The Muses' solution to Pythia's hiccups — throwing water over her — actually seems to make her condition worse:

> Облей ее водою,
> И полегчает ей.
> — Смотри, глаза полезли
> И пена из ушей.
>
> [Throw some water over her,
> That'll help calm her down.'
> 'Look, her eyes are bulging
> And froth's coming out her ears.']

Poem VI may depict the harmful effects of the Muses' inspiration: this would make Pythia an ominous warning to Shvarts herself.

---

87 'Khomo musaget [1]', p. 6, ESHA P.

VII

The seventh poem is the most wintry of all the poems in *Homo Musagetes*. It connects poetic inspiration with (im)mortality even more strongly than poems III–V, informed like them by the *Odes*' preoccupation with poetic immortality. Clio, Muse of history, is therefore the Muse of poem VII.

Shvarts asks: 'Музы (замерзли!) — белые мухи* | Вас завлекли сюда?' ['Muses (you're frozen!) — have the white flies* | Enticed you here?']. White flies are a development from the white bees in poem V. A footnote explains the flies' source:

> * One of Goethe's poems is 'Die Musageten' [Musagetes]. He believes that Musagetes are flies, as both of them appear in summer. Here, flies are also Musagetes, but winter ones — 'white flies'.

Goethe's 'Musagetes' considers the poetic potential of each season, and concludes that summer is best for writing poetry. Flies, which are only present in summer, make that season the most productive for the poet:

> Lastly, came the glorious summer;
> What aroused me then from dreaming,
> At the earliest dawn of morning?
> 'Twas the buzzing of the flies!
> [...]
> Straightway start I from my pillow,
> Leave the close-beleaguered chamber,
> Sally out to seek the Muses,
> [...]
> Thus I owe you, libelled insects.
> [...]
> And I thank you, as a poet,
> Ranking you, beyond all others,
> As the ushers to the Muse.[88]

Shvarts relocates Goethe's Musagetes flies from summer to winter, in the wintriest poem of the cycle, to underscore still more deeply the anomaly of the Muses' presence in Russia.

Poem VII is the first poem in *Homo Musagetes* that unambiguously locates the Muses in Russia:

> — Мир оттеснил нас, глухая вода,
> В гиперборею.
> Долго скользили во тьме седой
> Над морем Белым

> ['The world, the deaf water, has pushed us out
> Into Hyperborea.'
> Long had we slipt through the grey-haired gloom
> Over the White Sea]

---

[88] Johann Wolfgang von Goethe, *Poems and Ballads of Goethe*, trans. by W. Edmondstoune Aytoun and Theodore Martin (Edinburgh; London: W. Blackwood, 1859), pp. 159–61.

Specifically, the Muses are in north-west Russia, to the north of St Petersburg. This suggests that they *are* lost, as Shvarts supposed in poem II: there is no sensible route from Italy to St Petersburg that would go via the White Sea.

The Muses identify their northerly location as Hyperborea. Hyperborea is a symbolically loaded concept within both Russian and classical literature, connected by classical and Russian authors alike with Scythia (see above). Shvarts's Hyperborea in this poem is particularly affected by the cold of Scythia, indicating the influence of the epigraph ode III.4, which features the Geloni, a semi-mythical Scythian tribe redolent of extreme cold (*gelu*) and extreme north-easterliness.[89] But the most important Horatian intertext for Shvarts's Hyperborea in poem VII is Horace's declaration at the close of *Odes* Book II that he/his fame/his eternal poetry will visit Hyperborea:

> Soon, more famous than Daedalus' Icarus
> I shall see [...]
> [...], as a melodious
> bird, the Hyperborean plains. (II.20.13–16)

Hyperborea and the swan were both symbols of immortality in antiquity, because of Hyperborea's reputation as a 'resting-place for the dead', and because of the swan's miraculous dying song and 'distant northern flight', which connected swans with Apollo and 'the felicity of the Hyperboreans'.[90] The 'глухая вода' [deaf water], which has pushed the Muses to the frozen North, echoes Shvarts's protestation against the Muses' arrival in the first poem: 'Уже год у нас не певчий, | А глухой водоворот' [This year with us is no longer songful, | But a tone-deaf whirlpool]. This suggests that, despite Hyperborea's connections with unearthliness and Apollo, the Muses will receive a cold reception on the edge of the (Roman) civilised world. The Muses, saying 'Мир оттеснил нас' [The world [...] has pushed us out], also imply that Hyperborea/Russia is outside the world. From the perspective of the ancient map, Scythia and certainly Hyperborea were both beyond the civilised, known world. From the perspective of the modern map, in 1994 Russia had just been displaced from the heart of a huge empire to become a (comparatively) lone country on the periphery of Europe and Asia, a shift that Shvarts had felt keenly (see chapter 4).

Horace's defiance of death and visit to Hyperborea in ode II.20 is predicated on the lasting renown of his poetry. He embodies his eternal poetry by metamorphosing into a bird:

> On no common or flimsy wing shall I be borne aloft through the clear air, a poet of double shape. [...] I [...] shall not die, shall not be confined by the waters of the Styx.
> Now as I speak, rough skin forms on my legs; I am changing into a white bird in my upper part, smooth feathers sprout from finger to shoulder. (II.20.1–12, p. 139)

---

89 Nisbet and Hubbard, *A Commentary on Horace I*, p. 400.
90 R. G. M. Nisbet and Margaret Hubbard, *A Commentary on Horace: Odes, Book II* (Oxford: Clarendon Press, 1978), pp. 346, 333–34.

Shvarts reverses Horace's image — rather than turning the poet and their immortal poetry into a bird, her Muses turn a bird into an inspired, immortal poet:

> Видим — на льдине живой воробей
> Оледенелый.
> Мы и согрели его собой,
> Синими языками
> Молний живых, и на свет голубой
> Дале рванулись.
> А он плывет там и поет
> На девяти языках,
> С синим огнем в ледяной голове,
> Невидимым в очах.

[We glimpse — a sparrow, alive, on an ice floe,
Frozen through.
So we warmed him with ourselves,
With blue tongues
Of living lightning, then we tore onwards
To daylight.
And he floats there and sings
In nine tongues,
With blue fire in his icy head,
Imperceptible in his eyes.]

Both poems are a defiance of death, achieved through poetry, and enacted through a metamorphosis. But while Horace's metamorphosed poet-swan is majestic, Shvarts's reanimated sparrow-poet is disturbing. Once again, Shvarts is receiving Horace in the form of a dead thing.

In the final lines of poem VII the sight of the undead sparrow, reanimated by the Muses, breaks Proserpina's heart: 'Лопнуло накрест в подвалах Эреба | Сердце седой Прозерпины' [In the basements of Erebus the heart | Of hoary-headed Proserpina broke in two]. This refers to Horace's narrow escape from 'dusky Proserpine' (II.13.21, p. 123), as well as the universal truth Horace states that 'merciless Proserpine never shuns a head' (1.28.19–20, p. 77). The sparrow could be taken from *Dvenadtsat'* VIII: 'Ты лети, буржуй, воробышком! | Выпью кровушку' [Fly away, bourgeois, like a sparrow small! | I will drink your blood].[91] The connection of Proserpina with a dead bird also responds to a trio of poems by Mandel'shtam that depict a swallow in the underworld: 'Kogda Psikheia-zhizn'' spuskaetsia k teniam', 'Lastochka', and 'Chut' mertsaet prizrachnaia stsena'. In 'Kogda Psikheia-zhizn'' spuskaetsia k teniam' the name 'Персефоной' [Persephone] is immediately followed by the lines 'Слепая ласточка бросается к ногам | С стигийской нежностью и веткою зеленой' [A blind swallow tumbles at her feet | With Stygian tenderness and a green twig]. In the near-repetition of these lines in 'Lastochka', the swallow becomes an embodiment of a/the word:[92] 'беспамятствует слово. | [...] | То мертвой ласточкой бросается к ногам' [the

---

91 Blok, p. 9.
92 Taranovsky, p. 77.

word falls into senselessness. | [...] | Now, a dead swallow, it tumbles at my feet] (etc.). Shvarts parallels Mandel'shtam's metaphor: the Muses fill their dead sparrow with words. Finally, in 'Chut' mertsaet prizrachnaia stsena' Mandel'shtam aligns the same swallow with Eurydice through pervasive allusions to Gluck's opera *Orfeo ed Euridice*: Eurydice is called 'голубка'[93] [my dove] and situated in Russia's 'студеная зима' [freezing winter]; in the final lines — 'И живая ласточка упала | На горячие снега' [And a living swallow fell | Onto the burning snows] — Mandel'shtam must be referring to Eurydice's second death. This Mandel'shtamian reference by way of Proserpina brings Eurydice into *Homo Musagetes* — where Orpheus is prominent but she is all but absent.

Shvarts's selection of a sparrow rather than Horace's swan or Mandel'shtam's swallow, or any other bird, points towards three additional intertexts — and Shvarts has previously alluded to both of the classical ones (see chapters 2 and 3). The first is Shvarts herself, who called herself a 'Leningrad sparrow' (v.139). The second is Catullus, whose sparrow is the most famous in literature:

> And now he's off on the dark journey
> From which they say no one returns.
> Shame on you, shameful dark of Orcus,
> For gobbling up all the pretty things!
> You've robbed me of so pretty a sparrow.
> (Cat. III.11–15, p. 5)

The Muses' reanimation of the sparrow contradicts the lesson Catullus derives from the sparrow's death, that death is permanent, but also acts on his complaint against the underworld — Shvarts gets the sparrow back. The third is Sappho, whose *Hymn to Aphrodite* has the next most famous sparrows in literature: 'beautiful swift sparrows whirring fast-beating wings'.[94] Poem VII is in Sapphics (arranged unusually in couplets), a metre that both underscores her reference to Sappho's sparrows and comments on the Muses' ongoing mission to recruit her as their tenth, in Sappho's place. The Sapphic-Catullan-Blokian-Mandel'shtamian-Horatian sparrow is a proxy for Shvarts herself, should she relent — and its fate is a dire warning.

VIII

The eighth poem, 'Voskhvalenie drug druga u Nikol'skogo sobora' [Encomium of Each Other before Nikolsky Cathedral], is the first to invoke individual Muses by name. Its tragic plot and emphasis on song indicate that Melpomene, Muse of both song and tragedy — and among the Muses invoked — is this poem's Muse.

By this penultimate poem the Muses have reached St Petersburg:

> Аркады желтые, в проплешинах, Никольского рынка,
> Где делают с цветочками посуду
> Эмалированную, — там в длинную флейту ветер
> Дует ночами.

---

93 Simultaneously a bird and an endearment (see chapter 2).
94 Sappho, trans. by Campbell, pp. 53–55.

Fig. 5.1. View of the Nikolsky Market, Nikolsky Cathedral, and Kriukov Canal from above. Photograph by vasia_morskoi. Published on LiveJournal.

[The yellow arcades, paint peeling in patches, of the Nikolsky Market,
Where they make enamelware with little flowers
On it — there, down the long flute the wind
Blows through the night hours.]

The reference to the market's produce situates the poem in contemporaneity.[95] The image of the market as a flute is motivated by the appearance of the Nikolsky Market's brownish yellow arcades, with hole-like gaps spaced evenly along its length.[96]

Although the classical image of the flute helps to integrate the Muses into the modern setting, they are still hopelessly out of place. Their clothing is entirely unsuitable, and they are compared not to modern beings but to ancient Greek philosophers of the Aristotelian school: 'подпоясанные небрежно, босые, | Как перипатетики' [carelessly girded, barefoot, | Like Peripatetics].

It is perhaps because the Muses have arrived in the poet's vicinity that Shvarts names individual Muses at this point, for the first time. Out of the four whom Shvarts names, three are among the six Muses mentioned in Horace's *Odes*. Erato, Muse of lyric and erotic poetry, who is not present in Horace, appears first. Shvarts describes the inspiration she gives as a form of desire:

> — Молний сноп на поясе у тебя, Эрато,
> Без тебя не сложится ни гимн, ни песня,
> Подойдёшь ближе, глянешь — кровь быстрее
> В словах рванется.

---

95 'After 1917 an industrial manufacturing association producing enamelled tableware was established in the Nikolsky market building.' Aleksandr Chernega, 'Nikol'skii rynok (Sadovaia ul., 62)', *Progulki po Peterburgu* (2005), <http://walkspb.ru/zd/sadovaya62.html> [accessed 6 June 2016].
96 vasia_morskoi, 'Sankt-Peterburg s vozdukha: 20 foto', <http://yandex.livejournal.com/194741.html> [accessed 31 October 2014].

> ['You have a shaft of lightning at your belt, Erato,
> Without you neither hymn nor song will take shape,
> If you approach closer, bestow a glance — the blood rushes
> Faster through the words.']

Next comes Polyhymnia. Polyhymnia appears just once in Horace's *Odes*, but prominently, near the end of the first ode, just before Horace's catasterism among the Greek lyric poets: 'provided [...] Polyhymnia does not refuse to tune the Lesbian lyre' (I.1.33, p. 25). But whereas Horace invokes Polyhymnia to indicate the multiplicity of his Greek lyric sources, Shvarts depicts Polyhymnia exclusively as the Muse of sacred poetry:

> Ну а ты, Полигимния, не скромничай, дева,
> Взор певца устремляешь в небо,
> Без тебя он ползал бы по земле, извиваясь,
> Тварью дрожащей.

> ['As for you, Polyhymnia, be not so modest, maiden,
> You direct the singer's gaze towards the sky,
> Without you he would crawl o'er the earth, squirming
> Like a quiv'ring beast.']

Polyhymnia's depiction as a religious Muse is part of the cycle's movement towards Christianity. The other two get only brief mentions: ' — Без тебя, Мельпомена, без тебя, Клио...' ['Without you, Melpomene, without you, Clio...']. Melpomene, Muse of song and tragedy, is the Muse most frequently invoked by Horace (I.24, III.30, IV.3), while Clio, Muse of history, is invoked just once by Horace (I.12). In the same stanza, the Muses dance into the form of a crown, echoing the 'final poem' of Horace's *Odes*, III.30, in which Horace asks Melpomene to crown him with laurel, as a closural motif.[97] Typically, Shvarts subverts both the closure and the classical motif of the laurelled poet — the Muses will not be allowed to crown her.

Although the 'crown' that the Muses form as they dance must still be their circle dance from poem I, it is now imbued with Christian imagery: 'сливались в темнисто-светлый | Венец терновый' [they merged into a dark-bright | Crown of woven thorns]. The transformation of their pagan circle dance from the first poem into a symbol of Christ in the penultimate poem demonstrates once more that the Muses' time — paganism — is over. Christ's crown evokes the final lines of *Dvenadtsat'* XII, when Blok reveals that the soldiers are being led by Christ, wearing a crown of roses:

> ... Так идут державным шагом —
> Позади — голодный пес,
> Впереди — с кровавым флагом,
> И за вьюгой невидим,
> И от пули невредим,
> Нежной поступью надвьюжной,
> Снежной россыпью жемчужной,

---

97 Eidinow, 'Horace: Critics, Canons and Canonicity', in *Perceptions of Horace*, ed. by Houghton and Wyke, p. 89.

> В белом венчике из роз —
> Впереди — Исус Христос.
>
> [... And so they keep a martial pace,
> Behind them follows the hungry dog,
> Ahead of them — with bloody banner,
> Unseen within the blizzard's swirl,
> Safe from any bullet's harm,
> With gentle step, above the storm,
> In the scattered, pearl-like snow,
> Crowned with a wreath of roses white,
> Ahead of them — goes Jesus Christ.][98]

Parallels with Blok continue through the rest of poem VIII — but with a poem earlier in the cycle, *Dvenadtsat'* IX: the Muses' wish to intoxicate someone parallels the Guardsmen urging each other 'Гуляй, ребята, без вина!' [frolic, friends, though there's no wine!];[99] both poems are set by a cathedral tower (Nikolsky and Nevsky); and in both an unfortunate man becomes animal-like (the beggar and the bourgeois). But the fact that *Homo Musagetes*' clearest intertext with *Dvenadtsat'* is with this moment — the cycle's shocking and puzzling conclusion, where Blok reveals Christ as the leader of the Red Guard's march — suggests that it is Blok's commentary on religion that Shvarts finds most relevant to *Homo Musagetes*. And when the Muses dance into a crown-of-thorns formation, this symbolises the man who has come at the end to lead them, as in *Dvenadtsat'*: Christ. With this Shvarts affirms Blok's apparent message: that Christ will continue to be relevant, no matter what is happening in Russian politics. Shvarts's allusion to Blok here, in combination with the Christian imagery that increasingly overtakes the Muses towards the end of *Homo Musagetes*, opens up a new interpretation of the cycle's title: perhaps the Homo Musagetes, replacing the dead Apollo, is not Shvarts, but Christ.

Given Shvarts's continued refusal to join them, the Muses seek someone to inspire:

> Ах, кому нам девяти, бедным,
> Передать свою поющую силу,
> Ах, кого напоить водой кастальской,
> Оплести хмелем?
>
> [Ah, to whom are we nine, oh, poor maidens!,
> To bequeath our power of song,
> Ah, whom are we to intoxicate with Castalian water,
> Entwine with hop vines?]

The Muses' inspiration methods have already been encountered and discredited earlier in the cycle: the dismembered Orpheus, the hiccupping Pythia, the dead sparrow. The Castalian water, which was used in Pythia's cult at Delphi,[100] is presumably the same water that worsens Pythia's condition in poem VI. The hop

---

98 Blok, p. 12.
99 Ibid., p. 9.
100 '101 Castalian Spring', *Livius* (2015), <http://www.livius.org/articles/place/delphi/101-castalian-spring/> [accessed 2 June 2017].

vines are presumably the same as the entwining vine in poem v, which is described ominously as 'хмельная, | Ледяная, в слезах' [heady, freezing, tear-dewed]. Accordingly, the chosen recipient of inspiration, a homeless man, is driven mad and throws himself into the Kriukov canal (which runs along the left of the picture above, past the market and belltower). The beggar's madness suggests either that inspiration would be hazardous for Shvarts, too, or that Shvarts is the only one whom the Muses can safely inspire.

Yet the form of poem VII underlines Shvarts's refusal to take Sappho's former place among them. Even though it imitates the Sapphic stanza, which may seem to contradict Shvarts's refusal, it has only nine stanzas — just as the cycle has only nine poems, and just as the Muses will remain only nine in number.

IX

The ninth poem, 'Muzy pered Ikonoi' [Muses before the Icon], is Polyhymnia's, the Muse of sacred poetry — the Christian Polyhymnia whom Shvarts presents in the previous poem. The Muses have ended up where Shvarts told them to go in the final line of the first poem: 'Ах, оставьте человека, | Позовите Бога вы' [Ah, leave mankind alone, | Call ye upon God instead]. They enter a cathedral in the guise of, if not repentant, then cold and somewhat guilty sinners, bowing to the icon:

> По очередности — пред Троеручицей
> Творят — и в сторону — поклон короткий.
> Меж рук Иконы неземной
> Скользят отчетливо, как четки.
>
> [In order of precedence, before the Virgin of the Three Hands
> They make her — and to the side — a brief bow.
> Through the hands of the unearthly Icon
> They slip one by one, like rosary beads.]

Their transformation before it into a rosary echoes their transformation into a crown of thorns in the previous poem, with its Blokian connotations; their respect for the icon contradicts the Red Guardsman's blasphemy in *Dvenadtsat'* x: 'От чего тебя упас | Золотой иконостас?' [Did the golden icon screen | Ever save you from a thing?][101] The Muses' concession to the power of religion goes beyond the ambiguous ending of *Dvenadtsat'* to decisively declare the importance of religion to Russia's new social order. It also recalls Horace's gesture of defeat in love, when he hangs up a votive offering to the gods: 'a votive tablet on his temple wall records that I have dedicated my drenched clothes to the deity who rules the sea' (1.5.13–16, p. 35). The icon to which the Muses bow hangs in Nikolsky Cathedral, and Shvarts visited it regularly (v.107, 155), even calling it 'my Troeruchitsa' (v.90) and addressing a poem to it.[102]

---

101 Blok, p. 10.
102 'Troeruchitsa v Nikol'skom sobore' [Virgin of the Three Hands in Nikolsky Cathedral] (1996, 1.345).

Fig. 5.2. Troeruchitsa Icon, Nikolsky Cathedral, 2013.
'Ikona Bozhiei Materi Troeruchitsa', *Nikolo-Bogoiavlenskii morskoi sobor* (2013), <http://www.nikolskiysobor.ru/svyatynya/drugie-svyatyni-sobora/38-chudotvornyj-obraz-svyatitelya-nikolaya-arkhiepiskopa-mir-likijskikh-chudotvortsa-2>
[accessed 22 February 2019].

In the final stanza, the Muses recognise what the cycle's clash of antiquity with modernity, the death of the pagan gods, their unnatural resurrection of the dead and unsuccessful inspiration of the lowly, and the encroaching Christian symbolism all imply — that their time has passed: ' — Все наши умерли давно.' ['All our kindred died long ago.']. Their response can accordingly only be in Christian terms: 'Заупокойный заказали' [They commissioned a requiem mass'].

Conclusion

Shvarts's receptions of Horace in *Homo Musagetes* seem designed to demonstrate that the world of Horace's *Odes* is obsolete. The Scythia-like Hyperborea of wintry St Petersburg is entirely inimical to the Mediterranean Muses; all the other representatives of classical antiquity in the cycle are dead or associated with death;[103] and the Muses ultimately fail in their mission and abandon their culture. Even the trajectory of the cycle — away from paganism and towards Christianity, into Russia, into winter, towards old age and death — encodes the obsolescence of Horatian values and Graeco-Roman antiquity. The ultimate effect of Shvarts's Horatian reception is, paradoxically, to question the relevance of the classical world to Shvarts in 1990s St Petersburg. The epigraph framing the cycle becomes less a statement than a question: 'Yours, Muses, am I yours?' Her response wavers through the cycle: initial *recusatio* (I), Pushkinian 'Prorok'-style temptation (II), honouring the Muses (III), embarking on an inspired journey (IV), being forcibly inspired (V), negative examples of inspiration (VI, VII, VIII), and finally, the Muses surrendering to Shvarts's religion (IX). Such ambivalence marks a watershed between *Homo Musagetes* and Shvarts's earlier embracings of classical poets/inspirers, with all the pain and danger they bring (see chapter 2). Shvarts's final answer to 'Yours, Muses, am I yours?' is, apparently, 'No': she leads them into her modernity, but never takes Sappho's place as their tenth.

What has changed, for Shvarts to reject Horatian inspiration? The simple answer repeats her response in poem I: she is older now. Yet the cycle's depictions of Russia as cold and hostile, its pervasive citations of Mandel'shtam's poems about the Muses, the underworld, and a lost classical golden age, and its overarching narrative paralleling (and overtaking) of Blok's revolutionary *Dvenadtsat'*, point to a more complex cause of Shvarts's cynicism. When *Homo Musagetes* was written (1994), Russia was undergoing the aftermath of the USSR's collapse. Writing a cycle that is about ageing and winter and the ending of eras and the death of gods at such a time must reflect upon Shvarts's disappointment and bewilderment with, and difficulty adapting to, the new, more marginal, less poetry-centric, and generally harsher reality — as she also expressed in her Roman poems of this period.

In *Homo Musagetes* Shvarts is not the Muses' poet as Horace was. But a crucial paradox remains: *Homo Musagetes*' pervasive Horatian reception. In particular, Shvarts's engagement with Horace's themes of his own reception of lyric

---

103 Pan (II), the bees (III, V), the pagan gods (III), Orpheus (IV), Dionysus (IV, V), Apollo (IV, VI), Pythia (VI), the sparrow (VII).

predecessors, and of fleeting time versus poetic immortality, draws attention to the fact that the very presence of Horace in her poetry proves he is still relevant. As he predicted in ode II.20, Horace has indeed avoided death by visiting the Hyperborean plains. Even the obsolescence of Horace's Muses in the cycle is Horatian: in the *Odes* Horace constantly reiterates that all things (with the possible exception of poetry) pass and are subject to time and fortune. In *Homo Musagetes* the Muses seize their last day in true Horatian fashion.

AFTERWORD

> За то, что видела Рим
> Because I saw Rome
> E. A. Shvarts, 'Blagodarenie'
> [Thanksgiving], 2009

Eight days after an operation, and five months before her death, Shvarts wrote a prose work that is somewhere between a poem and a prayer, thanking God for her life: 'Blagodarenie' [Thanksgiving] (6 October 2009, v.219). It eloquently summarises Shvarts's interests and achievements over her lifetime, in a self-characterisation which displays the same shifting syncretism as all her poetic interactions with classical antiquity. Here is 'Blagodarenie' in full:

> Благодарю Тебя за то, что Ты создал меня поэтом Твоей милостью,
> За то, что я родилась вблизи Невы и за то, что сейчас смотрю на нее и Исакий из окна больницы,
> За то, что меня растили мама и Берта,
> За то, что росла в тени Театра,
> За то, что видела Рим и мир и Иерусалим,
> За чудесных друзей и животных, что сопровождали меня (и сейчас),
> За счастья вдохновения и радости чистого разума,
> За дар правильного чтения стихов, за свое легкомыслие,
> И за то, что Ты всегда спасаешь меня и порой я нахожу в себе силы благодарить Тебя и за муки.

> [I give thanks to You, because in Your mercy You made me a poet,
> Because I was born by the Neva and because I am looking at it and St Isaac's from the hospital window now,
> Because Mama and Berta brought me up,
> Because I grew up in the shadow of the Theatre,
> Because I saw Rome and the globe and Jerusalem,
> For the wonderful friends and animals who have accompanied me (and still do),
> For the blessings of inspiration and the joys of pure reason,
> For the gift of correct reading of poetry, for my frivolity,
> And because You always save me and sometimes I find the strength in myself to also thank You for the misfortunes.]

All the key themes of her poetry appear: religion, poethood, St Petersburg, female experience, theatre, travel, classical antiquity and Christianity (represented by Rome and Jerusalem), animals, intellectual pursuits, changefulness, playfulness, and pain. Rome quite literally holds the central place in this list: it is the middle word

Fig. 6.1. Elena Shvarts. Photograph courtesy of Kirill Kozyrev.

of the middle line. Rome's prominence in this retrospective on her life accords with antiquity's importance within her oeuvre.

Over the course of this book, we have learnt about Shvarts's lifelong poetic engagement with classical antiquity. First we witnessed incontrovertible proofs of Shvarts's knowledge and love of Latin. Next we saw Shvarts adopting alter egos from Graeco-Roman myth and literature: Narcissus, Aphrodite/Venus, Selene/Luna, Odysseus, Hades, Persephone, the Dioscuri, Orpheus, Eurydice, Dionysus and Apollo's victims, Pythia, and Ariadne. Her classical alter egos placed her in a poetic tradition stretching from Ancient Greece and Rome to nineteenth- and twentieth-century Russia. She used the alter egos to reflect on aspects of herself, primarily the painful vocation of poet, and to put herself into an altered state of consciousness associated with inspiration. Then we met Shvarts's most famous and sustained classical alter ego: Kinfiia, who was created from Shvarts's wide-ranging reading of classical authors, foremost among them Propertius, Catullus, Martial, Ovid, and Plato. But, as we discovered, Leningrad lay underneath the Roman façade just as Shvarts's own poetic idiom lay underneath Kinfiia's voice. Yet this did not make Kinfiia's poetic voice — a voice only barely permitted to Cynthia by Propertius — any the less rounded or believable. After this we visited Shvarts's Rome — both as she imagined it and as she experienced it in real life. She saw Rome as central to history, and fundamentally connected with St Petersburg. The Third Rome myth prompted Shvarts to apply Rome's imperial connotations and the fall of its empire to Russia when the USSR collapsed; and so Rome came to exemplify decline and the ravages of time. Yet after she had seen Rome for herself, a fragment of her life stuck to its ancient ruins forever. Finally, we delved into the Horatian cycle *Homo Musagetes*, which showed the Muses seeking Shvarts in an inimical, wintry St Petersburg. Far from embracing them like her classical poet/inspirer alter egos, Shvarts, cynical and aged, rejected the Muses' Horatian inspiration as obsolete in the face of the new Christian Russia. Her refusal of the position of classical poet was motivated by the bewildering and difficult conditions of the post-Soviet 1990s. Yet so pervasive was *Homo Musagetes*' Horatian reception that Shvarts created a paradoxical continuation of a long tradition of (Russian) poets assuming the mantle of Horace.

A narrative of sorts emerges from Shvarts's classical reception when viewed across her whole life. In her early poetry Shvarts transcends *byt* (everyday existence) by enstranging it as she inhabits her numerous classical alter egos. But in the face of the obsolescence of poetry in the post-communist era and then her own mortality, in her later poetry Shvarts stages the defeat of the classical world by *byt*. The trajectory is due to how much of herself Shvarts invested in her representations of antiquity: far from being fixed, unchanging, *dead*, classical antiquity in Shvarts's poetry ultimately bears the character not only of Shvarts's Russia but of Shvarts herself.

APPENDIX

1.1 'Ах если б все жили так дружно'

Ах если б все жили так дружно
Как слова латыни медной
Без ее бы пятаков
Я была б глубоко бедной.
~~Там *participia* подруги~~   Вкруг sum, esse — Катилина
~~Для существительных, они же~~   Verba anomalia [братья ?] чудес!
~~даже к *verba anomalia*~~   Но глядят они лукаво
~~быть готовые поближе.~~   Правильными быть хотят
И там по талии глагола
Ты ~~вдруг~~ узнаешь, чем чреват он
В каком сегодня наклонении
Каким он времен[ем] брюхатый.
~~Латынь мой город зачарованный~~   ~~весь запрятанный~~
~~там есть тюрьма для несклоняемых~~   Язык ~~теперь~~ как мамонт ископаемый
~~какой прекрасной паутиною~~   А некогда такой болтаемый
~~висит он некогда болтаемый.~~
там есть ~~и~~ центр *где* ~~и окраины~~ *проулки*
~~базар~~-синонимов обилие
~~они все разные, но все~~
~~давно зна[к]омые с Вергилием.~~   И каждый слог как мальчик наг
~~Латынь — ты и колосс и колос~~   Когда-то ночевал с Вергилием
~~поющее~~~~медное растение [??]~~ *медное [????] растений*
~~к злату сердцу ходит транспорт~~
~~падежей, местоимений.~~

[1974?]

* typewritten / *handwritten* / [corrected] / [illegible ?]

1.2 Надгробная надпись императора Адриана

    Душенька странная бродяжка
    Гостья тела и собеседница
    Где ты теперь блуждаешь
    Смутным испуганным облачком,
    И уж шуткам своим не смеешься ты.

1.1 'Ah, if only everyone could live as harmoniously'

Ah, if only everyone could live as harmoniously
As copper Latin's words
Without its pennies
I would be profoundly poor.

<s>There *participia* are friends</s>   *All around sum, esse — Catiline*
<s>With nouns, who are even</s>   *Verba anomalia [brothers ?] of marvels!*
<s>prepared to get close</s>   *But they look around slyly*
<s>to *verba anomalia*.</s>   *They want to be regular*
<s>And</s> there by a verb's waistline
You'll <s>suddenly</s> know what he's pregnant with
What mood he is in today
How tense the expectant father.
<s>Latin, my enchanted city</s>   <s>*all hidden away*</s>
<s>there are prisons for indeclinables</s>   *Language <s>now</s> like a fossilised mammoth*
<s>what a beautiful spider's web</s>   *But once so chattered*
<s>left dangling, once chattered.</s>
there is <s>both</s> a centre where <s>and outskirts</s> the alleys are
<s>a bazaar</s> — an abundance of synonyms
<s>they are all different, but all are</s>   *And every syllable like a boy — naked —*
<s>old acquaintances of Virgil.</s>   *At one time spent the night with Virgil*
<s>Latin — you are both helios and helianthus</s>
<s>a singing-copper plant [??] copper [????] of plants</s>
<s>towards the golden heart goes a transport</s>
<s>of cases, of pronouns.</s>

[1974?]

* typewritten / *handwritten* / [illegible ?]

1.2 Funerary Inscription of Emperor Hadrian

    Lil' soul strange wanderer
    Guest of body and interlocutrix
    Where do you now meander
    Like a hazy frightened lil' cloud,
    And at your own jokes you no longer laugh.

2.1 'Нарцисса я сужу за недостаток'

Нарцисса я сужу за недостаток
К себе любви.
Уж я-то не поверю отраженьям —
В воде ль, в крови.
Ах, angels, духи, когда бы вы могли
Хоть на мгновенье
Глухонемого 'я' извлечь коренья
И стебли бледные из бешеной земли.
Когда б устроили одно
Мне с ним короткое свиданье,
Чтоб прошептало мне оно
Свои желанья.
Его слегка поцеловав,
Я буду знать, что я жива,
Я буду знать, что 'я' во мне
Спит в черноземной глубине.

1979

2.1 'I find Narcissus guilty of an insufficiency'

I find Narcissus guilty of an insufficiency
Of self-love.
Me, now, I wouldn't trust reflections —
In water, or in blood.
Ah, *dukhi*, angels — when could you,
For just a moment,
Extract the roots and the pale stalks
Of my deaf and dumb 'I' from mad soil.
When could you arrange one
Short date for me with it,
So it might whisper to me
Its desires.
Once I have lightly kissed it,
I will know that I am alive,
I will know that the 'I' inside me
Is asleep in black-earth depths.

1979

2.2 Афродита улетает в ночь на субботу

Бледная полночь,
Фарфоровая сирень,
Пятница ускользает из сада.
Вдруг я услышала шелест и плеск,
Запах розы и серы,
Изнемогая, навзничь, сияя двойною луною зада
В голубях и венках проплывала Венера.
Я таких голубей еще не видала —
Жертву тучную им приготовь.
Пели, как соловьи, из клюва свесилось жало,
Капала темная кровь.
Изумрудные, алые — тяжесть не птичия тел.
Рядом, конечно, мальчик летел,
Натянул тетиву пчелиную,
Выстрелил, не целясь, цветком и, смеясь,
Пропищал — вот еще одну ранил я!
Вытянула гладиолуса стрелу длинную
И сказала (а в глазах все туманнее):
«На рассвете цветы ваши будут липкая грязь.
Где сестра твоя чистая — Афродита Урания?
Может, заперли в гору, может, съел ее змей,
Я видала ее, поклоняюсь я ей».
А она закружалась смерчом, свечой,
Прошептав — суббота, пора домой.
И из пены сирени взлетела на птицах,
Розами их погоняя и взявши под мышку козла.
В белой ночи по горло стояла столица,
Средь деревьев блестели везде зеркала.
И уже с облаков, торжествуя, она оглядела
Поле, полное жертв, — на постели, в траве, в саду,
Каменея лежали уже, холодея...
Ах, до пятницы новой укола я в сердце не жду!

1978

2.2 Aphrodite Flies off at the End of Friday Night

Pale midnight,
Porcelain lilac,
Friday slinks out of the garden.
All of a sudden I heard a rustle and a splash,
I smelled rose and sulphur,
Worn out, on her back, shining with the twin moon of her buttocks,
Amidst pigeons and garlands Venus wafted past.
I had never seen such pigeons —
Prepare them a fatted victim.
They sang, like nightingales, from their beaks dangled stings,
Dark blood dripped.
Emerald, scarlet bodies — of an unbirdly heaviness.
Alongside, of course, the boy flew,
Bent his honeybee bow,
Fired a flower without aiming, and, laughing,
Squealed: 'That's another girl I've wounded!'
I drew out the long gladiolus arrow
And said to them (though my sight was blurring):
'By dawn your flowers will be slimy mud.
Where is your pure sister — Aphrodite Urania?
Perhaps she's been locked in a mountain, or eaten by a snake,
I have seen her, I shall bow to her.'
But she began to spin like a whirlwind, a candle,
Whispering: 'It's Saturday, time to go home.'
And from a foam of lilac blossom she flew up on her birds,
Spurring them with rose stalks — an old goat stashed under one arm.
The capital stood up to its neck in white night,
Amidst the trees everywhere mirrors glinted.
And from the clouds now, triumphant, she surveyed
The field, full of victims — in beds, in grass, in gardens,
They lay already turning stone cold...
Ah, I cannot wait till next Friday for a prick in the heart!

1978

2.3 Рассказ Аида, проглоченного Кроном

Когда папаша, старый крокодил,
Меня, сестер и брата проглотил
И пасть захлопнул —
Гудящий розовый поток
Стучал в огромный бок,
Шумело, булькало вокруг,
Потом из тьмы всплывали вдруг,
Белея, ребра.
Из моря красного, шумящего все глуше,
Сестер вылавливал, вытаскивал на сушу.
И снова с бревен скользких
Ползли, крича, куда-то,
А небо над нами было
Черным и розоватым.
Сердце его стучало гулко,
Чавкая страшно,
И долго мы росли меж ребер в закоулке,
И розовом, и влажном,
Под небом розовым без облаков,
Давяся кашей холеных боков.
Было ненавистное родным,
И темница была родная,
И прогрыз бы я толстый бок,
Но за ним была темница другая.
И с трудом, задыхаясь во сне,
Мы глотали распаренный воздух,
И казалась вселенная мне
Жадной гадиной в белых звездах.

[*не позднее февраля 1973*]

2.4 'Сжальтесь, милые тени'

> Глюк теперь — сверчок запечный,
> Баба старая, — предвечный.

«Сжальтесь, милые тени,
Отпустите мою Эвридику!» —
Его слушают дикие звери,
По щекам текут сладкие слезы.
В Аид опустелый и пыльный
Теней не привозят ныне, —
Собачий вальс играет старый цербер
На глюковом забытом клавесине.

1967

2.3 The Tale of Hades, Swallowed by Kronos

When that old crocodile, daddy,
Swallowed my sisters, my brother, and me,
And clapped shut his jaws —
A booming pink flood
Pounded on the enormous gut,
Noise and bubbling was all about,
Then from the dark suddenly bobbed out
Whiteness — ribs.
From the sea of red, its din dying down,
I fished out my sisters, dragged them to land.
And over and over we crawled off our
Slippery perches, shouting, going somewhere,
But the sky above us
Was black and pinkish.
His heart beat boomingly,
Squelching scarily,
And for ages we grew up between ribs in a nook
That was pink and dank,
Under a pink cloudless sky,
Choking down a porridge of pampered insides.
The detestable became lovable,
And the dungeon became homey,
And I would have gnawed through the thick abdomen,
But beyond it was another dungeon.
And, gasping in our sleep, with difficulty
We gulped the air all stewy,
And it seemed to me the universe was
A greedy reptile in white stars.

[*no later than February 1973*]

2.4 'Sweet shades, take pity'

> Gluck is now the cricket behind the stove,
> An old woman — ancient of days.

'Sweet shades, take pity,
Set my Eurydice free!' —
He is heeded by wild beasts,
Sweet tears stream down their cheeks.
To a deserted and dusty Hades
They now no longer bring any shades —
Old cerberus plays 'dogsticks'
On an abandoned harpsichord of Gluck's.

1967

2.5 Орфей

На пути обратном
Стало страшно —
Сзади хрипело, свистело,
Хрюкало, кашляло.

Эвридика: По сторонам не смотри, не смей,
          Край — дикий.
Орфей: Не узнаю в этом шипе голос своей
          Эвридики.
Эвридика: Знай, что пока я из тьмы не вышла, —
          Хуже дракона.
          Прежней я стану когда увижу
          Синь небосклона.
          Прежней я стану — когда задышит
          Грудь — с непривычки больно.
          Кажется, близко, кажется, слышно —
          Ветер и море.

Голос был задышливый, дикий,
Шелестела в воздухе борода.

Орфей: Жутко мне — вдруг не тебя, Эвридика,
          К звездам выведу, а...

Он взял — обернулся, сомненьем томим —
Змеища с мольбою в глазах,
С бревно толщиною, спешила за ним,
И он отскочил, объял его страх.
Из мерзкого брюха
Тянулись родимые тонкие руки
Со шрамом родимым — к нему.
Он робко ногтей розоватых коснулся.
 — Нет, сердце твое не узнало,
Меня ты не любишь, —
С улыбкою горькой змея прошептала.
Не надо! не надо! —
И дымом растаяла в сумерках ада.

1982

Line	Published Version	Variant	
3	хрипело, свистело	свистело, хрипело	[verbs inverted]
4	Хрюкало	Харкало	Hawked
7	Не узнаю в этом шипе голос своей	Не узнаю ~~голос~~ в этом ~~басе~~ хрипе голос своей	I don't recognise ~~the voice~~ in that ~~bass~~ wheeze the voice of my
17-18	Голос был задышливый, дикий, | Шелестела в воздухе борода.	Голос был то мужской, то дикий, | Озвучивал жалобно - Никогда	The voice was now manly, now wild, | It vocalised piteously – "Never"

2.5 Orpheus

On the path back
He started to get scared —
From behind him issued
Croaks, grunts, coughs, whistles.

Eurydice: Don't look about you, don't you dare, this —
Is wild territory.
Orpheus: I don't recognise in that hiss the voice of my Eurydice.
Eurydice: Know that until I emerge from the dark, I am —
Worse than a dragon.
I will become my former self when I see the blue
Of the horizon.
I will become my former self when my chest begins
To breathe — unaccustomedly, painfully.
It seems like it's close, it seems like I can hear it —
The wind and the sea.

The voice was breathy, wild,
In the air a beard rustled.

Orpheus: I'm frightened — what if it's not you, Eurydice,
That I lead out to the stars, but instead...

He went and — turned around, tormented by doubt —
A huge serpent with a prayer in her eyes,
As thick as a log, was hurrying after him,
And he leapt away, seized by fear.
From the foul belly
Reached out familiar slender hands
With their familiar scar — to him.
Hesitantly he touched the pale pink fingernails.
'No, your heart did not recognise me,
You do not love me,'
Whispered the serpent with a bitter smile.
'Don't! Don't!'
And she melted away like smoke in the twilight of hell.

1982

Line	Published Version	Variant	
19	Эвридика	~~дорогая~~	~~dearest one~~
After l. 20: 2 or 3 extra lines		ну что тебя уже сожрала / сзади тихо | крадется змея?	well what if you've already been eaten / from behind quietly | a serpent is sneaking?
26	родимые	Родные	own/dear/familiar
27	родимым	знакомым	familiar
28	ногтей розоватых коснулся	к руке прикоснулся	lightly touched the hand

2.6 Подражание Буало

Э. Л. Линецкой

Мне нравятся стихи, что на трамвай похожи:
Звеня и дребезжа, они летят, и все же,

Хоть косо, в стеклах их отражены
Дворы, дворцы и слабый свет луны,

Свет слепоты — ночного отблеск бденья,
И грубых рифм короткие поленья.

Поэт собой любим, до похвалы он жаден.
Поэт всегда себе садовник есть и садик.

В его раздорранном размере, где Дионис живет,
Как будто прыгал и кусался несытый кот.

Неистовство и простота всего в основе,
Как у того, кто измышлял составы крови.

Родной язык как старый верный пес, —
Когда ты свой, то дергай хоть за хвост.

Но, юный друг, своим считаю долгом
Предупредить, что Муза схожа с волком,

И если ты спознался с девой страшной,
То одиночества испробуй суп вчерашний.

Поэт есть глаз, — узнаешь ты потом, —
Мгновенье связанный с ревущим божеством.

Глаз выдранный — на ниточке кровавой,
На миг вместивший мира боль и славу.

1971

2.6 Imitation of Boileau

To E. L. Linetskaia

I like a poem that is like a tram:
Clanging and rattling, it flies along, and,

Though crookedly, its windows do still reflect
Backyards and mansion-fronts and feeble moonlight,

Light of blindness — glare from vigils in the night-times,
And the short logs of rough-and-ready rhymes.

The poet loves himself, he craves adoration.
The poet is always both gardener and garden.

In his dismembered metre, where Dionysus abides,
It is as if a hungry cat leaps and bites.

Frenzy and simplicity underpin all,
Like with he who invented blood's formula.

The mother tongue is like an old hound, faithful —
When in your element, you can pull its tail.

But my young friend, I consider it my duty
To warn you: the Muse is like a coyote,

And if you have come to know the dread maiden,
Then try the leftover soup of desolation.

The poet is an eye — you'll learn eventually —
Linked for an instant with a roaring deity.

The eye is torn out — on a thread all gory,
For a moment it contained the world's pain and glory.

1971

2.7 Свалка

Нет сил воспеть тебя, прекрасная помойка!
Как на закате, разметавшись, ты лежишь со всклоченною головой,
И черный кот в манишке белой колко
Терзает, как пьянист, живот тяжелый твой.
Вся в зеркалах гниющих — в их протресках
Полынь высокая растет —
О, ты — Венеция (и лучше, чем Венецья),
И гондольером кот поет.
Турецкого клочок дивана
В лиловой тесноте лежит
И о Стамбуле, о кальяне
Бурьяну тихо говорит.
В гниющих зеркалах дрожит лицо июля.
Ворона медленно на свалку опустилась,
И вот она идет, надменнее чем Сулла,
И в цепкой лапе гибель или милость.
Вот персик в слизи, вспухи ягод, лупа,
Медали часть, от книги корешок,
Ты вся в проказе, или ты — ожог,
Ребенок, облитый кипящим супом.
Ты — Дионис, разодранный на части,
Иль мира зеркальце ручное.
Я говорю тебе — О Свалка,
Зашевелись и встань. Потом,
О монстр, о чудовище ночное,
Заговори охрипло рваным ртом.
Зашевелись и встань, прекрасная помойка!
Воспой — как ты лежишь под солнцем долго,
Гиганта мозгом пламенея, зрея,
Все в разложенье съединяя, грея.
Большою мыслью процвети. И гной
Как водку пей, и ешь курины ноги.
Зашевелись, прекрасная, и спой!
O rosa mystica, тебя услышат боги.

1983

2.7 Dump

No, I have not strength to sing your praise, beauteous midden!
How you lie stretched out at sunset, all tousle-headed,
And a cat, all in black but for white shirt front, poignantly
Tears, like a pianist, at your swollen belly.
Strewn with mouldering mirrors — wormwood growing
High amidst their shatterings —
O, you are Venice (which is better than Wenecja),
And the cat's your singing gondolier.
A scrap of a Turkish divan
Lies in lilac constraint
And softly weaves the weeds a tale
Of hookahs, of Istanbul.
In the mouldering mirrors quivers the face of July.
A crow has descended slowly upon the dump,
See, it struts more haughtily than Sulla,
And in its vice-like claws — death or mercy.
Here's a peach slice in slime, swellings of berries,
A magnifying glass, half a medal, the spine of a book.
You are all-over leprous, or you are a scald,
A child, drenched in boiling soup.
You are Dionysus, dismembered into bits,
Or the world's hand mirror.
I say to you: O Dump,
Rise up and walk. Then,
O ogre, o monster of the night,
Open your ragged mouth and speak.
Rise up and walk, beauteous midden!
Sing — of lying long under the sun,
Your giant's brain blazing, ripening,
Incorporating, warming all in decay.
Effloresce with great thoughts. And drink
Pus like vodka, and eat hens' feet.
Rise up, my beauty, and sing!
O rosa mystica, the gods will hear you.

1983

2.8 Пифии

И я как все — я червь земли,
Годов дубовых древоточец,
Но иногда и я могу
Пророчествовать за пророчиц.
Живет в пещере дымный Бог,
Он светлый, но во тьме как дома.
Мы будто ветер прошумим
От дальнего осколка грома.
Безжалостно нас учат, строго,
Живем в колоннах мы без крыши.
Всё страшное случилось с нами,
Не устрашит нас что услышим.
Мы голову бросаем в пропасть,
Приподнимая тайны глыбу,
И вот о вашей смерти новость —
Выуживаем злую рыбу.
Бесстыжей смерти сладок дом,
Стучат лопаты, дышат груди,
И мир уже идет на слом,
При этом — счастливы мы будем.

1988

2.8 Pythias

I, too, am like everyone — a worm of the earth,
A carpenter moth of the oaken years,
But sometimes I, too, can
Prophesy for the prophetesses.
In a cave there lives a smoky God,
He is radiant, but feels at home in the dark.
We, like the wind, will resound
From a distant shard of thunder.
Our training is merciless, strict,
We live in columns without a roof.
Every frightful thing has happened to us,
We will not be frightened by what we hear.
We throw our heads into the abyss,
Lifting up a clod of mystery,
And as for news of your deaths —
We go angling for those malignant fish.
The house of shameless death is sweet,
Spades are knocking, chests are breathing,
And the world's already going for scrap,
When it does — we will be happy.

1988

2.9 Пифия

Ванге

— Деушка, деушка, темный канал,
Тот, по которому сны проплывают
Или виденья грозно плывут, —
Ты нам поведай, что знаешь.
Деушка, деушка — посох в руке,
Хвост в облаках твой сокрылся,
А голова, волочась по земле,
Изрыгает темную воду,
Воду знамений, реки печалей:
«Знаю — тот день, которого ждали, —
Прах человеческий в недрах земли
Тяжесть руд и камней превысит —
Вот тогда и съежатся дали,
Разверзнутся трубные выси.
Станет тогда седая земля
Говорящею головой,
Каждый будет, как мысль, судим,
Или, как слово, спасен,
Или, как чувство, развеется в дым,
Или, как имя, забыт».
А пока что мертвыми рвет ее,
Тенями она говорит,
А потом, как котенок слепой, она
На овчине, свернувшись, сопит.
Утонула она — потому что тесна
Водопаду, что в горле спит.
Сон из дальних сочится стран,
Говорит она тихо в сторонку:
«Мне тяжело — через воронку
Переливают океан».

1992

2.9 Pythia

To Vanga

'Mi-iss, mi-iss, the dark channel,
The one that dreams float along,
Or visions malignly sail down —
Tell us what you know.
Mi-iss, mi-iss — staff in your hand,
Your tail is hidden in the clouds,
And your head, trailing on the ground,
Spews out the dark water,
Water of signs, rivers of sorrows.'
'I know — the day you have waited for —
Human ashes in the bowels of the earth
Will rise above the weight of ore and rock —
On that day the horizons will huddle together,
And the trumpeting firmament will open.
At that time the grey-haired earth
Will become a talking head,
Each will be, like a thought, judged,
Or, like a word, saved,
Or, like a feeling, melted into thin air,
Or, like a name, forgotten.'
In the meantime she vomits the dead,
She speaks in the voices of shades,
And after, like a blind kitten,
She sniffles, curled up in sheepskin.
She drowned — because she was too tight
For the waterfall sleeping in her throat.
A dream seeps in from far-away countries,
Quietly she says, in an aside:
'It's hard for me — through a funnel
They are decanting an ocean'.

1992

2.10 'Корабль Жизни уносился вдаль'

Корабль Жизни уносился вдаль.
Я с вашего упала корабля.
Не различить где небо, где земля,
Где воздух, звезды, череп иль лицо.
Зачем заветное глотаю я кольцо?
Мне ничего в себе не сохранить,
Сгнила в воде и Ариадны нить.
Птенца самосознанья утопить
(Но он не хочет исчезать, хоть и устал),
И вольною волной средь волн уплыть.
Ах, зубы скалить белые у скал.
Сверкать сиять в ночи привольно
И морю не бывает больно.
Бывает болен Бог? Он ведь боль.
А ей не больно. И меня уволь.

Нач. января 2010

2.10 'The Ship of Life scudded into the distance'

    The Ship of Life scudded into the distance.
    I have fallen off the ship — yours, everyone's.
    There's no telling where is sky, where is land,
    Where is air, where stars, a skull or face.
    Why am I swallowing the hallowed ring?
    I cannot keep anything safe inside me,
    Water's rotted even the thread of Ariadne.
    Oh, to drown the chick of self-awareness
    (But though it's tired, it does not want to vanish),
    And float away, a wave, free among the waves.
    Ah, to gnash white teeth at the cliffs.
    To shimmer, to shine in the night, at will,
    And the sea is never hurt or ill.
    Can God be ill, in pain? For He is pain.
    But she is not in pain. Let me go as well.

Early January 2010

3.1 Кинфия

Кинфия — римская поэтесса I века до н. э., героиня элегий Проперция, прославившаяся не только талантом, но и дурным нравом. Стихи ее не дошли до наших дней, однако я все же попыталась перевести их на русский язык.

КНИГА ПЕРВАЯ

I. К служанке

Дай мне мази багровой —
Ветрянку у губ успокоить,
Дай, постель подогрев,
Чемерицы в горячем вине.

Ливень льет с утра —
Ледяными хлыстами
Рим сечет, как раба,
Пойманного в воровстве.

В клетке кричит попугай —
Разговорился, проклятый!
Край наш под мокрым застыл одеялом,
Только там — далеко, в Пиренеях —

На германца идут легионы.
В ущельях — как мизинец они,
Что в агонии долго дрожит,
Когда тело уже омертвело.

В Риме никто переменчивей нравом
Меня не рождался, —
Нынче куда ни взгляну —
Все раздражает меня.

Все верещит попугай —
Жалкого жалкий подарок,
Задуши его быстро, рабыня.
Тельце зеленое после в слезах поплывет,
Буду тебя проклинать, но сейчас задуши поскорее.

Ревут водостоки — сегодня никто —
Ни вор, ни любовник — из дому не выйдет.
Тщетно в трактире напротив
Мутных не гасят огней.

3.1 Cynthia

Cynthia was a Roman poetess of the first century BC, heroine of the elegies of Propertius, famed not only for her talent, but also for her bad temper. Her poems are no longer extant; however, I have tried nevertheless to translate them into Russian.

BOOK ONE

I. To a Slave Girl

Give me the crimson ointment
To soothe the sore on my lip,
Give me — once you've warmed the bed —
Hellebore in hot wine.

Pouring rain since morning —
Icy switches that
Cut Rome like a slave
Caught thieving.

In its cage the parrot shrieks —
Talking at last, cursed creature!
These parts lie congealed under a damp blanket,
While there — far away, in the Pyrenees —

The legions march against the Germani.
In the gorges — they're like a little finger
That twitches in agony long
After the body has grown stiff in death.

In all Rome none more volatile of temper
Than me has ever been born —
Nowadays wherever I look
Everything irritates me.

The parrot keeps jabbering —
Pitiful present of a pitiful man,
Strangle him quickly, slave girl.
The little green body will swim in tears after,
I shall curse you, but now strangle him quick as you can.

The gutters bellow — today no one —
Not thief, nor lover — will leave the house.
Vainly the inn opposite
Keeps its smoky lamps burning.

II

Снова сунулся отец с поученьем:
— Надо жить, мол, не так, а этак.
— Хорошо, — говорю ему, — папа,
Больше этого не будет, папаша. —

Смотрю я, кроткая, на голову седую,
На руки скрюченные, слишком красный рот.
Говорю я рабам: — Немедля
Киньте дурака в бассейн. —

Волокут его по мраморному полу,
Он цепляется, а не за что цепляться,
Кровь течет по лицу и слезы:
— Доченька, — кричит, — прости, помилуй! —

Нет! Некормленым муренам на съеденье
Ты пойдешь, развратник и ханжа.
Или представлю — как лев в цирке
Дожевывает его печень.

— Ладно, ладно, — говорю, — я исправлюсь,
Ах ты бедный мой, старый папа.
Когда тигр вылизал даже пар от крови —
Мне стало его чуточку жалко.

В уме казню его по-разному — тыщу
Раз и еще раз тыщу, —
Чтоб однажды и в самом деле,
Молоток подняв, — по виску не стукнуть.

III. К служанке

Как посмела ты, подлая, как посмела!
Тебя мало сослать в деревню,
Выдать замуж за кельтибера,
Что мочою себе зубы чистит,
Иль под цвет души — за абиссинца.
О наглая! Катулла я твердила,
Бродя по дому тихо, — и светильник,
В углу стоявший, тень мою длинил.
Она вбежала, топая, из кухни,
Таща макрель на золоченом блюде,
И наступила прямо мне на — тень —
На голову, а после на предплечье!
А тень моя ее дубленой кожи —
Ведь знает же! — болимей и нежней.
Когда б тебя на той же сковородке
Зажарить с благородною макрелью,
И то тебе бы не было так больно,
Как мне — когда ты к полу придавила
Своей ножищей — тень от завитка.

II

Again father stuck his nose in with a lecture:
'You ought not,' he's like, 'to live this way, but that.'
'Fine,' I say to him, 'Dad,
I'll stop it at once, Daddy.'

I, meek, look at his grey head,
At his gnarled hands, his too-red mouth.
I say to the slaves: 'This instant,
Throw the fool into the pool.'

They drag him across the marble floor,
He clings, but there's nothing to cling to,
Blood flows over his face, and tears:
'Daughter dearest,' he cries, 'forgive me, have mercy!'

No! To the hungry moray eels to eat
You'll go, you debaucher and hypocrite.
Or I'll imagine: a lion in the circus
Chews on the last of his liver.

'OK, OK,' I say, 'I'll mend my ways,
Oh, poor you, my poor old dad.
When a tiger had licked up even the steam from his blood —
Then I became a teensy bit sorry for him.

In my mind I punish him variously — a ton of
Times and another times a ton —
In order, one day, and for real this time,
Hammer raised — to strike his cranium...not.

III. To a Slave Girl

How dare you, bitch, how dare you!
I should pack you off to the countryside,
Marry you off to a Celtiberian
Who cleans his teeth with urine,
Or to an Abyssinian, to match the colour
Of your soul — but that'd be too good for you.
O, hussy! I was reciting Catullus,
Roaming quietly through the house — and a lamp
Standing in the corner lengthened my shadow.
She ran in, clomping, from the kitchen,
Lugging a mackerel on a gilt platter,
And stepped right on my — shadow —
On my head, and after that my forearm!
And my shadow is more sensitive and tender —
As she well knows! — than her leathery hide.
If you were to be fried in that pan
With that noble mackerel,
Then you would still not feel as much pain
As me — when with your hoof you ground
Into the floor — the shadow of my ringlet.

IV. Купидону

Боль всегда с тобой, сосунок крылатый.
Хоть и разлюбишь — проститься больно.
У тебя в колчане — стрел всегда вдоволь,
Так зачем, жадный,
В горло упершись,
Стрелку рвешь так сильно
Из засохшей ранки?
Или мстишь, что больше мне не хозяин?
Лучше уж запусти другую,
Не тяни эту, не рви, не трогай —
Запеклась кровь уж.
Так лети себе, не жадничай, мальчик.

V. Молодому поэту

Чего ты, Септим, пристал к Музе?
Зря гнусавишь, зря ручонками машешь,
Такт отбивая. Надоел ты смертно
Каллиопе, Эвтерпе, а Эрато
И куда бежать от тебя не знает.
Не дергай Музу за подол больше.
Не то смотри — на площади людной
Вселится в тебя громовой голос,
И не захочешь — скажешь при людях:
«Таким, как я, — хозяевам счастливым
Мордашек гладких, наглых,
Каких стадами на Форум водит
День римский длинный,
С мозгами птичьими и языком длинным, —
Лишь к смертным женам вожделеть можно.
Раз сдернул я туфлю с Музы,
Раз оцарапал я ей лодыжку.
Чтоб гнев богини мимо пронесся —
Поскорей спрячьте от меня подальше,
Люди добрые, таблички и грифель».

IV. To Cupid

Pain is always with you, o wingèd suckler.
Though we fall out of love — parting is painful.
In your quiver are always arrows aplenty,
So why d'you, miser,
Clamped to my throat,
Wrench at this arrow
In its dried-up wound?
Is it vengeance, 'cause you're my master no more?
You had better fire off a brand-new arrow,
Don't tug at this one, don't tear it, don't touch it —
The blood's clotted now.
Off you fly, then, don't be stingy, little boy.

V. To a Young Poet

Why, Septimus, did you harass the Muse?
In vain you elocute, in vain you flail your arms
Beating out the time. You have bored Calliope
And Euterpe to death, and Erato
Has run out of places to hide from you.
Don't go tugging at the Muse's skirts any more.
Or else, watch out — in a crowded square
A thunderous voice will possess you,
And, all unwilling, you will declaim to the crowd:
'Those, such as I — lucky owners of
Bare, unblushing physiognomies,
Whom the long Roman day
Drives out onto the Forum in herds,
With bird brains and long tongues —
May lust after only mortal women.
Once I pulled the Muse's shoe off,
Once I scratched her ankle.
So the goddess's anger might pass over —
Quickly, hide far, far away from me,
Good people, tablets and stylus!'

VI. Клавдии

Клавдия, ты не поверишь — влюбился в меня гладиатор,
Третий сезон поражений он в цирке не знает,
Мне уже сорок, а он молод еще и красив —
Он целомудренный, честный, смуглый, огромный, печальный,
Слон Ганнибалов носил меньше шрамов, чем он.
В цирке всегда, говорит, ищет меня он глазами,
Но не найдет никогда — я ведь туда не хожу.
Сумерки только падут — в двери мои он стучится,
Вечер сидит, опираясь на остроблещущий меч.
Тяжко, с усилием, дышит он через рот и глядит
Страстно и жалобно вместе...
Любовник мой до слез над ним хохочет.
Конечно, не в лицо, ведь он — ты знаешь — трус,
Пороки все в себе соединяет,
Чуть гладиатора видит — прыгает прямо в окно.
«Страсть, — говорит гладиатор, — мешает сражаться,
Если так дальше пойдет, в Галлию я не вернусь,
Я побеждаю и так уж без прежнего блеска,
Кто-нибудь бойкий прирежет вот-вот».
Что он находит во мне? Хладно смотрю на него,
На глаз оленьих блеск и мощных темных рук.
Что делать, Клавдия, Амур причудлив —
Люблю, несчастная, я лысого урода,
Что прячется, как жалкий раб, за дверью,
Чтобы кричать потом: гони убийцу вон!
Но, подлой, жалко мне его прогнать,
Когда еще такой полюбит молодец,
А старости вот-вот они, туманы...
Как сытый волк и на зиму овца...
Я муки длю его, а если, — зачахнув от любви, —
Падет он на арене, — как жить тогда мне, Клавдия, скажи?

VI. To Claudia

Claudia, you won't believe who's fallen in love with me — a gladiator,
Three seasons in the circus he's not had a single defeat,
I'm already forty, and he's young still, and beautiful —
He is chaste, honest, swarthy, huge, sorrowful,
An elephant of Hannibal's bore fewer scars than he.
In the circus, he says, he always looks about for me,
But never sees me — for I don't go there.
As soon as dusk falls — he comes knocking at my door,
All evening sits there, leaning on his sharp-shining sword.
Heavily, strenuously breathing through his mouth, he gazes
Passionately and plaintively at the same time...
My lover cries laughing at him.
Of course, not to his face, since he — as you know — is a coward,
Unites all the vices within himself,
Scarcely glimpses the gladiator — straight out the window he jumps.
'Passion,' says the gladiator, 'interferes with my fighting,
If it keeps on this way, I shall never return to Gaul,
Even now I vanquish without my former flair,
Some keen young thing will up and skewer me soon.'
What does he see in me? I look at him coldly,
At the gleam of his doe eyes and his powerful dark hands.
What can I do, Claudia, Cupid is freakish —
Wretched me, I love a bald monstrosity
Who hides like a pitiful slave behind the door,
Only to shriek afterwards: 'drive that killer hence!'
But, despicably, I am loath to drive him away —
When will another such gallant love me again?
And they're almost upon me, the fogs of age...
Like a sated wolf wanting a sheep for the winter...
I draw out his torment, but what if — wasted away from love,
He should fall in the arena — how should I live then, Claudia, tell me?

VII

Как я вам завидую, вакханки,
Вы легко несетесь по нагорьям,
Глаз белки дробят луны сиянье,
Кобылицами несетесь вы степными.
Как-то раз в сторонке я стояла —
Привела меня подружка — мы смотрели —
Вдруг она, не выдержав, забилась
Тоже в пьяной пляске и рванулась
Вслед за вами, про меня забывши.
Я смотрела — ваши рты кривились
И съезжали набок ваши лица,
Будто бы с плохих актеров маски.
Вы быка живого растерзали
И, давясь, его сжирали мясо
И горячей кровью обливались,
Разум выплеснули, как рабыня
Выливает амфору с размаха.
И на вас в сторонке я глядела.
А домой пришла — смотрю — все руки
Расцарапаны — в крови до локтя...
Вот удел твой, Кинфия, несчастный —
На себя ты страсть обрушить можешь,
На себя одну, и ни страстинке
Улететь вовне не дашь и малой.
За быком не побежишь нагая...

VIII. К провинциалке

Может, ты не знала, абдерянка, —
Кинфию обидеть очень страшно —
Кинфия такие знает травы,
Чары есть у Кинфии такие...
Что спадешь с лица ты, почернеешь,
Будешь ты икать и днем и ночью,
Повар-грек твой будет в суп сморкаться,
Потому что порчу наведу я,
И залечит тебя твой хваленый
Врач-египтянин.

Даже пьяный негр, матрос просоленный,
В долгой по любви стосковавшийся дороге,
Даже он в постель к тебе не ляжет.
Так что лучше ты, абдерянка,
Кинфию забудь, оставь в покое.
Впрочем, пальцем я б не шевельнула,
Если сделаешь мне что дурное —
Все равно Юпитер, знай, накажет.
Кинфию обидеть — очень страшно.

1974

VII

How I envy you, bacchantes,
You tear lightly across the plateaux,
The whites of your eyes splinter the moonlight,
You gallop like mares on the steppe.
One time I stood on the sidelines —
A friend had brought me — we were watching —
Suddenly she succumbed and convulsed
Too in the drunken dance and rushed
After you, with me forgotten.
I watched — your mouths contorted
And your faces slipped down on one side,
Like masks on bad actors.
You tore a live bull to pieces
And, jostling, gorged yourselves on his meat
And doused yourselves with hot blood,
Tossing out all reason, as a slave girl
Sluices out an amphora with a swing.
And from the sidelines I looked on at you.
But when I get home — I see — my arms
Are all scratched — bloodied up to the elbow...
There's your unhappy lot, Cynthia —
On yourself you can unleash your passion,
On yourself alone, and not a speck of passion
Will you let fly outwardly — not the smallest.
You will never run after a bull naked...

VIII. To a Provincial Woman

Perhaps you did not know, Abderian woman —
To offend Cynthia is a fearful thing —
Cynthia knows such herbs,
Cynthia has such spells...
That your face will shrivel, you'll turn black,
You will hiccup day and night,
Your Greek cook will hawk up in your soup,
Because of the curse put on you by me,
And you will be physicked by your vaunted
Egyptian doctor.

Even a drunk negro, a salty sailor,
Who all voyage long has thirsted for love,
Even he will not get into bed with you.
So, Abderian woman, you'd better
Forget Cynthia, leave her in peace.
Besides, I wouldn't have to lift a finger,
If you do anything bad to me —
Know this: Jupiter will punish you anyway.
To offend Cynthia — is a fearful thing.

1974

КНИГА ВТОРАЯ

I

Вьется в урнах предков пепел — нынче Диониса ночь.
Все закрыты на просушку Эсквилинские сады,
Где исходит черной пеной вечно юный Дионис.
Равноденствие, и в чанах сада квасится весна.
Он исходит черной грязью, мраком, блеском и забвеньем,
Умирает, чтобы снова возродиться в эту ночь.
Будь ты богом или смертным — если только существуешь —
Занесет тебя налетом, житой жизнью занесет,
Как заносит в море дальнем затонувшие галеры
Илом, галькой и песком.
Я забвенью, полусмерти научусь у Диониса,
Очищает только смерть. Умирай же вместе с богом,
Что, перелетев чрез Форум, упадет в закрытый сад.
Налакайся черной грязи, изойди же черной грязью,
Ты воскреснешь чистым, юным — воскресит тебя Загрей.

II

Кто при звуках флейты отдаленной
Носом чуть поводит, раздувает ноздри,
Кто на помощь слуху зовет обонянье,
Тот музыку тонко понимает.
Кто, поставив пред собою блюдо,
Сладкий запах, острый дым вкушает,
Наклонив к нему слегка и ухо,
Толк тот знает не в одной лишь пище.
И любому чувству из шести — какому
Ни нашлось бы дело и работа —
Смежное он тотчас приплетает,
Тотчас же их все зовет на помощь.
Поступает он как грек умелый,
Управляющий большою виллой, —
Хлынет дождь — он выставит кувшины,
Не один, а все, что только в доме.

BOOK TWO

I

The ancestors' ashes wreathe in their urns — tonight is the Dionysia.
The Esquiline gardens are all closed to dry out,
There ever-young Dionysus froths black at the mouth.
Equinox, and in the garden's vats spring is brewing.
He exudes black mud, murk, lustre, and oblivion,
He dies, to be born again on this night.
Be you god or mortal — so long as you exist —
You will be buried under accretions of rust or lichen — under lived life,
Like sunken galleys in the far sea get buried,
Under silt, shale, and sand.
I shall learn oblivion, half-death from Dionysus.
Death alone can purify. Die together with the god,
Who, flown through the Forum, will fall into the closed garden.
Lap up black mud 'til you've drunk your fill, exude black mud,
You will rise from the grave pure, young — Zagreus will resurrect you.

II

Whoever, when strains of a distant flute drift by,
Pricks up their nose, flares their nostrils;
Whoever calls smell to the aid of hearing —
That person has a refined taste in music.
Whoever, having placed before themself a dish,
Savours the sweet smell, the sharp smoke
By inclining towards it, slightly, one ear —
That person has a feel for things — not just food.
And for whichever of the six senses
That has been found a task to work on,
They involve instantly the adjacent one,
Instantly they call on all of them to help.
In this they act like the prudent Greek,
Manager of a large villa:
If it pours with rain, he puts out amphorae —
Not one, but all the ones in the house.

III

Что хорошего в Саратоге дальней?
Для чего ты живешь в глуши юга?
Все мы ютимся, правда,
На дальнем дворе вселенной,
А далёко — в господской вилле
Музыка, свет и пенье.
Мы, как жертвенные ягнята,
В щели видим отблеск и отзвук
И дрожим, что вот рукой грубой
Дверь откроется резко настежь...
Ты приедешь, но будет поздно,
Ты вернешься потом в столицу,
Но меня не найдешь и даже
Не найдешь и моей гробницы,
Потому что в ворота мира
Волосато-железный кулак
Стучится.

IV. Клавдии — после посещения больной бабки

Неужели та,
Что была мне домом,
Столбом, подпирающим мирозданье,
Очага жаром, овечьей шерстью, —
Ныне
Жирно-сухим насекомым,
За косяк взявшись и провожая
Невидящим взглядом,
Слыша — не слышит,
И шелушась стоит.

V

Много, гуляя в горах, камней пестроцветных нашла я.
Этот валялся в пыли, унюхала тот под землей.
Этот формой прельстил, цветом понравился тот.
Все побросала в мешок и его волоку за спиною.
Может, в долине потом блеск их и цвет пропадет,
В утреннем свете булыжной растает он грудой,
Ведь ошибиться легко, по пояс бродя в облаках.
Все же — надеюсь, когда их рассыплю в таверне,
Скажет: как ярки — плебей, скажет: как редки — знаток.

III

What is the attraction of remote Saratoga?
Why do you live in the backwoods of the South?
We all, it is true, huddle
In the remote backyard of the universe,
But far off — in the masters' villa
There is music, light, and song.
Through a crack, like sacrificial lambs, we
See the reflection and hear the echo,
And tremble, lest of a sudden some rude hand
Should brusquely throw the door wide open...
You will come, but too late,
You will return then to the capital,
But you will not find me, nor
Will you find my tomb, even,
Because at the gates of the world
A hairy iron fist
Is knocking.

IV. To Claudia, after Visiting my Sick Granny

Surely she,
Who was my home,
The pillar propping up all Creation,
Hearth's heat, sheep's fleece,
Is not now
That greasy, dry insect,
Clinging to the doorjamb and following me
With sightless gaze,
Who hearing — does not hear,
And sloughs off her skin where she stands.

V

While strolling in the mountains I came across a host of multicoloured stones.
This one was rolling around in the dirt, I sniffed out that one under the earth.
This one beguiled me with its shape, I liked the colour of that one.
I toss them all into my sack, and drag it along behind me.
Perhaps, later, in the valley, their shine and colour will fall away,
In the morning light they will melt into a heap of cobblestones,
For it is easy to make mistakes, when wandering waist-deep in clouds.
All the same, I hope that when I strew them out in the taberna,
A plebeian will say: 'How bright!', and a connoisseur: 'How rare.'

VI

Сами смотрят кровавые игры,
Жрут ягнят, телят и голубей —
И плетут, что очень я жестока.
Я в таком ни в чем не виновата.
Правда, раз я обварила супом
Наглого и мерзкого мальчишку —
Пусть под тунику не лезет за обедом,
Суп имею право я доесть.
Раз в клиента запустила бюстом
Брута, кажется. Его мне жалко —
Черепки-то выбросить пришлось.
Раз нарушила закон гостеприимства —
Со стены сорвавши дедушкину пику,
Понеслась я с нею на гостей.
Уж не помню почему. Забыла.
И они ушли с негодованьем,
Говоря, что больше не придут.
И меня ославили свирепой!
Я же кроткая, я кротче всех.
Мной рабы мои всегда довольны,
Муравья я обойду сторонкой,
У ребенка отниму жука.

VI

They watch blood sports,
Scoff down lambs, calves, and doves —
And spin tales of my terrible cruelty.
Of this I am not in the least bit guilty.
True, I once threw scalding soup
Over an impertinent and odious little boy —
He should not grope under my tunic at lunch,
I have a right to finish eating my soup.
One time I hurled a bust of Brutus,
I think it was, at a client. I was sorry about that —
I had to throw the shards away.
Once I broke the rule of hospitality —
I tore my grandfather's pike from the wall
And rushed at my guests with it.
I don't remember why, now. I've forgotten.
And they left in deep dudgeon,
Saying that they would not come again.
And they call *me* ferocious!
But I am meek, I am meeker than anyone.
My slaves are always happy with me,
I would step around an ant,
I would take a beetle away from a child.

VII. На пляже в Байи

Падает Солнце в златых болячках,
Нежный агнец спускается с гор
Черных.
Свалялась шерсть его —
В репьях и колючках,
И дрожит,
Перерезана надвое кем-то,
На песке мокром
Звезда морская.
Видно, богу бессмертному это угодно,
Мне же, смертной, даже и стыдно —
Вечно бледной пифией в лихорадке
Вдыхать испарения злые
И вцепляться в невидимое, как собака
В кус вцепляется, головой мотая...
Но послушна я веленью бога,
Шьющего стрелой золотые песни.
Я иду — на плечах моих пещера
Тяжелым плащом повисла,
И невидимый город Дельфы
Дышит зловеще.
Варится жизнь моя в котле медном,
Золотые солнца в крови кружатся.
Тянут Парки шелковые нити.
Тащат рыбаки блестящие сети.
Задыхаясь, я жабрами хлопаю быстро,
И вокруг меня золотые братья
Сохнут, извиваясь — в тоске
Смертной.

VII. On the Beach at Baiae

The Sun is sinking in golden sores,
The gentle lamb descends from the black
Mountains.
Its fleece is matted
With burrs and thorns,
And cut in two by someone,
On the damp sand
A starfish
Shivers.
Apparently the immortal god wills this,
But even I, a mortal, am ashamed —
To be perpetually a pale pythia, fevered,
Breathing in baleful vapours
And grabbing on to the unseen, just as a dog
Grabs on to a scrap and shakes its head...
But I am obedient to the bidding of the god
Who sews golden songs with his arrow.
I walk; from my shoulders the cave
Hangs heavy like a cloak,
And the unseen city Delphi
Exhales ill omens.
My life is stewing in a bronze cauldron,
Golden suns swirl through my bloodstream.
The Parcae tug at the silken threads.
Fishermen haul in the glistening nets.
Gulping for breath, I flap my gills fast,
And all around me my golden brothers
Dry out, squirming —
In mortal anguish.

VIII. Разговор

Кинфия
Грек, ты помнишь ли — во сколько обошелся?
Вместо виллы тебя я купила,
Чтобы ты, пресыщенный годами,
Мудростью старинной начиненный,
Помогал мне понимать Платона —
В греческом не очень я сильна.
Чтобы ты в египетские тайны
Посвятил меня, александриец,
Но всего-то больше для того ведь,
Чтобы ты в скорбях меня утешил.
Завтра мне, ты знаешь, стукнет сорок.
Что такое возраст? Научи.
Как это я сделалась старухой,
Не вчера ль в пеленках я лежала?
Как это случилось? Объясни.

Грек
Знаешь ты сама, меня не хуже, —
Цифры ничего не означают,
И для всех течет неравно время.
Для одних ползет, для прочих скачет.
И никто не знает час расцвета,
И тебе быть может в сорок — двадцать.

Кинфия
Если будешь чепуху молоть ты,
То продам тебя иль обменяю
На врача и повара. Подумай.

Грек
В первой люстре мы голубоваты,
Во второй — душа в нас зеленеет,
В третьей — делается карминной,
А в четвертой — в двадцать восемь, значит,
Фиолетовою станет, в пятой — желтой,
Как в страду пшеница.
А потом оранжевой, и дальше
Все должна душа переливаться,
Все пройти цвета, а мудрой станет —
Побелеет, а бывает вовсе
И таких цветов, что глаз не знает.
Все она проходит превращенья,
Измененья, рост и переливы,
Ведь нельзя всю жизнь багрово-красным
Надоедливым цветком висеть на ветке,
Голой, побелевшей от морозов.
Только у богов да их любимцев так бывает —
Цвет отыщет свой и в нем пребудет,
Артемида ведь не станет дряхлой.
И Гефест младенцем не бывал.

VIII. Conversation

Cynthia
Greek, do you remember how much you cost me?
I bought you instead of a villa,
So that, over-endowed with years,
Stuffed full of ancient wisdom, you
Would help me to understand Plato —
Greek is not really my strong suit.
I bought you, an Alexandrian, who
Could initiate me into the Egyptian Mysteries.
But above all else, I bought you
To bring me comfort in times of affliction.
Tomorrow, as you know, I will turn forty.
What is age? Teach me.
How is it that I have turned into an old woman,
Was it not yesterday that I was lying in swaddling clothes?
How has this happened? Explain.

Greek
You yourself know, no worse than I do,
That numbers mean nothing,
And time does not flow equally for everyone.
For some it crawls, for others it gallops.
Nobody knows at what hour they will bloom,
And at forty you can be, actually, only twenty.

Cynthia
If you are going to talk drivel,
Then I will sell you or swap you
For a doctor or a cook. Think on it.

Greek
In our first lustre we are sky-blueish,
In our second, our soul grows green,
In our third, it flushes carmine,
And in the fourth — that is, at twenty-eight,
It turns violet, in the fifth — yellow,
Like corn at harvest time.
And then orange, and from then on
The soul should constantly iridesce,
Go through all the colours. But when it becomes wise —
Then it will go white, and be composed of
Such colours, that the eye cannot discern.
It goes through all these transformations,
Changes, growth and modulations,
For one cannot spend one's whole life as a
Bright red, tedious flower hanging on a branch
That is bare and bleached by frosts.
Only the gods and their favourites can live thus —
Each seeks out their own colour and abides in it,
For Artemis will never grow decrepit.
And Hephaestus was never an infant.

Кинфия
Что заладил про богов да про младенцев?
Ну а если я на дню меняю цвет свой
Сотню раз — то синий, то зеленый?

Грек
Кинфия, душа твоя — растенье
И не может в росте уменьшаться,
Но растет, и зреет, и трепещет.
Есть у цвета смысл сокровенный,
Есть у цвета тайное значенье.
Дождь — есть снег, глубоко постаревший,
Оба же они — одна вода,
Так душа собою остается у младенца и у старика.
Всё же знать нам нужно — снег ли, дождь.

Кинфия
Снег не может вдруг пойти в июне,
Дождь не льется мутно в январе.
Краснобай ты жалкий и нелепый.
И от всех от этих разговоров
Почернела вся моя душа.

1978

Cynthia
Why are you going on about gods and infants?
Well, what if in a day I change my colour
A hundred times — now blue, now green?

Greek
Cynthia, your soul is a living, growing plant,
And it cannot decrease in size,
But only grows, and matures, and pulsates.
Colour holds a mysterious meaning,
Colour holds a secret significance.
Rain is snow, profoundly aged,
Yet both of them are one and the same water:
Just so, the soul remains itself in man and boy.
Even so, we need to know if it's snow or rain.

Cynthia
Snow cannot come in June all of a sudden,
Rain doesn't tip dully down in January.
What a pitiful and clumsy windbag you are.
And from all this conversing
My soul has turned completely black.

1978

РАЗРОЗНЕННОЕ

I

В хижину вошла и огляделась:
Будто привиденья увидала —
В том углу однажды я рыдала,
В том молилась...
Если б эти призраки былого,
Вдруг воскреснув, — плотью-костью стали,
То-то давка здесь бы началась —
Как на скачках в праздники большие.
Сами бы себя передушили,
Сами бы себя перекусали,
И девчонки по-спартански, молча,
Кулаком наотмашь взрослых били,
Ну а те — разнеженно визжали, —
Так я вдруг представила ту свалку,
Эту бочку жизни мной отжитой...

Но душа бы искрой убегала
От одной — в другую — до живущей,
До меня, мгновенно долетая,
Оставляя позади все толпы
Тающих, одетых, неодетых,
Гневных, и веселых, и печальных —
Будто город после изверженья
Равнодушно-дикого вулкана.

II

Вновь Проперций мой ко мне вернулся —
Счастие для Кинфии какое!
Исцарапанный, залапанный, помятый,
Облысевший, грязный, исхудавший.
Бегают глаза его так жалко.
Отчего же ты в глаза не смотришь?
И кого стыдишься — не меня ли?
Третьего стыдишься ты — любови,
Ведь она противу нашей воли
Бегает за мною и тобою
И на стыд и горе снова сводит.
Ах, тебя прогнать отсюда взашей
Так бы мне хотелось — только жалко
Бедную сестрицу ту — любвишку,
Жалкую, но все-таки живую.
Поменяй же тогу, эта в пятнах,
Залечи царапины, умойся,
После серой окурись от скверны.
Видно, уж судьба моя такая...

ODDMENTS

I

I walked into the hut and looked about me:
It seemed I was seeing ghosts —
In that corner I sobbed one time,
In that one I prayed...
If these spectres of the past, risen
Suddenly from the dead, became flesh and bone,
What a squeeze it would be in here —
Like at the races on a public holiday!
They would all strangle their own selves,
They would all bite their own selves,
And gals, in Spartan fashion and in silence,
Would beat up the adults with swinging punches,
Who then would howl like mollycoddled brats —
All at once I saw before me that rubbish dump,
That vat of all the life outlived by me...

But the soul, flying spark-like, would flee
From one — to another — until it found life,
Until, honing in, it flew instantly to me,
Leaving behind all the crowds of
Phantoms — fading, clothed, unclothed,
Wrathful, and merry, and sorrowing —
Like a city after the eruption
Of an indifferent and savage volcano.

II

My Propertius has returned to me again —
What luck, what joy for Cynthia!
Scratched, mauled, bedraggled,
Balding, dirty, scrawny.
His eyes dart about so pitifully.
Why won't you look me in the eyes?
Surely you aren't ashamed in front of me?
You must be ashamed before someone else — love,
For against our will
She runs after me and you
And to our shame and woe brings us back together again.
Ah, how I would like to throw you out
On your ear — only I feel sorry
For that poor little sister, love,
In a pitiful state, but alive, all the same.
Go and change your toga, this one's all stained,
See to your scratches, get washed,
Then fumigate yourself from the filth with sulphur.
Apparently, such is my fate...

III

Только вчера я хотела
Югер земли отсудить у соседа —
Там растет виноград кудрявый,
Ползают мохнатые улитки, —
И сейчас сужусь за этот югер,
Но к нему как будто охладела.
Нынче я хочу совсем другого:
Я хочу достать шафранной краски
Для волос — шафранной, с переливом,
Рыжей стать хочу — лисицей в поле,
И к глазам зеленым цвет подходит.
Нам всегда хоть что-нибудь желанно,
Нынче это, завтра что другое.
О желанья, вы — скороходы,
Что, сменяясь, жизнь влекут
К мете заветной.
Вы — погонщики, вы и кони...

IV. К Морфею

Бог, души любящий нагими, без прикрас,
Страстишек скрытых бог и тайных страхов,
Весталке в сон развратника ты шлешь,
Насильника, чтоб было не обидно —
Мол, не сама я отдалась, а взяли.
Ревнивцу снится — он в железной клетке
Глядит, как тешится его с другим подружка
И смехом заливается жестоким...
Младенца чистого — того не пожалеешь,
Он весь дрожит во сне и цепенеет,
Вдруг закричит ужасно и проснется,
И тайный ужас в нем до самой смерти.
Морфей, как ночь, ты со свечой крадешься
Тропою тайной в мозг. Так знай, что если
Не будешь слать ты снов мне светлых,
Как паруса морские — чистых, ясных,
То ввек тебе назло я не засну.
Всю ночь водой холодной обливаться
Я буду, а служанок заставлю петь до утренней зари.
Пусть мне, Морфей, одно Ничто лишь снится.

III

Only yesterday I wanted
To sue a neighbour for a iuger of land —
Curly vines grow on it,
Shaggy snails crawl on it —
So now I am going to court over that iuger,
But I have, as it were, turned cold towards it.
Now I want something else entirely:
I want to get saffron dye
For my hair — saffron, with a shimmer,
I want to become ginger — like a fox in the field,
What's more, the colour sets off my green eyes.
There is always something we desire,
Now this, tomorrow some other thing.
O wishes, you are seven-league boots,
Which, taking turns, drag life along
Towards the ultimate *meta*.
You are both jockey and horses...

IV. To Morpheus

God who loves souls naked, unadorned,
God of hidden infatuations and secret fears,
You send a Vestal virgin a debaucher in her sleep,
A rapist, so it wouldn't be shameful —
Like, I didn't want to really, he made me...
A jealous man dreams he is in an iron cage
Watching his girlfriend dally with another man,
And she breaks into cruel laughter...
You do not even take pity on the pure infant,
He trembles all over and grows rigid in his sleep,
Suddenly gives a terrible cry and wakes up,
And the secret terror is in him until his dying day.
Morpheus, like night, you steal with your candle
By a traceless track into people's brains. So be warned,
If you do not send me dreams as sweet
As sea-sails — clean and clear,
Then to spite you I will never, ever go to sleep.
All night long I will pour cold water over myself,
And I will force my slave girls to sing until dawn.
Let me, Morpheus, dream of only Nothing.

V

...Прибегали тут колдуньи,
Приползали ведьмы злые
И вопили: здесь она,
Здесь, по нашим всем приметам,
Здесь волшебница живет.
По ее то заклинаньям
Третьи сутки, ночь и утро
Город бьет волна сырая,
Заливает Рим и мир.
Выходил префект навстречу,
И рабы с ним выходили,
Говорили: здесь гражданка
Рима честная живет,
Вы же, ведьмы, уходите
В свои норы поживей.
Я скосила глаз безумный,
Глаз свой левый небольшой
(Для других, а мне — огромный,
Он вмещает даже море,
Он вмещает Рим и мир),
Опустилась на колени,
Зашептала — Дионисе!
Пусть встает волна, кружася,
В пене, вое, плеске, соли,
Пусть очнется мир и Рим!
В мутных волнах птицерыбой
В смерче синем я помчусь.
Слышу — волны в окна бьются,
Затопило злых колдуний,
Затопило площадь, Форум,
Затопило Рим и мир!
Я плыла в водоворотах,
Души по волнам босые
Пробегали и носили
Низко палки чадных звезд,
При высоком полнолуньи......

V

Then hags came running,
Evil witches creeping up,
And they screeched: she is here,
Here, all our omens tell us,
Here is where the enchantress lives.
Her spells have summoned
The dank tide, which three days, now,
Night and day, batters the city,
Floods Rome and the Globe.
The Praefectus came out to take a look,
And his slaves came with him;
They said: here lives an honest
Roman citizeness,
Begone, you witches, back
To your burrows, lickety split.
I squinted my mad eye,
The left one, the smaller one
(As others see it, but to me it's immense,
It encompasses even the sea,
It encompasses Rome and the Globe),
I fell to my knees,
Whispered — 'Dionysus!'
Let the tide arise, swirling,
In foam and howl and splash and salt,
Let the Globe and Rome awake!
In the roily waves, a birdfish
I will tear through the caerulean vortex.
I hear — waves are beating at the windows,
Drowned are the evil hags,
Drowned is the Square, the Forum,
Drowned is Rome and the Globe!
I swam amidst the whirlpools,
Spirits ran barefoot over the waves
And carried held low
Their torch-sticks of fuming stars
Beneath a high full moon...

VI

Сделай, мастер, мне, — Пасифая Дедалу
Быстро шепчет, — ну, постарайся, телки
Сделай образ и недавней укрой
Содранной шкурой.

Кинется ль она быку на шею?
Нет, пылая, ждет она, терпит.
Кто в любви терпелив, кто служанок подкупит
Всех до единой,

Кто, пути к тебе торя, — с подругой твоею
Шашни затеет — чтобы ты ревновала,
Чтобы ты вернее попалась
Ловцу в сети, —

Сердца его не измеришь, вечно
Будет расчетлив. Ввек не растает
На дне его глаз влюбленных
Снег прошлогодний.

VII

Что меня бросило в объятья Диомида?
Пусть ответит знаток
Дел этих темных.
Может быть — месть, нелюбовь,
Ненависть ли к себе?
Хоть напыщенный, важный,
Глупый — но все же влюбленный,
Все же — сенатор и воин.
Даже рубец вдоль ребра,
Нанесенный вражеской пикой, —
Будь у любимого, сколько бы нежности вызвал,
Как бы его целовала!
А Диомидов рубец равнодушно
Чиркнула ногтем.
Нет, не на радость ему
Домоганьям его уступила —
От нелюбви за ночь
Стерся как будто и пол.
Рассвет нашел нас волками,
От ненависти дрожащих,
Некормленых и свирепых
По углам цирковой клетки.

VI

'Master, make me,' Pasiphaë to Daedalus
Whispers quickly, 'please, try to make me a heifer
Outfit, from a recent hide, so I can make cow-eyes
At that hot hoofer.'

Does she throw herself headlong at the bull?
No: aflame, she waits, she endures.
He who bides his time in love, who bribes your slave girls,
Every last one,

He who, beating a path to you, contrives a
Dalliance with your friend, so you'll be jealous,
So that you fall all the more surely into
The hunter's net —

You cannot ever gauge his heart, he will be
Eternally calculating. Last winter's
Snow at the depths of his loving eyes
Will never quite melt.

VII

What threw me into the arms of Diomedes?
Let an expert in these shadowy affairs
Answer this.
Was it, perhaps, revenge, unlove,
Self-loathing?
So, he's bombastic, and pompous,
And stupid — so what? He's in love with me,
And what's more, he's a senator and a soldier.
Even the scar along his rib,
Inflicted by an enemy spear —
If my beloved's, how much tenderness would it elicit,
How I would kiss it!
But the scar was Diomedes';
I scraped my fingernail along it, boredly.
No, it brought him no pleasure,
Me giving in to his pestering.
In the course of the night, even our sexes
Seemed to rub away, from lack of love.
Daybreak discovered us wolves,
Quivering with hatred,
Unfed and ferocious,
At either corner of a circus cage.

VIII

Раньше я сама любила кошек,
Но отныне хватит — надоели!
Приск, слуга мой верный, старый воин,
Хоть и потерял ты руку в Альпах,
Но второй, здоровою, рукою
Всех сыщи и выброси из дома.
Мой возлюбленный вчера взял на колени
Рыжую с глазами золотыми,
А она и рада — развалилась,
Будто опьяненная гетера.
Он чесал ей щеки, гладил брюхо
И смотрел в глаза ее смурные,
Кто из них мурлыкал громче — он ли
Иль она — не знаю. Все поплыло
В ревности багровом злом тумане.
— Что, блаженствуешь? — его спросила тихо.
Он, зажмурившись ответил: несказанно. —
Так что, Приск, слуга мой старый, верный,
Чтоб сегодня не было их в доме,
А особенно мордатой этой, рыжей.
Их хватай за что ни попадися,
За хвосты выкидывай за двери,
Если вдруг услышу визг кошачий,
Не сошлю тебя я на галеры.

IX

Надо было ехать в столицу —
Чему-нибудь поучиться.
Трудно теперь беглянке
Путь отыскать обратный.
Никто не слыхал здесь даже
О захудалом поместье.
Где наши луна и солнце?
Спросишь — никто не знает.
Где-то за топкою тьмой.
Нету вестей оттуда,
Разве битая птица
К нам иногда прилетает
На праздник, да та все молчит.

VIII

I used to love cats too,
But no more — I am sick of them!
Priscus, my faithful attendant,
You old campaigner, seek them all out,
And — with your good arm, not the one you lost
In the Alps — throw them out of the house.
Yesterday my beloved took onto his lap
That ginger one with the golden eyes,
And she sprawled in rapture
Like a drunken hetaera.
He scratched her cheeks, stroked her tummy,
Gazed into her doleful eyes...
Which of them purred louder — him
Or her — I don't know. The scene swam
In a blood-red, malevolent haze of jealousy.
'Do you like that, hmm?' she asked him softly.
He replied, eyes tight shut: 'Unutterably.'
So, Priscus, my faithful old attendant,
I want them out of my house today —
Especially that jowly, ginger one.
You may grab hold of them any which way,
Sling them out the doors by their tails,
And if I should hear a sudden feline yowl,
I won't send you to the galleys.

IX

I had to travel to the capital —
To study something or other.
But now it's hard for the fugitive
To find her way back home.
No one here has even heard
Of our one-horse estate.
Where is our moon, our sun?
You ask — no one ever knows.
Somewhere beyond the miry gloom.
Nary a breath of news comes thence,
Except on occasion, when
A plucked bird flies in for a festival,
But her beak is invariably sealed.

X

Розовые плывут облака над Римом.
Проплывают носилки мимо
Золотого столба верстового.
Сверну к рынку.
Перечитаю письмо. Погоди же!

«Пусть твое некогда столь любимое тело,
Знакомое до боли, до на ступне складки
Станет пеплом
В золоте костра погребального — прежде
Чем я вернусь из Лузитании дикой.
Да! Записываюсь центурионом
В легион Жаворонка, прощай же!»

Пахнут устрицами таблички,
Жареным вепрем, вином сицилийским, духами.

На рынке куплю я в лавке
Нитку тяжелых жемчужин
Цвета облаков,
Что сейчас над Римом.

80-е годы

X

Rosy-hued clouds are drifting over Rome.
Sedan chairs float past
The golden milestone.
I shall turn off here to the market.
I read the letter again. Hark at this!

'May your body, formerly so beloved,
Achingly familiar, down to the very wrinkles on your soles,
Turn to ashes
In the gold of a funeral pyre, before
I return from barbarous Lusitania.
Yes! I shall sign up as a centurion
In the Gaulish Foreign Legion — farewell!'

The tablets smell of oysters,
Roasted wild boar, Sicilian wine, perfume.

From a stall in the market I shall buy
A string of heavy pearls
The colour of the clouds
That are now over Rome.

1980s

3.2 *Кинфия* Apocrypha

A1 'Черный, как весло Харона, грязный'

[Разрозненное] III

Черный, как весло Харона, грязный,
Жиром нечистым налит от пят до макушки —
И не страшно тебе на языке липком
Искаженное мое носить подобье,
Будто статую варварской работы —
В пятнах и с отбитым напрочь мозгом?
Жалкий! Ведь на языке скользком
Ей не устоять. И рухнет
На твои же гнусные лапы.
Выплюнь и позабудь мое имя.

[1978?]

* *Variant, titled [2] V, breaks off after line 9:*

прямо на башку тебе. Стой, жалкий,

A2 'Есть у меня 4 небесных супруга'

Кинфия

Есть у меня 4 небесных супруга
Хоть и живые еще, брак наш небесный уже
К женам земным я их не ревную нисколько
Да и к друг другу они не ревнуют меня
Дай нам до смерти, Зевес, в формальном согласьи дожить

[27 December 1978?]

3.2 *Cynthia* Apocrypha

A1 'Black, like Charon's paddle, dirty'

[Oddments] III

Black, like Charon's paddle, dirty,
Soaked in foul grease from head to toe —
And aren't you scared to carry my likeness
On your sticky tongue — distorted,
Like a statue of barbarian workmanship,
Stained and with brains knocked clean out?
You're pitiful! Don't you see she can't stay standing
On a slippery tongue? And she'll collapse
Onto your own nasty little paws.
Spit out my name and forget it.

[1978?]

* *Variant, titled [2] V, breaks off after line 9:*

right onto your bonce. Stop, pitiful man,

A2 'I have 4 heavenly husbands'

Cynthia

I have 4 heavenly husbands
Though they're still alive, our marriage is made in heaven
I am not jealous at all of their earthly wives
And they are not jealous of each other with me
Let us live in legal concord, Zeus, till death

[27 December 1978?]

A3 Завистнику

    Кинф.

    Завистнику

    Ах зачем ты меня обидел?
    Ах зачем ты мне строил козни?
    Накажет тебя Юпитер.
    Налетят злые Музы
    Пчелиным роем
    искусают всего, исколют
    Прилетит Дионис ветром
    Бросит вниз будто лист ~~котор~~
    Пожухлый.
    Аполлон же проткнет тебя острой
    Золотою своею острогой
    и в котел тебя кинет кипящий
    Фессалийской прожорливой ведьмы
    Где ты будешь вариться рядом
    Со смердящей жабой лопаткой
    Разложившимся глазом спрута
    Превратишься в мазь и колдунья
    Тебя вмажет в свои морщины
    И тогда мне тебя будет жалко
    И сейчас уже тебя жалко
    Жалко! Жалко! Ужасно жалко!
    Жальте Музы!
    Мне жаль, но жальте!

[between 24 and 28 September 1980]

* whole poem struck through

A3 To the Envier

    Cynth.

    To the Envier

    Ah, why did you offend me?
    Ah, why did you plot against me?
    Jupiter will punish you.
    Ireful Muses will swoop down
    As a swarm of bees
    and sting and prick you all over
    Dionysus will fly up as the wind
    And throw you down like a leaf ~~whi~~
    All withered.
    Then Apollo, he'll impale you
    With his sharp golden harpoon
    and chuck you into a gluttonous
    Thessalian witch's bubbling cauldron
    Where you will be boiled alongside
    A pongy toad, a shoulder blade,
    An octopus's putrefied eyeball
    You'll turn into ointment and the hag
    Will rub you into her wrinkles
    And then I'll pity you
    And now I already pity you
    Pitiful! Pitiful! Terribly pitiful!
    Prick him, Muses!
    It's a pity, but prick him!

    [between 24 and 28 September 1980]

    * whole poem struck through

A4 'Горь—ка́ / я ты лю— / бовь'

Два стиха на особый распев

~~Из Кинфии~~   I

Горь—ка́—   бовь
        я ты лю—
Серд—це́   в кровь
        измучено
Птичь—им
        гнездом
                темне—ет.
Ра—зум
        щебета полн
Голо—
        дных
            немолчных птиц.

В черной ракушке Бог
Спит под
        звездой морей
В соли сребре
        розовеет.
Жалко, жалко
        любимых всех,
Спрятали б их в живот
Только
        тленный и он.

Плюньтесь зрачками, глаза
К морю во тьме летите
Плачьте над теплою тенью
Над посиневшей любовью —
Слабой сестрою смерти.

Прут раскаленный возьму
Язву души прижгу
Смерти нет вообще
Жизнь неизводна в нас.
Будто клейменный зверь
Станешь себя уносить
Кинешься в море рыбой
Вынут — крюком за губу.

Раскалю кочергу
Поставлю ее на лоб
Буду прыгать в горах
Буду — богов ворошить
Буду — бессмертных язвить,
Знайте же знайте боль,
Что во юдоли цветет.

80

* typewritten / *handwritten*

A4 'Bit—tér / are you / love'

Two Poems to a Special Chant

~~From Cynthia~~   I

Bit—tér   love
       are you
Heart cáre—   blood
             worn to
Bird's—nest—
          like it
               dark—ens.
Rea—son
      full of chatter
Of hun—
      gry
          unquieting birds.

In a black shell God
Sleeps under
        the star of seas
In salt silver
      he pinkens.
Pity, pity
      all the loved ones,
We'd hide them away in our belly
Only
     it too is mortal.

Eyes — spit your pupils
Fly to the sea in the dark
Cry over warm shade
Over blued love —
Death's weak sister.

I'll take the red-hot rod
I'll sear the soul's ulcer
There is no death at all
Life's inextricable in us.
Like a branded beast
You'll start to speed away
You'll plunge fishlike into the sea
They'll hoik you out — hooked by the lip.

I'll heat up a poker
I'll fix it to my forehead
I will cavort in the mountains
I will — stir up the gods
I will — wound the immortals,
Know ye, then, know ye the pain
That flowers in this vale.

[28 September 1980]

* typewritten / *handwritten*

A5 Цирцея

И я была в Цирцеиных садах
Там было много хрюканья и визга —
На борове, на кошках и ослах
Плясала, раздеваясь, одалиска.

Она свое лупила стадо
Тройною плеткой все сильней —
За то, что так легко (досада!)
Вы превращаетесь в свиней.

83

A6 Пасифая

[Виратиня ?]

Страсти зданье Пасифаи,
Похоть злая — на века,
Не то, что ваши похотишки,
Не распалитесь на быка.

Ее недра развихрялись в буре,
Жилы выли, в алчность ее лона
Чуть не утекли и бык и поле,
Зло, добро и очи небосклона.

83

⋆ [illegible ?]

A7 'повсю[д]у в дворах стояли поленницы'

повсю[д]у в дворах стояли поленницы,
в кладовках сырели дрова,
весь город засыпан был
деревом мертвым

дворник, мигая, ходил с колуном
повсюду кололи, рубили, пилили,
таким лабиринтом змеились дворы
в них было не[л]ьзя не поймать Минотавра
с детским лицом ~~минотавр~~
в перешитом пальтишке
казак же разбойника мог потерять

почти что телесная пряталась тайна
она ускользала, на пал[ь]цах занозы
так тесно в дворах, так ~~теснились~~ дрова
и *что* мрачный огонь из тебя высекали.

⋆ typewritten / *handwritten* / [corrected]

A5 Circe

    I, too, have been in the gardens of Circe
    There were a lot of grunts and squeals —
    Atop a hog, some cats, and donkeys
    She danced and undressed — the odalisque.

    Harder and harder she flogged her flock
    With her three-tailed whip — because it was
    So easy (how disappointing!)
    For all you guys to turn into pigs.

    1983

A6 Pasiphaë

    [~~Virago~~ ?]

    Pasiphaë's edifice of passion,
    Evil lust to last down the ages,
    A far cry from your little lustlets,
    None of you would get hot for a bull.

    Her innards whisked up a maelstrom,
    Her veins howled, the greed of her loins
    Nearly sucked in both bull and pasture,
    Evil, good, and the eyes of the horizon.

    1983

    * [illegible ?]

A7 'all round the courtyards were woodpiles'

    all round the courtyards were woodpiles,
    firewood was getting damp in storerooms,
    the whole city was awash with
    dead wood

    a street sweeper walked blinking with a hatchet
    all around was chopping, felling, sawing,
    the courtyards snaked about so labyrinthinely
    you couldn't not catch a Minotaur in them
    ~~a minotaur~~ one with a child's face
    in a little rehemmed coat
    even a Cossack could lose a bandit

    an almost bodily secret hid here
    it slipped away, in fingers — thorns
    the yards were so cramped, the wood so crammed
    ~~and~~ *that* they struck a gloomy light from you.

    * typewritten / *handwritten*

A8 'Ты опять о Тите речь заводишь'

    Ты опять о Тите речь заводишь
    ты влюблен в него — мне эт[о] ясно
    хоть ты не похож на мужеложца
    Темной сливой полежалой
    тронутой гнилью
    предста[в]лялся мне он,
    позабытой в кладовке случайно.
    [д]умать я уже о нем забыла.
    Ныне от твоих восхвалений
    тихо и моя любовь затлела
    если он в тебе даже
    никого от рожденья не любившем
    может вызвать страсть..
    Мотыльком была моя любовь
    умерла она едва родившись
    Видно и у мотыльков есть тени
    продлевать их жизнь короткую не стоит
    вызывать их заклинаньями не нужно

    * [corrected]

A9 Из восп. Кинф.

    женское обыкновенное —
    на тьмы, на сонмы
    сущест[в]
    в первый раз она ужас наводит.
    было тогда полнолунье
    цепко светила луна
    не отвести зрачок
    нравится ей
    в темном крови кольце
    отражаться.
    казалось ~~ей~~ страшно ~~ужас ее объял~~ ей было
      ~~обеим.:~~ *больше че* . Было мне *жутче*
    будто стучишься ты в лачугу
    где живет старичок знакомый,
    вдруг растворяется дверь
    птицы из дома летят
    черной рекою.
    столько их — в доме том
    им поместиться б неможно.
    так испугалась тогда
    своего же родимого тела
    и обещала себя
    в брачную жертву луне

    * typewritten / *handwritten* / [corrected]

A8 'Yet again you turn to talk of Titus'

>   Yet again you turn to talk of Titus
>   you're in love with him — it's obvious to me,
>   although you don't seem like a sodomite
>   A dark plum, past its best,
>   touched by mould
>   — that's how he seemed to me —
>   left too long in the larder by mistake.
>   I've already forgotten to think about him.
>   Now, because of your encomia,
>   my love, too, has quietly rotted
>   if he can incite passion in you,
>   of all people, who have never
>   loved anyone in all your years...
>   My love was a moth
>   It died moments from birth
>   Apparently even moths have shades
>   there's no use prolonging their short lives
>   no need to summon them with spells

A9 From Cynth.'s Mem.

>   the custom of women —
>   darknesses, hordes of
>   creatures
>   are terrified by her the first time.
>   it was then full moon
>   the moon shone tenaciously
>   can't tear the pupil away
>   she likes
>   to be reflected
>   in the dark ring of blood.
>   it seemed ~~to her~~ *she was* afraid ~~horror seized her~~
>   ~~to both of us.:~~ ~~more tha~~ *I was more horrified*
>   as if you knocked at a hovel
>   where a little old man you know lives,
>   suddenly the door swings open
>   from the house birds fly out
>   in a black river.
>   so many of them — the house
>   could not possibly hold them.
>   then I was so frightened
>   by my own body
>   and I promised myself
>   as a nuptial sacrifice to the moon
>
>   * typewritten / *handwritten*

298 APPENDIX

3.3 *Cynthia* Variants

Poem	Published Version	Variant	
1.6	шрамов	шрамов и ссадин	scars and scrapes
	в двери мои он стучится	он у моих уж дверей,	he's already at my door
	остроблещущий меч	меч свой блестящий.	his shining sword
	Люблю, несчастная, я лысого урода	Жаль мне его — люблю, несчастная, я лысого урода	I feel sorry for him — wretched me, I love a bald monstrosity
	Но, подлой, жалко мне его прогнать, Когда еще такой полюбит молодец, А старости вот-вот они, туманы... Как сытый волк и на зиму овца...	Подлой жалко мне и гладиатора гнать — Жадный я волк, что не знает — съест ему агнца иль нет Несчастного пресыщенный сжирает И я вот так же мучаюсь и мучу Старости близко туманы — когда еще такой полюбит молодец.	Despicably, I am loath to drive even the gladiator away — I'm a greedy wolf, that doesn't know whether to eat the sheep or not Satiated, it'll gobble the unlucky man up And just like that I am tortured and I torture The fogs of age are near — when will another such gallant love me again.
R	РАЗРОЗНЕННОЕ	Аппендикс	Appendix
R.8	мордатой этой	золотоглазой	golden-eyed
R.9	Надо было ехать в столицу — Чему-нибудь поучиться. Трудно теперь беглянке Путь отыскать обратный. Никто не слыхал здесь даже О захудалом поместье. Где наши луна и солнце? Спросишь — никто не знает. Где-то за топкою тьмой.	Пора мне ехать в столицу, чему-нибудь поучиться. тр[у]дно будет путь отыскать обратный никто здесь не знает — где деревенька наша больно уж захудала, где наши луна и солнце, всякий кого ни спросишь мне отвечает — не знаю где-то за топкою тьмой.	It's time for me to travel to the capital, to study something or other. it will be hard to find the way back home no one here knows where our little village is it's really very run-down, where is our moon, our sun whoever I ask tells me — I don't know somewhere beyond the miry gloom.

* I only give substantive variants; i.e., differences in punctuation, spelling, numbering, or word order are not noted. All variants come from ESHA M unless otherwise stated.

| R.10 (BT 137) | Розовые плывут облака над Римом. | Розовые плывут облака над вечерним Римом.

табличка на подушке рядом
почерк знакомый

Знаю — тебя не дождется варвар
С саблей короткой
и напрасно ждут в нетерпеньи прыгая океана волны
Пойду в лавку на Священной дороге | Rosy-hued clouds are drifting over evening-time Rome.

tablet on the pillow beside me
familiar handwriting

I know — you'll never make it to the barbarian
With his short sabre
and the ocean's waves, jumping in their impatience, are waiting in vain
I'll go to a stall on the Sacred Road |

3.4 *Cynthia* Metres

Cynthia	Metre
I.1 'To a Slave Girl'	Elegiac-ish (dactylic hexameter, pentameter, and heptameter, usually split over two lines)
I.2	Dolnik (four-stress)
I.3 'To a Slave Girl'	Iambic pentameter
I.4 'To Cupid'	Sapphics (but not in the usual stanza pattern)
I.5 'To a Young Poet'	Hendecasyllables and decasyllables
I.6 'To Claudia'	Elegiac-ish (dactylic hexameter and pentameter, but not alternating in pairs)
I.7	Trochaic pentameter (regular)
I.8 'To a Provincial Woman'	Trochaic pentameter (regular)
II.1	Trochaic octameter
II.2	Trochaic pentameter (regular)
II.3	Logaoedic trimeter and tetrameter (anapaests with amphibrachic line endings)
II.4 'To Claudia, after Visiting My Sick Granny'	No fixed metre
II.5	Elegiac-ish (very regular dactylic hexameter and pentameter, but alternating in threes instead of pairs)
II.6	Trochaic pentameter
II.7 'On the Beach at Baiae'	Dactylic tetrameter and pentameter, and trochaic pentameter
II.8 'Conversation'	Trochaic pentameter
R.1	Trochaic pentameter
R.2	Trochaic pentameter (regular)
R.3	Dactylic trimeter and tetrameter, and trochaic pentameter
R.4 'To Morpheus'	Hendecasyllables
R.5	Trochaic tetrameter (regular)
R.6	Sapphics
R.7	Elegiac-ish (dactylic metres often split over two lines)
R.8	Trochaic pentameter (regular)
R.9	Elegiac-ish (dactylic heptameter and hexameter, usually split over two lines)
R.10	No fixed metre
A1 'Black, like Charon's paddle, dirty'	No fixed metre
A2 'I have 4 heavenly husbands'	Elegiac-ish (dactylic hexameter and pentameter, but not alternating in pairs)
A3 'To the Envier'	Logaoedic trimeter (anapaests with amphibrachic line endings)
A4 'Bit—tér | are you | love'	Logaoedic trimeter (dactyls, amphibrachs, anapaests)

A5 'Circe'	Iambic pentameter (stanza 1) and tetrameter (stanza 2) (very regular)
A6 'Pasiphaë'	Trochaic tetrameter (stanza 1) and pentameter (stanza 2) (very regular)
A7 'all round the courtyards were woodpiles'	Amphibrachic tetrameter
A8 'Yet again you turn to talk of Titus'	Trochaic pentameter
A9 'From Cynth.'s Mem.'	Elegiac-ish (dactylic metres often split over two lines)

* Metre is approximate or majority, unless otherwise stated.

3.5 *Cynthia* Classical References

Cynthia	Propertius	Catullus	Martial	Horace	Ovid	Others
I.1 'To a Slave Girl'	II.5, II.9, III.3, IV.7	II, III	I.56, III.100, IX.94, X.5, XII.29	*Satires* II.3, *Epistles* II.2	*Amores* II.6	
I.2			*Spec.* 9	*Satires* II.3, *Epodes* III		Pliny the Elder and Seneca the Younger re. Vedius Pollio
I.3 'To a Slave Girl'	II.32, II.34, IV.7, IV.8	XXXVII, XXXIX	II.66, VIII.73		*Ars Am.* III	Juvenal VI
I.4 'To Cupid'	II.12	XI, LI				(Sappho XXXI)
I.5 'To a Young Poet'	IV.2	XIV, XXII, XXXVI, XLV, CV	IV.41, VIII.20, IX.83, XII.63	*Satires* I.4		
I.6 'To Claudia'	I.16, III.25, IV.8			*Epodes* XIII		Juvenal VI
I.7	I.3, II.22, III.8	LXIII				Euripides, *Bacchae*
I.8 'To a Provincial Woman'	IV.5	XLIII, LXIX, XCIII	I.47, VII.87, X.77	*Satires* I.8, *Epodes* V, XVII		
II.1	III.17, IV.8			*Satires* I.8		
II.2						
II.3						Plato, *Republic*
II.4 'To Claudia, after Visiting my Sick Granny'			III.93			
II.5			V.11			(Posidippus *Lithika*)
II.6						Juvenal V
II.7 'On the Beach at Baiae'	I.11, II.31/32, III.18, IV.6		IV.30			
II.8 'Conversation'	III.10, III.25, IV.1			*Satires* II.7		Plato, *Phaedo*, *Phaedrus*, *Republic*, *Timaeus*, *Meno*; Sulpicia II
R.1	III.14		IV.44		*Met.* XV	
R.2	I.3, I.8, II.15, II.29, IV.8					
R.3	II.2, II.18, II.25, III.14, IV.1, IV.6		VI.19, X.50	*Epistles* I.1		Juvenal XIV

APPENDIX

Cynthia	Propertius	Catullus	Martial	Horace	Ovid	Others
R.4 'To Morpheus'	I.3, II.29	(metre)				
R.5	I.1			Satires I.8, Epodes XVII	Met. I	
R.6	II.23, II.31/32, III.19, IV.7	(XI/LI — metre)			Ars Am. I	(Sappho — metre)
R.7	II.5, III.8					
R.8			Spec. 31			
R.9			IX.54-55			
R.10	I.17, II.16, III.12, III.21, III.23, III.24, IV.7		VIII.81, XII.17			
A1 'Black, like Charon's paddle, dirty'	II.1, II.23/24, II.29, III.18, IV.2, IV.7, IV.8, IV.11	XCVIII	VIII.61, XI.102			
A2 'I have 4 heavenly husbands'	(metre)					
A3 'To the Envier'	I.1, I.5, II.1, III.24, IV.5			Epodes V		Apuleius, Met. II–III
A4 'Bit—tér | are you | love'						
A5 'Circe'	III.12					Homer, Odyssey X
A6 'Pasiphaë'	II.31/32, III.19, IV.7				Ars Am. I	
A7 'all round the courtyards were woodpiles'						
A8 'Yet again you turn to talk of Titus'			XII.42			
A9 'From Cynth.'s Mem.'	(metre)					

4.1 Монолог лодки

«Ты счастье Цезаря везёшь...»
Я повезу, а он меня потом из тысяч не узнает!
И счастья нет. Ведь не бывает.
Для Цезаря бывает.
Ему ведь славы хочется, как крови волку.
Не повезу. Чего болтать без толку.
Он кормчего грозит зарезать.
Но он же Цезарь, Цезарь, Цезарь!
Садись. Поехали. Ох, ветер нас относит.
Ведь он же брат мой. Ветер нас относит.
Ему через войска — ведь тоже через бурю.
Ему через века — ведь тоже через бурю.
И тоже носом.
А он кричит, а он клокочет, всё Рубикон да Рубикон.
И кормчему: «Правее, нет, левее!..»
Ох, если б взял меня конём —
бока широкие — кормить не надо, не похудею.
Я б на уключинах бежала,
я бы по воздуху летела.
Быстрее всех его желаний
и дальше всех его пределов.
Приехали. Ох, прямо в берег носом.
О Господи, избавь его от бед, от всех мечей, от всех дурных советов.
Прости ему, что кормчего он бросил,
прости ему зелёные монеты.

1963

* *Variant — extra couplet after line 21:*

Но берег близко. Едва дышу. Вода по колку.
Тяжелую гнедую воду несу как холку.

4.1 The Boat's Monologue

'You're carrying the luck of Caesar...'
I'll carry him, and afterwards he won't pick me out of a line-up!
And there's no such thing as luck. It doesn't exist.
For Caesar it exists.
You see, he wants glory like a wolf wants blood.
I won't carry him. There's no use going on about it.
He threatens to stab the helmsman.
But he is Caesar, Caesar, Caesar!
Sit down. Off we go. Oof, the wind's catching us.
But then, he is my brother. The wind catches us.
He goes through armies — that's sailing through storms.
He goes through centuries — that's sailing through storms.
And also nose-first.
How he hollers, how he froths, Rubicon this, Rubicon that.
And to the helmsman: 'Right a bit, no, left!...'
Oh, if he took me as his steed —
my sides are broad — I don't need feeding, I won't get thin.
I would run on my rowlocks,
I would fly through the air.
Faster than all his wishes
and further than all his limits.
We have landed. Ouch, right onto the bank, nose-first.
O Lord, deliver him from harm, from all the swords, from all the bad advice.
Forgive him for what he threw to the helmsman,
forgive him for the green coins.

1963

* *Variant — extra couplet after line 21:*

But the bank's close. Can hardly breathe. Water up to my rowlocks.
I carry the heavy chestnut-coloured water like withers.

4.2 Два надгробия

Вздрагивает весна. Телятся коровы.
Легионер умирает в далеком городе Убир,
Будущем Кёльне.
На берегу большой реки — последней, —
За которой круглится плечо Европы,
Опускаясь бессильно в море,
Глубокое море.

Еще не так стар. Перед смертью
Снесли его товарищи в Термы,
На дверях козлы с рыбьими хвостами.
Это новые веянья? Новые формы?
Нет, это древнее Рима.

— Поблиций, — говорят ему солдаты, —
Мы тебе воздвигнем такое надгробье —
Выше ворот, что твой Цезарь.
Посредине ты в полный рост, со свитком
Стихов любимых,
Чтоб они были с тобою и в смерти.
А мы останемся у твоей могилы,
Никуда не пойдем отсюда —
Потому что Империя наша крошится,
Как засохший хлеб,
Как гнилая палка. —

....

И вот чрез девятнадцать столетий
Мы стоим с моим другом в лесу под Кельном,
У новенького надгробья,
Под которым лежит жена его Лена,
Смотрим на светлый камень
С вбитым в него православным распятьем,
Там же выбито его имя —
«Это чтоб хлопот потом было меньше».
За спиной оседает, как снежная баба,
Империя наша.
Нету Рима, но нету Германии тоже.

В Рождество Германия в оспе свечек,
Теплый туман льется в леса дубовые,
Что стоят на листьях лиловых,
Как на щитах медных,
Как на славе римской.

1990

4.2 Two Headstones

Spring is quivering. Cows are calving.
A legionary is dying in the remote town of Ubiorum,
The future Cologne.
On the bank of a large river — the last river —
Beyond which the slumped shoulder of Europe
Sinks helplessly into the sea,
The deep sea.

He's not very old. Before he died
His comrades carried him off to the Thermae,
On its doors are goats with fishes' tails.
Are these new fads? New forms?
No, they are older than Rome.

'Poblicius,' the soldiers say to him,
'We will build you such a headstone —
Higher than the gates your Caesar built.
In the middle — you, life-size, with a scroll
Of your favourite poems,
So they will be with you even in death.
And we will stay by your tomb,
We won't budge from this spot —
Because our Empire is crumbling
Like stale bread,
Like a rotten stick.'

....

And so nineteen centuries later
My friend and I are standing in a forest near Cologne,
By a brand-new headstone,
Under which lies his wife Lena,
We look at the bright stone
With the orthodox crucifix hammered into it,
And there, too, is hammered out *his* name —
'That's so there'll be less hassle later'.
Behind us our empire founders
Like a snowman.
There's no Rome, but there's no Germany, either.

At Christmas Germany is pocked with candles,
Warm fog pours into the oak forests,
That stand on purple leaves,
Like on shields of bronze,
Like on the glory of Rome.

1990

4.3 'Стамбул не пал, не пал Константинополь'

Стамбул не пал, не пал Константинополь,
А с грохотом расшибся третий Рим,
На дне морей, под изумрудной коркой
В его развалинах, в золе горим.
Проливов не видать, теперь уж это ясно,
На что они? На что мне Рим?
Мне мира мало, да и он опасен,
Он рухнул весь, мы в головне дрожим.
На что мне мир? Мне нужно только,
Чтоб ангелы не слышали меня,
Все ж слушая, и всхлипывали горько,
Подглазья синевою затемня.

1996

4.4 Римская тетрадь (selected poems)

4.4.1 *Circo Massimo*

Вот только повернёт автобус
У Circo Massimo, тогда
Чувствую — в седой арене
Стынет тьмы зацветшая вода.
Днём он дремлет, сохнет позвоночник
С сломанной навек метой,
Ночи поперёк он ржавой ванной
Стынет с заболоченной водой.
Император, если бы ты видел,
Как несутся в мраке колесницы,
Никогда меты не достигая,
Падают, ломая в смерть ключицы.
Цезарь, Цезарь, подавившись ядом,
Не стесняйся, выплюнь. Не глотай.
Чашу цирка поднимать не надо —
Там отрава — будущее там.

2002

4.3 'Istanbul did not fall, nor did Constantinople'

> Istanbul did not fall, nor did Constantinople,
> But the Third Rome came crashing down,
> On the bottom of seas, under an emerald crust
> In its ruins, in its ashes we burn.
> I shan't see the gulfs, that is now quite clear,
> Why should I want them? Why should I want Rome?
> The world's not enough for me, and it's not safe,
> It's all collapsed, we shiver in the embers.
> Why should I want the world? All I need
> Is for the angels not to hear me
> But to listen to me, and sob bitterly,
> Beclouding their under-eyes with circles of blue.

1996

4.4 Roman Notebook (selected poems)

4.4.1 *Circo Massimo*

> The very moment the bus turns
> By the Circo Massimo, I sense
> The icy water of darkness
> Stagnating in the grey-haired arena.
> By day it slumbers, its agèd spine —
> With *meta* broken forever — gets parched;
> All night long, like a rusty bath,
> It is gelid with swampy water.
> Emperor, if only you could see
> The chariots tearing through the gloom,
> Never reaching the *meta*,
> Falling, fatally breaking collarbones.
> Caesar, Caesar, poisoned and choking,
> Don't be shy, spit it out. Don't swallow.
> You do not have to raise the circus cup —
> There lies poison — the future lies there.

2002

4.4.2 'Рим как будто варвар-гладиатор'

Рим как будто варвар-гладиатор
Цепь накинул на меня стальную,
И уже готов был и прикончить,
Я уже готова умереть.
Только публика того не захотела
(Та, которая всегда нас видит).
Многие из плебса и сената
Вскинули тотчас большие пальцы —
Гибели моей не захотели.
Ну и я пошла себе, качаясь,
Превращаясь в самолётную снежинку,
На родной свой город опускаясь,
В северное страшное сиянье.

2002

4.4.3 Забастовка электриков в Риме

В ту ночь на главных площадях
Вдруг электричество погасло.
Луна старалась — только, ах —
Не наливайся так, опасно!

Фонтаны в темноте шуршали,
Но что-то в них надорвалось.
Как будто вместо них крутилась,
Скрипя и плача, мира ось.

И тьма, тревожима Селеной
Чуть трепетала, будто море.
И люди, сливки мглы, качались
Придонной водорослью в бурю.

Тьма нежная и неживая —
Живых и мёртвых клей и связь.
Вдруг вечный мрак и вечный город
Облобызались, расходясь.

2002

4.4.2 'Rome like a barbarian-gladiator'

> Rome like a barbarian-gladiator
> Threw a chain of steel over me,
> And was just ready to finish me off,
> And I was just ready to die.
> Only the public did not want that
> (The one that always comes to see us).
> Many of the plebs and senate
> Jerked up straightaway their thumbs —
> They were not in the mood for my death.
> And, well, I went on my way, swaying,
> Turning into an airborne snowflake,
> Descending on my native city,
> Towards the frightful northern light.
>
> *2002*

4.4.3 Electricians' Strike in Rome

> On that night in the main squares
> The electricity suddenly went off.
> Luna tried her best — only, ah! —
> Don't glow so much, it's dangerous!
>
> Fountains were pattering in the darkness,
> But something inside them ruptured.
> As if revolving there, in their place,
> Grating and groaning, was the world's axis.
>
> And the dark, disturbed by Selene,
> Palpitated slightly, like the sea.
> And people, the cream of the murk, swayed
> Like weeds on the ocean floor during a storm.
>
> Dark, you are gentle and inanimate —
> Glue and bond of the living and dead.
> Suddenly eternal gloom and eternal city
> Kissed as they parted.
>
> *2002*

4.5 Жалоба Кинфии

«Чем виноват соловей — что в эпоху лесного пожара
Довелось ему сгинуть в огне?
Страшно ему
В час последний,
Глаза закрывая,
Видеть, как свитки родимых деревьев
В пепел сухой обратились —
Будто и не было вовсе.
Гибель родного всего.
Варваров новых язык —
Вот до чего суждено
Было судьбою дожить.
Разве мне жаль было б жалкое тело покинуть,
Если б душа моя в свитках родимых жила?»

С жалобой этою римской свою я свивала
Сидя в развалинах римских в слезах:
В городе сняли трамвай,
Не на чем в рай укатиться,
Гнусным жиром богатства
Измазали стены.
Новый Аларих ведёт войско джипов своих.
Седою бедною мышкой
Искусство в норку забилось,
Быстро поэзия сдохла,
Будто и не жила.

Римлянка, плач твой напрасен —
Через века возродится многое, пусть изменясь.
Ныне ж всё кажется мне безвозвратным,
Столь безнадёжным, что лучше —
Хрупкий стеклянный поэзии город
Грубо о землю разбить.

2006

4.6 Воспоминание о Риме

Меня, как сухую ветвь,
К Риму долго несла река,
И очнулась я, чуть отпив
Древле волчьего молока,
Что сочится из всех щелей,
Что от самых младых ногтей
Каждый римлянин жадно пьёт
Из Волчицы, простёршей над Градом
Голубой и бездонный живот.
Вот я шла и брела под ним,
Бормотала себе, и незримо
Обломок жизни моей
Прилепился к руинам Рима.

6 марта 2009

4.5 Cynthia's Complaint

'Is the nightingale to blame, if in the epoch of forest fire
It chances to perish in the flame?
It is frightened
In its final hour,
Shutting its eyes,
To see the scrolls of its native trees
Turn to dry ashes —
As if they had never been at all.
The death of everything dear.
The tongue of new barbarians —
So this is what fate has doomed
It should live to see.
Would I be loath to quit this pitiful body,
If my soul lived on in its native scrolls?'

Together with this Roman complaint I span out my own,
Sitting in the Roman ruins in tears:
In the city they've taken up the tram tracks,
There's nothing to trundle off to paradise on,
They've smeared the walls
With the odious fat of wealth.
New Alaric leads the war host of his jeeps.
Poor grey mouse
Art hid cowering in a burrow,
Poetry quickly dropped dead
As if it had never lived.

Roman woman, your weeping is in vain —
In centuries to come much will revive, albeit in altered forms.
Right now, though, everything seems irrevocable,
So hopeless, to my eyes, that 'twere better
To dash this brittle glass city of poetry
Roughly to the ground.

2006

4.6 Remembering Rome

I was carried, like a dry branch,
Long by the river to Rome,
And I came to with a small sip
Of the ancient wolf's milk,
Which oozes out of all the cracks,
Which even in their cradles
Every Roman greedily drinks
From the She-Wolf, who spreads o'er the City
Her blue and fathomless stomach.
So I walked and wandered beneath it,
Muttering to myself, and imperceptibly
A fragment of my life
Stuck to the ruins of Rome.

6 March 2009

5.1 Хомо Мусагет

(Зимние Музы)

> Vester, Camenae, vester...
> *Horatius*★

I

Ветер шумит за стеклами,
Вид на задний двор.
Ветер подъемлет кругами,
Носит во мне сор.
Всякий вор
В душу мне может пролезть,
Подкупит
И низкая лесть.
Но поднимается жар
И разгорается хор,
Легких сандалий лепет,
Босой разговор.

Не тяните меня, Музы, в хоровод,
Я устала, я сотлела.
Не во что ногою топнуть —
Под ногами топлый плот.
Я уже вам не десятый,
И уже не мой черед.

Пахнет льдом, вином и мятой,
Травы горные в росе.
Вертишейкою распятой★★
Закружили в колесе.

Музы кружатся, как бусы
Разноцветные, — пестрей!
И одна из них как прорубь,
А другая как Орфей.
И одна из них как морфий,
А другая как Морфей.
И одна как сон тягучий.
А другая — сноп огней.
Не тяните меня, Музы, в хоровод —
Уже год у нас не певчий,
А глухой водоворот.

Легче ветра, темней света
И шумней травы.
Ах, оставьте человека,
Позовите Бога вы.

★ Я ваш, Музы, я ваш... (*Гораций*) (*лат.*).
★★ Вертишейку, распятую в колесе, приносили в жертву Афродите.

5.1 Homo Musagetes

(Winter Muses)

> Vester, Camenae, vester...
> *Horatius*★

I

Wind whistles outwith windowpanes
Overlooking the rear courtyard.
The wind, circling, rises,
Stirs up my innermost dregs.
Any thief
Can creep into my soul,
The basest flattery
Will buy me off.
But the heat is rising
And the choir igniting,
Light sandals' lisping blether,
A barefoot conversation.

Do not pull me, Muses, into the circle dance,
I'm tired, I'm burnt out.
There's nothing to tap my feet on —
Underfoot is a sodden, sinking raft.
I am no longer your tenth,
And it is no longer my turn.

Scent of ice, wine, and mint,
Mountain grasses in the dew.
A crucified wryneck★★
Has been spun in a wheel.

The Muses spin, like beads
Multicoloured — yet more motley!
And one of them is like a hole in the ice,
Yet another is like Orpheus.
And one of them is like morphine,
Yet another is like Morpheus.
And one of them is like clinging sleep,
Yet another is a shaft of lights.
Do not pull me, Muses, into the circle dance —
This year with us is no longer songful,
But a tone-deaf whirlpool.

Lighter than wind, darker than light,
And louder than grass.
Ah, leave mankind alone,
Call ye upon God instead.

★ I am yours, Muses, I am yours... (*Horace*) (*Latin*).
★★ Wrynecks, crucified on a wheel, used to be brought as a sacrifice to Aphrodite.

II

Музы! Девушки! Зима уж навалилась.
Снег под кожею — где флейта, где тимпан?
С верткою поземкой вы впервой явились
С углями в ладонях... или заблудились?
Сгинули, как Пан?

Моряки-эгейцы на недвижном море
Услыхали голос: — Умер Пан! —
Вздох слетел с вершины, солнце побелело,
В мареве Олимп пропал.

Только Музы живы, им десятый нужен
В разноцветный их и пьяный хоровод.
С первою порошей, по ледку босая,
С черно-красным камнем первая бредет.

III

Вот выпал первый снег.
Багровое вино
В сугробы возливая,
Чтобы почтить озябших Муз,
И дикие стихи
На свечке сожигая,
Я Смерти говорю:
Пчелой в тебя вопьюсь.

О, как она бывает рада,
Когда ее встречают
Не с отупелостью потухшей,
Не с детским ужасом,
И не бредут к теням унылой тенью —
А как любовника: и с трепетом в очах,
И сладострастьем нетерпенья.

Камены бедные
В снегу переминались —
Все боги умерли,
Оне одне остались.
Они и в смерть перелетают —
Как захотят летят они,
Горя вкруг древа мирового
Как новогодние огни.

II

Muses! Ladies! The winter really has closed in.
Snow under the skin — where's the flute, where's the timpani?
It was with the twisting blizzard you first appeared
With coals in your palms... or have you lost your way?

Vamoosed, like Pan?
The Aegean sailors on the becalmed sea
Heard a voice: 'Pan is Dead!'
A breath dropped from the mountaintop, the sun turned pale,
In a haze Olympus fell.

Only the Muses are alive, they need a tenth
To join their multicoloured, drunken circle dance.
With the first dusting of snow, barefoot over frost,
With her black-red stone the first goes wandering.

III

So, the first snow has fallen.
Libating blood-red wine
Onto the snowdrifts
To honour the frozen Muses,
And burning wild poems
Over a candle,
I say to Death:
As a bee I will suck of thee.

Oh, how happy she is
When she is met
Not with snuffed-out stupidity,
Not with childish fear,
And not by a dreary shade, shuffling into the shadows,
But as a lover: with tremulousness in their eyes,
And concupiscent impatience.

The poor Camenae shifted
In the snow from foot to foot —
All the gods were dead,
They alone were left.
The others — even unto death they flit —
Flying howsoever they will,
Burning round the world tree
Like so many New Year's lights.

IV

Снега насыпьте в красный
Стакан с тяжелым вином,
Может быть, я забудусь
Горько-утешным сном.
Может быть, мне приснится
Орфеева голова —
Как она долго по морю
Пророчила и плыла.
Как ее колотило
Солью, и тьмой, и волной!
Как она небо корила
Черным своим языком
И ослепляла звезды
Бездонным пустым зрачком.

Кажется мне — это лодка,
Остроносая лодка была,
И я в ней плыла матросом,
Словесной икрой у весла.
Пред нею летели боги —
Дионис и Аполлон.
Они летели обнявшись:
Он в нас обоих влюблен.
С тех пор, как я прикоснулась
К разодранному рту,
Я падаю тяжким камнем
В соленую пустоту.
С тех пор, как я посмотрела
Глазами в глаза голове,
Я стала выродком, нищим,
Слепою, сестрой сове.

Вмешайте в вино мне снегу,
Насыпьте в череп льду,
Счастье не в томной неге —
В исступленно-строгом бреду.
О снег, ты идешь все мимо,
Белизною не осеня.
Кружатся девять незримых,
В снегопадных столбах звеня.

IV

Sprinkle some snow into a red
Cup with some heavy wine,
And perhaps I will find oblivion
In a bitter-consoling dream.
Maybe in the dream I will see
Orpheus's head,
At sea for so long,
Prophesising and floating.
How it was pounded
By the salt, and the dark, and the waves!
How it reproached the heavens
With its black tongue
And blinded the stars
With bottomless empty pupils.

It was a boat, I think,
A sharp-nosed boat,
And I was a sailor paddling it,
The verbal calf muscle at the oars.
In front of it flew the gods —
Dionysus and Apollo.
As they flew they embraced:
He is in love with us both.
Ever since I touched
That dismembered mouth
I have been a heavy stone falling
Into salty emptiness.
Ever since I looked
The head in the eyes
I am become degenerate, indigent,
Sightless, a sister to the owls.

Mix my wine with snow,
Sprinkle some ice into my skull;
Happiness is not in languorous luxury —
It is in ecstatic-strict delirium.
O snow, you keep on falling by,
Your whiteness not settling on my mind.
The nine are wheeling unseen,
Amidst flurries of snowy columns they chime.

V

Мохнато-белых пчел,
Под фонарем скользящих,
Я отличу легко
От хладных настоящих.
У этих из-под белизны
Косится темный глаз блестящий
И жальца острые ресниц
Нацелены на предстоящих.

Замерзшие колют ресницы,
Ледяные глядят глаза,
Тебя оплетает хмельная,
Ледяная, в слезах, лоза.
Музы, ужели вы только
Пьющие душу зрачки?
Девять звезд каменистых,
Кружась, ударяют в виски.

V

Fuzzy white bees,
Skimming beneath a lamp —
I can tell them easily
Apart from these frosty ones.
From under their whiteness, these
Squint with a dark, glittering eye,
And the sharp stings of their eyelashes
Are pointed at whoever's in their sights.

Frozen eyelashes prick,
Icy eyes inspect,
You are entwined
By a heady, freezing, tear-dewed vine.
Muses, surely you are not merely
Pupils for imbibing the soul?
Nine stony stars,
Spinning, strike me in the temples.

VI. Пифия

Сидит, навзрыд икает...
— Да вот я и смотрю.
Ударь ее по спинке,
Скорей, я говорю!
— Ничто! Она икает
Все громче и больней.
Облей ее водою,
И полегчает ей.
— Смотри, глаза полезли
И пена из ушей.
— Да что же с ей такое?
Иль умер кто у ней?

VII

Музы (замерзли!) — белые мухи*
Вас завлекли сюда?
— Мир оттеснил нас, глухая вода,
В гиперборею.
Долго скользили во тьме седой
Над морем Белым,
Видим — на льдине живой воробей
Оледенелый.
Мы и согрели его собой,
Синими языками
Молний живых, и на свет голубой
Дале рванулись.
А он плывет там и поет
На девяти языках,
С синим огнем в ледяной голове,
Невидимым в очах.
Когда он повис на гребне
На клочке ломаемой льдины,
Лопнуло накрест в подвалах Эреба
Сердце седой Прозерпины.

* У Гете есть стихотворение «Мусагеты». Ими он считает мух — и те, и другие, мол, появляются летом. Здесь тоже мухи — мусагеты, но зимние — «белые мухи».

VI. Pythia

She just sits, hiccups uncontrollably...
'Well, I can see that for myself.
Give her a thump on the back,
Quickly, do as I say!'
'No effect! She's hiccupping
Even more loudly and painfully.
Throw some water over her,
That'll help calm her down.'
'Look, her eyes are bulging
And froth's coming out her ears.'
'What on earth's the matter with her?
Has there been a death in the family?'

VII

Muses (you're frozen!) — have the white flies*
Enticed you here?'
'The world, the deaf water, has pushed us out
Into Hyperborea.'
Long had we slipt through the grey-haired gloom
Over the White Sea,
We glimpse — a sparrow, alive, on an ice floe,
Frozen through.
So we warmed him with ourselves,
With blue tongues
Of living lightning, then we tore onwards
To daylight.
And he floats there and sings
In nine tongues,
With blue fire in his icy head,
Imperceptible in his eyes.
When he rode a wave-crest
Upon a flake from the fragmenting ice floe,
In the basements of Erebus the heart
Of hoary-headed Proserpina broke in two.

* One of Goethe's poems is 'Die Musageten'. He believes that Musagetes are flies, as both of them appear in summer. Here, flies are also Musagetes, but winter ones — 'white flies'.

VIII. Восхваление друг друга у Никольского собора

Аркады желтые, в проплешинах, Никольского рынка,
Где делают с цветочками посуду
Эмалированную, — там в длинную флейту ветер
Дует ночами.

Там гулькает голубь, постовой свистнет,
Да подпоясанные небрежно, босые,
Как перипатетики, бродят девы
Глухой ночью.

— Молний сноп на поясе у тебя, Эрато,
Без тебя не сложится ни гимн, ни песня,
Подойдешь ближе, глянешь — кровь быстрее
В словах рванется.

Ну а ты, Полигимния, не скромничай, дева,
Взор певца устремляешь в небо,
Без тебя он ползал бы по земле, извиваясь,
Тварью дрожащей.

— Без тебя, Мельпомена, без тебя, Клио... —
Так наперебой друг дружку хвалили
И, танцуя, сливались в темнисто-светлый
Венец терновый.

Ах, кому нам девяти, бедным,
Передать свою поющую силу,
Ах, кого напоить водой кастальской,
Оплести хмелем?

У Никольской, видят, колокольни
Притулился, согнувшись, нищий.
Он во сне к небесам тянет руку,
Стоя спит, горький.

Тут они на него набежали —
Закружили, зашептали, завертели.
Замычал он, мучимый сладкой
Пения болью.

Ладонями захлопал в бока гулко
И, восторгом переполненный тяжким,
Взял и кинулся в неглубокий
Канал Крюков.

VIII. Encomium of Each Other before Nikolsky Cathedral

The yellow arcades, paint peeling in patches, of the Nikolsky Market,
Where they make enamelware with little flowers
On it — there, down the long flute the wind
Blows through the night hours.

There the pigeon coos, the postman whistles,
And carelessly girded, barefoot,
Like Peripatetics, maidens wander
In the dead, deaf night.

'You have a shaft of lightning at your belt, Erato,
Without you neither hymn nor song will take shape,
If you approach closer, bestow a glance — the blood rushes
Faster through the words.'

'As for you, Polyhymnia, be not so modest, maiden,
You direct the singer's gaze towards the sky,
Without you he would crawl o'er the earth, squirming
Like a quiv'ring beast.'

'Without you, Melpomene, without you, Clio...'
Thus they vied in singing each other's praises,
And, as they danced, they merged into a dark-bright
Crown of woven thorns.

Ah, to whom are we nine, oh, poor maidens!,
To bequeath our power of song,
Ah, whom are we to intoxicate with Castalian water,
Entwine with hop vines?

By the Nikolsky's belltower, they see,
A beggar is huddled, hunched over.
In his sleep he reaches out his hand to heaven,
Sleeps standing, hapless.

At once they fell upon him —
Started turning, whispering, whirling him.
He set to mewling, tormented by the sweet
Pain of songfulness.

With both hands he slapped his sides resoundingly,
And, overflowing with weighty rapture,
He went and threw himself into the fairly shallow
Kriukov Canal.

IX. Музы перед Иконой

Вокруг Никольского собора
Во вьюжном мчатся хороводе,
Озябнув, будто виноваты,
Цепочкой тянутся при входе.

По очередности — пред Троеручицей
Творят — и в сторону — поклон короткий.
Меж рук Иконы неземной
Скользят отчетливо, как четки.

— Все наши умерли давно. —
Со свечками в руках мерцали.
И сами по себе молебен
Заупокойный заказали.

ноябрь 1994

IX. Muses before the Icon

Around Nikolsky Cathedral
They race in snowstorm circle dance,
Feeling cold, and kind of guilty,
Form a chain strung out at the entrance.

In order of precedence, before the Virgin of the Three Hands
They make her — and to the side — a brief bow.
Through the hands of the unearthly Icon
They slip one by one, like rosary beads.

'All our kindred died long ago.'
They flickered, candles in their hands.
And of their own accord, alone,
They commissioned a requiem mass.

November 1994

5.2 *Homo Musagetes* Variants

	Published Version	Variant	
I	сноп	2. сирп	sickle
II	Сгинули, как Пан?	1. Сгинули туда, где Пан?	Vamoosed to the same place as Pan?
III	одне	1. одни	alone (m. pl.)
IV	Счастье	1. О счастье	O happiness
V	глядят	1. смотрят	look
VI	Пифия	1. Талия	Thalia
VIII	Никольского	1. Андреевского	Andreevsky
	там в	1. в их	in their
	сливались	1. & 2. свивались	coiled
	горький	2. бедный	poor man
	восторгом переполненный тяжким	1. восторгом преисполненный темным	filled up with dark rapture
IX	отчетливо	1. & 2. отчетисто	precisely

* I only give substantive variants; i.e. differences in punctuation, spelling, numbering, or word order are not noted. All variants come from two manuscripts in ESHA P, containing two versions of the entire cycle (1. and 2.) plus a third, earlier variant of poem VII (0.).

VII	entire poem	0. что завлекло вас, музы, в гиперборею под снегопады мир оттеснил нас жестокий на льдину мы летели над морем белым видим птенчика полуживого мы согрели его девятью языками он теперь плывет по бурному морю на девяти вопрошает наречьях небо и от этого вечное расскололось сердце мрака трещины пошли по эребу подземелья качнулись	what enticed you, muses, to Hyperborea? under the snowfalls 'the cruel world pushed us out onto an ice floe we flew over the white sea we see a little chick half-alive we warmed him with nine tongues now he floats on the turbulent sea he beseeches the sky in nine dialects and from this the eternal heart of dark split asunder cracks went across erebus the dungeons rocked
	Музы (замерзли!) — белые мухи	1. Белые мухи, водители Муз,	White flies, leaders of the Muses
	Мы и согрели	1. Как мы согрели	How we warmed
	Когда он повис на гребне На клочке ломаемой льдины, Лопнуло накрест в подвалах Эреба Сердце седой Прозерпины.	~~1. И от бесстрашья и жара его~~ ~~от серенькой буквы и знака~~ ~~Качнулись подвалы Орка~~ ~~Треснул[о] сердце мрака.~~ И от песни бесстрашья и бреда от треска ломаемой льдины Лопнуло накрест в подвалах Эреба Сердце седой Прозерпины.	~~And from his fearlessness and heat~~ ~~from the grey little letter and the sign~~ ~~The basements of Orcus rocked~~ ~~The heart of dark cracked.~~ And from the song's fearlessness and delirium from the cracking of the fragmenting ice floe, In the basements of Erebus the heart Of hoary-headed Proserpina broke in two.'

* [corrected]

5.3 *Homo Musagetes* Metres

Homo Musagetes	*Metre*	*Rhymed?*
I	No fixed metre	Loosely
II	Sapphics/trochaic hexameter	Partially
III	Iambic trimeter and tetrameter	Partially
IV	Dol'nik (3-stress)	Loosely
V	Iambic trimeter and tetrameter → 3-stress dol'nik	Loosely
VI 'Pythia'	Iambic trimeter (regular)	Loosely
VII	Sapphics (in couplets)	Loosely
VIII 'Encomium of Each Other before Nikolsky Cathedral'	Sapphics	No
IX 'Muses before the Icon'	Iambic tetrameter	Loosely

* Metre is approximate or majority, unless otherwise stated.

5.4 *Homo Musagetes* Classical References

Homo Musagetes	*Horace Odes*	*Other*
Title	III.4, *Carmen Saeculare*, IV.6	
Subtitle	I.2, I.4, I.9, I.11, II.10, IV.7, IV.12	
Epigraph	III.4	
I	I.9, I.37, III.4, IV.1	Plato, *Palatine Anthology* IX.506
II	I.2, III.4	Plutarch, *On the Obsolescence of Oracles*; Plato, *Palatine Anthology* IX.506; Sappho
III	I.4, I.9, I.11, I.16, I.19, I.31, III.8, III.18, IV.2	Pindar, *Pythian* X
IV	I.12, I.24, II.7, II.11, II.19, III.19, III.25	(Sappho)
V	I.1, IV.2	Homer, *Iliad* II; Virgil, *Georgics* IV; Varro, *De Re Rustica* III; Pindar, *Pythian* X; *Homeric Hymn to Dionysus* (VII); (Sappho/Corinna)
VI 'Pythia'	I.16, IV.6	
VII	I.28, II.13, II.20, III.4, IV.2	Catullus III; Sappho I
VIII 'Encomium of Each Other before Nikolsky Cathedral'	I.1, I.12, I.24, III.30, IV.3	Aristotle; Sappho
IX 'Muses before the Icon'	I.5	

6.1 Благодарение

Благодарю Тебя за то, что Ты создал меня поэтом Твоей милостью,
За то, что я родилась вблизи Невы и за то, что сейчас смотрю на нее и Исакий из окна больницы,
За то, что меня растили мама и Берта,
За то, что росла в тени Театра,
За то, что видела Рим и мир и Иерусалим,
За чудесных друзей и животных, что сопровождали меня (и сейчас),
За счастья вдохновения и радости чистого разума,
За дар правильного чтения стихов, за свое легкомыслие,
И за то, что Ты всегда спасаешь меня и порой я нахожу в себе силы благодарить Тебя и за муки.

6 октября 2009
(восемь дней после операции)

6.1 Thanksgiving

I give thanks to You, because in Your mercy You made me a poet,
Because I was born by the Neva and because I am looking at it and St Isaac's from the hospital window now,
Because Mama and Berta brought me up,
Because I grew up in the shadow of the Theatre,
Because I saw Rome and the globe and Jerusalem,
For the wonderful friends and animals who have accompanied me (and still do),
For the blessings of inspiration and the joys of pure reason,
For the gift of correct reading of poetry, for my frivolity,
And because You always save me and sometimes I find the strength in myself to also thank You for the misfortunes.

6 October 2009
(eight days after an operation)

BIBLIOGRAPHY

Unpublished Manuscript Sources

Elena Shvarts Archive / *Elena Shvarts Dom-Arkhiv* (St Petersburg), curated by Kirill Kozyrev. (See Note on Abbreviations and Editions.)
Forschungsstelle Osteuropa / The Research Centre for East European Studies at the University of Bremen:
——Elena Shvarts collection (FSO 01–194 Švarc)
——Evgenii Pazukhin collection (FSO 01–265 Pazuchin)

Works by Elena Shvarts

Books

Sochineniia Eleny Shvarts, 5 vols (St Petersburg: Pushkinskii fond, 2002–13)
Stikhi iz 'Zelenoi tetradi'. Stikhotvoreniia 1966–1974 godov, ed. by Pavel Uspenskii and Artem Shelia (St Petersburg: Poriadok slov, 2018)
Voisko, Orkestr, Park, Korabl': chetyre mashinopisnykh sbornikov, ed. by Artem Shelia and Pavel Uspenskii (Moscow: Common place, 2018)

Webpages

'Dikopis' poslednego vremeni', *Vavilon* (2001), <http://www.vavilon.ru/texts/shvarts4.html> [accessed 13 September 2018]
'Elena Shvarts', *The Blue Lagoon Anthology of Modern Russian Poetry*, ed. by Konstantin Kuzminskii and Grigorii Kovalev, 9 vols (Newtonville, MA: Oriental Research Partners, 1980–86), 2B (1985). <http://kkk-bluelagoon.ru/tom2b/shvarts.htm> [accessed 11 April 2019]
'"Khrustia, rastsvetaet zvezda Aventina…" (vstrecha Ol'gi Martynovoi i Eleny Shvarts v Rime, stikhi i fotografii)', *Novaia kamera khraneniia*, <http://www.newkamera.de/roma.html> [accessed 24 January 2019]
'"Mundus Imaginalis": neobiazatel'nye poiasneniia', *Vavilon* (2001), <http://www.vavilon.ru/texts/shvarts1-6.html> [accessed 12 September 2016]
'Nadgrobnaia nadpis' imperatora Adriana', *Novaia kamera khraneniia*, <http://www.newkamera.de/shwarz/escwarz_12.html> [accessed 1 November 2014]
'Na povorote v Gefsimaniiu', *Sovremennaia russkaia poeziia*, <http://modernpoetry.ru> [accessed 12 September 2016]
'Non dolet', *Znamia*, 8 (2001), <http://znamlit.ru/publication.php?id=1502> [accessed 21 November 2019]
'Pesnia ptitsy na dne morskom', *Vavilon* (1995), <http://www.vavilon.ru/texts/shvarts3.html> [accessed 25 April 2019]
'Prorochestvovat' za prorochits: neizdannye stikhi', ed. by Pavel Uspenskii and Artem Shelia, *Novyi mir*, 11 (2015), <http://www.nm1925.ru/Archive/Journal6_2015_11/Content/Publication6_6188/Default.aspx> [accessed 4 May 2020]

'Stikhi', *Novaia kamera khraneniia*, <http://www.newkamera.de/shwarz/escwarz_08.html> [accessed 8 September 2016]

Interviews and Correspondence

BARSKOVA, POLINA, Interview by Georgina Barker, Amherst, Massachusetts, 2016
DOLININ, VIACHESLAV, 'pro "obez'iannik"', 27 July 2020 [e-mail]
KOZYREV, KIRILL, Interview by Georgina Barker, St Petersburg, Russia, 2019
—— 'Razreshenie postavit' perevod stikhotvoreniia Eleny Andreevny', 23 August 2018 [e-mail]
KUTIK, ILYA, 'A Small Question', 11 August 2020 [e-mail]
OSTANIN, BORIS, Interview by Georgina Barker, St Petersburg, Russia, 2019
PANCHENKO, DMITRII, Interview by Georgina Barker, St Petersburg, Russia, 2019

Other Primary Sources

AKHMATOVA, ANNA, *Stikhotvoreniia i poemy* (Moscow: Eksmo, 2008)
BARATYNSKII, EVGENII, 'Razuverenie', *Kul'tura.RF* <https://www.culture.ru/poems/25943/razuverenie> [accessed 8 February 2022]
BARRETT BROWNING, ELIZABETH, *The Poetical Works of Elizabeth Barrett Browning*, 6 vols (London: Smith, Elder & Co, 1890)
BARSKOVA, POLINA, 'pamiati vsiakikh besed i nabliudenii — davno', *pbarskova* (2010), <http://pbarskova.livejournal.com/20977.html> [accessed 13 November 2015]
BERG, MIKHAIL, 'Momemury' <http://mberg.net/proza/momemuri/> [accessed 6 August 2020]
BISHOP, SARAH CLOVIS, 'In Memoriam: Elena Andreevna Shvarts (17 May 1948–11 March 2010)', *Slavonica*, 16.2 (2010), 112–30
BLOK, ALEKSANDR, *Izbrannaia poeziia/Selected Poems*, ed. by James B. Woodward (London: Bristol Classical Press, 1992)
—— 'Twelve', trans. by Maria Carlson, <https://kuscholarworks.ku.edu/bitstream/handle/1808/6598/BlokTwelve_RusEngTxt.pdf?sequence=1&isAllowed=y> [accessed 22 February 2019]
BOILEAU-DESPRÉAUX, NICOLAS, *The Art of Poetry Written in French by the Sieur de Boileau; Made English*, trans. by William Soames and John Dryden (London: R. Bentley and S. Magnes, 1683)
—— 'Bualo: poeticheskoe iskusstvo', trans. by E. L. Linetskaia <http://fgpodsobka.narod.ru/poetica.htm> [accessed 29 September 2018]
—— *Œuvres poétiques*, 2 vols (Paris: Imprimerie générale, 1872)
BRODSKY, JOSEPH, *Chast' rechi: izbrannye stikhotvoreniia* (St Petersburg: Azbuka-klassika, 2009)
—— *On Grief and Reason: Essays* (London: Penguin, 1995)
BULGAKOV, MIKHAIL, *Izbrannoe: roman 'Master i Margarita'; rasskazy* (Moscow: Khudozhestvennaia literatura, 1982)
CATULLUS, *The Poems of Catullus*, trans. by Guy Lee (Oxford: Oxford University Press, 1991)
CHERNEGA, ALEKSANDR, 'Nikol'skii rynok (Sadovaia ul., 62)', *Progulki po Peterburgu* (2005), <http://walkspb.ru/zd/sadovaya62.html> [accessed 6 June 2016]
DUFF, ARNOLD M., and J. WIGHT DUFF, trans., *Minor Latin Poets, Volume II: Florus. Hadrian. Nemesianus. Reposianus. Tiberianus. Dicta Catonis. Phoenix. Avianus. Rutilius Namatianus. Others* (Cambridge, MA: Harvard University Press, 1934)
ELISEEV, NIKITA, '"Triumf" dlia Eleny', *Ekspert Severo-Zapad*, 5 (2004), <https://expert.ru/northwest/2004/05/05no-scult_50671/> [accessed 11 April 2019]

FILIPPOV, VASILII, 'Pamiati Iashi', *Vavilon*, <http:// www.vavilon.ru/texts/filippov1-3. html> [accessed 27 April 2019]

GOETHE, JOHANN WOLFGANG VON, *Poems and Ballads of Goethe*, trans. by W. Edmondstoune Aytoun and Theodore Martin (Edinburgh; London: W. Blackwood, 1859)

GRAVES, ROBERT, *The Greek Myths*, 2 vols (Harmondsworth: Penguin Books, 1962)

HESIOD, *The Homeric Hymns and Homerica*, trans. by Hugh G. Evelyn-White (London: Heinemann, 1914)

—— *Theogony; Works and Days; Testimonia*, trans. by Glenn W. Most (Cambridge, MA: Harvard University Press, 2018)

HOMER, *The Odyssey*, trans. by A. T. Murray, 2 vols (Cambridge, MA; London: Harvard University Press, 1974)

HORACE, *Odes and Epodes*, trans. by Niall Rudd (Cambridge, MA; London: Harvard University Press, 2004)

—— *Ody*, trans. by N. I. Shaternikov (Moscow: Izdatel'stvo 'Khudozhestvennaia literatura', 1935)

—— *Ody. Epody. Satiry. Poslaniia*, ed. by M. L. Gasparov (Moscow: Izdatel'stvo 'Khudozhestvennaia literatura', 1970)

—— *Satires, Epistles and Ars Poetica*, trans. by H. Rushton Fairclough (London: Heinemann, 1926)

—— *Sobranie sochinenii*, ed. by S. V. Chistobaev (St Petersburg: Biograficheskii institut 'Studiia biografika', 1993)

IVANOV, V. I., *Sobranie sochinenii*, 4 vols (Brussels: Foyer Oriental Chrétien, 1971–87)

Joseph Brodsky Fellowship Fund, 'Elena Shvarts — Joseph Brodsky', <http://www. josephbrodsky.org/fellow13> [accessed 22 January 2019]

JUVENAL, and PERSIUS, *Juvenal and Persius*, trans. by Susanna Morton Braund (Cambridge, MA: Harvard University Press, 2015)

KAZ'MYRCHUK, G. D., 'Dzhedzhula Andriy Omelianovych', *Entsyklopediia Kyivs'kogo natsional'nogo universytetu imeni Tarasa Shevchenka* (2013), <http://eu.univ.kiev.ua/ departments/istorychnyy-fakul%60tet/dzhedzhula-andriy-omelyanovych/> [accessed 17 April 2019]

KOLESOV, V. V., 'Biblioteka literatury Drevnei Rusi, tom 9: Poslaniia startsa Filofeia', *Elektronnye publikatsii Instituta russkoi literatury (Pushkinskogo Doma) RAN*, 2006 <http:// lib.pushkinskijdom.ru/Default.aspx?tabid=5105#> [accessed 10 August 2020]

KOZYREV, KIRILL, 'Ot publikatora', *NLO*, 115 (2012), <http://magazines.russ.ru/nlo/2012/ 115/kk25.html> [accessed 3 March 2014]

LABÉ, LOUISE, *Complete Poetry and Prose: A Bilingual Edition*, ed. by Deborah Lesko Baker, trans. by Annie Finch (Chicago: University of Chicago Press, 2006)

MANDEL'SHTAM, OSIP, *Slovo i kul'tura*, ed. by Pavel Nerler (Moscow: Sovetskii pisatel', 1987)

—— *Sochineniia v dvukh tomakh*, ed. by A. D. Mikhailov and P. M. Nerler (Moscow: Khudozhestvennaia literatura, 1990)

MARTIAL, *Epigrams*, trans. by D. R. Shackleton Bailey, 3 vols (Cambridge, MA; London: Harvard University Press, 1993)

—— *Epigrammy*, trans. by F. Petrovskii (Moscow: Khudozhestvennaia literatura, 1968)

MARTYNOVA, OL'GA, 'S nebes v nakazan'e na zemliu poverzhennyi', *Novaia kamera khraneniia* (2010), <http://www.newkamera.de/martynova/omartynova13.html> [accessed 28 February 2014]

—— 'V lesu pod kel'nom', *Novaia kamera khraneniia* <http://www.newkamera.de/ martynova/omartynova12.html> [accessed 30 April 2015]

MARTYNOVA, OL'GA, and ELENA SHVARTS, '"Khrustia, rastsvetaet zvezda Aventina..." (vstrecha Ol'gi Martynovoi i Eleny Shvarts v Rime, stikhi i fotografii)', *Novaia kamera khraneniia*, <http://www.newkamera.de/roma.html> [accessed 24 January 2019]

Monty Python, 'Life of Brian Script — Scene 10: Before the Romans Things Were Smelly', *Another Bleedin' Monty Python Website* <http://montypython.50webs.com/scripts/Life_of_Brian/10.htm> [accessed 23 January 2019]

Nikolo-Bogoiavlenskii morskoi sobor, 'Ikona Bozhiei Materi Troeruchitsa', 2013 <http://www.nikolskiysobor.ru/svyatynya/drugie-svyatyni-sobora/38-chudotvornyj-obraz-svyatitelya-nikolaya-arkhiepiskopa-mir-likijskikh-chudotvortsa-2> [accessed 22 February 2019]

Obolensky, Dimitri, ed., *The Heritage of Russian Verse* (Bloomington; Indianapolis: Indiana University Press, 1976)

Ovid, *Heroides; Amores*, trans. by Grant Showerman, ed. by G. P. Goold (Cambridge, MA; London: Harvard University Press, 1977)

—— *Metamorphoses*, trans. by Frank Justus Miller, 2 vols (Cambridge, MA: Harvard University Press, 1977)

—— *The Art of Love, and Other Poems*, trans. by J. H. Mozley, ed. by G. P. Goold (Cambridge, MA; London: Harvard University Press, 2004)

Parker, Dorothy, *Dorothy Parker* (New York: Viking Press, 1954)

Petrovskii, F., ed., *Valerii Katull, Al'bii Tibull, Sekst Propertsii: perevod s latinskogo* (Moscow: Gosudarstvennoe izdatel'stvo khudozhestvennoi literatury, 1963)

Petrushkin, Aleksandr, 'Elena Andreevna Shvarts', *Megalit Evraziiskii Zhurnal'nyi Portal*, <http://www.promegalit.ru/personals/1917_shvarts_elena_andreevna.html> [accessed 17 April 2019]

Pindar, *Olympian Odes, Pythian Odes*, trans. by William H. Race (Cambridge, MA: Harvard University Press, 2015)

Plato, *Lysis; Symposium; Gorgias*, trans. by W. R. M. Lamb (Cambridge, MA; London: Harvard University Press, 1925)

—— *Republic*, trans. by Jeffrey Henderson, 2 vols (Cambridge, MA: Harvard University Press, 2013)

Pliny, *Natural History: Books 8-11*, trans. by H. Rackham (London: Heinemann, 1940)

Plutarch, *Moralia: Volume V*, trans. by Frank Cole Babbitt (London: Heinemann; New York: G. P. Putnam's Sons, 1936)

Propertius, *Elegies*, trans. by G. P. Goold (Cambridge, MA; London: Harvard University Press, 2006)

Pushkin, Aleksandr, *Izbrannye sochineniia v dvukh tomakh* (Moscow: Khudozhestvennaia literatura, 1978)

Rich, Adrienne, *Snapshots of a Daughter-in-Law* (London: Chatto & Windus: The Hogarth Press, 1970)

Rubinshtein, Lev, 'Lev Rubinshtein, Elena Shvarts, D. A. Prigov, Mikhail Sheinker. 1989 g. Germaniia. "Otpechatki": fotografii iz arkhiva L'va Rubinshteina', *OpenSpace.ru*, <http://os.colta.ru/photogallery/30314/281166/> [accessed 22 April 2019]

Russian and East European Institute, 'In Memoriam: Nina Perlina', <https://reei.indiana.edu/news-events/newsletter/archive/Fall-2019/In Memoriam Nina Perlina.html> [accessed 6 May 2020]

Sappho, and Alcaeus, *Greek Lyric, 1: Sappho, Alcaeus*, trans. by David A. Campbell (Cambridge, MA; London: Harvard University Press, 1982)

Seneca, *Moral Essays*, trans. by John William Basore, 3 vols (London: Heinemann; Cambridge, MA: Heinemann, 1928)

Shklovsky, Viktor, 'Art, as Device', trans. by Alexandra Berlina, *Poetics Today*, 36.3 (2015), 151–74

—— *O teorii prozy* (Moscow: Sovetskii Pisatel', 1983)

Shvarts, Dina, *Dnevniki i zametki* (St Petersburg: Inapress, 2001)

Sinel'nikov, Mikhail, *Peterburg, Petrograd, Leningrad v russkoi poezii* (St Petersburg; Moscow: Limbus Press, 2013)

Soiuz pisatelei Sankt-Peterburga (2019), 'Premii', <http://pisateli-spb.ru/award.html> [accessed 24 April 2019]
TIBULLUS, ALBIUS, LYGDAMUS, and SULPICIA, *The Complete Poems of Tibullus*, trans. by Rodney G. Dennis and Michael C. J. Putnam (Berkeley; Los Angeles; London: University of California Press, 2012)
TKACHENKO, NINA-INNA, '"I ves' sostav moi budet napoen stradan'ia svetom..." Interv'iu s O. A. Sedakovoi v pamiat' poetessy Eleny Shvarts', *Gazeta KIFA* (2010), <http://gazetakifa.ru/content/view/3454/38/> [accessed 25 April 2019]
TSVETAEVA, MARINA, *Stikhotvoreniia i poemy v piati tomakh* (New York: Russica publishers, 1980–90)
VASIA_MORSKOI, 'Sankt-Peterburg s vozdukha: 20 foto', <http://yandex.livejournal.com/194741.html> [accessed 31 October 2014]
Vestnik novoi literatury 3 (Leningrad: Assotsiatsiia 'Novaia literatura', 1991) <https://imwerden.de/pdf/vestnik_novoj_literatury_3_1991__ocr.pdf> [accessed 6 August 2020]
VIRGIL, *Eclogues. Georgics. Aeneid I–VI*, trans. by H. Rushton Fairclough, 2 vols (Cambridge, MA; London: Harvard University Press, 1999)
VKontakte (2020), '"KINFIIA" 14 fev v 21:35', <https://vk.com/event191088171> [accessed 29 June 2020]

Secondary Sources

ANPILOV, ANDREI, 'Svetlo-iarostnaia tochka', *NLO*, 35 (1999), 362–72
ARKINS, BRIAN, 'The Cruel Joke of Venus: Horace as Love Poet', in *Horace 2000: A Celebration: Essays for the Bimillennium*, ed. by Niall Rudd (London: Duckworth, 1993), 106–19
ARNOTT, W. GEOFFREY, *Ancient Birds from A to Z* (London and New York: Routledge, 2007)
ASOIAN, ARAM, *Semiotika mifa ob Orfee i Evridike* (St Petersburg: Aleteiia, 2017)
BAEHR, STEPHEN L., 'From History to National Myth: Translatio Imperii in Eighteenth-Century Russia', *Russian Review*, 37.1 (1978), 1–13
BARCHIESI, ALESSANDRO, *Speaking Volumes: Narrative and Intertext in Ovid and Other Latin Poets* (London: Duckworth, 2001)
BARKER, GEORGINA, 'Russia's Classical Alter Ego, 1963–2016: Classical Reception in the Poetry of Elena Shvarts, Il'ia Kutik, and Polina Barskova' (PhD thesis, University of Edinburgh, 2017)
—— 'Sofiia Parnok's Sapphic Cycle *Roses of Pieria*: A Commentary' (forthcoming)
BISHOP, M. C., 'Legio V Alaudae and the Crested Lark', *Journal of Roman Military Equipment Studies*, 1 (1990), 161–64
BISHOP, SARAH CLOVIS, 'Harmonious Disharmony: Elena Shvarts's *Trudy i Dni Lavinii, Monakhini iz Ordena Obrezaniia Serdtsa*', *The Slavic and East European Journal*, 56.2 (2012), 213–31
BOYM, SVETLANA, 'Estrangement as a Lifestyle: Shklovsky and Brodsky', *Poetics Today*, 17.4 (1996), 511–30
—— 'Poetics and Politics of Estrangement: Victor Shklovsky and Hannah Arendt', *Poetics Today*, 26.4 (2005), 581–611
BURGIN, DIANA LEWIS, *Sophia Parnok: The Life and Work of Russia's Sappho* (New York: NYU Press, 1994)
BYRD, CHARLES, 'Thunder Imagery and the Turn against Horace in Derzhavin's "Evgeniyu. Zhizn' Zvanskaya" (1807)', in *Russian Literature and the Classics*, ed. by Peter I. Barta, David H. J. Larmour, and Paul Allen Miller (Amsterdam: Harwood Academic, 1996), 13–34
CANCIK, HUBERT, and HELMUTH SCHNEIDER, eds, *Brill's New Pauly: Encyclopaedia of the Ancient World*, 15 vols (Leiden: Brill, 2002–09)

CARLSON, RACHEL D., 'The Honey Bee and Apian Imagery in Classical Literature' (PhD thesis, University of Washington, 2015)

CARPENTER, THOMAS H., and CHRISTOPHER A. FARAONE, eds, *Masks of Dionysus* (Ithaca; London: Cornell University Press, 1993)

CARTER, JESSE BENEDICT, *Selections from the Roman Elegiac Poets* (Boston: D. C. Heath & Company, 1909)

CLARK, KATERINA, 'Socialist Realism in Soviet Literature', in *The Routledge Companion to Russian Literature*, ed. by Neil Cornwell (London, New York: Routledge, 2001), 174–83

COMMAGER, STEELE, 'The Function of Wine in Horace's Odes', in *Horace: Odes and Epodes*, ed. by Michèle Lowrie (Oxford: Oxford University Press, 2009), 33–49

—— *The Odes of Horace: A Critical Study* (New Haven: Yale University Press, 1962)

CURTIS, JAMES M., 'Michael Bakhtin, Nietzsche, and Russian Pre-Revolutionary Thought', in *Nietzsche in Russia*, ed. by Bernice Glatzer Rosenthal (Princeton, NJ; Guildford: Princeton University Press, 1986), 331–54

DAVIDSON, PAMELA, *Cultural Memory and Survival: The Russian Renaissance of Classical Antiquity in the Twentieth Century* (London: UCL School of Slavonic and East European Studies, 2009)

——, ed., *Russian Literature and its Demons* (New York, NY; Oxford: Berghahn, 2000)

DELBRUCK, HANS, *History of the Art of War*, trans. by Walter J. Renfroe, Jr., 4 vols (University of Nebraska Press, 1990)

DOBRENKO, EVGENY, and ILYA KALININ, 'Literary Criticism during the Thaw', in *A History of Russian Literary Theory and Criticism: The Soviet Age and Beyond*, ed. by Evgeny Dobrenko and Galin Tihanov (Pittsburgh, PA: University of Pittsburgh Press, 2011), 184–206

DOLININ, VIACHESLAV, BORIS IVANOV, BORIS OSTANIN, and DMITRII SEVERIUKHIN, *Samizdat Leningrada, 1950-e–1980-e: literaturnaia entsiklopediia*, ed. by Dmitrii Severiukhin (Moscow: Novoe literaturnoe obozrenie, 2003)

EASTERLING, P. E., and J. V. MUIR, *Greek Religion and Society* (Cambridge: Cambridge University Press, 1985)

EDMONDS, RADCLIFFE, 'Tearing Apart the Zagreus Myth: A Few Disparaging Remarks on Orphism and Original Sin', *Classical Antiquity*, 18.1 (1999), 35–73

EIDINOW, J. S. C., 'Horace: Critics, Canons and Canonicity' in *Perceptions of Horace: A Roman Poet and his Readers*, ed. by L. B. T. Houghton and Maria Wyke (Cambridge; New York: Cambridge University Press, 2009), 80–95

EPSTEIN, MIKHAIL, ALEKSANDR GENIS and SLOBODANKA VLADIV-GLOVER, *Russian Postmodernism: New Perspectives on Post-Soviet Culture* (New York; Oxford: Berghahn, 1999)

FEENEY, DENIS, 'Horace and the Greek Lyric Poets', in *Horace: Odes and Epodes*, ed. by Michèle Lowrie (Oxford: Oxford University Press, 2009), 202–31

FENNELL, JOHN, *A History of the Russian Church to 1448* (London: Longman, 1995)

FLASCHENRIEM, BARBARA L., 'Speaking of Women: "Female Voice" in Propertius', *Helios*, 25.1 (1998), 49–64

GASPAROV, BORIS, ROBERT P. HUGHES, and IRINA PAPERNO, eds, *Cultural Mythologies of Russian Modernism: From the Golden Age to the Silver Age* (Berkeley, Los Angeles, Oxford: University of California Press, 1992)

GESSEN, KEITH, 'The Gift: Joseph Brodsky and the Fortunes of Misfortune', *The New Yorker*, 23 May 2011, <http://www.newyorker.com/arts/critics/atlarge/2011/05/23/110523crat_atlarge_gessen?currentPage=all> [accessed 16 July 2014]

GOLD, BARBARA K., '"But Ariadne Was Never There in the First Place": Finding the Female in Roman Poetry', in *Feminist Theory and the Classics*, ed. by Nancy Sorkin Rabinowitz and Amy Richlin (New York; London: Routledge, 1993), 75–101

—— 'The Natural and Unnatural Silence of Women in the Elegies of Propertius', *Antichthon*, 41 (2007), 54–72
GOL'DBERG, A. L., 'Tri "poslaniia Filofeia" (Opyt tekstologicheskogo analiza)', *Trudy otdela drevnerusskoi literatury*, 29 (1974), 68–97
GOLDHILL, SIMON, *Victorian Culture and Classical Antiquity: Art, Opera, Fiction, and the Proclamation of Modernity* (Princeton, NJ: Princeton University Press, 2011)
HALES, SHELLEY, 'Aphrodite and Dionysus: Greek Role Models for Roman Homes?', in *Role Models in the Roman World: Identity and Assimilation*, ed. by Sinclair Bell and Inge Lyse Hansen (Ann Arbor: University of Michigan Press, 2008)
HARDIE, ALEX, 'Etymologising the Muse', *Materiali e discussioni per l'analisi dei testi classici*, 62 (2009), 9–57
HARDIE, PHILIP R., *The Cambridge Companion to Ovid* (Cambridge: Cambridge University Press, 2002)
HARDWICK, LORNA, and CHRISTOPHER STRAY, *A Companion to Classical Receptions* (Malden, MA; Oxford: Blackwell, 2008)
HARTOG, FRANÇOIS, *The Mirror of Herodotus: The Representation of the Other in the Writing of History* (Berkeley; London: University of California Press, 1988)
HASTY, OLGA PETERS, *Tsvetaeva's Orphic Journeys in the Worlds of the Word* (Evanston, IL: Northwestern University Press, 1996)
HAWES, GRETA, 'Circean Enchantments and the Transformations of Allegory', in *A Handbook to the Reception of Classical Mythology*, ed. by Vanda Zajko and Helena Hoyle (Chichester; Malden, MA: Wiley-Blackwell, 2017), 123–38.
HEJDUK, JULIA T. DYSON, 'The Lesbia Poems', in *A Companion to Catullus*, ed. by Marilyn B. Skinner (Malden, MA: Blackwell, 2007), 254–75
HELDT, BARBARA, 'The Poetry of Elena Shvarts', *World Literature Today*, 63.3 (1989), 381–83
HENDRY, MICHAEL, 'Martial's Gloomy Ethiopian (7.87)', *Curculio*, 38 (2017), 1
HERDMAN, JOHN, *The Double in Nineteenth-Century Fiction* (Basingstoke: Macmillan, 1990)
HINDS, STEPHEN, *Allusion and Intertext: Dynamics of Appropriation in Roman Poetry* (Cambridge: Cambridge University Press, 1998)
HOLLAND, TOM, *Rubicon: The Triumph and Tragedy of the Roman Republic* (London: Hachette UK, 2011)
HORSFALL, NICHOLAS, 'Bees in Elysium', *Vergilius*, 56 (2010), 39–45
ICHIN, KORNELIIA, '"Orfei" Eleny Shvarts v kontekste poeticheskoi traditsii', *Poetika iskanii ili poisk poetiki: materialy mezhdunarodnoi nauchnoi konferentsii-festivalia 'Poeticheskii iazyk rubezha vekov i sovremennye literaturnye strategii' (16–19 maia 2003 goda)*, ed. by Natal'ia Fateeva (Moscow: Izdatel'stvo Instituta russkogo iazyka RAN, 2004), 356–67
INGLEHEART, JENNIFER, '"Greek" Love at Rome: Propertius 1.20 and the Reception of Hellenistic Verse', *EuGeStA Revue*, 5 (2015), 124–53
IVANITS, LINDA J., *Russian Folk Belief* (Armonk, NY; London: M. E. Sharpe, 1989)
IVANOV, BORIS, *Istoriia Kluba-81* (St Petersburg: Izdatel'stvo Ivana Limbakha, 2015)
KAHN, ANDREW, 'Ovid and Russia's Poets of Exile', in *A Handbook to the Reception of Ovid*, ed. by John F. Miller and Carole Elizabeth Newlands (Chichester: Wiley-Blackwell, 2014), 401–15
—— *Pushkin's Lyric Intelligence* (Oxford; New York: Oxford University Press, 2008)
—— 'Readings of Imperial Rome from Lomonosov to Pushkin', *Slavic Review*, 52.4 (1993), 745–68
KALB, JUDITH E., *Russia's Rome: Imperial Visions, Messianic Dreams, 1890–1940* (Madison: University of Wisconsin Press, 2008)
KALLENDORF, CRAIG, 'Allusion as Reception: Virgil, Milton, and the Modern Reader', in *Classics and the Uses of Reception*, ed. by Charles Martindale and Richard F. Thomas (Malden, MA; Oxford: Blackwell, 2006), 67–79

KEITH, ALISON, *Propertius: Poet of Love and Leisure* (London: Duckworth, 2008)
KELLY, CATRIONA, *A History of Russian Women's Writing, 1820–1992* (Oxford: Clarendon Press, 1994)
KNABE, G. S., ed., *Antichnoe nasledie v kul'ture Rossii* (Moscow: Rossiiskii nauchno-issledovatel'skii institut kul'turnogo i prirodnogo naslediia, 1996)
—— *Russkaia antichnost': Soderzhanie, rol' i sud'ba antichnogo naslediia v kul'ture Rossii* (Moscow: Rossiiskii gosudarstvennyi gumanitarnyi universitet, 2000)
KORENEVSKIY, ANDREY, 'Kem i kogda byla "izobretena" teoriia "Moskva — Tretii Rim"?', *Ab Imperio*, 1–2 (2001), 87–124
LEKMANOV, OLEG, ed., *Mandel'shtam i antichnost'* (Moscow: Radiks, 1995)
LEVIN, IURII, 'Zametki o "krymsko-ellinskikh" stikhakh O. Mandel'shtama', in *Mandel'shtam i antichnost'*, ed. by Oleg Lekmanov (Moscow: Radiks, 1995), 77–103
Livius (2015), '101 Castalian Spring', <http://www.livius.org/articles/place/delphi/101-castalian-spring/> [accessed 2 June 2017]
LYGO, EMILY, *Leningrad Poetry 1953–1975: The Thaw Generation* (Oxford, Bern, Berlin, New York: Peter Lang, 2010)
LYNE, R. O. A. M., *Collected Papers on Latin Poetry* (Oxford: Oxford University Press, 2007)
MACIVER, CALUM A., 'Representative Bees in Quintus Smyrnaeus' *Posthomerica*', *Classical Philology*, 107.1 (2012), 53–69
MALTBY, ROBERT, 'Major Themes and Motifs in Propertius' Love Poetry', in *Brill's Companion to Propertius*, ed. by Hans Christian Günther (Leiden; Boston, MA: Brill, 2006), 147–81
MANS, M. J., 'Humour, Health and Disease in Martial', *Akroterion*, 39 (1994), 105–20
MARKOV, A. V., 'Latinizmy v poeticheskikh knigakh "Dikii shipovnik" Ol'gi Sedakovoi i "Trudy i dni monakhini Lavinii" Eleny Shvarts', *Vestnik Permskogo universiteta: rossiiskaia i zarubezhnaia filologiia*, 9.1 (2017), 122–29
MARTINDALE, CHARLES, 'Introduction: Thinking through Reception', in *Classics and the Uses of Reception*, ed. by Charles Martindale and Richard F. Thomas (Malden, MA; Oxford: Blackwell, 2006), 1–13
—— 'Reception', in *A Companion to the Classical Tradition*, ed. by Craig Kallendorf (Malden, MA; Oxford: Blackwell, 2007), 297–311
MASING-DELIC, IRENE, *Exotic Moscow under Western Eyes* (Boston, MA: Academic Studies Press, 2016)
MERRIAM, CAROL U., 'Sulpicia and the Art of Literary Allusion: [Tibullus] 3.13', in *Women Poets in Ancient Greece and Rome*, ed. by Ellen Greene (Norman: University of Oklahoma Press, 2005)
MILLER, JOHN F., 'Horace's Pindaric Apollo (Odes 3.4.60–64)', *The Classical Quarterly*, n.s., 48.2 (1998), 545–52
MONTEFIORE, JAN, *Feminism and Poetry: Language, Experience, Identity in Women's Writing* (London: Pandora, 1987)
MORFORD, MARK P. O., and ROBERT J. LENARDON, *Classical Mythology* (Oxford University Press, 1999)
NELIN, IOSIF, '"i gornii angelov polet, i gad morskikh podvodnyi khod"', *Zvezda*, 10 (1997), 208–13
NESTEROV, ANTON, 'Germenevtika, metafizika i "drugaia kritika"', *NLO*, 61 (2003), 75–97
NISBET, R. G. M., and MARGARET HUBBARD, *A Commentary on Horace: Odes, Book I* (Oxford: Clarendon Press, 1970)
—— *A Commentary on Horace: Odes, Book II* (Oxford: Clarendon Press, 1978)
NISBET, R. G. M., and NIALL RUDD, *A Commentary on Horace: Odes, Book III* (Oxford: Oxford University Press, 2004)

NUSSBAUM, MARTHA C., 'Nietzsche, Schopenhauer, and Dionysus', in *The Cambridge Companion to Schopenhauer*, ed. by Christopher Janaway (Cambridge: Cambridge University Press, 1999), pp. 344–74
ORLITSKII, IURII, 'Geteromorfnyi (neuporiadochennyi) stikh v russkoi poezii', *NLO*, 73 (2005), <http://magazines.russ.ru/nlo/2005/73/or19.html> [accessed 3 June 2015]
OSTAPENKO, I. V., 'Priroda v russkoi lirike 1960–1980-x godov: Ot peizazha k kartine mira' (PhD thesis, Kamenets-Podol'skii natsional'nyi universitet, 2012)
PANCHENKO, DMITRII, '"Kinfiia" Eleny Shvarts', *NLO*, 103 (2010), <http://magazines.russ.ru/nlo/2010/103/pa22.html> [accessed 4 March 2014]
PAVLOU, MARIA, 'Pindar Olympian 3: Mapping Acragas on the Periphery of the Earth', *The Classical Quarterly*, n.s., 60.2 (2010), 313–26
POLUKHINA, VALENTINA, *Brodsky through the Eyes of his Contemporaries* (Basingstoke: Macmillan, 1992)
PUTNAM, MICHAEL C. J., *Artifices of Eternity: Horace's Fourth Book of Odes* (Ithaca and London: Cornell University Press, 1996)
—— *Horace's Carmen Saeculare: Ritual Magic and the Poet's Art* (New Haven, CT; London: Yale University Press, 2000)
RISSANEN, MIKA, 'Was There a Taboo on Killing Wolves in Rome?', *Quaderni Urbinati di Cultura Classica*, 107 (2014), 125–47
ROGOV, OLEG, 'Elena Shvarts. Solo na raskalennoi trube: novye stikhotvoreniia', *Volga*, 2 (1999), <http://magazines.russ.ru/volga/1999/2/shvarc.html> [accessed 12 September 2016]
ROMM, JAMES S., *The Edges of the Earth in Ancient Thought: Geography, Exploration, and Fiction* (Princeton, NJ: Princeton University Press, 1992)
ROSENTHAL, BERNICE GLATZER, ed., *Nietzsche in Russia* (Princeton, NJ; Guildford: Princeton University Press, 1986)
ROSENZWEIG, RACHEL, *Worshipping Aphrodite: Art and Cult in Classical Athens* (Ann Arbor: University of Michigan Press, 2004)
RYZHENKO, IULIIA, 'Chto takoe muzyka stikha? Ol'ga Sedakova o slovesnoi khoreografii — i o tom, zachem poetu nuzhno legkoe serdtse', *colta.ru* <http://www.colta.ru/articles/specials/1090?page=3> [accessed 3 June 2015]
SANDLER, STEPHANIE, 'On Grief and Reason, on Poetry and Film: Elena Shvarts, Joseph Brodsky, Andrei Tarkovsky', *Russian Review*, 66.4 (2007), 647–70
—— 'A Poet Living in the Big City: Viktor Krivulin, among Others', in *Poetics, Self, Place: Essays to Honor Anna Lisa Crone*, ed. by Nicole Boudreau and Catherine O'Neil (Columbus, OH: Slavica, 2007), 675–93
—— 'Poetry after 1930', in *The Cambridge Companion to Twentieth-Century Russian Literature*, ed. by Evgeny Dobrenko and Marina Balina (Cambridge: Cambridge University Press, 2011), 115–34
—— 'Thinking Self in the Poetry of Ol'ga Sedakova', in *Gender and Russian Literature: New Perspectives*, ed. by Rosalind J. Marsh (Cambridge: Cambridge University Press, 1996), 302–25
SCHERR, BARRY P., *Russian Poetry: Meter, Rhythm, and Rhyme* (Berkeley, CA.: University of California Press, 1986)
SCHÖNLE, ANDREAS, and ANDREI ZORIN, *On the Periphery of Europe, 1762–1825: The Self-Invention of the Russian Elite* (DeKalb, IL: Northern Illinois University Press, 2018)
SCHUR, DAVID, 'A Garland of Stones: Hellenistic *Lithika* as Reflections on Poetic Transformation', in *Labored in Papyrus Leaves: Perspectives on an Epigram Collection Attributed to Posidippus (p. Mil Vogl. Viii 309)*, ed. by Benjamin Acosta-Hughes, Manuel Baumbach, and Elizabeth Kosmetatou (Washington, D.C.: Center for Hellenic Studies, 2004), 118–22
SEDAKOVA, OLGA, 'L'Antica Fiamma Elena Shvarts', *Novoe Literaturnoe Obozrenie*, 3 (2010),

<https://magazines.gorky.media/nlo/2010/3/l-8217-antica-fiamma-elena-shvarcz.html> [accessed 16 November 2013]

SEDAKOVA, OLGA, VALENTINA POLUKHINA, and ROBERT REID, 'Collective Analysis of Olga Sedakova's "The Wild Rose"', *Essays in Poetics*, 22 (1997), 237–57

SEGEL, HAROLD, 'Classicism and Classical Antiquity in Eighteenth- and Early-Nineteenth-Century Russian Literature', in *The Eighteenth Century in Russia*, ed. by J. G. Garrard (Oxford: Clarendon Press, 1973), 48–71

SHUBINSKII, VALERII, 'Elena Shvarts (Tezisy doklada)', in *Istoriia leningradskoi nepodtsenzurnoi literatury: 1950–1980-e gody: sbornik statei*, ed. by B. I. Ivanov and B. A. Roginskii (St Petersburg: Dean, 2000), 110–15

SINITSYNA, NINA VASIL'EVNA, *Tretii Rim: Istoki i evoliutsiia russkoi srednevekovoi kontseptsii (XV–XVI vv.)* (Moscow: Indrik, 1998)

SMITH, ALEXANDRA, *The Song of the Mocking Bird: Pushkin in the Work of Marina Tsvetaeva* (Bern; Berlin; New York: Peter Lang, 1994)

STEVENSON, JANE, *Women Latin Poets: Language, Gender and Authority, from Antiquity to the Eighteenth Century* (Oxford: Oxford University Press, 2005)

SULLIVAN, J. P., *Propertius: A Critical Introduction* (Cambridge: Cambridge University Press, 2010)

SURI, JEREMI, 'The Promise and Failure of "Developed Socialism": The Soviet "Thaw" and the Crucible of the Prague Spring, 1964–1972', *Contemporary European History*, 15.2 (2006), 133–58

SVIIASOV, E. V., *Antichnaia poeziia v russkikh perevodakh XVIII–XX vv.: Bibliograficheskii ukazatel'* (St Petersburg: Dmitrii Bulanin, 1998)

SVITNEVA, EVGENIIA, 'Elena Shvarts. Dikopis' poslednego vremeni', *Novyi mir*, 9 (2001), 189–92

SWORD, HELEN, 'Orpheus and Eurydice in the Twentieth Century: Lawrence, H. D., and the Poetics of the Turn', *Twentieth Century Literature*, 35.4 (1989), 407–28

TARANOVSKY, KIRIL, *Essays on Mandel'štam* (Cambridge, MA: Harvard University Press, 1976)

TERRAS, VICTOR, 'Classical Motives in the Poetry of Osip Mandel'štam', *The Slavic and East European Journal*, 10.3 (1966), 251–67

THOMAS, RICHARD F., ed., *Horace: Odes Book IV; and Carmen Saeculare* (Cambridge: Cambridge University Press, 2011)

TORLONE, ZARA MARTIROSOVA, *Russia and the Classics: Poetry's Foreign Muse* (London: Duckworth, 2009)

—— *Vergil in Russia: National Identity and Classical Reception* (Oxford: Oxford University Press, 2014)

TULCHINSKY, GRIGORY, 'Culture and Mythocracy', in *Re-entering the Sign: Articulating New Russian Culture*, ed. by Ellen E. Berry and Anesa Miller-Pogacar (Ann Arbor: University of Michigan Press, 1995), 62–78.

ULANOV, ALEKSANDR, 'Postposlednii romantik?', *Znamia*, 9 (1999), 216–17

UNGURIANU, DAN, 'The Wandering Greek: Images of Antiquity in Joseph Brodsky', in *Russian Literature and the Classics*, ed. by Peter I. Barta, David H. J. Larmour, and Paul Allen Miller (Amsterdam: Harwood Academic, 1996), 161–91

VINGE, LOUISE, *The Narcissus Theme in Western European Literature up to the Early 19th Century* (Lund: Gleerups, 1967)

VOITEKHOVICH, ROMAN, 'Dopolneniia k interpretatsii stikhotvoreniia O. Mandel'shtama "Da, ia lezhu v zemle, gubami shevelia..."', *Toronto Slavic Quarterly*, 13 (2005), <http://sites.utoronto.ca/tsq/13/vojtehovich13.shtml> [accessed 26 February 2019]

WACHTEL, MICHAEL, *The Development of Russian Verse: Meter and its Meanings* (Cambridge: Cambridge University Press, 1998)

WALDE, CHRISTINE, BRIGITTE EGGER, DUNCAN SMART, and MATTHIJS H. WIBIER, eds, *Brill's New Pauly: The Reception of Classical Literature* (Leiden; Boston: Brill, 2012)

WALKER, BARBARA, 'Kruzhok Culture: The Meaning of Patronage in the Early Soviet Literary World', *Contemporary European History*, 11.1 (2002), 107–23

WARRINGTON, JOHN, *Everyman's Classical Dictionary: 800 B.C.–A.D. 337* (London: J. M. Dent, 1961)

WELLS, DAVID N., 'Classical Motifs in the Poetry of Aleksandr Kushner', in *Russian Literature and the Classics*, ed. by Peter I. Barta, David H. J. Larmour, and Paul Allen Miller (Amsterdam: Harwood Academic, 1996), 143–60

WILLIAMS, CRAIG A., *Roman Homosexuality: Ideologies of Masculinity in Classical Antiquity* (Oxford; New York: Oxford University Press, 1999)

WYKE, MARIA, 'Mistress and Metaphor in Augustan Elegy', *Helios*, 16 (1989), 25–47

—— *The Roman Mistress: Ancient and Modern Representations* (Oxford: Oxford University Press, 2002)

—— 'Written Women: Propertius' Scripta Puella', *The Journal of Roman Studies*, 77 (1987), 47–61

ZAV'IALOV, SERGEI, 'Retromodernizm v leningradskoi poezii 1970-x godov', in *'Vtoraia kul'tura': Neofitsial'naia poeziia Leningrada v 1970–1980-e gody*, ed. by Zhan-Filipp Zhakkar, Violen Fridli, and Iens Kherl't (St Petersburg: Rostok, 2013), 30–52

ZETZEL, JAMES E. G., 'Poetic Baldness and its Cure', *Materiali e discussioni per l'analisi dei testi classici*, 36 (1996), 73–100

ZHDANOV, IVAN, 'Igra na ponizhenie', in 'Andegraund vchera i segodnia', ed. by Mikhail Aizenberg, *Znamia*, 6 (1998), 187–98

ZHITENEV, A. A., *Poeziia Neomodernizma* (St Petersburg: INAPRESS, 2012)

ZIOLKOWSKI, JAN M., 'Middle Ages', in *A Companion to the Classical Tradition*, ed. by Craig Kallendorf (Malden, MA; Oxford: Blackwell, 2007), 17–29

ZITZEWITZ, JOSEPHINE VON, 'From Underground to Mainstream: The Case of Elena Shvarts', in *Twentieth-Century Russian Poetry: Reinventing the Canon*, ed. by Katharine Hodgson, Joanne Shelton, and Alexandra Smith (Cambridge: Open Book Publishers, 2017), 225–63

—— *Poetry and the Leningrad Religious-Philosophical Seminar 1974–1980: Music for a Deaf Age* (Oxford: Legenda, 2016)

—— 'The "Religious Renaissance" of the 1970s and its Repercussions on the Soviet Literary Process' (DPhil thesis, University of Oxford, 2009)

GENERAL INDEX

Abel'skaia, Natal'ia 9 n. 36
Achilles 72
Actium, Battle of 108, 166
Adamovich, Georgii, 'Eshche i zhavoronkov khor' 194
Admiral'skii, Aleksei 9
Aeneas 30, 84
Aesop 136 n. 106
Akhmadulina, Bella 17
Akhmatova, Anna 3, 26, 44, 169 n. 18, 187, 215
    meeting with 4, 24 n. 116
    Severnye elegii 186
    'Tainy remesla 2' 81–82
Aksel'rod/Konstriktor/Vantalov, Boris 19
Alaric 180, 184, 312–13
Alexandria 108, 215, 272–73
Amalthea 135 n. 100
Anacreon 27
Annenskii, Innokentii 18, 26 n. 129, 123
Anon., 'Letiat utki' 143
Anpilov, Andrei 43–44, 173
Antigone 136 n. 105
Antinous 135 n. 102
Antony, Mark (Marcus Antonius) 166
Aphrodite 24, 25, 29, 40, 48–54, 56, 64, 68 n. 46, 93, 148, 150, 203, 210 n. 73, 220, 230, 238–39, 314–15
    see also Venus
Apollo 26 n. 129 & 131, 29, 40, 65, 77, 78–80, 87, 93, 153, 189, 206, 223, 226 n. 103, 230
    and Dionysus 23–24, 76–80, 84, 157, 212–13, 290–91, 318–19
    in Horace 193–94, 207, 213 n. 78, 216
    and Hyperborea 197, 199, 218
    in Propertius 98, 104, 108
    and Pythia 84–85, 87, 216, 248–49, 270–71
Apt, Solomon 98
Apuleius 97
    Metamorphoses 35 n. 164, 154, 159, 303
architecture 7, 22, 25, 163, 168–70, 171–72, 175, 177–78, 179, 180–82
Ariadne 5, 35, 40, 88–92, 93, 230, 252–53
Aristotle 33–34, 42, 221, 331
Artemis 135 n. 101, 272–73
Asoian, Aram 70–71
Attila 180
Attis 122–23
Atwood, Margaret:
    Circe/Mud 135

The Penelopiad 96, 136
'Siren Song' 135
Augustus (Gaius Octavius) 22 n. 100, 35, 95, 108, 118, 166, 189

Bacchanalia, the 101
    see also Dionysia, the
bacchantes/maenads 83, 105–06, 122–23, 136 n. 105, 142, 144–45, 148, 210, 213, 262–63
Bacchus 29, 78, 106, 107, 148
    see also Dionysus
Baiae 84, 85, 107–08, 126, 270–71
Baratynskii, Evgenii, 'Razuverenie' 48
Barker, Pat, *The Silence of the Girls* 136
Barkova, Anna 4
Barrett Browning, Elizabeth, 'The Dead Pan' 205–06
Barskova, Polina 28
Basmanova, Marina 137
bees 51, 155, 157, 189, 202–03, 206–08, 213–15, 217, 226 n. 103, 238–39, 290–91, 316–17, 320–21
Belyi, Andrei 3 n. 7
Berezhnova, Iuliia 9, 163
Beshenkovskaia, Ol'ga 13 n. 62
Bezprozvannaia, Polina 9 n. 36
Blok, Aleksandr 3 n. 7, 18, 192
    Dvenadtsat' 191, 192–93, 201, 204, 206, 213, 215, 216, 219, 220, 222–23, 224, 226
    Na pole Kulikovom 142
    'O doblestiakh, o podvigakh, o slave' 91, 92
    'Skify' 198
Bogdanovich, Ippolit 169–70 n. 21
Boileau-Despréaux, Nicolas, *L'Art poétique* 77–78, 184, 195 n. 29, 244–45
Boreas 65, 198
Brezhnev, Leonid 5, 9, 13, 25 n. 125
Brodskii, Iosif 9, 18, 25 n. 125, 26
    'Anno Domini' 136–37
    'Letter to Horace' 198
    Pis'ma rimskomu drugu 96
Brutus 147, 268–69
Budini, the 198
Bukovskaia, Tamara 9 n. 36, 10
Bulgakov, Mikhail, *Master i Margarita* 22, 52 n. 25
Burikhin, Igor' 172
byt 36, 43–44, 80, 83, 231
Byzantium 21, 168, 174, 308–09

Caligula (Gaius Julius Caesar Germanicus) 165–66, 172
Callimachus 98, 130, 131
    Aetia 104
Calypso 65, 135 n. 101
Carlson, Rachel 207–08
Cassandra 135 n. 100
Cassius, Gaius 164
Castalian Spring, the 85–86, 193, 223, 324–25
catasterism 215, 222
Catherine II: 22
Catiline (Lucius Sergius Catilina) 32, 234–35
Catullus, Gaius Valerius 24 n. 120, 33, 34–35, 95–96,
    98, 99, 100, 104, 116–24, 128, 130, 135 n. 102,
    138–39, 152, 156, 159, 199, 230, 256–57
    2: 116, 302
    3: 116–17, 220, 331, 302
    5: 117 n. 52
    11: 119–20, 130, 302, 303
    14: 120–21, 302
    22: 121, 302
    36: 121, 302
    37: 118, 302
    39: 98, 118, 302
    43: 123, 302
    45: 120 n. 54, 302
    51: 120, 130, 302, 303
    63: 106, 122–23, 302
    64: 90–92, 93
    69: 124, 302
    93: 124, 302
    98: 152, 303
    105: 121, 302
    see also Ariadne; Attis; Lesbia
Ceaușescu, Nicolae 173 n. 29
Cerberus 68, 240–41
Charon 29, 150, 152, 288–89
Chaucer, Geoffrey, *Troilus and Criseyde* 129
Cheigin, Petr 9 n. 36
Chloe 135 n. 100
Christ/Jesus 56, 63, 65, 66–68, 76, 83–84, 92, 137, 140,
    165, 206, 222–23
Cixous, Hélène, *Le Rire de la Méduse* 136 n. 108
Cybele 106, 122
Circe 65, 135, 136, 151, 154, 294–95
circus, the 30, 113, 118, 144, 154, 177, 178, 256–57,
    260–61, 268–69, 276–77, 278–79, 282–83, 308–09,
    310–11
Cleopatra VI: 165–66, 168
Clytemnestra 136 n. 104
Coleridge, Samuel Taylor, *The Rime of the Ancient
    Mariner* 64
Commager, Steele 196, 207
commedia dell'arte 43
Corday, Charlotte 165
Corinna (Greek poet) 97, 135 n. 102, 138, 215, 331

Corinna (Ovid's creation) 116–17
Crates of Thebes 190 n. 7
Cupid 51, 54, 104, 120, 134–35, 148, 149–50, 238–39,
    258–59, 260–61
    see also Eros
Cynthia (Propertius's creation) 95, 96, 97–98, 101–15,
    118–20, 131–32, 133–34, 136, 138–39, 143, 152–53,
    157, 183, 230

Daedalus 144, 218, 282–83
Daniel', Iulii 9
D'Annunzio, Gabriele 18
Daphnis 29, 135 n. 100
Davidson, Pamela 80
Deianira 136 n. 105
Delia 98, 133
Delphi 65, 84, 85, 108, 223, 270–71
Demeter 66, 135 n. 101, 136
Derzhavin, Gavrila, 'Evgeniiu. Zhizn' Zvanskaia' 191
Diomedes (*Iliad*) 129
Dionysia, the 139, 264–65
    see also Bacchanalia, the
Dionysus 40, 65, 77, 78–80, 82–84, 87, 93, 107, 124,
    139–40, 144, 145, 148, 150, 193, 226 n. 103, 230,
    244–45, 246–47, 264–65, 280–81, 331
    and Apollo 23–24, 76–80, 84, 157, 212–13, 290–91,
        318–19
    and Ariadne 88
    Dionysian 1, 79, 80, 82, 83, 84, 148, 193, 210, 215
    in Euripides 142
    in Horace 189, 212–13
    in Propertius 148
    Zagreus 139–40, 264–65
    see also bacchantes/maenads; Bacchus; *Homeric Hymn
        to Dionysus* (VII)
Dioscuri, the (Castor & Pollux) 40, 66, 67–68, 93, 230
Dolinin, Viacheslav 11, 12
Dostoevskii, Fedor 3 n. 7, 44, 88, 169 n. 18, 170
    Prestuplenie i nakazanie/Raskol'nikov 170
Double, the 43, 44, 62, 68
Dragomoshchenko, Arkadii 13
drinking (alcohol) 5, 8, 39, 66, 82, 93, 109–10,
    190 n. 7
    alcoholism 10, 18
    vines/hop bines 65, 82, 128, 215, 223–24, 278–79,
        320–21, 324–25
    vodka 12, 82, 246–47
    wine 67, 82, 102, 114, 117, 126, 130, 147, 149,
        178 n. 42, 189, 194, 202, 206–07, 209–10, 213,
        223, 254–55, 286–87, 314–15, 316–17, 318–19
Dubuque, Alexandre & Aleksei Razorenov, 'Ne brani
    menia rodnaia' 143
Duffy, Carol Ann, *The World's Wife* 136
Dunaevskaia, Elena 9 n. 36
Dzhedzhula, Andrei 6, 18

Echo 48
Eidinow, J.S.C. 200
elegy, Latin love 96, 97–98, 101, 102–04, 116, 119, 130,
    131–35, 136, 156
  domina/mistress 104, 112, 117, 133–35, 138
  form 99, 100, 103, 104, 107, 113, 125, 153, 157, 199,
    300–01
  genethliacon 108, 126–27
  militia amoris 103, 113–14
  paraclausithyron 104–05
  parrots 116–17, 132, 133, 254–55
  servitium amoris 134–35
empire 21, 23, 25, 26, 28, 163, 165, 166–67, 169–70,
    172–75, 185, 187, 218, 230–31, 306–07
enstrangement/*ostranenie* 40–45, 231
Erl', Vladimir 12
Eros 29, 238–39
  see also Cupid
Esenin, Sergei 18
Esquiline gardens, the 107, 124, 143, 264–65
Euripides, *Bacchae* 116, 123, 142, 302
Euryclea 135 n. 102
Eurydice 29, 40, 68–76, 93, 135 n. 101, 136, 204, 210,
    220, 230, 240–41, 242–43

Feeney, Denis 215
Filippov, Vasilii 4, 13 n. 60
Filofei 21–22, 167–68, 174
fire 47, 74–75, 98, 102, 112, 114, 121, 125, 127, 166,
    173, 182–83, 185, 194, 195, 203–04, 205, 219,
    312–13, 322–23
  in flat 5 n. 26, 18, 33, 34, 49, 148
Flaschenriem, Barbara 132, 136
Francis of Assisi 165
Furies 179

Gallus, Gaius Cornelius 98, 104 n. 39?, 130
  see also Lycoris
Gaul 141, 260–61, 286–87
Geloni, the 197, 198, 218
gender 1, 40, 44, 69–70, 80, 85, 87–88, 96, 106, 109,
    111, 131–39, 142, 154–56, 193, 202, 215, 229
  feminism 1, 10, 69, 87, 96, 131, 135–36, 137–38
  male gaze 69–70
Germani, the 103, 254–55
Germany 14–16, 18, 170, 172–73, 306–07
Getae, the 198
Gippius, Zinaida 3
gladiators 104–05, 121–22, 129, 145, 178–79, 186,
    260–61, 298, 310–11
glasnost' 10, 13–15, 26
Gluck, Christoph Willibald, *Orfeo ed Euridice* 68–69,
    220, 240–41
Gnedich, Nikolai, 'Inostrantsam gostiam moim' 198
God 5, 8, 30–31, 54 n. 29, 56, 63, 76, 82, 90, 92, 140,
    164, 165, 203, 224, 229, 252–53, 292–93, 314–15

Goethe, Johann Wolfgang von:
  'Die Musageten' 194 n. 26, 217, 322–23
  West-östlicher Divan 173 n. 31
Gogol', Nikolai 3 n. 7, 22, 44, 169 n. 18, 175 n. 35,
    180, 187
  Mertvye dushi 142
Gol', Nikolai 9 n. 36
Gold, Barbara K. 103, 131, 132, 134, 137
Gorbachev, Mikhail 13
Gorbovskii, Gleb 9 n. 36
Goricheva, Tat'iana 12
Gozzi, Carlo 43
Graves, Robert, *The Greek Myths* 67 n. 45
Grebenshchikov, Boris 17
Greece (Ancient) 4, 5, 19, 25, 29, 42, 65, 84, 130, 138,
    197, 198, 200, 207, 208, 215–16, 222
  vs. Rome (Ancient) 22, 23, 28, 30, 34, 36, 116, 148, 153
Greek, Ancient (language) 22, 27, 30–31, 41, 58, 141
Grois, Boris 12
Grossman, Vasilii, *Zhizn' i sud'ba* 16
Grudinina, Natal'ia 9
Gumilev, Nikolai, 'Zabludivshiisia tramvai' 183–84

Hades (god) 40, 66, 93, 230, 240–41
  see also Pluto; for Hades (place) see underworld, the
Hadrian (Publius Aelius Hadrianus) 32–33, 234–35
Hannibal 260–61
Hasty, Olga Peters 87
Hauser, Emily, *Golden Apple Trilogy* 136
Haynes, Natalie:
  The Children of Jocasta 136
  A Thousand Ships 136
H.D.:
  Collected Poems 1912–1944: 135 n. 101
  Helen in Egypt 135
Heldt, Barbara 96, 99, 169 n. 18
Helen 28, 119, 135, 136
Helicon 29, 165 n. 2, 208
Hephaestus 272–73
Hercules 127, 136 n. 105, 145, 153 n. 144
Hermes 29
Herodotus, *Histories* IV: 197
Hesiod 196
  Theogony 199
  Works and Days 30 n. 154
Hipparchia of Maroneia 190 n. 7
Hippolyta 135 n. 101
history 5–6, 11, 19, 28, 29, 40, 163, 164–68, 170, 174,
    175, 178, 179, 180, 182, 192, 217, 222, 230
Homer 19, 25, 31, 34, 93, 116, 159, 197
  Iliad 129, 214, 331; see also Achilles; Cassandra;
    Diomedes
  Odyssey 64–65, 67, 136, 154, 303; see also Calypso;
    Circe; Eurycleia; Lotus-eaters; Odysseus;
    Penelope; Polyphemus; Sirens
Homeric Hymn to Dionysus (VII) 65, 83, 215, 331

Homeric Hymn to the Dioscuri (XXXIII) 67 n. 45
homosexuality 151, 156–57, 296–97
Horace (Quintus Horatius Flaccus) 5, 27 n. 139, 33, 34–35,
    77, 95, 116, 130, 159, 160, 189–227, 231, 314–15
  Carmen Saeculare 193, 198 n. 42, 331
  Epistles 189
    I.1: 128, 302
    I.17: 190 n. 7
    II.2: 117, 302
  Epodes 189, 191
    3: 117, 302
    5: 123, 154, 302, 303
    13: 122, 302
    17: 123, 128, 302, 303
  Odes 189–227
    I.1: 215–16, 222, 331
    I.2: 194, 206, 331
    I.4: 194, 209, 331
    I.5: 224, 331
    I.9: 194, 200, 207, 331
    I.10: 200
    I.11: 191, 192, 194, 200, 207, 227, 331
    I.12: 210, 213, 222, 331
    I.16: 216, 331
    I.19: 207, 331
    I.24: 210, 222, 331
    I.28: 219, 331
    I.31: 207, 331
    I.37: 201, 331
    II.7: 210, 331
    II.10: 194, 331
    II.11: 210, 331
    II.13: 191, 219, 331
    II.19: 213, 331
    II.20: 192, 197, 218–19, 220, 227, 331
    III.1: 196
    III.4: 189, 193, 196–97, 202, 204, 218, 314–15, 331
    III.8: 207, 331
    III.18: 207, 331
    III.19: 210, 331
    III.25: 213, 331
    III.30: 191, 222, 331
    IV.1: 201, 331
    IV.2: 207–08, 213, 331
    IV.3: 222, 331
    IV.6: 216, 331
    IV.7: 194, 331
    IV.12: 194, 331
  Satires 189
    I.2: 190 n. 7
    I.4: 120, 302
    I.8: 123, 124, 128, 302, 303
    II.2: 190 n. 7
    II.3: 117, 302
    II.5: 190 n. 7
    II.7: 126, 302

Hubbard, Margaret 200
Hyperborea 197–99, 217–18, 226, 227, 322–23, 329

Iasnov, Mikhail 9 n. 36
Icarus 136 n. 106, 218
Ichin, Korneliia 70, 72
Ignatova, Elena 9 n. 36, 13 n. 62
invective 35, 95, 116, 118, 120–21, 125, 130, 152, 156,
    159, 189, 207
Irigaray, Luce, *Speculum* 136 n. 108
Iurskii, Sergei 164
Ivan III: 21
Ivanov, Viacheslav 3, 24, 79, 83, 140, 193
  Dionis i pradionisiistvo 79
  'Orfei' 210

John, St 139–40, 176
Julius Caesar, Gaius 124, 164–65, 304–05
Jupiter 106–07, 128, 262–63, 290–91
  see also Zeus
Juvenal (Decimus Iunius Iuvenalis) 34, 116, 119, 130
  V: 126, 302
  VI: 119, 121, 302
  XIV: 128, 302

Kahn, Andrew 76, 191
Kantemir, Antiokh 22, 191
Karamzin, Nikolai, *Istoriia Gosudarstva Rossiiskago* 198
Kazantzis, Judith, *The Wicked Queen* 136
Khlebnikov, Velimir 4
Khrushchev, Nikita 25
Kniazeva, Nina 9
Korovin, Sergei 14
Kovaleva, Natal'ia 12
Kozyrev, Kirill 18–19
Krivulin, Viktor 4, 9, 10, 12, 13, 14, 27
Kupriianov, Boris 9 n. 36, 10, 13 n. 62
Kurochkina, Tat'iana 9 n. 36
Kushner, Aleksandr 9 n. 36, 26
  Apollon v snegu 26 n. 131
  'Ne slishkom slozhen byl professorskii vopros'
    26 n. 129
  'O da, ona mogla b vnushit' Orfeiu' 26 n. 129
  'Razmashistyi sovkhoz Temriukskogo raiona'
    26 n. 129
Kutik, Il'ia 28
Kuzmin, Mikhail 4, 18

Labé, Louise, *Elegy* I: 135
Latin (language) 22, 27, 29–34, 40–41, 54, 58, 98, 106,
    129, 152, 169–70, 177, 189 n. 1, 190, 193–94, 196,
    198–99, 230, 234–35, 314–15
Lavinia (*Aeneid*) 30, 96, 136
Leda 29
legions, the 102–03, 114, 141, 165, 171–72, 254–55,
    286–87, 306–07

Le Guin, Ursula, *Lavinia* 96, 136
Leningrad: x, 3, 5, 10, 14, 26, 28, 33, 36, 48, 67, 76, 144, 145, 185, 220, 230
   Blockade 6, 83, 184
   see also Petersburg, St
Lermontov, Mikhail 18
Lerner, Sergei 145–46
Lesbia 98, 116–17, 118–20, 129, 138–39
Linetskaia, El'ga 11, 77, 244–45
literary prizes 12, 17, 18
Lomonosov, Mikhailo 22, 191
Lotus-eaters 65
Louÿs, Pierre, *Les Chansons de Bilitis* 96
Lucifer/Satan 55
Lucretia 135 n. 100
Luna 40, 57–58, 60–64, 65, 68 n. 46, 76, 93, 166, 179, 210 n. 73, 230, 310–11
   see also Selene
Lusitania 30, 286–87
Lycoris 98
Lygo, Emily 25–26
Lyne, R.O.A.M. 109, 127

Maecenas, Gaius Cilnius 95, 107, 143, 189
magic/witchcraft 52 n. 25, 95, 100, 106–07, 111–12, 123, 124, 128, 143, 151, 153–54, 262–63, 280–81, 290–91, 296–97
Maiakovskii, Vladimir 3, 18
Maliarova, Irina 9, 10
Mandel'shtam, Osip 18, 22, 24–25, 26, 27, 28, 36, 44, 187, 191–93, 226
   'Cherepakha' 192, 201–03
   'Chut' mertsaet prizrachnaia stsena' 192, 194, 201–02, 219–20
   'Eto kakaia ulitsa?' 170 n. 23
   Kamen' 192
   'Kogda Psikheia-zhizn' spuskaetsia k teniam' 192, 219–20
   'Lastochka' 192, 219–20
   'Silentium' 48, 53
   'Vek' 177
   'Voz'mi na radost'' iz moikh ladonei' 192, 202–03, 208
Marat, Jean Paul 165
Marcellus, Marcus Claudius 108
Marcus Aurelius 22 n. 100
Marie Antoinette 165 n. 5
Markov, A.V. 56
Marsyas 40, 78–79
Martial (Marcus Valerius Martialis) 34, 96, 116, 116–20, 124–30, 153, 156–57, 159, 230
   Spectacles 8: 118
   Spectacles 9: 118, 302
   Spectacles 12: 118
   Spectacles 17: 118
   Spectacles 21: 118
   Spectacles 26: 118
   Spectacles 31: 129, 303
   Spectacles 32: 118
   I.47: 124, 302
   I.56: 117, 302
   II.66: 119, 302
   III.93: 125, 302
   III.100: 117, 302
   IV.13: 125
   IV.30: 126, 302
   IV.41: 120, 302
   IV.44: 127, 302
   V.11: 125–26, 302
   VI.19: 127–28, 302
   VII.60: 125
   VII.87: 124, 302
   VIII.20: 120, 302
   VIII.61: 153, 303
   VIII.73: 119, 302
   VIII.81: 130, 303
   IX.54–55: 129, 303
   IX.83: 120, 302
   IX.94: 117, 302
   X.5: 302
   X.50: 128, 302
   X.77: 124, 302
   XI.27: 142
   XI.53: 125
   XI.102: 153, 303
   XII.17: 130, 303
   XII.29: 302
   XII.42: 156–57, 303
   XII.63: 120, 302
   XIV.176: 153 n. 144
   XIV.178: 153 n. 144
   XIV.189: 101 n. 35
Martynova, Ol'ga 147, 172, 175–76, 182
Mary (mother of Jesus) 56, 137
Mary Queen of Scots 165
Masing-Delic, Irene 142
masks 41, 42–43, 44, 144–45, 153 n. 144, 262–63
Massagetae, the 198
Maz'ia, Mark 9 n. 36
Medici, Ferdinando de' 180
Medusa 136 n. 106 & 108, 177
menstruation 57, 157–59, 296–97
Merezhkovskii, Dmitrii, *Voskresshie bogi: Leonardo da Vinchi* 83 n. 80
meta/turning post 30, 98, 110–11, 128, 177, 278–79, 308–09
metempsychosis 127, 167, 276–77
metre 1–2, 3, 4, 78, 99–100, 220, 245, 300–01, 330
   in Graeco-Roman poetry 35, 95, 99, 100, 102, 119, 129, 189, 199–200
   in *Homo Musagetes* 199–200, 206, 220, 224, 330
   in *Kinfiia* 99–100, 103, 104, 107, 113, 119–20, 121, 126, 128, 129, 130, 153, 157, 199, 300–01, 303
   in Russian poetry 22, 25, 99–100
Midas 136 n. 106
Miller, Madeline, *Circe* 136

Minerva 22 n. 100
Minotaur, the 88, 156, 294–95
Mironov, Aleksandr 4, 9 n. 36
Mnemosyne 29
Montefiore, Jan 137–38
moon, the 40, 48, 57–64, 68 n. 46, 106, 111–12, 128, 158–59, 166, 179, 194, 238–39, 244–45, 262–63, 280–81, 284–85, 296–97, 298, 310–11
  see also Luna; Selene
Morits, Iunna 17
Morozkina, Zinaida 98 n. 17
Morozova, Tat'iana 160, 161
Morpheus 16, 29, 111, 150, 203–04, 278–79, 314–15
Moscow 24, 27
  as the Third Rome 21–22, 163, 167–68
Muse(s) 25, 29, 76 n. 63, 77–78, 80, 82, 120–21, 157, 189, 192, 193–97, 199–200, 200–10, 213–24, 226–27, 231, 244–45, 258–59, 290–91, 314–31
  Calliope 29, 97, 195, 199, 202, 204, 206, 210, 258–59
  Camenae, the 189, 192, 193, 196, 215, 314–15, 316–17
  Clio 29, 199, 210, 217, 222, 324–25
  Erato 29, 135 n. 100, 195, 199, 206, 221–22, 258–59, 324–25
  Euterpe 29, 195, 199, 209, 215–16, 258–59
  Melpomene 29, 199, 201–02, 210, 220, 222, 324–25
  Polyhymnia 29, 199, 215–16, 222, 224, 324–25
  Terpsichore 29, 199, 200
  Thalia 29, 193, 199, 216, 328
  Urania 29, 195, 199, 213
myth (Graeco-Roman) 4, 5, 19, 24, 28, 29, 34, 35, 40, 42, 44, 45, 46–48, 65–66, 68–72, 80, 88, 89, 93, 95, 100, 103, 112, 132, 135, 136, 144, 212, 218, 230

Napoleon Bonaparte 84, 170
Narcissus 5, 35, 39, 40, 45–48, 56, 64, 68 n. 46, 93, 230, 236–37
Nekrasov, Nikolai, 'Dedushka Mazai i zaitsy' 195
Nemesis 29
Nero (Nero Claudius Caesar Augustus Germanicus) 13, 165–66, 170, 185
Nesterovskii, Vladimir 13 n. 62
Nietzsche, Friedrich 23–24, 79
  The Birth of Tragedy 23–24 n. 113
Nisbet, Robin 200

Obez'iana/Chimposia 11–12, 86 n. 88
Odysseus 40, 62, 64–65, 66–67, 93, 154, 190 n. 7, 230
Okhapkin, Oleg 4, 9 n. 36, 10, 13
Olympus 67, 199, 205–06, 316–17
Oppidum Ubiorum 170, 306–07
Orion 135 n. 101
Orpheus 24, 26 n. 129, 29, 40, 66, 68–76, 79, 87, 93, 136 n. 105 & 107, 189, 203–04, 210–13, 220, 223, 226 n. 103, 230, 240–41, 242–43, 314–15, 318–19
Osherov, Sergei 98 n. 17
Ostanin, Boris 12, 86 n. 88

Ostapenko, I. V. 60
Ostroumov, Lev 98–99
Ovid (Publius Ovidius Naso) 23, 24 n. 120, 26, 27, 34–36, 93, 98 n. 16, 116–17, 119, 128–29, 130, 132, 133, 156, 159, 198, 230
  Amores II.6: 117, 132, 302
  Ars Amatoria 119, 128–29, 302, 303
  Heroides 132
  Metamorphoses 45–48, 71, 87, 127, 128, 302, 303
  Remedia Amoris 101 n. 35
  see also Corinna

Pan 204–06, 226 n. 103, 316–17, 328
Panchenko, Dmitrii 96, 98 n. 18, 100–01, 108 n. 44, 116, 117, 123, 141, 143, 190
Parcae/Fates 29, 91, 108, 270–71
Parker, Dorothy, 'From a Letter from Lesbia' 138–39
Parnassus 29
Parnok, Sofiia, Rozy Pierii 96, 99 n. 25
Pasiphaë 112, 128–29, 144, 151, 154, 156, 282–83, 294–95
Pasternak, Boris 9, 10, 25 n. 125
  'Gamlet' 92
Paul I: 165
Pausanias 52, 197–98
Pazukhin, Evgenii 12
Penelope 135 n. 101, 136
perestroika 13, 170
Perlina, Nina 88
Persephone 25, 40, 66–67, 93, 136 n. 104, 208, 219, 230
  see also Proserpina
Peter I: 3, 22, 65, 142, 143–44, 165, 168–70
Peter, St 60, 63
Petersburg, St: x, 3, 4, 5, 18, 22, 24, 27, 65, 150, 179, 180, 189, 192, 200, 218, 220–21, 226, 229, 231, 238–39, 310–11
  as Hyperborea 198–99
  Neva, the 65, 143, 186, 229, 332–33
  as Rome 22, 141–44, 150, 163, 168–70, 173–75, 183–87, 230
  see also Leningrad
Petrovskii, Fedor 98
Pindar 196, 197, 208
  Pythian IV: 214 n. 82
  Pythian X: 207–08, 213, 331
Piotrovskii, Adrian 98 n. 17
Plato 33–34, 116, 126, 130, 202, 230, 272–73, 302, 331
  Meno 126, 302
  Phaedo 126, 302
  Phaedrus 126, 302
  Republic 124–25, 126, 302
  Symposium 52
  Timaeus 126, 302
Platonov, Andrei, Kotlovan 16
Pleshcheev, Aleksei 170
Pliny (Gaius Plinius Secundus) 118, 302
Plutarch, On the Obsolescence of Oracles 205, 331

Pluto 29
  see also Hades
Poblicius, Lucius 171–72, 306–07
poethood 2–3, 4, 5, 16, 18, 23–25, 28, 35–36, 39–40, 44, 47–48, 50–51, 53, 56, 65, 75–80, 84–88, 90, 93, 95, 115, 117, 125–26, 136, 139, 148–50, 185, 191, 193, 196, 205, 207–08, 210–13, 215, 216, 217–19, 226–27, 229–31, 244–45, 264–65, 266–67, 332–33
  inspiration (divine) 1, 2, 23, 24, 26 n. 129, 40, 50, 51, 63, 64, 65, 75–80, 82, 84–88, 93, 95, 98, 108, 148–49, 166, 189, 190, 193, 194, 195, 196, 201, 203, 205, 207–08, 210, 211–13, 215, 216, 217, 219, 221, 223–24, 226, 229, 230, 231, 332–33
  madness/lunacy 40, 62–64, 71, 84, 117, 122–23, 128, 210, 224
  self-sacrifice 40, 63, 67, 76–77, 84, 87, 142, 150, 158, 262–63, 296–97
  transcendence 1, 4, 5, 40, 42, 87
  see also Apollo; Dionysus; Eurydice; Muse(s); Orpheus; Pythia
Polyphemus/cyclops 65, 179
Posidippus, *Lithika* 126, 302
post-Soviet era, the 16, 28, 174, 231
Priapus 29
Prigov, Dmitrii 15
Propertius, Sextus 33, 34, 95–96, 97–98, 99, 100, 101–15, 116, 117, 118–19, 120, 123, 128, 130, 131–32, 133, 134, 137, 138, 139, 140, 143, 148, 149, 150, 152–54, 156, 157, 159, 183, 230, 254–55, 276–77,
  I.1: 101, 104 n. 39, 111–12, 115 n. 48, 134–35, 154, 303
  I.2: 97
  I.3: 105, 109–10, 111, 115, 132, 302, 303
  I.4: 104 n. 39
  I.5: 104 n. 39 & 40, 154, 303
  I.6: 104 n. 39
  I.7: 97, 104 n. 39
  I.8: 109, 115 n. 48, 139, 302
  I.9: 104 n. 39
  I.10: 104 n. 39
  I.11: 85, 107–08, 115 n. 48, 302
  I.12: 104 n. 39
  I.13: 104 n. 39
  I.16: 104, 115 n. 48, 302
  I.17: 113–14, 115 n. 48, 303
  I.18: 104 n. 40
  I.20: 104 n. 39, 156
  I.22: 104 n. 39
  II.1: 152, 153, 303
  II.2: 110, 115 n. 48, 302
  II.3: 97
  II.4: 156
  II.5: 99, 103, 113, 115, 302, 303
  II.6: 97, 104 n. 40
  II.9: 98, 115 n. 48, 302
  II.10: 131
  II.11: 97
  II.12: 104, 115 n. 48, 302
  II.13: 97, 104
  II.15: 109, 115 n. 48, 302
  II.16: 114, 115 n. 48, 303
  II.18: 110, 115 n. 48, 302
  II.22: 106, 115 n. 48, 302
  II.23: 101 n. 35, 112–13, 115 n. 48, 129, 153, 303
  II.25: 111, 115 n. 48, 302
  II.29: 109–10, 111, 115, 132, 152, 302, 303
  II.31/32: 108, 112, 115, 118–19, 302, 303
  II.34: 115 n. 48, 119, 156, 302
  III.3: 103, 115 n. 48, 302
  III.6: 154
  III.8: 105, 113, 115, 302, 303
  III.10: 108, 115 n. 48, 302
  III.12: 114, 115 n. 48, 154, 303
  III.14: 109, 115, 302
  III.17: 107, 115 n. 48, 302
  III.18: 85, 107–08, 115 n. 48, 152 n. 143, 302, 303
  III.19: 99, 112, 115 n. 48, 128–29, 156, 303
  III.21: 113–14, 115 n. 48, 303
  III.23: 97, 107, 114, 115 n. 48, 303
  III.24: 114–15, 153–54, 303
  III.25: 105, 109, 114, 115, 115, 302
  IV.1: 98, 108, 111, 114, 115, 302
  IV.2: 104, 115 n. 48, 153, 302, 303
  IV.3: 107
  IV.5: 106–07, 115 n. 48, 154, 302, 303
  IV.6: 108, 110, 115, 302
  IV.7: 97, 101, 102, 104, 112, 114, 115, 132, 150, 153, 183, 302, 303
  IV.8: 98, 101, 102, 105, 107, 109–10, 114, 115, 132, 152, 160, 302, 303
  IV.11: 114, 152 n. 143, 303
  see also Cynthia
Proserpina 29, 219–20, 322–23, 329
  see also Persephone
Pudovkina, Elena 9 n. 36
Pushkin, Aleksandr 2, 3 n. 7, 23, 24, 25, 26, 29, 44, 65, 87, 93, 196
  'Arion' 23
  'K Ovidiiu' 23, 198
  Mednyi vsadnik 142, 143–44
  'Pamiatnik' 23, 191
  'Poet' 77
  'Poet i tolpa' 23
  'Prorok' 23, 76–77, 205, 226
  Ruslan i Liudmila 86–87
Pygmalion 136 n. 106
Pythagoras 127
Pythia/Delphic oracle, the 40, 65, 84–88, 93, 108, 148–49, 150, 197–98, 199, 204, 214 n. 82, 216, 223, 226 n. 103, 230, 248–49, 250–51, 270–71, 322–23
  see also Castalian Spring; Delphi

reception theory 5, 19–21
recusatio 81, 201–02, 203, 226
religion 1, 4, 5, 12, 21, 27, 36, 52, 55, 56, 100, 167–68,
    169–70, 173–75, 176, 199, 206, 222–23, 224, 226,
    229, 332–33
  Buddhism 12
  Christianity 10, 23 n. 107, 27, 139, 36, 55–56, 63,
      66, 83, 125, 139–40, 150, 156, 157, 163, 167,
      176–77, 179, 193, 203, 209, 213, 222–26
    Bible, the 43, 54, 55, 92, 135 n. 100, 156, 157, 173
    Catholicism 30, 83, 167–68, 179 n. 43
    Christmas/New Year 54 n. 29, 56, 140, 173, 209,
        306–07, 316–17
    Easter 22 n. 105, 83, 140, 168
    iurodstvo/holy foolishness 63
    Orthodoxy 12, 21–22, 36, 55, 167, 213, 224–25,
        306–07
    see also Christ/Jesus; God; Mary
  Hinduism 76
  Islam 55
  paganism 19, 36, 63, 66, 83, 139, 165 n. 4, 193, 194,
      203, 206, 209, 213, 216, 222, 226
Remus 186
reptiles (dragon/lizard/salamander/serpent/snake) 69,
    70, 72, 74–75, 76, 238–39, 242–43
rhyme 1, 42–43, 77–78, 99, 100, 199, 244–45, 330
Rich, Adrienne, *Snapshots of a Daughter-in Law* 135,
    137–38
Riding, Laura:
  'Poems of Mythical Occasion' 135
  A Trojan Ending 136
Roginskii, Arsenii 12
Roma (goddess) 180–81
Romanticism 4, 23, 24, 44, 87
Rome (Ancient) 4, 5, 19, 25, 34, 35, 40, 41, 42, 81, 95,
    96, 102–03, 107, 111, 113, 114, 117, 124, 139, 140,
    141–44, 145, 156 n. 147, 160, 163–87, 208, 229–31,
    254–55, 284–85, 286–87, 299, 306–07, 308–11,
    312–13, 332–33
  Forum, the 101 n. 35, 104, 120, 144, 153, 175–76,
      258–59, 264–65, 280–81
  vs. Greece (Ancient) 22, 23, 28, 30, 34, 36, 116,
      148, 153
  (modern) 5, 16, 58, 175–82, 185–87, 229–31, 308–11,
      312–13, 332–33
  plebs 30, 266–67, 310–11
  rim i mir 36, 128, 143, 180, 187, 229, 280–81, 332–33
  sack of 180, 183–85
  Senate, the 4, 30, 282–83, 310–11
  see also Third Rome, the
Romulus 176, 186
Rubicon, the 164–65, 304–05
Rubina, Berta 6, 7, 145, 229, 266–67, 332–33
Rubina-Shvarts, Liubov' 6, 18
Rubinshtein, Lev 15
Rudd, Niall 200

Rudkevich, Lev 12
Rus' 21, 30, 142

samizdat 9–10, 12, 26, 30, 43, 72 n. 55, 126, 131, 166,
    190 n. 7
Sandler, Stephanie 16
Sappho 34, 48, 50–53, 96, 100, 116, 119–20, 129, 130,
    135, 136, 138, 160, 199, 200, 202, 206, 212, 215,
    220, 224, 226, 303, 330, 331
  1: 48, 50–53, 220, 331
  16: 135
  31: 51, 120, 130, 302
Satyr 29
Schneider, Myra, 'Eurydice's Version' 136
Schopenhauer, Arthur 23 n. 113
Scythia 196–99, 213, 218, 226
Sedakova, Ol'ga 3, 4, 26, 27, 29 n. 150, 96, 160,
    166–67, 190, 194
Selene 40, 57–61, 63, 64, 68 n. 46, 76, 93, 179,
    210 n. 73, 230, 310–11
  see also Luna
Sel'vinskii, Il'ia 98 n. 17
Semenov, Gleb 9
Seneca, Lucius Annaeus 118, 302
Sextus Empiricus 33–34
Shakespeare, William:
  Antony and Cleopatra 166 n. 7
  Hamlet 28, 92
  Julius Caesar 164
  Troilus and Cressida 129
Sheinker, Mikhail 12, 15, 16, 18
Shervinskii, Sergei 98 n. 17
Shklovskii, Viktor, 'Iskusstvo, kak priem' 41–42
Shneiderman, Eduard 13 n. 62
Shul'ts, Iurii 98 n. 17
Shvarts, Dina 5–8, 10–11, 12, 16–17, 19, 33, 42, 89, 92,
    158, 182, 229, 252–53. 332–33
Shvarts, Elena:
  biography 5–18
  death 18–19, 90–92, 186–87, 191, 229, 252–53,
      332–33
  family 5–6; mother, *see* Shvarts, Dina; great
      aunt/'grandmother', *see* Rubina, Berta; father,
      see Dzhedzhula, Andrei
  works, *see* Index of Elena Shvarts's Works
Shvarts, Lilia 6
Shvarts, Moris 6
Shvarts (Panfilova), Roza 6
Sibyl, the/Cumaean oracle, the 24, 84, 85, 87
Silver Age, the/Modernism 3–4, 23, 25, 26, 27, 36
Siniavskii, Andrei 9
Sinitsyna, Nina 167, 174
Sirens 65, 135 n. 103
Sisyphus 136 n. 106
slaves/slavery 30, 86, 95, 102, 103–04, 105, 108, 112,
    116, 118–19, 126, 129, 132, 133–35, 142, 145, 156,

254–55, 256–57, 260–61, 262–63, 268–69, 278–79, 280–81, 282–83
Socialist Realism 25, 26, 44, 180
Socrates 126, 165–66
Solov'ev, Vladimir 23 n. 112
Solzhenitsyn, Aleksandr, *Arkhipelag GULAG* 16
sparrows 48, 50, 67–68, 116–17, 119, 138, 182, 219–20, 223, 226 n. 103, 322–23
Sparta 109, 147, 276–77
Stagnation, the 5, 9, 10, 27, 43
Stalin, Iosif 7, 24, 25, 28, 192
Stratanovskii, Sergei 4, 9 n. 36, 12
Sulla (Lucius Cornelius Sulla Felix) 81, 246–47
Sulpicia 98, 116, 130, 133, 136
  II: 126–27, 302
sun, the 50, 66–68, 75–76, 108 n. 44, 124, 205–06, 246–47, 270–71, 284–85, 298, 316–17
Sword, Helen 69–70

tablets (writing) 97, 114, 115, 130, 139, 224, 258–59, 286–87, 299
tamizdat 12, 14
Terence (Publius Terentius Afer) 33–34
Thaw, the 7, 9, 17, 25–27, 43
theatre 1, 5, 6, 8, 10, 12, 42–43, 69 n. 47, 82, 92, 144–45, 160, 161, 164, 173, 195, 229, 332–33
Theseus 88, 90–92
Thessaly 112, 153–54, 290–91
Thetis 136 n. 106
Third Rome, the 21–22, 23, 25 n. 121, 36, 163, 167–68, 170, 173–75, 185, 187, 230–31, 308–09
Thoth 7
Tibullus, Albius 33, 98, 133
  see also Delia
Tiresias 136 n. 106, 190 n. 7
Tiutchev, Fedor 4
Tomoshevskii, Iurii 161
Toporov, Viktor 9 n. 36
Tovstonogov, Georgii 12
Trediakovskii, Vasilii 22, 191
Tsar'kova, Tat'iana 9 n. 36
Tsvetaev, Ivan 24
Tsvetaeva, Marina 3, 4, 18, 24, 25, 26 n. 129, 44, 65, 85, 93, 215
  'Evridika — Orfeiu' 71–72
  'Khvala Afrodite' 48, 50–51, 53
  Sivilla 85, 87–88

Skifskie 198
'Tak plyli: golova i lira' 211–12

Ulanovskaia, Bella 12
underground, the 4, 10–11, 16, 27, 36, 145
underworld, the 40, 64, 65–74, 76, 84, 88–89, 112, 175, 192, 219–20, 226, 240–41, 242–43, 248–49, 250–51, 322–23, 329
  katabasis 65–68
  Lethe 29, 88, 102
  Styx 29, 127, 218, 219
  see also Cerberus; Charon; Dioscuri, the; Eurydice; Hades; Orpheus; Persephone; Pluto; Proserpina
USSR/Soviet Union 4, 12, 13, 14, 26, 29, 33, 36
  fall of 14–16, 25, 73, 163, 172–75, 183, 187, 192, 226, 231

Vargaftik, Elena 170
Varro, Marcus Terentius, *De Re Rustica* 214, 331
Vedius Pollio, Publius 118, 302
Venus 40, 48, 50, 52 n. 25, 53–57, 64, 65, 68 n. 46, 76, 93, 127, 148, 210 n. 73, 230, 238–39
  in Horace 194, 201, 203
  in Propertius 107, 153–54
  see also Aphrodite
Venzel', Evgenii 9 n. 36, 10, 18
Vesta/Vestal virgins 111, 150, 278–79
Vesuvius/Pompeii/Herculaneum 127, 140–41
Virgil (Publius Vergilius Maro) 1, 27, 31, 32, 95, 210, 234–35
  Aeneid 30, 84; *see also* Aeneas; Lavinia
  Georgics 71, 214
Vladimir, Prince 21

Wandor, Michelene, *Gardens of Eden* 136
Wittig, Monique, *Le Corps lesbien* 136 n. 108
wolves 113, 122, 144, 154, 186, 260–61, 282–83, 298, 304–05, 312–13
Wyke, Maria 97 n. 13, 131–32, 133, 134

Zabolotskii, Nikolai 3
Zeus 29, 52, 67, 153, 199, 288–89
  see also Jupiter
Zitzewitz, Josephine von 5 n. 26, 44, 76, 142 n. 126, 169
Zubova, Liudmila 9 n. 36

INDEX OF ELENA SHVARTS'S WORKS

Index of transliterated BOOK TITLES, *Cycle/Collection Titles*, Poem Titles, 'First lines', and <u>Prose Pieces</u>, with [English translations]. 'Poems' and <u>Prose Pieces</u> are grouped under the *Cycle/Collection* in which they appear, in publication order. Page numbers are in **bold** where the poem is given in full, and in *italics* where the manuscript is pictured.

Afrodita uletaet v noch' na subbotu [Aphrodite Flies off at the End of Friday Night] 48, *49*, 50–53, 54, 55, 56, 60, 80 n. 74, 148, **238–39**
'Akh esli b vse zhili tak druzhno' [Ah, if only everyone could live as harmoniously] 1, 31–32, 152, **234–35**
Animus 30
Apologiia solntsevorotnogo sna [Apology of Solstice Sleep] 16 n. 72
Arboreiskii sobor [Arboreal Cathedral] 30
'A v oknakh u tsygan' [But in gypsies' windows] 54 n. 29, 55, 56

Blagodarenie [Thanksgiving] 36 n. 165, 180, 187, **229–30**, **332–33**
'Bogi spiat raskinuv nog[o/i]ruki' [The gods sleep with leg-arms spread] 80 n. 72
Bokovoe zrenie pamiati [The Lateral Vision of Memory] 76 n. 62
Burliuk 65 n. 39

Chernaia paskha [*Black Easter*]
  2. Gde my? [Where Are We?] 10, 22 n. 105, 168–70, 173
Cogito ergo non sum 30

DIKOPIS' POSLEDNEGO VREMENI [MADU-SCRIPT OF THE LAST HOUR] 16 n. 73
Dva aspekta [*Two Aspects*] 82–83
Dva stikhotvoreniia na osobyi raspev [*Two Poems to a Special Chant*] 151, 292–93
Dve satiry v dukhe Goratsiia [*Two Satires in the Spirit of Horace*] 190

Elegiia na rentgenovskii snimok moego cherepa [Elegy on an X-ray of my Skull] 78–79, 213 n. 80
Elegii na storony sveta [*Elegies on the Corners of the Earth*]
  IV. Zapadnaia [Western] 66
EXERCITUS EXORCITANS 30, 166
  PRAETORIANI 30
  EQUITATUS 30
  MACHINAE OBSIDIALES 30

Genius loci 30
Geopoliticheskii trilistnik [*Geopolitical Triptych*] (May 1990)
  2. Smutnye strofy [Troubled Stanzas] 30 n. 153, 73
Gorbatyi mig [Hunchbacked Moment] 195 n. 29
  'O nesdannye butylki' [O unreturned bottles] 82
Gostinitsa Mondekhel' [Hotel Mondehell] 54 n. 29, 57, 62–63
Grubymi sredstvami ne dostich' blazhenstva [Rough Methods Won't Get You Bliss] 30, 148, 195 n. 29
'Grustno smotriu ia pod kryl'ia tiazhelye' [I look sadly under the heavy wings] 80 n. 72

<u>*Istinnye proisshestviia moei zhizni*</u> [<u>*True Events of My Life*</u>]
  <u>Gabala</u> [<u>Kapala</u>] 213 n. 80
  <u>Komarovo</u> 57, 58, 157–58
'Iz-za ugla Venera vyskochila' [Venus leapt out from behind the corner] 54

'Kak eta ulitsa zovetsia — ty na doshchechke prochitai' [What this street is called — you can read it off the sign] 170
'Kak stydno starit'sia' [How shameful ageing is] 160 n. 149
Kh'iumbi [*Humbe*]
  6. Dostoevskii i Pleshcheev v Pavlovskom parke [Dostoevskii and Pleshcheev in Pavlovsk Park] 170
Khomo musaget [*Homo Musagetes*] 5, 34, 35, 130, 187, 189–227, 231, **314–27**, 328–31
  I. 'Veter shumit za steklami' [Wind whistles outwith windowpanes] 200–04, 205, 207, 208, 210, 215, 224, 226, **314–15**, 328, 330, 331
  II. 'Muzy! Devushki! Zima uzh navalilas'' [Muses! Ladies! The winter really has closed in] 199, 204–06, 218, 226, **316–17**, 328, 330, 331
  III. 'Vot vypal pervyi sneg' [So, the first snow has fallen] 203, 206–09, 214, 217, 226, **316–17**, 328, 330, 331
  IV. 'Snega nasyp'te v krasnyi' [Sprinkle some snow into a red] 73, 79, 204, 207, 209–13, 217, 223, 226, **318–19**, 328, 330, 331

v. 'Mokhnato-belykh pchel' [Fuzzy white bees] 157, 203, 208, 213–16, 217, 224, 226, **320–21**, 328, 330, 331

vi. Pifiia [Pythia] 84 n. 83, 86, 149, 204, 216, 223, 226, **322–23**, 328, 330, 331

vii. 'Muzy (zamerzli!) — belye mukhi' [Muses (you're frozen!) — have the white flies] 199, 217–20, 223, 226, **322–23**, 329, 330, 331

viii. Voskhvalenie drug druga u Nikol'skogo sobora [Encomium of Each Other before Nikolsky Cathedral] 199, 220–24, 226, **324–25**, 328, 330, 331

ix. Muzy pered Ikonoi [Muses before the Icon] 209, 224–26, 226, **326–27**, 328, 330, 331

Kinfiia [Cynthia] 5, 26, 30, 34, 35, 40, 41, 93, 95–161, 163, 182, 183, 185, 187, 190, 199, 230, **254–87**, 298–303

Kniga pervaia [Book One] 100–01, 102–07, 116–24, 130, 134, 136, 148, **254–63**

i. K sluzhanke [To a Slave Girl] 98, 99, 101, 102–03, 134, 116–17, 130 n. 69, 70, 72, & 73, 133–34, 139, 141, 149, **254–55**, 300, 302

ii. 'Snova sunulsia otets s pouchen'em' [Again father stuck his nose in with a lecture] 30, 134, 117–18, 130 n. 70 & 73, 133–34, 142, **256–57**, 300, 302

iii. K sluzhanke [To a Slave Girl] 98, 103–04, 134, 118–19, 130 n. 69, 70, 72, & 74, 133–34, 142, **256–57**, 300, 302

iv. Kupidonu [To Cupid] 51, 199, 134, 104, 119–20, 129, 130 n. 69, 134–35, 148, **258–59**, 300, 302

v. Molodomu poetu [To a Young Poet] 104, 120–21, 195 n. 29, 130 n. 69, 70, & 73, 139, **258–59**, 300, 302

vi. Klavdii [To Claudia] 104–05, 109, 121–22, 125, 130 n. 73 & 74, 145, 148, 150, **260–61**, 298, 300, 302

vii. 'Kak ia vam zaviduiu, vakkhanki' [How I envy you, bacchantes] 44, 101, 105–06, 122–23, 130 n. 69, 142, 144–45, 148, **262–63**, 300, 302

viii. K provintsialke [To a Provincial Woman] 106–07, 112, 123–24, 130 n. 69, 70, & 73, 151, **262–63**, 300, 302

Kniga vtoraia [Book Two] 100–01, 107–09, 124–27, 130, 150, 151, **264–75**

i. 'V'etsia v urnakh predkov pepel — nynche Dionisa noch" [The ancestors' ashes wreathe in their urns — tonight is the Dionysia] 83, 101, 107, 124, 130 n. 73, 139–40, 143, 148, **264–65**, 300, 302

ii. 'Kto pri zvukakh fleity otdalennoi' [Whoever, when strains of a distant flute drift by] 99, 101, **264–65**, 300, 302

iii. 'Chto khoroshego v Saratoge dal'nei?' [What is the attraction of remote Saratoga?] 101, 124–25, 130 n. 71, 140, **266–67**, 300, 302

iv. Klavdii — posle poseshcheniia bol'noi babki [To Claudia, after Visiting my Sick Granny] 101, 104, 125, 130 n. 70, 145, **266–67**, 300, 302

v. 'Mnogo, guliaia v gorakh, kamnei pestrotsvetnykh nashla ia' [While strolling in the mountains I came across a host of multicoloured stones] 30, 101, 125–26, 130 n. 70, **266–67**, 300, 302

vi. 'Sami smotriat krovavye igry' [*They* watch blood sports] 101, 103, 126, 130 n. 74, 143, 147, **268–69**, 300, 302

vii. Na pliazhe v Baii [On the Beach at Baiae] 84, 85, 101, 107–08, 126, 130 n. 70, 148–49, **270–71**, 300, 302

viii. Razgovor [Conversation] 100–01, 108–09, 126–27, 130 n. 71, 73, & 75, 145, 147, **272–75**, 300, 302

Razroznennoe [Oddments] 96, 100–01, 109–15, 127–30, 149, 150, 151, 152, **276–87**, 288–89, 298, 302

i. 'V khizhinu voshla i ogliadelas'' [I walked into the hut and looked about me] 101, 109, 127, 130 n. 70 & 72, 140–41, 147, 149, **276–77**, 300, 302

ii. 'Vnov' Propertsii moi ko mne vernulsia' [My Propertius has returned to me again] 30, 98, 101, 109–10, 143, 148, 149, 150, 152, **276–77**, 300, 302

iii. 'Tol'ko vchera ia khotela' [Only yesterday I wanted] 30, 177, 98, 101, 110–11, 127–28, 130 n. 70, 73, & 74, 149, **278–79**, 300, 302

iv. K Morfeiu [To Morpheus] 111, 128, 130 n. 69, 148, 150, **278–79**, 300, 303

v. 'Pribegali tut koldun'i' [Then hags came running] 36 n. 165, 180, 101, 107, 111–12, 128, 130 n. 72 & 73, 143–44, 151, **280–81**, 300, 303

vi. 'Sdelai, master, mne, — Pasifaia Dedalu' ['Master, make me,' Pasiphaë to Daedalus] 99, 112–13, 119, 199, 128–29, 130 n. 69 & 72, 144, 148, 151, 156, **282–83**, 300, 303

vii. 'Chto menia brosilo v ob"iat'ia Diomida?' [What threw me into the arms of Diomedes?] 30, 113, 129, 144, 148, **282–83**, 300, 303

viii. 'Ran'she ia sama liubila koshek' [I used to love cats too] 30, 103, 129, 130 n. 70, 147, **284–85**, 298, 300, 303

ix. 'Nado bylo ekhat' v stolitsu' [I had to travel to the capital] 101, 129, 130 n. 70, 140, **284–85**, 298, 300, 303

x. 'Rozovye plyvut oblaka nad Rimom' [Rosy-hued clouds are drifting over Rome] 30, 101–02, 113–15, 130, 141, **286–87**, 299, 300, 303

Apocrypha 95, 96, 150–59, **288–97**
- [1] 'Chernyi, kak veslo Kharona, griaznyi' [Black, like Charon's paddle, dirty] 150, 152–53, 157, **288–89**, 300, 303
- [2] 'Est' u menia 4 nebesnykh supruga' [I have 4 heavenly husbands] *151*, 153, **288–89**, 300, 303
- [3] Zavistniku [To the Envier] 79, 151, 153–54, *155*, 157, 196, 213, 214, **290–91**, 300, 303
- [4] 'Gor' — ká | ia ty liu — | bov" [Bit — tér | are you | love] 151, 157, **292–93**, 300, 303
- [5] Tsirtseia [Circe] 65 n. 39, 151, 154, **294–95**, 301, 303
- [6] Pasifaia [Pasiphaë] 151, 154, 156, **294–95**, 301, 303
- [7] 'povsiu[d]u v dvorakh stoiali polennitsy' [everywhere stacks, all round the courtyards] 151, 156, **294–95**, 301, 303
- [8] 'Ty opiat' o Tite rech' zavodish" [Yet again you turn to talk of Titus] 151, 156–57, **296–97**, 301, 303
- [9] Iz vosp. Kinf. [From Cynth.'s Mem.] 152, 157–58, *159*, **296–97**, 301, 303

'Kogda ia pod utro usnula [When I fell asleep towards morning] 35
Kolodets-dub [Well-Oak] 86–87, 149
KORABL' [SHIP] 72 n. 55
'Korabl' Zhizni unosilsia vdal" [The Ship of Life scudded into the distance] 90-92, 186, **252–53**
Kostroma-Dionis [Kostroma-Dionysus] 83

Lestnitsa s dyriavymi ploshchadkami [*Staircase with Holey Landings*] 66
  'Ia opushchus' na dno morskoe' [I sink to the seabed] 66
  'Ia znaiu, chego ia khotela' [I know what I wanted] 160 n. 149
  'Krov'iu Motsarta atlasnoi' [With Mozart's satin blood] 79
Laif-vita [Life-vita] 30, 66 n. 43
Letnee Morokko [*Summer Moroque*] 13, 30
  Svalka [Dump] 40, 80–*81*–83, 149, 150, **246–47**
  Ostrovok na Kamennom [Islet on Kamennyi (Stony) Island] 54 n. 29
<u>Literaturnye gastroli</u> [<u>*Literary Tours*</u>] 15–16
Luna bez golovy [Luna Loses her Head] 58, 60–64, 65
  1. 'Se li ty?' [C'est toi là?] 60, 63
  3. 'Za oknami nelovko' [Beyond the windows awkwardly] 60–61
  4. Telo Luny i golova ee zhe [Luna's Body and her Head Too] 61, 62, 63
  5. 'Kogda Lunu veli na gil'otinu' [When Luna was led to the guillotine] 61–62, 63
  6. 'Zima. Lunatik po karnizu' [Winter. A lunatic along a cornice] 62–63
  7. 'Telo Luny' [Luna's body] 63

Malen'koe puteshestvie sredi ostrovov i zvezd [A Little Journey among Islands and Stars] 54 n. 29, 64–65, 80 n. 72, 83, 154
Martovskie mertvetsy [*March Corpses*]
  4. Vesnoi mertvye riadom [In Spring the Dead Are Near] 83
<u>Maski komedii del' arte vo f'iabakh Karlo Gotstsi [Masks of Commedia dell' Arte in the Fiabe of Carlo Gozzi]</u> 43
Moisei i kust, v kotorom iavilsia Bog [Moses and the Bush God Appeared in] 54 n. 29, 56
Monolog lodki [The Boat's Monologue] 163-64-65, **304–05**
MUNDUS IMAGINALIS: KNIGA OTVETVLENII [MUNDUS IMAGINALIS: BOOK OF OFFSHOOTS] 41
  <u>Neobiazatel'nye poiasneniia [Optional Explanations]</u> 41, *42*, 43, 144–45, 148

Nadgrobnaia nadpis' imperatora Adriana [Funerary Inscription of Emperor Hadrian] 32-33, **234–35**
Neugomonnyi istukan [Indefatigable Idol] 54 n. 29
Nevidimyi okhotnik [Invisible Hunter] 79 n. 69
Nochnaia tolcheia [*Night-Time Throng*] 47
  Dialog [Dialogue] 5 n. 25
  'Nartsissa ia suzhu za nedostatok' [I find Narcissus guilty of an insufficiency] 39, 45-46-48, **236–37**
Nochnoe kupan'e [Night Bathing] 58, *59*

<u>O Marine Tsvetaevoi [About Marina Tsvetaeva]</u> 24 n. 116
Opiat' Venera [Venus Yet Again] 54
<u>Opredelenie v durnuiu pogodu</u> [<u>*Definition for a Rainy Day*</u>]
  Luch [Ray] 75–76, 166
  Liubov' [Love] 147
Orfei [Orpheus] 69-72, 73, 74, 75, **242–43**
O tom, kto riadom [*About the One Who's Nearby*]
  6. 'Tot, kto prostranstvo istorg' [The one who issued space] 83

Perekhod cherez Neman i dal'she na Vitebsk [Crossing of the Neman and on to Vitebsk] *39*, 84
Pifii [Pythias] 85, 86, 87, 149, **248–49**
Pifiia [Pythia] 85–87, 149, **250–51**
Pis'mo [Letter] 88–89, 175
Podrazhanie Bualo [Imitation of Boileau] 77–78, 184, 195 n. 29, **244–45**
Podzemnyi ogon' [Subterranean Fire] 195
Poetica — more geometrico 30
<u>*Poetika zhivogo*</u> [<u>*Poetics of the Alive*</u>]
  Poetika zhivogo [Poetics of the Alive] 1–2, 208
  Tri osobennosti moikh stikhov [<u>Three Characteristics of My Poems</u>] 35
  I-tszin [*I Ching*] 190–91
Pokhorony rifmy [Burial of Rhyme] 42–43, 80 n. 72
Posledniaia noch' [The Last Night] 58

Pravota Nerona [The Rightness of Nero] 185
Preryvistaia povest' o kommunal'noi kvartire [*Discontinuous Story about a Communal Flat*] 173–74
　'Glava 7. Prodolzhenie (eshche bolee bessviaznoe)' [Chapter 7. Continuation (Even More Incoherent)] 173–74
Pri lunnom zatmenii [During a Lunar Eclipse] 54 n. 29, 57
Pri zatmenii Luny [During an Eclipse of the Moon/Luna] 57

Rasprodazha biblioteki istorika [Sale of a Historian's Library] 165–67, 168, 170, 185
Rasskaz Aida, proglochennogo Kronom [The Tale of Hades, Swallowed by Kronos] 66, 240–41
Razlilas' Venera v shest' luchei [Venus spilled forth into six rays] 54
Razvlecheniia Demiurga [*Amusements of the Demiurge*]
　1. Filologicheskie razvlecheniia Demiurga [Philological Amusements of the Demiurge] 30–31, 32
Rimskaia tetrad' [*Roman Notebook*] 175–82, 187
　1. Vospominanie o freske Fra Beato Andzheliko "Kreshchenie" pri vide golovy Ioanna Krestitelia v Rime [Remembering Fra Beato Angelico's 'Baptism' Fresco upon Seeing the Head of John the Baptist in Rome] 176–77
　2. Ploschad' Mal'tiiskikh rytsarei v Rime [Knights of Malta Square in Rome] 177
　4. Circo Massimo 177, 178, 179, 183 n. 47, **308–09**
　5. Ten' u fontana na P'iatstsa del' Popolo [Shade by a Fountain on the Piazza del Popolo] 177–78, 179
　6. 'Rim kak budto varvar-gladiator' [Rome like a barbarian-gladiator] 178–79, 186, **310–11**
　7. Sluchai u pamiatnika Dzhordano Bruno [Incident by the Monument to Giordano Bruno] 179
　9. Zabastovka elektrikov v Rime [Electricians' Strike in Rome] 58, 179, **310–11**
　10. U Panteona [At the Pantheon] 65 n. 39, 179
　11. Sad villy Medichi [Medici Villa Garden] 180, 183
Rondo s primes'iu patriotizma [Rondeau with a Dash of Patriotism] 53–54 n. 29, 76 n. 62, 195 n. 29

Salamandra [Salamander] 75
Slepaia vesna [Blind Spring] 65 n. 39
Smotriu na goriashchii sobor [I Watch the Burning Cathedral] 185
Sochineniia Arno Tsarta [*Collected Works of Arno Tsart*] 27, 148, 149
　Vtoroe puteshestvie lisy na severo-zapad [The Fox's Second Journey to the North-West] 199
Solntse spuskaetsia v ad [The Sun Descends into Hell] 66–68, 74–76
　1. Bormotan'e snega (Vstuplenie) [Muttering of Snow (Prelude)] 66

　2. Orfei opiat' spuskaetsia v ad [Orpheus Descends into Hell Yet Again] 74–76
　3. K Solntsu — pered Rozhdestvom [To the Sun — before Christmas] 66
　4. Zhazhda tenei [The Shades' Thirst] 66–67
　5. Kol'tso Dioskurov [Ring of Dioscuri] 67–68
　6. 'Gliadia na belyi porokh' [Gazing at the white powder] 66
　7. Rozhdestvo na chuzhbine [Christmas in a Foreign Land] 66
　8. Epilog [Epilogue] 66
SOLO NA RASKALENNOI TRUBE [SOLO ON A RED-HOT TRUMPET] 16 n. 73, 89, 90
'Stambul ne pal, ne pal Konstantinopol'' [Istanbul did not fall, nor did Constantinople] 174–75, 183, **308–09**
Stikhi o Germanii [*Poems about Germany*]
　Dva nadgrobiia [Two Headstones] 170–73, **306–07**
　Primechaniia k stikham o Germanii [Notes to *Poems about Germany*] 170 n. 25, 173
Stikhi o Gore-Zloschast'e i beskonechnom schast'e byt' mechennoi Bozh'ei rukoi [*Poems on Grief-Ill-Fortune and the Endless Joy of Being Marked by God's Hand*]
　III. Chem byla i chem stala [What I Was and What I Have Become] 75, 148, 183
STORONY SVETA [CORNERS OF THE EARTH] 14
'"Szhal'tes', milye teni' ['Sweet shades, take pity] 68–69, **240–41**

'Taiat' mozhet' [It could melt away] 72-73
Troeruchitsa v Nikol'skom sobore [Virgin of the Three Hands in Nikolsky Cathedral] 224
Trudy i dni Lavinii, monakhini iz ordena obrezaniia serdtsa [*The Works and Days of Lavinia, a Nun from the Order of the Circumcision of the Heart*] 30, 54 n. 29, 56, 63–64 n. 36, 75, 84, 140, 148, 149–50, 157
　11. Temnaia Rozhdestvenskaia pesn' [Dark Christmas Song] 54 n. 29, 56
　25. Soblaznitel' [Seducer] 150
　29. 'Vy lovites' na to zhe, zhto i vse' [You are hooked on the same things as everyone else] 149
　43. Ognennyi urok [Fiery Lesson] 75, 149

V bolezni — Navarin [In Sickness — Navarin] 195 n. 29
Verchen'e [Whirling] 54 n. 29
Vidimaia storona zhizni [*The Visible Side of Life*]
　Ditia liubvi [Love Child] 6
　Predki [Forebears] 6
V monastyre bliz albanskoi granitsy [In a Monastery near the Albanian Border] 54 n. 29, 55
Volosovedenie [Hair-Direction] (1998) 89–90, 91
Vospominanie o reanimatsii s vidom na Nevy techen'e [Remembering Resuscitation with a View of the Neva Flowing By] 186
Vospominanie o Rime [Remembering Rome] 163, 185–86, **312–13**

Vremiaprovozhden'e [Passing Time] 190
Vzryvy i gomunkuly [*Explosions and Homunculi*] 127

ZAPADNO-VOSTOCHNYI VETER [WEST-EAST WIND] 173
Zapiski na nogtiakh [*Notes on my Nails*]
   O bezumii v poezii [On Madness in Poetry] 84 n. 85
   Ded Mazai i Muzy [Grandpa Mazai and the Muses] 195
   Nesmyvaemoe gore [Indelible Grief] 17

'Zemlia, zemlia, ty esh' liudei' [Earth, earth, you eat people] 72, 85–86
Zhaloba Kinfii [Cynthia's Complaint] 95, 160, 182–85, 312–13
Zimniaia Florentsiia s kholma [Wintry Florence from a Hill] 175 n. 35, 195
Zver'-tsvetok [Animal-Flower] 198

www.ingramcontent.com/pod-product-compliance
Lightning Source LLC
Chambersburg PA
CBHW060230240426
43671CB00016B/2898